FAMILY RESOURCE MANAGEMENT

FAMILY RESOURCE MANAGEMENT

Principles and Applications

SECOND EDITION

Ruth E. Deacon
Iowa State University

Francille M. Firebaugh
The Ohio State University

ALLYN AND BACON, INC.
Boston London Sydney Toronto

A Division of Simon & Schuster
160 Gould Street
Needham Heights, Massachusetts 02194-2310

Library of Congress Cataloging-in-Publication Data

Deacon, Ruth E.
Family resource management: principles and applications / Ruth E.
Deacon and Francille M. Firebaugh.—2nd ed.
Bibliography:
Includes index.
ISBN 0-205-11138-6
1. Family life education—United States. 2. Home economics—United States.
I. Firebaugh, Francille M., 1933– . II. Title.
HQ10.5.U6D43 1988
640–dc19
87-31855
CIP

Printed in the United States of America
10 9 8 7 6 5 4 3 2 1 92 91 90 89 88

Dedicated to our parents

in memory of
Madge B. and Floyd T. Deacon
and Delton V. Maloch
and
with appreciation to
Lucille Maloch

Contents

PART TWO: APPLICATIONS TO RESOURCES

PART THREE: APPLICATIONS TO SITUATIONS

Preface

In this second edition of *Family Resource Management: Principles and Applications* following *Home Management: Context and Concepts,* we hold the same firm commitment to the strategic role of families and households in society. Knowledge and skills in resource management are basic to their capacity to utilize their human and material resources optimally as interchanges of individual members within the unit and externally on behalf of the unit.

Society is as dependent on the quality of these day-to-day living decisions and interchanges as are the individuals and families themselves. Their composite activity is reflected not only in their own quality of life, but also in that of their communities and in the broader society as well.

Systems concepts are again utilized and built upon as the organizing framework within which management functions. The family system has been more fully developed, however. Subsystems within the personal system have been expanded to illustrate the interdependent relationships of the personal and managerial subsystems. Subsystems within the personal system for developing personal capacities and for evolving value systems are identified. These are shown to be important processes, just as managerial processes, in turn, provide the "laboratory" for the development of personal capacities and experiences and insights through which values are formulated. The centrality of decision making to all of these developments continues to be emphasized.

Management concepts for families have been reviewed in relation to their contexts. Universal interpretations of basic management components in all functional settings are utilized in a manner consistent with their differing contexts. This contribution to cross-cultural and interdisciplinary interpretation indicates the integrative nature of management concepts and their application in a systems format.

While the introductory chapters in this edition are sequenced somewhat differently, each of the major components of management continues to receive attention as an updated chapter. Supportive processes—communication and decision making—have also been revised.

The applied chapters have been completely recast. The Work and Family chapter in the current edition replaces the former chapter Management of Household Work. More emphasis is given to the problem of balancing home and paid work, which so many families now experience. Chapters on situational applications have all been updated, and a chapter entitled Blended Families has been added.

We are concerned that the full significance of management be understood for its role in everyday life. The system presented and the management concepts and applications discussed are intended to give reality to these processes. We trust that will be so.

Our special appreciation goes to Doris Beard, Mary Winter, Rosemary Key, Revathi Balakrishnan, Carla Jacobson, and the students in the introductory family resource management class at The Ohio State University who endured an earlier draft and made helpful suggestions. To others with whom we regularly work and live, our appreciation for your patience and encouragement, including John Firebaugh for his assistance on the revision and his support of "work and family" challenges.

Part one

Family system and management

1

Introduction to family resource management

Management is a basic tool for creative living, for achieving desired goals and purposes by using resources to advantage. The focus of this book is on managerial processes that promote meaningful, effective living of individuals and families. The approach has relevance for understanding and interpreting management activity from both a personal and professional perspective.

Most of us acquire managerial skills through experience or conscious effort. But differing situations may affect the significance we place on them.

As a process of maturing, some people acquire managerial skills that serve them well as they move from situation to situation, and these modes of action become so ingrained that they seem "natural." Other people are in situations that permit only a limited range of managerial responses.

Sometimes we find ourselves on a plateau where life is pretty routine, or we may avoid changes that require new managerial responses. Some people find it difficult to cope with change, and they may correctly blame uncontrollable factors in their situation.

But, more often, situations can be controlled, at least to some degree. Problem situations can often be anticipated, and orientations and responses that permit, or even invite new, creative management opportunities can be acquired. Management helps people control the events of life and influence the outcomes of situations. It influences the quality of life of the individual and the family through the way resources are directed toward goals.

Circumstances that affect the significance of family resource management as well as an overview of basic ideas common to management perspectives are presented.

Circumstances affecting family resource management

For managerial processes to be applied creatively, changing realities of living need to be understood. These are explored from four perspectives: (1) increasing complexities of living, (2) family stability, (3) role changes in the family system itself, and (4) technology.

COMPLEXITIES OF LIVING

Individuals and families are a part of a continuous transition as they go about the business of daily living. The passage of time brings inevitable change, if only for reasons of aging and life cycle changes. Such transitions occur even when society in general is stable. But when societal changes are relatively rapid, as has been the case in recent decades, some individuals and families will accept or even promote change, adjusting readily, while others will question or resist change—the former embracing complexity for anticipated gains, the latter preferring current modes and values.

Living involves a changing scene, a continuous sequence of events to which some response is required. People need to develop the ability to anticipate change and to involve themselves in management processes that give direction to their daily lives. To manage creatively in a changing world, a high degree of flexibility and sensitivity is required as environmental and personal shifts occur. Helping to mold community situations to be more compatible with individual or family goals may be as important as management within the family. The manager must hold intended objectives in perspective and make considered adjustments within changing frames of reference. A realistic manager is sensitive not only to conditions that affect goals but also to the potential of obtaining resources to reach intended objectives.

FAMILY STABILITY

Observers of the family have noted changes in family composition, mobility, levels and styles of living, roles of members, and patterns of interaction with the larger society and have come to various conclusions. Technological developments and growth have prompted sociologists and historians to suggest that when the more traditional and extended family system yielded to modernization, an isolated and vulnerable nuclear family was promoted.

More recent historical analyses have led to revision of this view. Many families continue economic and emotional support between generations in times of stress in spite of geographical separation. Intergenerational support is probably more representative of present extended kin relationships, compared to earlier traditions of protection and control by the parent generation.

Viewing families through a systems format provides a way to capture the dynamics of family life in full range. The activities of families can be interpreted in relation to the life-styles of the total family group as well as of individual members, both at a given time and over their respective life cycles.

While in 1985 almost three of four households were composed of members related by marriage, birth, or adoption (compared to four of five in 1970), there has been considerable change in the patterns of living arrangements. In 1985, for example, there were relatively fewer husband–wife households with children under eighteen at home and relatively more single-parent households than in 1970.

There has been a sharper increase in the number of single-parent households headed by females than by males. Within this group, the proportion of black families with women assuming the single-parent role was three in ten in 1985, compared to one in ten for white families.

By far the largest composition change is represented by nonfamily households; that is, where there was no other person related to the householder by birth, marriage, or adoption. More than one fourth were so classified in 1984, compared to less than one fifth in 1970, and four of five of these were maintained by individuals living alone.

This reduction in the traditional intact family with children has been the source of much concern. The underlying apprehension is that important social values and the related role of families as a major source of social stability are threatened.

Impacts of individualism and the focal role of the family in molding and responding to societal changes are critical influences on family stability. No other social unit has been so strategically involved in or broadly affected by the developing networks of complex and interdependent social-economic-political systems. All other social systems, in fact, depend on interchanges with individual and family units for their functioning. Most social institutions, however, primarily interact with individual family members rather than with the family unit, with a few exceptions, such as churches. These interchanges present opportunities, conflicts, and pressures for individual family members. Some family members may be confused about the relative importance of individual versus family goals and functions. Others cannot cope successfully in responding to diverse complex demands under accelerated conditions of change.

FAMILY ROLES AND CHANGES

Society's expectations for families continue to lie in two major areas: (1) procreation and socialization of children and (2) support and development of family members.

Procreation and socialization of children. Although the focus of this book is not on the values and processes that underlie and contribute to the procreation and socialization of children, recognition must be given to their importance. Understanding and developing concepts of family resource management can contribute to decision making about family size, spacing of children, and the many components of child rearing.

It is in the family setting that children receive their first orientation to the values and the reasoning (or lack of same) that (1) are sources of acceptability of or displeasure with behavior, (2) structure the day, (3) make possible or constrain the doing of or obtaining of something, or (4) define the setting for or style of living. Concepts evolve about the family's own and external demands, about the material world, about the costs of and gains from prompt or postponed gratification (planning), and the nature of skills and other resources that make some outcome more or less possible. Families have the initial responsibility, but educational, religious, and other institutions play important roles.

Support and development of family members. Providing for the fundamental needs of each individual in the family continues to be a function families are expected to fulfill. Housing and clothing provide protection, privacy, and a source of expression for individuality and belonging. Food sufficient to meet nutritional needs, to maintain health, and to provide energy for activities to be pursued is an assumed responsibility. In addition, rest, exercise, and recreation accompany food, clothing, and shelter as basic commitments of families. Barring accidents or other unforeseeable health hazards, the development of practices that minimize preventable illness and foster a positive level of health, fitness, and well-being is encouraged.

The family system is among the most—if not *the* most—complex of social systems in an increasingly complex society. The family addresses the responsibilities and opportunities accruing from life changes that the varying skills and perspectives of different generations present. Changing tasks are associated with stages in the life cycle of the unit itself. While critics may contend that families are taking on the transient characteristics of other social groups, the mutual commitments of family members remain primary, sustaining, and unique.

Changes in role patterns are occurring within the family, although deeply instilled role patterns are slow to change. The increase in the number of women who have children and are also working outside the home contributes to the role changes. The acceptance of women into the world of paid employment seems easier than the reverse interest and involvement of men in household and family tasks (see Figure 1.1).

Some contend that women were previously underemployed in the home and now they are overemployed in the combined household and

FIGURE 1.1 *Family role changes—balance of household and work-force commitments between men and women*

Source: DOONESBURY, copyright © 1986 by G. B. Trudeau. Reprinted with permission of Universal Press Syndicate. All rights reserved.

work-force roles. A balance in combined household and work-force commitments by men and women seems necessary for equity and enrichment to prevail.

Women today are concerned about comparable worth in employment, in the interest of increased income and general equity. The economic value of household work is not clearly established, so the question of equity in household work must be considered in terms of the expenditure of time and the amount of responsibility.

"What is involved here is not the old battle of the sexes, which was a battle for dominance, but a process of mutual liberation on behalf of that gentler and more creative generation to come—our children's children."[1]

TECHNOLOGY

Technological changes have been instrumental in their impacts on conditions and styles of individual and family life. Over time, productivity increases in developed societies have brought shifts in life styles, including movement from rural to urban population centers, greater segmentation of social structures and roles, and geographic separation of families. These changes have been balanced by higher levels of living and a reduction in laborious work. Both at home and in industry, technological improvements in mechanical devices have helped us accomplish our routine work faster or with less energy. Interesting trade-offs occurred in the process. Life became at the same time more complex, yet more routine; more opportunistic, yet more vulnerable; more independent, yet more dependent in some of its aspects.

More recently, technological developments have added a different dimension to how we accomplish our objectives. Probably the most striking example is in electronic devices. Sophisticated data and word processors expedite and extend our individual productive and analytical capacities, adding flexibility to our working hours and locations, as well. Both routine and precision tasks are increasingly performed by robots. Our work force is shifting dramatically to information and service roles from the manual and industrial endeavors of earlier decades.

The family resource management system—An overview

Throughout this book, the family is viewed as a system with two major subsystems: personal and managerial. The family system will be described in Chapter 2, but here it is essential to note the roles of the personal system in (1) receiving input from external forces and clarifying values and (2) nurturing the individual capacities of family members. While management is the focus of this book, the great importance of the personal subsystem is fully recognized. Figure 1.2 is a schematic representation of the family system with a managerial subsystem emphasis.

The systems approach is especially useful as a format for presenting family and managerial concepts. Systems concepts have been formulated through interpretation of how major units function in our world, whether social or natural phenomena are under review.

Our technical definition of a *system* is that it is an integrated set of parts that function to accomplish a set of goals. We see this as a consistent framework for *management,* which is most simply defined as the judicious use of means to accomplish ends. Systems ideas also support our interest in focusing sometimes on the overview of families, at other times on subunits of the family or of management. At this point, the idea of a *subsystem* is relevant because it is defined as a set of components functioning together for a purpose fulfilling the same conditions as a system and playing a functional role in a larger system.

Through the managerial system, individuals and families strive to accomplish their goals by the acquisition and use of resources. A general

FIGURE 1.2 *Family system with managerial subsystem emphasis*

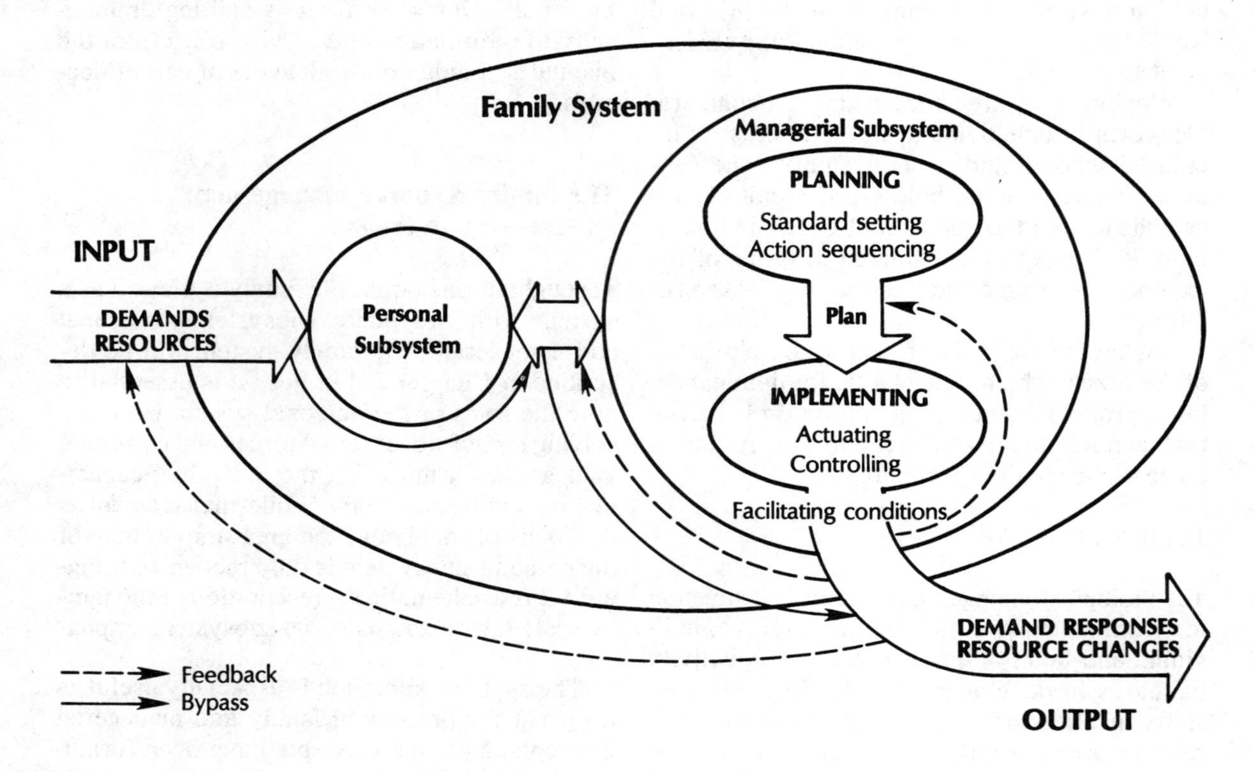

definition of management is planning for and implementing the use of resources to meet demands. Management enables individuals and families to cope with the pressures of changing conditions and serves as the avenue by which anticipations of the future become reality. Management is both affected by and affects its environment, the contexts within which it functions: the larger society, the community, and the more intimate living situation. Chapter 3 focuses on the environment of the family as an ecosystem.

Management is not a general, rigid set of rules and actions but a set of flexible responses to a particular situation. Managerial actions are goal oriented and are related to available or obtainable resources. Comprehending the totality of given situations is important to understanding them in terms of management. And the systems format is supportive to these managerial realities.

In the following sections, demands and resources as inputs, the throughput components of planning and implementing, and the output of demand response and resource change will be discussed as an introduction to management. The importance of these relationships will be considered in terms of their roles in identifying with management the continuity and dynamic qualities that families as open systems have as they interchange with their environment.

INPUT

Input is matter, energy, and/or information entering a system in various forms to affect throughput (transformation) processes in the achievement of outcome or output. Inputs provide the basis for answering such questions as why, what, and whether. Why resources are allocated in a given way, what resources are allocated, and whether or not resources are allocated depend on input factors that stimulate response. Inputs to family systems and their subsystems that provide such motivation are called demands. *Demands* are either goals or events that require action. *Goals* are defined as value-based objectives or anticipated outcomes that give direction and orientation to action; specifically, they provide directional criteria for standard setting. *Values* are essential meanings related to what is desirable or has worth, providing fundamental criteria for goals. *Events,* by comparison, are unexpected or low-probability occurrences that require action.

Thus, both goals and events place on individuals and families a level of demand that, whether high or low, is adequate to bring about a response. Demands, as with resources, may originate from inside or outside the family system. *Resources* are means capable of meeting demands, that is, they provide the properties or characteristics through which the goals and events are achieved or satisfied.

Demands. Goals and events form the demands that give direction for managerial activity. Goals may originate in the personal subsystems of the family members, or they may bypass the personal system and go directly to the managerial subsystem as shown in Figure 1.2. One obvious source of goal demands is the biological requirements of family members, such as for food and water. Besides the many goals individuals and families set for themselves and events to which they must respond, goal demands arise externally, as from the political system—for school attendance, obedience to laws, zoning restrictions, and from the sociocultural system expectations for gender roles.

The management subsystem helps focus and order goals into purposes or objectives that are specific enough to achieve. If a family holds many goals, its management is probably more complicated than if goals are few. Assessing goal priorities can be difficult; management can help by assisting in realistic appraisal of the goals.

If goal priorities are unclear because values are unclear, the chances for management to be effective are questionable. Clear goals are a function both of how well they relate to underlying values and the possibility that they can be met. The significance and development of values and their relation to goals will be discussed more fully in Chapter 4.

Events. Events as inputs are pertinent or unexpected low-probability occurrences that require action. External events that affect the family system represent demands that ordinarily bypass the personal system. They move directly to the management system for response. For example, a raging hurricane is an external event that requires action wherever it hits. An example of a minor event emanating from an external source is a traffic jam caused by a neighborhood parade.

Internal events, such as home accidents, may also occur. Families respond to events according to their values. The family has a standing commitment to some events, such as those that relate to health. When such events arise, the event demand bypasses the personal system.

Resources. Resources are means that provide the characteristics or properties capable of meeting the demands placed upon the family by goals and events. Resources may become available from productive activities internal to the family system or through interactions with other systems. In either case, the available resources are those that individuals or families own or over which they have control. Resources may be classified as human and material.

The human resources within the family system are the skills, abilities, and knowledge of the people who are members of the system. If the family sometimes prefers the knowledge, skills, or abilities of others outside the family, these may be obtained by exchanging money or time or by receiving assistance in the form of gifts. The tangible goods already available for consumption or that will be used to produce other goods, and the savings and investments, represent the material resources of the family. Resource characteristics and resource allocation are discussed more fully in Chapter 5.

THROUGHPUT

Throughput is the transformation of matter, energy, and/or information by a system from input to output. The components within the boundary of a system help explain its dynamics. Within the managerial system, throughput is the activity that pursues answers to questions of how, how much, how good, when, and where. A system's overall effectiveness can be measured by comparing the output (the results achieved) with input (what was wanted and available). Such an analysis of how well goals are met does not reveal why some families with similar resources more nearly achieve goals than do others. The answers lie in understanding internal processes.

The effects—but not the processes—of throughput are reflected in how well output coincides with input. The term "black box" describes the unknown throughput. If the nature of the management processing is not recognized, wrong conclusions about the output can be drawn. Boulding observes that "a pure 'black box' behavioral science, which studies only inputs and outputs and makes no attempt to pry off the lid of the behavior unit to see what is inside, suffers from almost fatal limitations."[2] Observing consumer behavior only at the marketplace could yield misleading conclusions regarding the actions.

For the management of home and personal affairs, throughput comprises planning and implementing—two of the components in the definition given earlier. *Planning* is a series of decisions concerning future standards and/or sequences of action. *Implementing* is actuating plans and procedures (standards and sequences) and controlling the actions. Figure 1.2 illustrates planning and implementing as major components within management.

Decision making is a process of evaluation in choosing or resolving alternatives. The decision-making process involves recognizing that a decision is needed and then identifying, weighing, and choosing among or resolving alternatives. The process is integral to all aspects of management, but decision making is not synonymous with management. Management is a more inclusive concept than decision making, even though good decision-making ability is critical in management. In Chapter 6, the basic decision-making process and related strategies and patterns are presented.

Planning. The inputs to planning are demands and resources. Planning decisions involve standards and sequences of action needed to meet demands. Planning is elaborated upon in Chapter 7; an introduction to standard setting and sequencing follows.

Although planning is always future oriented, plans vary in specificity from situation to situation. During the planning process, operational criteria evolve. *Standards* are operational criteria that reflect qualities and/or quantities that reconcile resources with demands. *Standard setting* is this reconciliation of resources with demands to bring them into a realistic relationship for meeting goals and events satisfactorily.

In buying a VCR, for instance, the processes of searching, developing alternatives, and weighing the alternatives need to be completed. Quality and quantity factors such as portability, tape format, and programming ease are decided, which is standard setting. Decisions about the relative importance of these and other features in relation to purpose and cost form the criteria or standards to guide buying.

A *sequence of action* is an order among or within tasks. In the illustration of shopping for a VCR, for instance, the plan development and execution may take place in one or several shopping trips. The major sequencing activity may be to schedule the shopping to make the best choice within the available time. A sequence (the order for doing the shopping, in this example) must be consistent with the established standards. If the store farthest away from home is more likely to have the widest choice, starting at that store may be the best sequence. Standards and sequences, ordinarily integral parts of a total plan, do not need to be developed at the same time.

Implementing. After standards and sequences are developed into a plan consistent with resources and demands, implementing the action is the other task of management. If the action is completed through implementation without complications, the plan's effectiveness can be evaluated.

To implement plans, actions must be taken by someone or something. *Actuating* is putting plans into effect. It is the responsibility of the manager to relate those actions to the larger plan. At times, family resource management has been distinguished from other types of management by the preponderance of actions by the manager. Although in many cases the same person may develop and implement the plan, this is not an essential difference in management by families and, for example, corporate management. The difference is in the management unit and the importance of the interaction with the personal subsystem in the family system. In corporations, personal values are ordinarily subordinate to corporate values.

Actuating plans may be easier in secure situations than in situations with high uncertainty. Inertia can occur when an unrealistic plan for action is made. For example, a plan to go to school next summer to speed graduation is unlikely to be actuated if estimates of earnings during the school year to cover expenses were unrealistic. Reasons for not implementing plans have been studied in only a limited way, but lack of sufficient resources is probably a major deterrent.

More realistic plans may not be actuated when others in a unit such as a family are uninterested in the plan. Inertia may also occur when actuating the plan depends on another person who has conflicting interests or responsibilities.

If a plan does not work out as anticipated during implementing, corrections can be made as a part of controlling. *Controlling* is checking actions and outcomes for conformity to plans and, if necessary, adjusting standards or sequences.

The role of controlling is to increase the likelihood that the expected outcomes toward which planning was directed will actually occur. *Facilitating conditions* are situation characteristics that assist the progress or flow of actions but are not directly accounted for as resources.

Suppose you agreed to work with a committee to develop a drug abuse program. You had arranged for an informative panel of persons having experiences ranging from overcoming addiction to living with addiction-related abusiveness. The date and location were set. When you followed up the day before the meeting, you learned that one member of the panel could not participate on the agreed date. Will you change the program and probably also the standard you had worked so hard to meet? Or will you set another time so you can keep the program intact? Similar issues are discussed in Chapter 8.

Communicating. *Communication* is the process of using messages to engender meaning in the minds of others. *Messages* are stimuli flowing from a sender to a receiver.[3] Effective communication precedes and contributes to effective decision making; the chances for meeting goals of a system are enhanced. Communication is a mutual process if barriers can be minimized or removed. Communication characterized by feedback in an open system is supportive and centers on information, advice, or counsel; in a closed system, the emphasis is on decisions and instructions. Communicating is the focus of Chapter 9.

Output. *Output* is matter, energy, and/or information produced by a system in response to input and from throughput (transformation) processes. As noted before, outputs of the managerial system are called demand responses and resource changes. They result from transformations inside the boundaries of the managerial system in response to demand and resource inputs.

Feedback is the portion of output that reenters a system as input to affect succeeding output. Feedback from the management output is a positive or negative response to action that conveys changes to the managerial and personal subsystems that make a difference in other decisions to follow. Demand responses and resource changes are briefly discussed here and will be enlarged upon in Chapter 10; input–output relations and feedback are also included in that chapter.

Demand responses. *Demand responses* are the output from managerial actions relating to values and satisfactions. A portion of the output gained from responses to goal and event demands returns to the personal system. Output to the external environment of all families contributes to the molding of society.

Resource changes. *Resource changes* are the output from managerial actions relating to the composition of the stock of human and/or material means. Human resources are commonly incremented through managerial activity—as through more skill or knowledge. Material resources may be either increased or decreased. The shift may reduce resources, as when resources are consumed or shared.

If resources are exchanged, the outcome reflects a shift in the makeup if not the value of the resource stock of an individual and/or family unit. Producing, saving, or investing are reallocations intended to increase the stock of available means.

NONMANAGED ACTIONS

The management bypass line of Figure 1.2 needs a brief explanation. It is drawn outside the boundary of the management system from demand and resource inputs to the output arrow. *Nonmanaged actions,* or unconsidered responses in the managerial system, may occur as a result of a desire to respond directly via the personal system to a demand involving the use of resources, but managerial components and processes have not been activated. It may be a response to an impulse to see a movie and forget a paper due tomorrow or to buy an item solely on the basis of the seller's charisma. A common explanation is that "I wanted to do it no matter what." Such actions, albeit impulsive and/or prescribed by the personal system as overriding, have managerial implications because they are likely to affect later management. The feedback line from output to resources, demands, and the personal system reflects nonmanaged as well as managed actions.

The situations in the illustrations of nonmanagement just given might also have been managed. Even if the student had weighed the desire to go to a movie against the cost of staying up late or of being late with the paper, he or she might still have decided on the same action. The item that the persuasive salesperson promoted could have been one that the student needed and considered a good choice. The actions could have been managed through basic processes described here.

When actions are not managed, resources already planned for one purpose may be used for the nonmanaged action. The effects of this change in resource use feed back to affect succeeding resource inputs; the effects of demands that are met through nonmanagement also use feedback. The seriousness of the imbalance between resources and demands due to nonmanagement depends partly on the extent of resource use and their availability as well as on demands.

Applications to resources

No discussion of management is meaningful without acknowledging the central role of resources as essential means to meet demands. For households, there are two major contexts for resource use in providing for the demands of individuals and families. First is the potential of the market utilized through money expenditures. Secondly, within homes, time and skills are used to carry out tasks that provide for each other's needs and enhance the living situation. Skills are offered in the marketplace, as well, to obtain money resources to meet goals.

In Chapter 11, aspects of financial management are discussed in relating the application of management to earning and using money resources. Chapter 12 addresses the complexities of managing the roles of work in the workplace and at home in meeting individual and family needs.

Applications to situations

Special circumstances highlight the need for management if crises are to be avoided or minimized. Mismatches often occur between demands and resources over the life cycle. When young, for example, there is the need to take the long view and develop capacities for earning to meet the demands of a lifetime (see Chapter 13). Often, pressures on scarce resources are heavy when investments in education and training coincide with responsibilities of establishing and maintaining a growing family. Later, a family's responses to the needs of both their younger and older generations may compete with a concern to prepare for their own retirement (see Chapter 14). All managerial components need to mesh, although each may take precedence at various stages. The significance of long-range planning is basic to a life cycle discussion.

Besides the varying demands that inevitably affect us all, there are the environmental and societal impacts that introduce changes in life chances.

Special demands that arise when a family member is handicapped are considered in Chapter 15. Families who have a person with a handicapping condition face unique management situations, depending on the extent and type of disability or illness.

Managerial responses and challenges accompanying the complex circumstances of the increasing portion of families experiencing changes in form or structure will be analyzed with special reference to single parents (see Chapter 16) and blended families (see Chapter 17). Female-headed, single-parent families have particularly serious problems in meeting goals. Alternatives for acquiring sufficient resources to meet the demands of the family are often limited.

Differences in the economic climate, with effects on employment opportunities at critical life stages or of spending one's childhood and developmental years in poverty, are interpreted in relation to their management aspects in Chapter 18.

Managerial processes are presented within a systems format. A systems context facilitates the study of management in much the same way that factors not accounted for or taken as givens in individual managerial decisions serve as facilitators.

Nature of family resource management

INTERDISCIPLINARITY

Just as an understanding of management processes provides a basis for interpreting the scope of decisions confronting individuals and families in their daily lives, subject matter from diverse disciplines is integrated in the process. The components and processes to be expanded upon in the chapters that follow provide a framework for relating the content of many subjects into an integrated response in utilizing resources to meet needs or achieve goals. This is because evaluation processes throughout the system require that the significant criteria be consistently served as properties of resources capable of meeting them are weighed. Individuals may rarely identify their preference for designer jeans in psychological, sociological, aesthetic, or economic terminology. Nor are they likely to consider the agricultural, textile science, design, retailing, or other expertise required to provide the desired product. These and other factors combine to affect the properties unique to a final product with the design, fit, wear, care, and economic qualities and characteristics for the potential buyer to consider.

The many choices to be made are comprehensible through the system under study. This is because decisions that depend on values and the valuing process while specific to each stage are also dependent on previous stages, providing integrity and continuity to the system. The chapters most related to interdisciplinary relationships are those on values, resources, and planning—particularly the discussion on standard setting.

UNIQUENESS

While the same components are common to all types of management, each type also has its own uniqueness. This is because the nature of the problems that are faced, the mix of resources, and the way resources are utilized all vary. Both families and businesses plan, for example, but the goals and outcomes often differ. One of the differences characterizing the management of households or families is the fact that their problems and solutions are influenced not only by their management at home but also by their interactions with the market and other sectors of society.

The management of a household is viewed by many as mundane. Much of it is repetitive. But most of it has significance in fostering meaning—for life-styles, relationships, and life goals. Today's management problems may vary from grocery shopping to how best to invest savings. Tomorrow's special needs may be to get the yard work done and get the phone calling done for a community group's event. Accomplishing these projects focuses on the use of money for today's decisions and on time for tomorrow's, even though both time and money are involved in each. All affect life-styles and have implications beyond the activities themselves.

The management of families and households is characterized by situations having contrasting aspects, including formal versus informal arrangements, market versus nonmarket or paid versus unpaid costs and benefits, and external versus personal influences. Differences in managerial purposes, the substantive information pertinent to the issues, and situational circumstances determine major management types or subtypes. Each type, in turn, shares similarities that rest somewhere on a common continuum of purpose, resource availability, and contextual influences. Business firms are established to produce goods or services and to make a profit. Schools are founded to educate students. The resource management efforts of individuals and families are directed toward meeting day-to-day and future living demands and providing for an adequate and fulfilling life-style. Businesses, schools, and households represent unique management types.

CROSS-CULTURAL AND INTERNATIONAL APPLICATION

Along with the uniqueness of the family resource management context, the management of families from region to region, from ethnic group to ethnic group, and from country to country is both similar and different. But the fundamentals of the particular system are universal. For family or household resource management, there is the common challenge to provide for and use available means for day-to-day living (even survival) and to seek improved opportunities over the life cycle for one's self and one's dependents. Even so, major differences in cultural influences on life-styles and expectations, available resources and managerial skills and constraints affect the application of management, if not the concepts per se.

The degree of interface with other sectors of society varies sharply. Families in many developing countries are less dependent on the market system, being more self-sufficient than their counterparts in developed countries. That is, more relative emphasis is placed on the production of the household for meeting total needs, although some of the products may be sold and some goods purchased. Families in developed countries also make a considerable contribution to their needs through household production. Families in both developed and developing countries engage in household production, but they do so at different intensities and with different degrees of necessity.

Other differences, such as specification of roles or the influence of social norms on family goals, need to be recognized where individual or group situations are under study. The variations are unlimited, but the basic questions are common to all households to some degree. To recognize these differences and illustrate the broad application of family resource management concepts, illustrations are drawn from a number of cross-cultural settings.

Notes

1. Elise Boulding, ''Familial Constraints on Women's Work Roles,'' *Signs* 1 (Spring 1976): 117.
2. Kenneth E. Boulding, *Economics as a Science* (New York: McGraw-Hill, 1970), p. 54.
3. James C. McCroskey, Carol E. Larson, and Mark L. Knapp, *An Introduction to Interpersonal Communication* (Englewood Cliffs, N.J.: Prentice-Hall, 1971), pp. 3–4.

2

The family system and its subsystems

The systems format provides a frame of reference for analyzing the goal-directed behavior of families as they address their living situations. The family system's context changes partly because of previous responses and partly because of other systems. Viewing these interactions in a dynamic context is a special advantage of the systems approach to family analysis.

Relative openness and closedness

The *environment* is the external setting within which a system functions. The family is an *open system,* since it interrelates continually with its environment. *Openness* and *closedness* are relative terms, and systems are frequently called "relatively open" or "relatively closed." A *closed system* does not make significant exchanges with its environment. In a closed system, the internal transfers are far more important than the exchanges across the system's boundary. Relatively closed systems generally function within a specialized or narrow sphere, and exchanges across boundaries are limited. A young child with dangerously low resistance to disease who must live in a "germ-free" environment has intake from the environment, however filtered, and body wastes flowing across the system boundary to the environment. Nevertheless, such a child is in a "relatively closed" system.

System elements

Input-throughput-output. The *input* of basic systems consists of matter, energy, and information. Those specific forms of matter, energy, and information entering the family system are classified as resources and demands. As the family uses resources to meet demands, both the resource changes and the demand responses leave the family system and enter the environment as *output*. The processes of changing the inputs of matter, energy, and information into outputs is called *throughput,* or transformation.

The family as a system provides form and perspective to the basic inputs represented by matter in the observation "Matter without form is unintelligible; form without matter is empty. Form gives intelligibility to matter; matter gives content to form."[1] Demands are inputs that provide the stimulus, motivation, and meaning to the activity undertaken within the system.

The relative importance of matter, energy,

and information to the functioning of systems has been interpreted in terms of the degree to which they are self-regulating, adaptive, and goal oriented. Systems that are self-regulated and self-directed are more dependent on information, while those that have no internal, directive mechanism depend primarily for their functioning on matter and energy. They may receive information, in a sense, but they cannot make or do not have a choice. Human beings and their social systems are the most complex of self-regulating systems, although the simplest forms of animal life are also self-regulating to a degree.[2]

While information represents the fundamental resource for fostering family system processes, it is also the case that any social system is ultimately subject to matter–energy constraints. This relationship is illustrated by viewing the family and other social systems as residing within a context of elements responsive to natural laws. Use of these matter- and energy-based resources needs to be consistent with natural laws to preserve the vitality of the ecosystem. This book emphasizes the goal-oriented and adaptive nature of the family system in responsible interaction with its total environment.

Within self-regulating family systems, differences may occur in the throughput processes. Two systems concepts apply to these differences. With varying initial circumstances or conditions, the throughput process of two individuals or families may lead them to similar conclusions. This phenomenon is called *equifinality*. And yet, relatively similar opportunities and beginning orientations can lead to different outcomes: *multifinality*. Two couples that start married life with widely different resources may later attain resources that show approximately the same net worth when they retire—even though the composition of the assets and liabilities may vary. For example, families who purchase similar houses in the same neighborhood may sell them at considerably different prices because of differences in the maintenance of or improvements to the property, assuming that the same market conditions prevail at the time of both sales.

The concepts of equifinality and multifinality are important from the managerial perspective because they emphasize the need to consider factors that contribute to why families can take different approaches successfully. Variations among families in their present situations may be due to differences in their adaptive responses to other systems and to their decisions as growth-supporting units.

Feedback. Feedback is information about output that reenters the system as input. The feedback process is important because this return to the system can affect later transformation processes and/or outputs.[3] *Positive feedback* accepts deviations from anticipated effects and promotes rather than inhibits change.[4] Positive feedback is informational input that indicates that the system may benefit from change and should institute a new course. Positive feedback is deviation promoting.

For example, a librarian who participates in a workshop on new dimensions in computer services in libraries receives the conclusions (output of the workshop) about proposed library changes favorably, even though they would lead to major changes in the mode of operation. Awareness of conditions that might improve with changes contributes to the openness to positive feedback; a willingness to initiate changes is essential.

Positive feedback recognizes system processes that exceed expectations or introduce change that can be desirable. A number of factors may influence willingness to change. A person may be generally uncommitted to one outcome over another and would accept the change rather than reprocess it. One example might be when a child's sense of the possibilities of freer movement, as its first steps are taken, provides incentive to keep trying even in the face of the inevitable fall. Another is when we as adults participated reluctantly in a volunteer activity with an anticipated short commitment and found expanded horizons and contacts led us to long-range involvements and even redirections. Changed circumstances sometimes make a changed outcome as inviting or more so than the original situation. In an example from gardening, a rain may make weeding much easier even though it delays work a few hours.

Some people seek change and create circumstances that lead to change. An unending pursuit of new possibilities can make realizing any one goal difficult. Receptivity to positive feedback appears to vary by stages in the life cycle and orientation to change. *Morphogenic systems* are adaptive and growth supporting in response to change. Morphogenic literally means "evolution of form."

Morphogenic systems have permeable boundaries, use positive feedback, have flexible internal structures to deal with varying inputs, and adjust to change.[5] Through in-depth studies, healthy families have been found to have flexible structure and to be open to new directions; that is, functioning as open systems.[6] The family that has to cancel vacation travel plans but uses the time for enjoying local sites and restaurants may expand its experiences and horizons. A morphogenic system response is deviation promoting, through the information provided by positive feedback.

Negative feedback is output information returning as input to promote corrective measures to maintain the system in a desired state; it is "informational input which indicates that the system is deviating from a prescribed course and should readjust to a new steady state."[7] For example, a runner taking more time to reach a given point than intended or a family having spent more than they intended by midyear are processing negative feedback as they contemplate adjustments. The runner draws on inner resources to muster the energy to finish the distance at the hoped-for speed. The family needs to control expenditures more effectively when they have no leeway to cover increased tuition expenses for their college-bound daughter, whom they do not want to have to take a job until after her first term. Negative feedback is deviation correcting. In both illustrations, deviations were being responded to with corrective measures.

Although the family is characterized as adaptive, in some families and under certain circumstances the static tendencies may equal or exceed the dynamic qualities. While most families strike a balance, many families operate effectively with minimum or maximum change orientations. *Morphostatic systems*—literally, a fixed form—are stable, and deviation correcting in response to change. They are somewhat mechanistic and relatively closed. Characterized by relatively rigid boundaries, they accept limited new inputs, emphasize negative feedback, tend toward inflexible internal structures, and have difficulty in or resist adjusting to change.[8] A morphostatic system response to a need to change vacation travel plans would be postponement until the original plan could be implemented. Such an action would correct any deviation from original intentions, except for the time component.

From a systems perspective, family maintenance is a negative feedback orientation; development emphasizes positive feedback. Both contribute fundamentally to families' welfare and take their turn throughout the life cycle in providing needed stability and promoting creative change, even though the balance varies from family to family either by preference or circumstance. The feedback mechanism relates to the individual's or family's evaluation of its own activity or output. Environmental conditions and relative openness or closedness to other sources of inputs and how well the system components interact also make a difference in continuity of family functioning and adaptiveness.

Some families foster a life-style that emphasizes either relative stability or relative change as illustrative of their mode of life. Neither mode is right or wrong; both are needed to some degree in either general style. Within each general style, the balance will also shift during periods of transition or stress.

Subsystems

A system is a functioning unit, and any such unit may be identified for the primary focus. The functioning parts of the primary system are subsystems. Subsystems must be functioning units in their own right and could under certain circumstances become the primary objects of study with identified subsystems. Management, for example, will be discussed as a subsystem of the family system. Later, as our primary focus, the management system will be central with its own subsystems.

As with other primary systems, the regular functioning of the family system is interpreted through identification and understanding of interactions among its subsystems. Subsystems within the family system have been identified as personal and managerial. Since major emphasis in this book is on management, which has been introduced and will be expanded upon later, the personal subsystem and the overall family system are discussed more extensively in this chapter as they relate to management.

PERSONAL SYSTEM

It is through the personal system that the surrounding forces of family and society, of near and far environments, and of inner potential and constraints influenced by heredity and experience combine to shape our very being as individuals with unique personalities. These influences continue throughout individual life cycles and affect, in turn, evolutionary family processes (whether of the family of origin or procreation) and other significant relationships. Input, throughput, and output dimensions of the personal system are suggested in Figure 2.1.

Inputs to the individual personal system encompass physical surroundings, societal and cultural norms, community support systems (such as educational, religious, or recreational programs), family goals, available economic opportunities or living conditions, and the quality of life experiences, including the nature of interpersonal relationships. Some of these inputs place demands on us, as is the case of expectations of society regarding behavior of the family—perhaps to learn responsibility or to perform at a given level. Other inputs provide various kinds and levels of support, such as experiences or role models. Income and net worth impact personal resources indirectly through the managerial system—for example, the use of income to purchase building blocks to enhance the development of a child. The managerial system interrelates with the personal system in many ways, only one of which is through income and net worth.

The individual personal system is composed of two major subsystems: developmental and values. It is generally accepted that developmental potential is highly affected by our genetic endowment. The relative impact of inherent versus environmental influences on our eventual personalities and capacities remains an area of conjecture. Through the *developmental subsystem,* growth and development are commonly interpreted to foster four interrelated capacities: cognitive, emotional, social, and physical. The quality of early experiences and relationships is known to have important effects on later development and responses. The personal-system interaction with managerial processes is integral to the shaping of these developments. The *values subsystem* translates experience and understanding into intrinsic and extrinsic meanings. As experiences accrue and the consequences of choice are assimilated, a basic value system gradually evolves that, upon maturity, provides impetus for ongoing development within the limits of opportunity. Family management makes a primary contribution to developing capacities in the personal system.[9]

Outputs from the basic value subsystem are represented as value/goal orientations. Outputs

FIGURE 2.1 *Individual personal system*

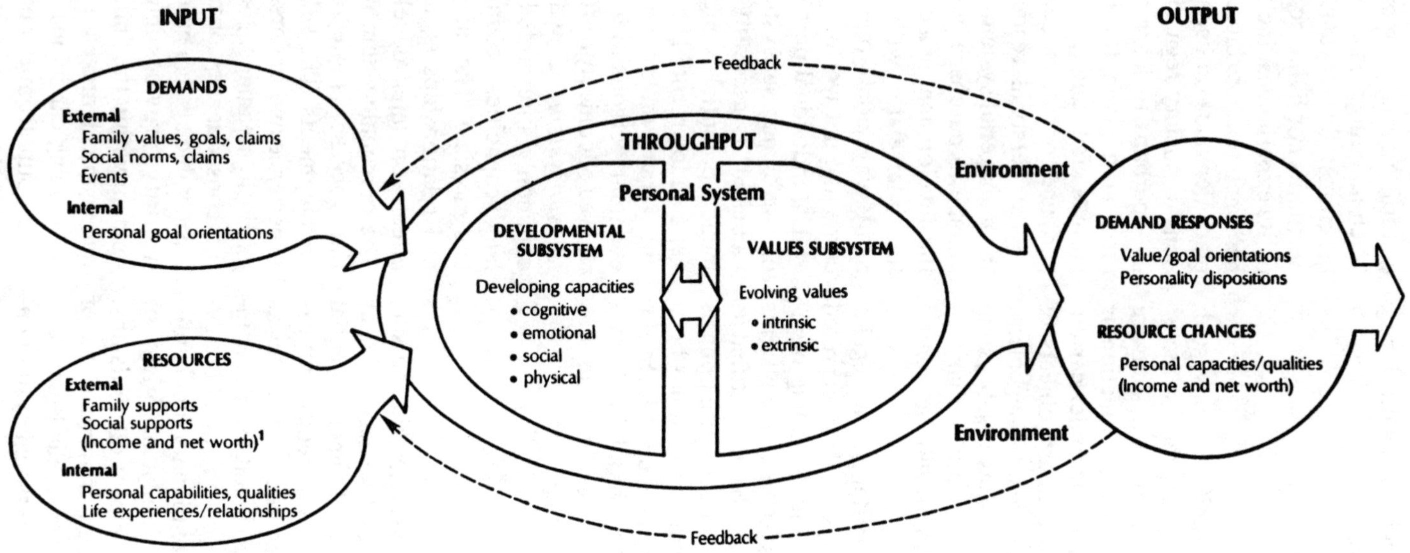

INPUT

DEMANDS

External
Family values, goals, claims
Social norms, claims
Events

Internal
Personal goal orientations

RESOURCES

External
Family supports
Social supports
(Income and net worth)[1]

Internal
Personal capabilities, qualities
Life experiences/relationships

Feedback

THROUGHPUT

Personal System

DEVELOPMENTAL SUBSYSTEM

Developing capacities
- cognitive
- emotional
- social
- physical

VALUES SUBSYSTEM

Evolving values
- intrinsic
- extrinsic

Environment

Environment

Feedback

OUTPUT

DEMAND RESPONSES

Value/goal orientations
Personality dispositions

RESOURCE CHANGES

Personal capacities/qualities
(Income and net worth)

[1] The income and net-worth items are indicated parenthetically to recognize their indirect role in the personal system.

from the developmental subsystem are reflected in accruing personal capacities and/or qualities that are in constant interchange with evolving values. They combine to form characteristic personality dispositions and patterns. Due to the dynamic nature of life, these patterns are continually evolving and changing. As can be seen in the diagram, feedback from the output returns as input to affect future development of the system. Positive feedback is supportive to changes in personal qualities or goal orientations. Negative feedback signals necessary adjustment to the system's state.

The generalized output is indicated as demand responses and resource changes. Since our life tasks are ongoing, these outputs do not imply that demands are met consistently and fully—rather that they are, to a greater or lesser degree, confronted and dealt with. Traumatic events may lead to setbacks, at least for a period—a frustration of values, emotional stress accompanying a broken relationship, or physical illness. However, the anticipated response to these as well as more fulfillment opportunities is that they are addressed. The greater the insight into processes of personal development and management, the more effective the result should be over time.

PERSONAL-MANAGERIAL SYSTEM

As daily lives are pursued and possibilities for the future are contemplated, the personal and managerial subsystems of individuals function as fully integrated entities. As Figure 2.2 illustrates, the personal system contributes value/goal orientations and underlying capacities supportive to managerial processes. Likewise, output from managerial processes over time provides the situational context and experiences from which much of our personal development evolves. Human and material resources are a combined output of both subsystems.

By definition, management is a process of thought and action through which resources are utilized in the meeting of demands. This means *all* resource decisions involve managerial processes. Information is brought to bear on such decisions as conflict resolution, choice of a life partner, and leisure reading, as well as decisions on the use of time and money. All developmental capacities are drawn on, although the cognitive dimension is central. The personal system can limit or enhance responses to given managerial processes through emotional or physical influences (e.g., feeling up or down).

Goal orientations may initiate a managerial response. But management, as a series of decisions throughout planning and implementing processes, constantly involves one's value system as choices are made. Contributions to the value system are made in turn.

The purpose of identifying a personal and a managerial subsystem is to recognize reinforcing aspects of the subsystems. They are parts of a whole. It is through our continual application and development of managerial skills that we are able to meet life's demands. Management activity contributes to—indeed, it is necessary, if not sufficient, for—our functioning. But it does not explain what and who we are as persons. The personal system represents the composite of social-psychological-physiological-spiritual development that gives integrity to management, providing bases for purposeful response processes for persons coping with and/or enhancing their lives in their individual and family settings.

The family system

Recognition of the importance of individual development becomes more complex as we move from consideration of life tasks of individuals to a broader view of individuals in their roles of membership in a family system. For not only does each of the family group have individual developmental tasks to accomplish throughout his or her individual lifetime, but the family as a system also represents a unique entity with its

FIGURE 2.2 *Individual personal/managerial system*

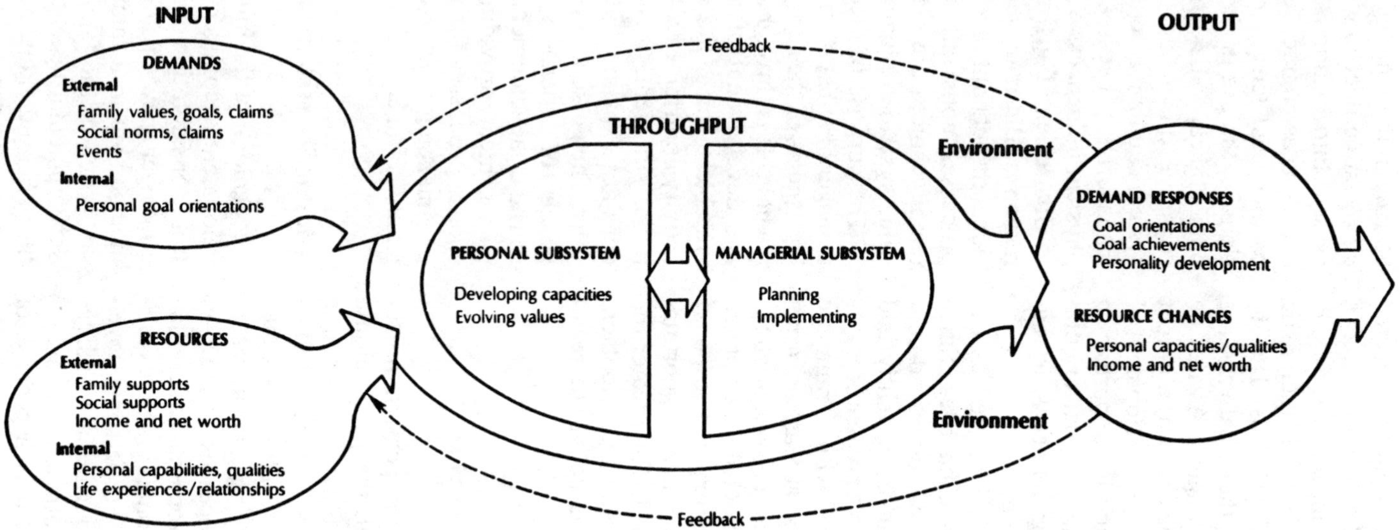

INPUT

DEMANDS
External
Family values, goals, claims
Social norms, claims
Events
Internal
Personal goal orientations

RESOURCES
External
Family supports
Social supports
Income and net worth
Internal
Personal capabilities, qualities
Life experiences/relationships

Feedback

THROUGHPUT

PERSONAL SUBSYSTEM
Developing capacities
Evolving values

MANAGERIAL SUBSYSTEM
Planning
Implementing

Environment

Environment

Feedback

OUTPUT

DEMAND RESPONSES
Goal orientations
Goal achievements
Personality development

RESOURCE CHANGES
Personal capacities/qualities
Income and net worth

own developmental characteristics.[10] Each family unit is composed of a special set of people whose relationships are established and maintained through their communication behavior; note that "insofar as family relations endure, they form patterns over time, and it is this patterning over time that is the essence of a family system."[11] And consistent with the nature of systems, the family system is a holistic concept that has a totality that cannot be adequately captured by concentrating only on the individuals involved and a summation of given interactions.

Three underlying dimensions that emerged from a comprehensive analysis of concepts utilized by researchers and theorists in the family field and developed into a "circumplex model" of the family behavior are: cohesion, adaptability, and communication.[12] These dimensions were utilized in a study of over 1,100 couples distributed over seven family life stages. While the particular demands and resources—such as health, financial, or emotional strain and social or financial support—differed at each stage, these three underlying dimensions were pertinent to all. While the details of models comprehensive enough to encompass the range of family processes continue under discussion, adaptability and cohesion have been agreed upon as the salient dimensions of family life by major interpreters from sociopsychological perspectives.[13]

Family processes from an economic perspective have been characterized as a form of production. The effects emanate from personal interaction—physical, mental, or emotional—and produce the intrinsic character of family life.[14]

The proposed model for the family system we are presenting incorporates dimensions of cohesion and adaptability, contributing to the developmental and interpersonal dynamics. Functionality is also included to represent the capacity of family members to keep day-to-day relationships and activities supportive to the overall needs and interests of the group. Functionality extends the intrasystem concepts of cohesion and adaptability to include the contributions both of ongoing interpersonal interaction and of managerial activity in the development and maintenance of effective overall family processes. Therefore, the *family system* is composed of personal and managerial subsystems that interact through communication processes to develop intrasystem dynamics: cohesion, adaptability, and functionality.

Along with communications as a facilitating component, these four dimensions are defined as follows:

- Cohesion
  The emotional bonding that family members have toward one another[15]
- Adaptability
  The ability of a marital or family organization to change its power structure, role relationships, and relationship rules[16]
- Functionality
  The ability of family members to use their human and material resources to anticipate and meet demands
- Communication
  The process of using messages to engender meaning in the minds of others,[17] it is critical to adaptability, cohesion, and functionality as a facilitating dimension.

Figure 2.3 presents the family system processes and shows that inputs to the family system are similar to those depicted for the personal system and the personal-managerial system. The family-related inputs are now inside the boundary of the family system. Figure 2.4 illustrates the facilitating role of interpersonal communication by arrows to and from individuals in the family. Output from each individual filters through the synergistic mechanism of intrasystem dynamics. This represents the evolving and unifying dimensions of cohesion, adaptability, and functionality through the fam-

FIGURE 2.3 *Family system*

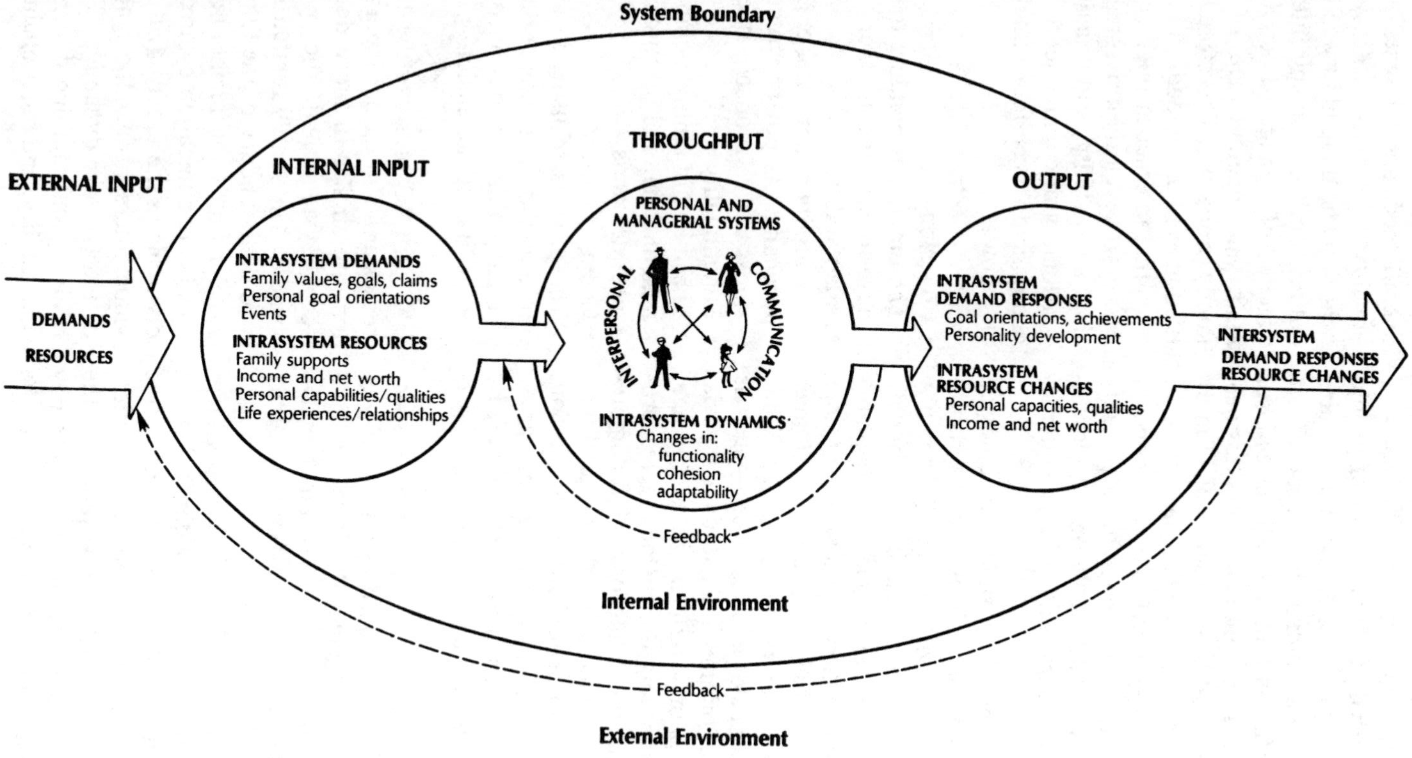

FIGURE 2.4 *Individuals as subsystems of family systems*

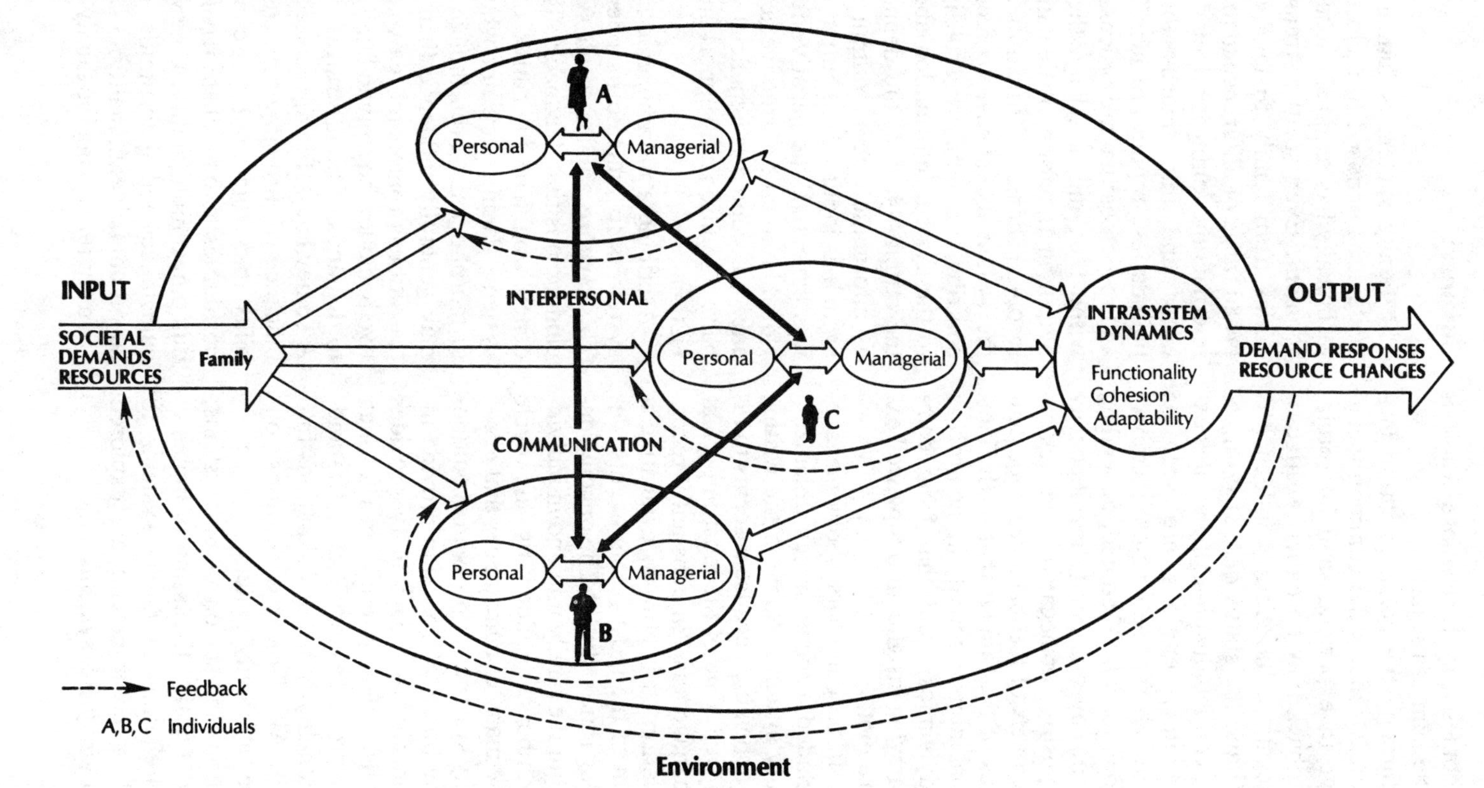

ily, which becomes a system whose whole is greater than the sum of its parts.

Feedback through the communication process to individuals reflects the common meanings responsive to experience and interpretation. Such feedback may be either positive or negative. If negative, the group's influence is toward control and the status quo. If positive, the response is continually changing as new experiences and interpretations are seen as growth opportunities for one or more members with implications for all. Of course, depending on the situation, any one family member may elicit either a positive or negative feedback response. Three levels of feedback are important to the dynamics of the family: that of the individual, that from internal activity in the process (intrasystem dynamics), and that from completed tasks carrying insights into how well expectations were met.

Discussions in recent years about management have included a focus on self-organizing and evolutionary systems. Some of the writing is particularly appealing because it seems to reflect reality so well. One of the most important functions of managers is "in constantly recognizing the situation as it now is, evaluating it and, in the light of the most recent events, deciding and acting rationally."[18] The ongoing development within the family unit and in individual family members, prodded by life cycle changes and the many circumstances that occur within the family system, supports an evolutionary nature. The bonds of cohesion provide integrity; the capacity for adaptability provides dynamic response; clear interchanges through communication processes facilitate understanding; and functionality translates situations into effective action. All of these dimensions contribute to a healthy family system.

Many situations impact on family systems, as was suggested in the discussion of inputs in this chapter. Relations of family systems to their near and far environments are explored in Chapter 3: Family Ecosystems.

Summary

The family system is fundamentally an open system, as opposed to a closed system, which technically has minimal exchange with its environment. Even so, the strength of boundaries varies from family to family, and there is a broad range of difference in the degree to which internal functioning is affected by external influences and interchanges that permeate the boundaries. Inputs are identified as demands and resources that are processed as throughput within the family and leave the family system as output in the form of demand responses and resource changes. Critical to a family system is the system's response to feedback. Feedback contributes a monitoring role in conveying back to the system information about the nature of the output—hence, the definition of feedback as information about output that reenters the system as input. If the output differs from what was expected, the negative feedback response would be to take corrective action. If the difference is accepted as beneficial, the positive feedback response is to support and amplify the deviation.

Ascribing a morphogenic nature to a family system is to indicate its openness to change. This posture applies to all system activity including positive feedback. The opposite tendency would be indicative of a morphostatic system. Families are not wholly morphostatic or morphogenic, even though those tendencies may generally influence their behavior. Life's transitions promote more expansive or contractive behavior, so a given family shifts according to demands of its life stages or circumstances. A somewhat different manifestation of the significance of throughput processes is the possibility that from similar circumstances and opportunities, two families arrive at quite different outcomes: multifinality. Likewise, different circumstances and opportunities may lead to similar outcomes: equifinality.

In characterizing the family system, two subsystems were identified as integral to throughput or transformation processes. They are the individual personal and managerial subsystems. These subsystems of individuals are in constant interaction. Through reinforcing interrelationships facilitated by communication among family members, a unique pattern of intrasystem dynamics evolves, represented by family cohesion, adaptability, and functionality. As positive forces, these dimensions are considered to be crucial to a healthy family and connote the synergism indicative of an effective system.

Within the family system, major components (or subsystems) of individual managerial subsystems are presented in Chapter 1 as planning and implementing. Major components of individual personal subsystems have been discussed in this chapter as developmental and values subsystems. Capacities and values from the personal subsystem become inputs to the managerial subsystem as sources of goal orientation and human capacities for managerial activity. Managerial activity, in turn, provides opportunity for further development of individual knowledge and skills (an example of resource changes) and for continued value evolution.

Notes

1. Mortimer J. Adler, *A Guidebook to Learning for the Lifelong Pursuit of Wisdom* (New York: Macmillan Publishing Co., 1986), p. 127.
2. Alfred Kuhn and Robert D. Beam, *The Logic of Organization* (San Francisco: Jossey-Bass Publishers, 1982), pp. 27–34.
3. Fremont E. Kast and James E. Rosenzweig, "General Systems Theory: Applications for Organization and Management," *Academy of Management Journal* 15 (December 1972): 450.
4. Walter Buckley, *Sociology and Modern Systems Theory* (Englewood Cliffs, N.J.: Prentice-Hall, 1967), p. 79.
5. Doris Beard and Francille M. Firebaugh, "Morphostatic and Morphogenic Planning Behavior in Families: Development of a Measurement Instrument," *Home Economics Research Journal* 6 (March 1978): 192, 194.
6. Jerry M. Lewis, W. Robert Beavers, John T. Gossett, and Virginia Austin Phillips, *No Single Thread* (New York: Brunner/Mazel, 1976), p. 50.
7. Kast and Rosenzweig, "General Systems Theory," p. 450.
8. Beard and Firebaugh, "Morphostatic and Morphogenic Planning," pp. 192, 194.
9. Kathryn Rettig and Glenda Everett, "Management, Crucial Subject Matter for the Home Economist in the '80's," *Canadian Home Economics Journal* 32 (Winter 1982): 20.
10. Jacqueline Fawcett, "The Family as a Living Open System: An Emerging Conceptual Framework," *International Nursing Review* 22 (July/August 1975): 113–116.
11. Janet Beavin Bavelas and Lynn Segal, "Family Systems Theory: Background and Implications," *Journal of Communications* 32 (Summer 1982): 102.
12. David H. Olson and Hamilton I. McCubbin with Howard Barnes, Andrea Larsen, Marla Muxen, and Marc Wilson, *Families: What Makes Them Work* (Beverly Hills, California: Sage Publications, Inc., 1983), p. 47.
13. W. R. Beavers and D. H. Olson, "Epilogue," *Family Process* 22 (1983): 97.
14. Mary Winter and Ivan F. Beutler, "Home Production as a Propinquous Activity," paper presented to North Central Regional Committee (NCR-116) on Family Resource Management, Columbus, Ohio, 1982.
15. Olson et al., p. 48.
16. Ibid.
17. James C. McCroskey, Carol E. Larson, and Mark L. Knapp, *An Introduction to Interpersonal Communication* (Englewood Cliffs, N.J.: Prentice-Hall, 1971), pp. 3–4.
18. F. Malik and G. Probst, "Evolutionary Management," *Cybernetics and Systems, an International Journal* 13 (1982): 153–174. Reprinted in *Self-Organization and Management of Social Systems,* H. Ulrich and G. J. B. Probst, eds. (Berlin: Springer-Verlag, 1984), pp. 105–120.

3

An ecosystem perspective of the family

Ecological systems (ecosystems) are the totality of organisms and environments that interact interdependently. We give focus by identifying individuals and families in their living settings as the units (organisms) whose environmental interrelationships are under review. In the previous chapter, information was presented as the fundamental or necessary resource supportive to the processes of family and other goal-oriented, self-regulating systems, while matter and energy flows are primary to plants and other systems responding to natural laws. But in the broad ecological perspective, everything is connected and interdependent. Changes in one dimension affect others. Ecologically, the basic resource flows of matter, energy, and information occur between and among units at all levels of comprehensiveness: global, national, regional, state, or local.

We are a very complex and interrelated world, by comparison to preindustrial periods. In the process of becoming so, imbalances have occurred in the relationship of ourselves as human beings and our environment. We see these imbalances as pollution, crowding, the endangerment of species, or the contrasting economic effects of deflation and inflation: unemployment and eroded savings. While imbalances in the natural environment tend to trigger self-correcting processes, human actions can knowingly or unknowingly thwart adjustments. The effects of the loss of nonrenewable resources are debated, for example. Recognizing, understanding, and minimizing such effects are important so that optimum benefits can be realized from the interdependencies we share—for our own welfare as well as that of future generations.

In this chapter, families and households are placed in the overall context of society and are recognized for their significant role as primary units in our complex ecosystem. We will explore the relationships of the family system between and among other units, all of which serve as environments for each other, rather than the internal processes occurring within the family. The discussion in the previous chapter of the family and its subsystems that receive inputs from and make outputs to the ecosystem presupposes this integral relationship.

The family depends on various external systems and vice versa. *External systems* are all of the functioning units outside the family—units that, as part of their environment, interact directly with the family or affect it indirectly. Families and individuals depend on businesses, all levels of government, churches, and other community groups. Schools and universities provide formal education; and vocational programs provide training for special skills that once may have been learned from a skilled craftsman in the home.

Consideration of a family's interrelationships with the various dimensions of its environment involves an expanded view of systems. The *microenvironment* includes the surrounding elements of the living environment common to all family systems. The microenvironment is made up of physical habitats, including homes and yards and social aspects relating to kin, friends, and neighbors. While the physical residence and members of any one family are integral to their own system, they are also a part of the microenvironment of other families with whom interchanges occur on a personal or support level. The larger *macroenvironment* surrounds the microenvironment through: (1) related societal systems: sociocultural, political, economic, and technological; and (2) the natural and structured surroundings or settings for all other ecosystem interchanges. These environments and their different components are presented diagrammatically in Figure 3.1, even though a two-dimensional illustration understates the complex intertwining of systems and ever-changing boundaries of most of the systems.

Boundaries separate a system's area of influence from that of other systems; *interface* is the common or shared boundary of systems. Notice that in the diagram the thickness of the lines (boundaries) that separate types of systems from each other become narrower from the outside circle to the inner circle. This is to illustrate the increasing permeability, or openness to interchange, of individual systems within and across encircled areas as we move from the outer area inward to the family system at the core. By contrast, man-made structures are often built with as much imperviousness to change as possible for safety or durability. Yet, natural forces inevitably make their impact. The boundaries of biological systems may be vulnerable, but their orientation is to maintain, not initiate, life-style changes—as is our human inclination.

The boundaries of many families or household units are flexible. For example, a divorced father lives in a mobile home on his parents' property. The father and his children eat frequently with his parents and share laundry facilities. On weekends when the children visit their mother, he may assume the role of a single man with little or no participation in activities or shared facilities with his parental family.

Or, as reported from an analysis of households as income-pooling units:

> . . . we have consistently run into a problem of household boundaries, membership, and composition. . . . Income-pooling practices clearly extend beyond biological kinship and bind individuals who are dispersed geographically. Consider a current example that is commonly found in very low-waged urban areas in the United States: The individual who eats in one household may sleep in another, and contributes resources to yet another. Can an individual be a member of multiple households? Income-pooling appears to have rather complex, circuitous and overlapping boundaries.[1]

The age-old question continues regarding the degree to which people shape or are shaped by their environments. The question is moot from an ecological perspective: Interdependent relationships among life forms and their physical environments are mutually beneficial and constraining. An ecosystem approach is a holistic one: It recognizes that the parts of the system function within larger systems that are ultimately planetary in scope.

Microenvironment

As Figure 3.1 indicates, the *microenvironment* provides the immediate setting for the family system: the physical and social surroundings of the family or household. The setting close to the family system involves the area of regular and

FIGURE 3.1 *The micro- and macroenvironment of the family system*

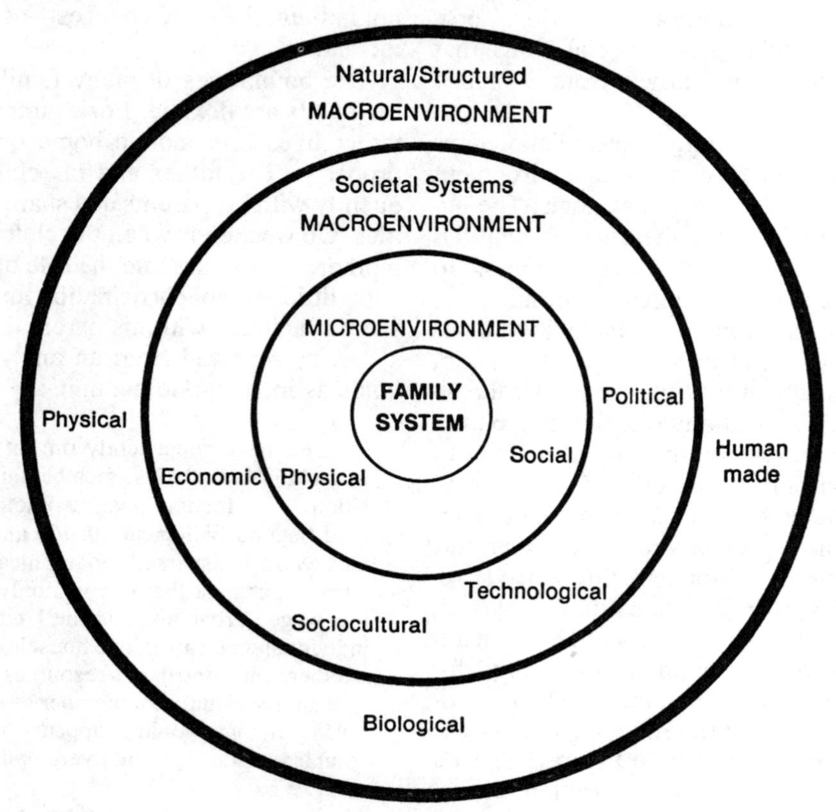

personal contact: (1) the living unit and surroundings, (2) all the objects available to enhance the environment or promote the purposes of each member, and (3) the biological systems, including plants, animals, and individual family members.

Permeating the boundaries of the family system is relatively easy, although there is much variation among individual units. For example, the people who live next door may not be neighbors who interact with the family, while a person or family several houses or apartments away may be. A given family's outer boundary for its microenvironment is actually a result of environmental interchanges. These boundaries are more definitional than physical, representing what experience identifies as the meaningful interrelationships beyond the family unit.

The opportunity for individuals and families to be able to determine their social relationship or the nature of the physical setting in which they live affects what describes a given family's microenvironment. In the process, a natural transition and filtering effect of the inputs from the macroenvironment occur.

PHYSICAL HABITATS

Within their own microenvironment, individuals and families occupy spatial territory, which may be marked by a house, apartment, or a room plus the edge of the lawn, hedges, or fences that circumscribe the area. In Western society, people ordinarily expect and are expected to have a place to live. Recent awareness of the growing number of homeless people brings both criticism and sensitive response—both supportive to the norm.

Space and time are principal frameworks within which people, in fact all living things, organize their lives. Space and time provide the context for experiences and might be expected to determine housing locations. However, the nature of housing, within limits, may carry more weight in its selection than the closeness of its location to employment.[2] The time constraints may be simply an acceptable commuting distance and convenience to other services. The quality and character of the space and location are apparently more significant. Housing furnishings provide the sense of place, opportunity for privacy, rest, development, and intimacy that serve the personal needs and interests of its residents.

Individual responses to housing and available space vary with backgrounds, preferences, and values. The responses are part of interactions of the physical and social environments with the family system. When space is seen as adequate, there is an uncrowded feeling; when there is crowding or overcrowding, psychological or physiological stress may occur. Such stress might evolve because there is a perceived deficit with respect to the cultural norm one's group holds for "needed" space. Such norms vary from culture to culture but can provide a strong influence on choices regarding the amount of living space—the number of bedrooms needed, for example.[3] The long-term effects of adapting to crowding need to be explored. Individuals are able to cope with crowded conditions, but the social, psychological, or related costs of this adaptation are not known.

Changes in household composition and shifts from traditional living arrangements can have an influence on the location and nature of housing selected. The question has been raised as to whether our increasingly independent lifestyles may have adverse effects on the social relations and mental health of persons living alone. According to a study of patterns of social "integration" across various living arrangements, this was not the case. While persons living alone spend less total time in the company of others, there is a clear compensatory process occurring, "so that for the most part persons living alone tend to show more extensive social integration outside the household than persons living with others in more conventional family situations."[4]

SOCIAL ASPECTS

The family system is shown in Figure 3.1 as having other primary social systems surrounding it (not necessarily in physical proximity)—specifically relatives, friends, and neighbors. Social aspects relate to the interaction family system members have with relatives, friends, and neighbors and the variations that relate to family life-cycle stage, age, socioeconomic status, and cultural background.

Over the life cycle, external relationships and influences vary from community to community and with the passage of time. A study of adolescent orientations toward peers and parents showed such changes over recent years. For example, though teenage boys were less inclined in 1976 than in 1965 to consult their parents on topics relating to money, education, careers, and social life, they were again more oriented to doing so in 1982. Stronger peer than parental orientations were reflected in all years on social events, hobbies, and how to dress.[5]

At later life-cycle stages, meaningful social interchanges may be affected by racial or ethnic patterns or by other influences, such as differences in local customs. Evidence from past studies of black families in various locations has indicated that substantial material, informational, and emotional support is extended from one to another. A national survey of black families in 1979–1980 provides a more comprehensive picture of these support patterns and corroborates earlier studies. Respondents interviewed in the national sample reported frequent interaction, close residential proximity, and extension of both material and emotional support among family members and relatives. Higher incomes were related to a higher probability of receiving material support, but older persons were less likely to receive support than were younger ones.[6]

Relationships and supports within and among families were compared in two isolated fishing communities, "Fishneck" and "Seafood".[7] The purpose was to determine whether family processes were comparable across such communities similar in size and other occupational and organizational characteristics. If family patterns were not comparable, the variations and their causes were a part of the investigation. What the researchers found were basic differences in the kinship structure of the communities. Fishneckers were dependent on kin for their sense of identity and of community, as the researcher reported:

> The Fishneck area can best be defined by tracing kinship rather than geographic lines. Fishneckers disagree over community boundaries, but they do not disagree about who does and does not belong to the community. In response to my question, "Is 'X' a Fishnecker?," the answers would typically be, "Yea, he's kin to 'Y' (another Fishnecker in the area)," or "No, he ain't kin to nobody down here." However, when I asked about geographic boundaries in the community, I received as many different responses as people I asked. . . . When I asked Seafooders about community membership, they responded in terms of the part of the Island on which they live, not in terms of kin. Extended-kin lines, once an important source of ties, are now less important for identification. Family patterns of Seafood have undergone a marked transition from large extended families to small and more isolated conjugal units.[8]

The changing friendship-kinship network of the aging is of particular interest as the number and percent of people sixty-five and older in the United States increase. Among grandparents, involvement with friends contributed more to differences in life satisfaction than involvement with grandchildren.[9] Age dissimilarity undoubtedly contributes to the lesser importance of grandchildren in life satisfaction, while common interests, experiences, and values held by friends enhance the role of friends in life satisfaction of the aging.

Neighborhoods, residential areas having some identifiable character, serve as a buffer to change. The neighborhood remains important today even with mobility and social change.

In summary, the interrelationships of the family and individuals with their immediate physical and social environments are important in understanding and promoting effective use of resources in meeting their goals. The physical setting provides a spatial context within which and from which primary social interactions take place. The microenvironment also provides a buffer through which what is most relevant from the larger, macroenvironment is channeled.

Macroenvironment

SOCIETAL SYSTEMS

Societal systems are a significant part of the ecosystem of the family, surrounding the microenvironment and providing comprehensive systems of interchange for meeting individual and family needs. Information, goods, and varied services are constantly exchanged with these related societal systems: sociocultural, political, economic, and technological. Most often, the impact of family systems on these related systems occurs by groups of families or individuals, rather than by the influence of one person. Transactions between the societal systems and individuals or families are less personal or intimate than in the microenvironment.

As part of the assumption that interchanges occur among the various systems of an ecosystem, the accompanying assumption of interdependency is also important. What one system does affects another. In systems terms, what one system "puts out" into the environment affects other systems either by being taken into other systems directly or by affecting the nature of the environment. These interchanges may be in the form of goals, needs, or expectations one system holds or provides for another or as tangible support or resources. Such interrelationships of the family system with societal systems are summarized in Table 3.1 as outputs from given systems directed as inputs and vice versa.

Sociocultural. Culture defines the meaning and content of a society: the values and the cumulative experiences, knowledge, skills, and material goods that comprise its heritage. Changes in cultural meanings occur through social processes. The process is two-way. Collectively, the choices of individuals and families bring about reinterpretations of sociocultural norms over time. The sociocultural system involves the processes through which the meaning and content of any society are reinforced or changed.

> . . . there is not one aspect of human life that is not touched and altered by culture. This means personality, how people express themselves (including shows of emotion), the way they think, how they move, how problems are solved, how their cities are planned and laid out, how transportation systems function and are organized, as well as how economic and government systems are put together and function.[10]

Usually the dominant culture represents the major influences affecting the character of the area. Subgroups are conscious of these dominating influences and may or may not seek to be absorbed into the fabric of the community.

Because of their strong cultural heritage, some groups remain apart from the general society. Members of the Amish community are such an example. Adjustments to change are made, but in relation to their group, not to society in general.

> . . . being Amish means living in a closely interwoven society that links religious, familial, societal, educational, and vocational beliefs into a complete whole. Totally immersed in the Old Order (descendants of 16th century Mennonites) traditions and participating in a society where members have the resources and desire to continually provide for each other, the Amish member experiences a sense of security that few non-Amish ever know. The degree of constraint on the individual is mitigated by a sense of separateness from the outside world and also by the freedom to relocate in another Old Order community where certain conditions might be slightly different and therefore more to the liking of a particular family.[11]

Finding mutual reinforcement in strong kinship ties can be fostered by immigration into a society. An illustration of this relates to the large influx of Koreans into the United States since 1970. Kinship ties were enhanced as a part of the adjustment to their new environment, apparently engendering closer ties than if they had stayed in Korea.[12]

Some ethnic groups have a strong desire to become a part of the dominant societal system. The interactions between the sociocultural and family systems can be influential. Adjusting to changed circumstances and a strong desire to become part of the dominant societal system are not necessarily the same, but the resulting impact on the family system can be similar. For example, seeing the need to move or learn new skills to earn a desired level of living may lead to involvement in the socioeconomic mainstream; a strong achievement motivation may lead to the same involvement.

Cultural values carry a sense of commitment and moral obligation to behave in a prescribed manner. Cultural expectations and societal norms tend to prescribe and sometimes limit the scope of managerial involvement (as will be dis-

TABLE 3.1 *Interrelationships of the family system with societal systems*

Interchange	*Goals or expectations to be fulfilled*	*Resources or support to be given*
From sociocultural to family system	Behaviors consistent with sociocultural values, accordingly, socialization of children.	Sense of identity, affiliation, and commendation for appropriate response in support of sociocultural consensus.
From family to sociocultural system	Recognition of special needs and pressures; latitudes for adapting as dynamics of changing societal conditions impinge.	Adherence to and appreciation of sociocultural values; continuation of heritage through socialization of children.
From political to family system	Anticipated adherence to laws and other regulations; politically socialized members.	Protection; provision of services, programs, and policies to meet needs.
From family to political system	Expressions of needs or values held—formal (in support of issues) or informal (letters, meetings).	Tax payments; obeying laws and other regulations; military service; court duty; voting.
From economic to family system	Quantity of goods and services purchased; labor and other productive resources provided at a reasonable price.	Reasonable return for labor and other productive outputs; dependable goods and services at acceptable prices.
From family to economic system	Goods and services available at an acceptable price; opportunities to participate in productive processes; reasonable protection at the market.	Expenditures for consumer goods and services; provision of labor and other productive resources at reasonable and agreeable terms.
From technological to family system	Availability of improved products and services consistent with level of alternatives needed.	Adoption of practices, products, and services, in keeping with optimum social and ecological interactions.
From family to technological system	Indication of products and services required to meet changing needs and social expectations.	Assumption of appropriate responsibility for shared ecological and societal needs and commitments.

cussed in Chapter 4). The family structure in the state of Kerala in India, a strong matriarchal society, identifies the woman as the decision maker and manager of the household. Another example would be festival time in some countries, which may place heavy demands on the limited resources of families, affecting their ability to provide for basic needs.

Parents are not the *only* transmitters of cultural learning today. In fact, the process may work in reverse. Ever-widening communication processes bring the outside world to children in schools and in less formal educational settings. For example, American Indian adults who learn from their children as well as from other American Indians may be better informed about many aspects of their heritage than their parents.

Political. The political system affects the family system through laws, regulations, protection, and other services. The political system encourages politically responsible citizens and requires adherence to laws and regulations. Goods and services, such as education and recreational facilities, are frequently made available through the public sharing of resources rather than by private means. Such public goods are equally available to all. One person's use of the good does not alter another person's enjoyment or basis for access to its use, except temporarily. An example of a public good is a lake with water recreation facilities. Community facilities and services like parks, playgrounds, libraries, police, and fire protection are important resources in family management. Knowledge about community resources is a prerequisite to the actual availability of a resource to an individual or family. This knowledge often depends on the person's being literate and exposed to other services or information.

Policies and regulations of the political system can have almost immediate impact on the family system. Examples include changes in the social security system or the prohibition of foodstuff additives that contain carcinogens. Zoning regulations affect choices made by families and other systems, such as business and industry. Care of children above a certain number must often have zoning commission approval.

Education is probably one of the most far-reaching and influential governmental services affecting family managerial behavior. Traditionally, government-supported education in the United States has been considered necessary to promote responsible decision making by citizens.

Families support the political system by tax payments, responsible voting, adherence to laws, and the fulfillment of other civic obligations, such as jury duty. Members of the family system and individuals can inform the political system of their values and needs in person, by appearing before the city council or the state or federal legislative committees. Others may become an integral part of the political system through appointment or election.

Economic. The economic system is based on the purchase of goods and services, and the aggregate choices make up market demand: total amount of a good or service that consumers will buy at a given time and at a given price. The family receives dependable goods and services and a fair return for its participation in production processes only to the extent that the economic system supports the family system's demands.

The family expects the economic system to make goods and services available that the family can purchase at acceptable prices within a context of reasonable protection of market values. The family makes purchases and provides productive resources on reasonable and/or agreeable terms of exchange, thus supporting the economic system. The family expects that the economic system will provide opportunities for family members to participate equitably in productive processes through their labor and investments.

The choices families make as producers and consumers influence the general economy and affect the available family resources. Spending decisions affect family lifestyle and create market demand. The family's capabilities and circumstances influence their choices among available alternatives within the opportunities and constraints of the general economy. The family's interaction with the general economic system is mutually responsive when consumers use information to make choices that reflect their needs.

Technological. Technology's basic role in a managerial sense is as a tool, as a means through which knowledge, material, and energy may be usefully applied. Science and technology relate to the development of products and services, while management promotes their considered choice and use. Changing technology has both personal and social welfare implications and increases the significance of management.

High technology is a much-used term that,

because of different interpretations and complex applications, apparently has no acceptable definition. Generally implied, however, is the shift from an emphasis on machines or product applications that fostered the industrial revolution to electronic or other fundamental changes in structures or functions. These fundamental changes are introducing ethical questions along with opportunities—as with genetic possibilities for correcting handicapping conditions as well as inadvertently introducing them.

Increasingly, families and individuals must consider their needs in relation to the impact of their choices on the environment and on the cost of the energy to operate and maintain the purchase. These concerns tie individuals and families integrally to their macroenvironment.

Involvement of individuals and families with their environment is illustrated by the responses of those living in the communities surrounding the Three Mile Island nuclear accident. Following the accident, a plan for purging the reactor met with resistance from residents of the area due to a decline in confidence in the information disseminated regarding proposed plans. To improve communication, a citizen radiation-monitoring program was initiated to involve residents in the process of reading radiation detectors for comparison of citizen and official data on radiation levels. With comparable readings plus strengthened efforts to address safety concerns, improvements occurred in the attitudes of members of the communities regarding how well informed and safe they felt.[13]

NATURAL AND STRUCTURED SYSTEMS

Social systems such as the family interact in a physical setting. *Natural and structured systems* are the physical and biological surroundings within which related societal systems function. These physical and biological systems include space, structured as buildings and highways, natural space such as parks and wilderness areas, and the accompanying biological systems such as marine, plant, and animal life.

Many family resources originate in the macroenvironment and society and families change matter and energy into forms they need. Probably the most familiar example is the alteration of food into desired forms through technological processing and by freezing, drying, and cooking.

Environmental concerns. An awareness of environmental concerns can increase recognition of systems interrelationships. Past changes made in the natural environment were often made to serve people better. Families and individuals contributed to altered land use through their preference for single-family dwellings. Changed courses of rivers and landscapes resulted from highway construction and urban sprawl. In the interest of economic development, industrial plants were located at sites with cheap water, cheap energy, and often cheap labor. Polluted air and streams resulted.

Increased attention to environmental concerns has led to regulations regarding industrial discharges, residential wastes, and pollutants from the transportation system. Products have been changed to reduce air and stream pollution. Families and individuals alter their systems exchanges with the natural environment by their consumer choices, such as biodegradable products, reuseable containers, and pump dispensers.

Energy consumption and conservation. Total energy consumption in the United States in the mid-1980s was at about the same level as it was ten years earlier. Consumption had increased through 1979 and then trended downward during the early 1980s. In 1984, likely in response to lower oil costs, the trend again reversed. Residential use is about 20 percent of the total. Efficiency in the fuel consumption of automobiles increased from 13.1 to 16.7 miles per gallon between 1973 and 1983. Since the miles driven per car did not change comparably, the actual fuel consumption per car decreased over the period. However, our energy usage for all transportation needs has been relatively constant.[14]

Household waste. Families as consumers contribute directly to elevated waste levels and pollution through automobile exhausts, gases from space heating and incineration, noise from machines (such as lawn mowers), sewage, and solid wastes (such as garbage and junked autos and appliances).

The extent and patterns of garbage generated by families have been examined by the University of Arizona's Garbage Project in Tucson over a ten-year period. A First Principle of Edible Food Loss has been derived, to the effect "that the *short-run* response to rapid price rises or shortages is likely to be high rates of consumer experimentation, or change, that result in increased food losses."[15] The study has also shown the reverse to be true: that when the patterns of food consumption are similar from day to day, there is less discarding of edible foods.

Another observation from the same study concerns the somewhat complex relationship between prepared packaged food, which has a low rate of waste, and fresh produce, which has the highest rate of waste. Households that have the greatest dependence on packaged foods also have the highest percentage loss of whatever fresh produce they purchased. These same households are presumed to have limited time for food preparation and for planning—hence, the purchase of prepared packaged foods and the inability to give the attention and handling needed to use fresh produce without waste. In contrast, households purchasing higher proportions of fresh foods had lower food losses. The opportunity to utilize these foods well would seem to be the corollary explanation. Also, regardless of household type or purchasing patterns, knowledge of food safety is the most apparent reason for reduced food losses.[16]

The Tucson Study has shown that around 10 percent of the solid, once-edible food purchased is discarded as waste. This represents 300 grams/household/day. In 1977, the U.S. General Accounting Office projected food losses in the United States at $11.7 billion a year.[17] This equals $20.8 billion in 1985 dollars.

Environmental effects. Our natural resources and surroundings are being seriously affected by the level of living desired by many of us in the United States. We have begun to evaluate the impact of alterations to the environment. Some decisions mean temporary problems; the limit on burning sulfur-containing coal means that we must pay higher prices to bring in other coal or to clean up the air. The concern for environmental quality will continue to be weighed against other problems, such as energy shortages.

We have tried to control and modify our environment, including climate, probably more than ourselves. Our increasing control over the environment, especially at the micro- and ecoclimate levels, may slowly reduce the biological, psychological, and social capability to adapt to new environmental conditions. Our emphasis always seems to be on modifying the environment rather than on modifying or controlling the human organism to give it the innate capability to cope with the environment.[18]

Adjustments to localized energy and water shortages have shown individuals to be open to making necessary changes when circumstances are adverse. One hopes such responsiveness is not limited to crisis situations.

Weather and climate effects on families. In developed countries, temperature extremes require heating and cooling of residences, weather patterns affect food crop production, and employment may be limited by weather. In developing countries, however, even everyday life must respond to weather changes. If cooking takes place outdoors or classes are held outdoors, dust storms may immediately affect the activities. Most critical is the family's relation-

TABLE 3.2 *Interrelationships of systems of the macroenvironment*

Interchange	*Goals or expectations to be fulfilled*	*Resources or support to be given*
From physical/biological to societal systems	Basic material and energy sources.	Raw materials for processing and distribution; natural environments for public use.
From societal to physical/biological systems	Consumption products; waste; available energy; regulation mechanisms.	Altered space, water, atmosphere; changed materials, supplies, and forms of energy.

ship to the land: In a subsistence-level agricultural setting, when the weather is bad for crops, many people will lack sufficient food.

Family systems and individuals regularly interact with human-made aspects of the macroenvironment. Roads, sidewalks, office buildings, stores, schools, shopping centers, churches, theaters—all around us are spaces that may or may not be conducive to the growth and development of individuals whose lives are affected.

Interactions of the macroenvironment with family systems. While interactions of the macroenvironment with family systems have been emphasized, interactions of physical and biological systems with societal systems in the macroenvironment provide important interchanges of the total ecosystem. These may be summarized according to their expected and actual contributions (resources or support) to the alternate system (see Table 3.2).

Summary

The interplay of individual and family systems with all external systems has been the emphasis of this chapter. As the primary social unit, families interact with all external systems (not all external systems interact with each other). For this reason, the boundaries of family systems tend to be more permeable, or subject to intersystem information flows, than other societal systems. Also, families are often strategic to changes occurring in other systems, either in terms of support or resistance. External systems, in turn, provide constraints and opportunities to families and individuals.

The microenvironment represents the living context within which families carry out their day-to-day activities and personal social interchanges—their more proximate habitats and social networks. The macroenvironment provides the larger societal mechanisms and settings. Included are the sociocultural, political, economic, and technological systems and the natural and built environments supportive to societal processes. The nature of the interchanges between the family and societal systems, in terms of the goals to be fulfilled and resources exchanged, are presented to clarify the nature of their interdependency.

Notes

1. Kathie Friedman, "Households as Income-Pooling Units," from *Households and the World Economy,* Joan Smith, Immanuel Wallerstein, and Hans-Dieter Evers, eds. (Beverly Hills: Sage Publications, 1984), p. 51.
2. Earl W. Morris and Mary Winter, *Housing, Family, and Society* (New York: Wiley, 1978), pp. 138–139.
3. Ibid., pp. 31–34.
4. Duane F. Alwin, Philip E. Converse, and Steven S. Martin, "Living Arrangements and Social Integration," *Journal of Marriage and the Family* 47 (May 1985): 329.
5. Hans Sebald, "Adolescents' Shifting Orientation toward Parents and Peers: A Curvilinear Trend

over Recent Decades," *Journal of Marriage and the Family* 48 (February 1986): 7.

6. Robert Joseph Taylor, "Receipt of Support from Family among Black Americans: Demographic and Familial Differences," *Journal of Marriage and the Family* 48 (February 1986): 67–77.

7. Carolyn Ellis, "Community Organization and Family Structure in Two Fishing Communities," *Journal of Marriage and the Family* 46 (August 1984): 515–526.

8. Ibid., p. 517.

9. Vivian Wood and Joan F. Robertson, "Friendship and Kinship Interaction: Differential Effect on the Morale of the Elderly," *Journal of Marriage and the Family* 40 (May 1978): 369–370.

10. Edward T. Hall, *Beyond Culture* (Garden City: Anchor Books, 1977), pp. 16–17.

11. Elmer Schwieder and Dorothy Schwieder, *A Peculiar People: Iowa's Old Order Amish* (Ames: The Iowa State University Press, 1975), pp. 78–79.

12. Pyong Gap Min, "An Exploratory Study of Kin Ties among Korean Immigrant Families in Atlanta," *Journal of Comparative Family Studies* 15 (Spring 1984): 59–75.

13. Barbara Gray Gricar and Anthony J. Baratta, "Bridging the Information Gap at Three Mile Island: Radiation Monitoring by Citizens," *Journal of Applied Behavioral Science* 19 (January 1983): 35–49.

14. U.S. Department of Energy, Energy Information Administration, National Energy Information Center, *Energy Facts 1984* (Washington, D.C.: U.S. Department of Energy, 1985, pp. 4, 7.

15. William L. Rathje, "The Garbage Decade," *American Behavioral Scientist* 28 (September/October 1984): 17–18.

16. Ibid., pp. 18–19.

17. Ibid., p. 17.

18. Paul Sommers and Rudolf Moos, "The Weather and Human Behavior," in *The Human Context,* Rudolf H. Moos, ed. (New York: Wiley, 1976), p. 102.

4

Values and demands

The norms of society have a continuing influence on the evolution of individual and family values and goals. Experiences throughout development gradually become integrated into a person's values, identifying what is more and less important. These evolving value processes within the personal subsystems and the shared meanings among family members (represented as a part of intrasystem dynamics) constitute the situational and unique valuing roles of individuals and families. Individual valuing processes, which involve interchanges with all segments of society, contribute in turn to the evolution of societal norms.

As illustrated in Figure 2.2, value/goal orientations are outputs of the values subsystem of the personal system to the managerial system. The nature of values is given first consideration in this chapter. Then their action-based manifestations as goals, giving direction to the management, will be addressed. Included also is a discussion of events as the other component along with goals that comprise the demand inputs in the managerial system.

Values

Values permeate all aspects of management, providing the bases for decisions. *Values* are the essential meanings relating to what is desirable or has worth, providing fundamental criteria for goals, thereby giving continuity to all decisions and actions. At the same time, management contributes to the clarification of values as goals. Values provide both the purpose toward which managerial activity is directed and criteria to identify the means through which demands are effectively met.

CHARACTERISTICS

An understanding of the nature of values is important to the analysis of managerial processes. Characteristics particularly relevant to management are their location on an absolute–relative continuum, their intrinsic–extrinsic nature, and their general–specific scope.

The absolute versus the relative aspects of values we hold refer to the extent to which they are independent of or dependent on surrounding conditions or situations. *Absolute values* are meanings that are unrelated to surrounding factors or conditions. They are firmly held and fixed. *Relative values,* on the other hand, are meanings that depend on their context for interpretation of what is desirable or of worth.

Absolute values. Absolute values are deeply rooted, associated with one's way of life, and subject to little change. Absolute values are appropriately justified on spiritual or other fundamental grounds. They give special direction and meaning to life and need to be carefully nurtured. Similar to absolute values for their effect on management are normative values, those which are reinforced through people's own experiences or by the expectations of those around them: neighbors, colleagues, community, the country. Absolute values are taken as givens, while normative values may have evolved by similar reevaluation of recurring situations.

Normative values, like absolute values, tend to be prescriptive and binding; they may change slowly, however, with shifts in social values and experience. Normative values are not "absolutely" unaffected by the special circumstances of a given situation unless they have reached a point where such factors are never taken into account. Absolute trustworthiness would mean that the individual never considers betraying a confidence, regardless of related consequences. Accepting a social and employer expectation of getting to work on time as a value becomes a behavioral norm, which may be subject to special circumstances, such as family illness.

Relative values. Relative values depend on their context for interpretation. In many situations, a student often has to weigh recreation relative to education values just as professors have to weigh personal enrichment relative to writing for professional advancement. Individual and group values can be more responsive to new situations if they are more relative than absolute, because relative values are open to new alternatives. However, relative values also make decisions more complex. A person who responds to a query about the importance of something with "It all depends" is giving a relative value response.

The more relative a person's values, the broader the managerial potential he or she has. Conversely, the person who primarily adheres to absolute values reduces alternatives and narrows the managerial potential. Absolute values may also simplify responses to many demands and be deeply significant to those who hold them. Some individuals and groups choose simplified life-styles through high commitment to certain absolute values. An example is the Amish, who have "religious ways of life dedicated to nonconformity to all worldly things."[1] Formal schooling beyond the eighth grade is rejected. The vocational training of boys for farming and of girls for homemaking is an unchanging pattern.

Basic values, whether absolute or interpreted for their differing significance in situations, are pervasive and meaningful. Basic values are rooted in one's evolving personality and so are identified with the personal subsystem of the family system, thus providing direction to goal development and managerial behavior.

Absolute–relative value interpretations. Finding a meaningful resolution of the tension between absolute and relative value interpretations is part of the process of coping with stability and change. In reality, changing situations may foster a shift from an absolute position on the continuum to a more relative one. Less-developed societies have more absolute values and stable frameworks for decisions and actions. Following is an example among the Sioux Indians:

> I think of a young Sioux I know whose family was preparing a giveaway feast. He went to the trading post for enough bread, meat, and coffee to feed 50 or 60 people. "We'll pay you when we get the lease money in two months," he told the trader.
>
> "You'll pay me now," said the trader, who was a new man in the area.
>
> "You know I can't pay you now," said the Sioux. "The trader before you always gave us credit."

"He went broke," said the trader.

"This is a religious ceremony," said the Sioux. "I'll have to take the stuff, whether you like it or not. Watch what I take and write it down. I'll pay you when I can." And the Indian took what he needed and loaded it onto his old pickup.

The trader called the police, and now my young friend is doing time for robbery. He can't understand. Neither can his family.[2]

The value placed by the Sioux family on the religious ceremony in providing food for guests was too high to change, as was the trader's policy for no credit. Such impasses and misunderstandings may accompany situations even when both parties, from their individual views, have good intentions and high integrity. In more complex societies, industrialization and rapid technological changes have influenced shifts from a more absolute or normative value stance to a more relative one.

Values held to be generally important may not be important in every situation if they are relative in their orientation. Also, values may be absolute for some situations and relative for others. For example, an absolute value for sharing an unvarying portion of income may be specific to one's church and/or special charities. Contributions to other groups or to family members may depend on the circumstances. The values held to be important and their absolute or relative interpretations represent the meanings that guide an individual's thoughts and actions. The basic internalized values evolve over time. The greater the relative nature of these basic values, the more important managerial processing is to the decisions and actions.

Usually, the balance of absolute and relative values is related to the individual's value system. Differences in values held between groups of a population or within a population group over time are also indicative of shifts in individual value systems. A 1984 survey of 500 undergraduate students from a representative sample of 310 colleges and universities provides an opportunity to compare educational objectives as well as more-general value-goal orientations.[3] With respect to objectives considered essential through their college education, about three-fourths of the students reported as essential meeting their occupational interests, compared to the less than 60 percent who indicated that obtaining a well-rounded general education or formulating life values and goals was essential to their college experiences (Table 4.1). These differences were even more strongly reflected by women than by men and by students in public as compared to private institutions. Learning to get along with people was an essential objective for about the same proportion of students as were interested in a general education and in formulating life goals, although relatively more students in private institutions held this as an essential objective. Interestingly, about two-thirds of the students in private institutions rated all five objectives as essential.

Among the life goals (values) rated very or fairly important by the students surveyed, health and happiness were identified by almost all of them. Religious or spiritual fulfillment received the lowest proportion of very or fairly important ratings.

A good marriage was rated above raising children. Career success was rated above financial success. There was less variation between men and women students and between students attending private and public institutions than was the case for college-focused objectives. The longer time perspective may affect these differences.

Intrinsic–extrinsic orientation. Intrinsic value is the inherent and self-sufficient quality of an experience, the joy of watching a beautiful sunset or the incoming ocean tide. Intrinsic values are ultimate in their meaning or they are ends in themselves. *Extrinsic value* is the meaning or worth derived from the relation of one thing to another. Extrinsic values depend on their role in serving either intrinsic or other (higher) extrinsic values. Activities can hold intrinsic or extrinsic value, depending on the purposes they

TABLE 4.1 *Student educational objectives and life goals, 1984*

Objectives/goals	*Total*	*Student response*			
		Sex		*Institution*	
		Men	*Women*	*Public*	*Private*
		Percent			
Essential objectives at college					
Detailed grasp of a special field	73.8	71.7	74.7	74.8	66.2
Well-rounded general education	58.7	54.0	61.1	57.7	65.8
Occupational training, skills	75.2	70.8	78.1	76.5	65.7
Learning to get along with people	56.1	55.0	56.6	54.3	69.8
Formulating life values, goals	59.1	55.2	61.3	57.9	67.6
Very/fairly important goals					
Career success	96.8	98.4	95.8	96.6	97.7
Happiness	99.1	99.6	98.7	99.1	99.7
A good marriage	95.1	94.1	95.7	95.1	95.4
Raising children	85.9	85.1	86.2	85.6	87.9
Financial success	92.2	94.0	91.0	92.5	90.0
A long life	88.8	88.4	88.8	89.2	84.7
Good health	99.4	99.5	99.3	99.4	99.3
New friendships	93.0	91.9	93.6	92.6	96.1
Religious, spiritual fulfillment	80.3	77.4	81.9	80.0	81.7
Intellectual development	97.0	96.0	97.6	96.9	98.1

Source: Robert L. Jacobson, "Most Students Are Satisfied with Their Education, Survey Indicates, but Frustrations Are Widespread," *The Chronicle of Higher Education* 31:29. Survey data are from the Carnegie Foundation for the Advancement of Teaching. Copyright 1986, The Chronicle of Higher Education. Reprinted with permission.

serve. The process of nurturing a rose bush may in itself give intrinsic pleasure. Or the process may have extrinsic or instrumental value in relation to the expected fuller enjoyment of the flowering rose.

Examples of intrinsic and extrinsic values and goals are given in Table 4.2. Goals help direct specific actions consistent with either extrinsic or intrinsic values. The goal to be employed part-time may be consistent with the extrinsic value of helping to earn a desired level of living, which in turn contributes to the intrinsic value of pleasure of achievement. Goals reflect intrinsic or extrinsic values in the objectives to be met.

General–specific scope. Specific values are fulfilled or satisfied by single actions or by achieving given goals. *General values* prevail over time and involve a variety of different kinds of actions, each inadequate in its ability to satisfy. An example of a general, more pervasive value is knowledge, which is not fulfilled by the accumulation of certain facts or the achievement of a given level of education. A sense of security is not fulfilled by the purchase of a new set of tires, a new insurance policy, or even the attainment of full retirement benefits, although all contribute. A general value may encompass an extensive series of activities, as in the case of a medical missionary whose preparation for ser-

TABLE 4.2 *Examples of intrinsic and extrinsic values and goals*

Intrinsic values	*Extrinsic values*	*Goals*
Pleasure in achievement	Earning or helping to achieve a desired level of living	To be a foreman To be employed part-time To be a gourmet cook
Sense of security	Having assets to meet needs	To have life insurance To own some mutual-fund shares To have a savings account
Sense of trustworthiness	Maintaining good credit rating	To meet financial commitments

vice may require many years of study, experience, and personal growth. General values are sometimes called higher-order values because so many actions build toward them.

A managerial activity may serve one or more values at any level of generality or specificity. A decision may be complex because more general or underlying values influence the goal choices. The selection of a university may be a complex decision when a number of important general values influence the choice—communication with family, educational opportunities beyond area of interest, and desirable living situation, for example.

In summary, these characteristics can be useful in clarifying the nature of values now held and identifying why something is or is not important to one's self or others in given situations. Situations that have brought about changes in viewpoints can be analyzed. All value combinations are appropriate to management even as they affect management styles differently.

CONTENT

Value content is the meaning associated with valuing processes in arriving at judgments. Value meanings are derived from how people feel (the affective domain) and think (the cognitive domain) about situations, decisions, and actions. Predispositions evolve over time and are a part of the interchange with the personal system. Cognitive and affective capacities have been identified as dimensions or domains of personality development within the personal system. As responsibilities for choices are assumed, managerial processes provide valuing opportunities that sharpen cognitive and affective development.

Affective domain. The *affective domain* is represented by the positive or negative feelings derived from experience. These feelings provide the emotional content that, when internalized, leads to the adoption of a value system—an important aspect of personality development. For any value to reach a point where some expressive feeling is identified with it, whether enjoyment of a ballet or repulsion of flagrant waste, an internalizing process has evolved. At first, a tentative response is registered; and with continuing association, more deeply rooted positive and/or negative responses become apparent.

Early experiences are internalized, including those of receiving and being aware of situations that have expressive or affective overtones. Through continued exposure and evaluations, more definite leanings toward particular value orientations occur. An individual's value system undergoes varying degrees of influence by societal norms and by the direction of one's social development, but what is internalized becomes one's own individual value norms.

These subjective value orientations have a certain stability about them, although they are likely to be in a constant state of flux as new experiences continue to influence the content of the affective domain. Continuing experiences may also reinforce value positions.

To illustrate, a couple married for eight years who have two children review their life-style and values. He is a civil-rights lawyer and she works in an architect's office. The wife says that she and her husband "have only recently realized and accepted their different backgrounds and different values about money."

> I have felt with some justification that he thought that I was materialistic. . . . But now I think, yes, I am materialistic and I'm going to continue to be materialistic. . . .
>
> I mean, it does matter to me to feel secure. It matters to me not to have the things that other people do not necessarily think are the important things, but things that are lovely. The things that I really like, I like to have them, and I no longer choose to feel ashamed to have them or to want them.[4]

Such reflection is illustrative of an internally integrated value system.

Cognitive domain. Values accrue over time through processes that involve constant testing of possible actions against values held. This mental valuing process involves management. All managerial processes have a cognitive, or conscious, dimension. Emotional overtones associated with values of primary importance should be recognized when managerial decisions are made on an intellectual level. The *cognitive domain* is the perception of values, goals, and related criteria and the potential of the situation for their fulfillment.

A fourfold division of all learning has been proposed: (1) obtaining or receiving information, (2) acquiring knowledge, (3) supplementing knowledge with understanding, and (4) reaching for wisdom.[5] These capabilities that accrue through intellectual activity are on an increasing scale, with wisdom at the highest level. Valuing is a process of relating means and ends, and some of the discussion of the capabilities applies to an understanding of means (resources) as well as of values.

Information is defined as a simple collection of data, bit by bit. Obtaining information is not, per se, an avenue through which intellectual growth occurs—it is more a function of memory. Building from the base of information, the higher intellectual levels are differentiated as ways of knowing—knowing *that,* knowing *what,* knowing *how,* knowing *why and wherefore*. Knowing *that* builds on information through possession of a body of knowledge that is organized beyond the acquisition of unrelated facts. There is systemization to the content. Knowing *what* is also a part of the knowledge level, illustrated by historical and scientific investigation that provides explanatory insight into the nature of things.[6]

Knowing *how* represents two types of activity. First, there are the imagination and productive skills through which artifacts are produced that do not exist or occur naturally. Second, there is the capacity for knowing how to act or to promote improvements in ourselves or in society. "These are all works of art, using the word 'art' in its broadest sense. . . ."[7] Management fits this category. Knowing *how* involves an understanding of the relevant knowledge that makes desired transformations possible. If activity moves beyond the more explanatory aspects of knowing what and why to a fuller consideration of the whys and wherefores, then understanding is being extended to wisdom.

Crucial to reaching the upper cognitive levels is the process of critical or reflective thinking. Here, the values or ends to be served by any action are carefully reviewed and justified. There is an ability to discern the significant qualities or relationships in situations and to make well rounded judgments.

Subjective–objective components. The reasoning process accompanying well-grounded decisions are those that have established why something is important (subjective) and what it will take to accomplish the desired outcomes (objective). All valuing decisions have subjective and objective components. The subjective and objective components of values parallel the management concepts of goals and resources. The *subjective value component* indicates a person's needs, wants, interests, aims, or purposes: his or her goals. Accompanying each goal is a set of value criteria that need to be met (Figure 4.1).

The *objective value component* relates to the attributes and properties of available resources that can meet the subjective criteria.[8] A basic role of management is to match the subjective criteria of goals to the appropriate properties or attributes of resources as advantageously as possible.

Personal–managerial subsystems relationships. While all of the characteristics and content dimensions are important within both the personal and managerial subsystems, the characteristics and content dimensions that are likely to be emphasized in interaction between the two systems are indicated by capital letters:

Personal Subsystem	*Managerial Subsystem*
ABSOLUTE/ relative	Absolute/ RELATIVE
INTRINSIC/ extrinsic	Intrinsic/ EXTRINSIC
SUBJECTIVE/ objective	Subjective/ OBJECTIVE
AFFECTIVE/ cognitive	Affective/ COGNITIVE

With these understandings, aspects and dimensions of goals as management inputs will now be addressed as a major demand. A discussion will follow of events that are not consciously evolved demands within the family system but require managerial response. Special attention to resources will be given in Chapter 5.

Goals

Goal orientations enter the management system from the personal system initially as value-related directions to be confirmed or clarified as goals. In the initial managerial process, the significant values to be fulfilled are clarified and formulated into *goals* as value-based objectives or anticipated outcomes. Goals provide criteria for standard setting in the planning process, giving direction and purpose to the managerial system.

The degree of specificity attached to goals arising from the personal system depends in part on whether they are based on absolute or relative values. Absolute values lead to more specific goals. If one's music interest is only in country and western, the desire to hear live performances or acquire tapes of special performers becomes a focused goal. By contrast, the person who enjoys a variety of music is constantly weighing alternative options to achieve a desired balance.

Goals develop from values through many sources: experiences, new knowledge, information feedback, and environmental changes. The value of health translates into a goal to increase physical exercise when one knows the importance of physical fitness for health. The insight may have been gained through instruction, reading, medical advice, personal experience, or friends with health problems.

Goals as anticipated outcomes are further confirmed or clarified by the planning process. Not only are the underlying values reviewed, but resources are also examined for their potential availability. The goal to buy a desk may be sharpened by the need for a more convenient and comfortable study area. A couple having a goal to take a vacation in Acapulco may have to revise their thinking in favor of a trip to a nearby area after facing reality regarding travel costs.

FIGURE 4.1 *Relation of values in cognitive and affective domains, goals, standard setting, resources, and standards*

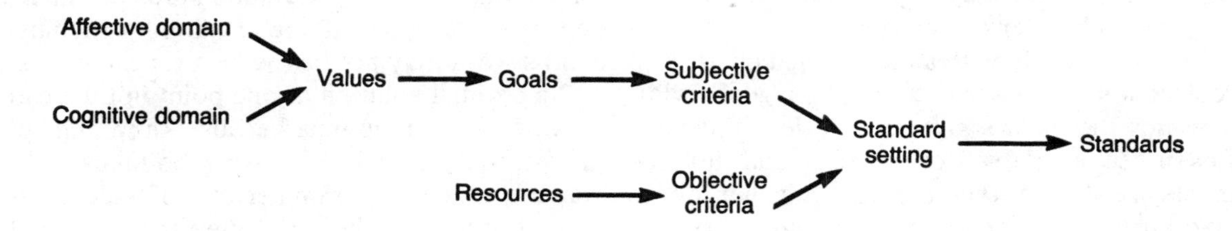

Choices among alternative goals are considered managerially: to rent or buy a house; to go to a movie or take a motorcycle ride; to be an extension worker or a teacher. Goal alternatives are examined during the planning process when the balance between resources and demands is considered. Information obtained during clarification of goals returns as feedback to the personal subsystem for verification or redefinition.

NATURE OF GOALS

Understanding the nature of goals helps to interpret their influence on other managerial subsystem components. Goals concern resources and actions and are integrally related to values. Three qualities of goals are important: duration, continuity, and interdependence.

Duration. Long- and short-term goals differ in the length of time projected to accumulate needed resources or to accomplish the goals. The goal to buy a lathe for my workshop "when my ship comes in" is indeterminant but probably long-term. Goals are long-term when their accomplishment takes a long time regardless of resources: specializing in radiology requires several years' work beyond the M.D. degree.

Short-term goals can help increase goal tangibility and provide a point for checking progress toward long-term goals. A long-term goal of getting ahead in a career may lead to a short-term goal of attending a workshop for career development. A long-term goal of maintaining the family dwelling may precede a short-term goal to replace the front steps with a specific standard of four concrete steps.

Are some families or individuals oriented primarily to short- or long-term goals? For many years, middle-class America subordinated gratification in sex, marriage, and material goods to educational achievements and occupational pursuits, but there have been changes. Technology has mass-produced material goods, including contraceptive aids; economic gains permit parental assistance to children in getting married or established in a career; and credit makes purchases readily available for many. Waiting to gratify wants is increasingly questioned.

Personality, family life stage, and economic well-being influence the balance between goals of long and short duration. A preoccupation with day-to-day activities can often be due to inadequate resources for facing the future with confidence rather than an inability to take a longer view. Most of us probably have a mixture of short- and long-term goals, however.

Continuity. Some goals require almost continuous effort and attention, as in parenting or preparation for classes and attendance to meet an educational goal. Other goals involve only short-term or sporadic attention. Meeting goals that require continuous attention can become routinized, an aspect discussed more fully in Chapter 7.

An event or shifts in resources can disrupt or

reorient goal expectations. A young person injured (an event) in an intramural game may face a lifetime of limited activity or confinement that may severely alter career goals.

A young family with an unplanned child may replace former asset-accumulation goals with aims for the child's growth and development. Resources available for savings and investments are altered when the wife quits her job to give birth and when child-raising costs are encountered. A family whose child has special physical, mental, or emotional problems may replace goals for a parent's educational achievement with goals for the child's self-functioning and independence in daily living.

Interdependence. Although some goals are relatively independent of other goals, many are so intermeshed that the pursuit of one goal affects another. The effect of interdependent goals is similar to a jigsaw puzzle: The puzzle is incomplete without all the interlocking pieces (Figure 4.2).

With interdependent goals, the best alternative to achieve one goal may be less than optimal for another goal. The goals of a husband and wife to find satisfying and rewarding work for both in the same commuting area are interdependent. The best living location for the husband's work may not be the best for the wife's.

FIGURE 4.2 *Interdependent goals*

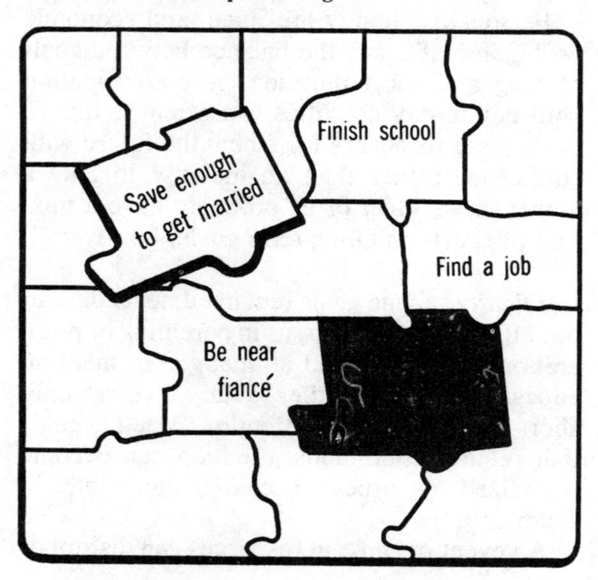

An optimal solution at one point in time can later become suboptimal because knowledge of the future is limited. A person who takes a liberal arts college program because of wide interests (an optimal solution at the time) may find the solution suboptimal upon graduation when available work is in specialized fields. On the other hand, specialized areas may become obsolete or oversupplied.

GOAL PRIORITIES

Individuals, families, and institutions face multiple goals with similar priorities. In a university setting, teaching, research, and continuing education may have similar priorities. But obviously, no individual, family, or institution can strive for all goals at the same rate. When priorities for goals of similar importance cannot be formed, one approach is to compartmentalize decisions related to one goal and to deal with one goal at a time as though the other goals of similar priority did not exist. People who separate career goals from family goals are compartmentalizing. The person who concentrates single-mindedly on matters at the office, but who also gives full attention to the family while at home, appears to have two sets of goals and may be compartmentalizing. Under some conditions, compartmentalization may be the only way to deal with goals that have similar priorities, but the interdependence of many goals may sometimes make it difficult.

Over the years, goal priorities for families and individuals change, even though values remain relatively stable. Family needs and resources affect aims. Early years of marriage are times of intensive goal setting related to getting established. Couples in developmental years may have an opportunity to get ahead and prepare for heavy demands of the middle years.

Families in the middle years often have heavy demands in educating or launching their own children while at the same time wanting to respond to the needs of elderly parents. Another less-demanding period often follows, permitting preparation for retirement.

A family's many goals with each member's separate priorities make "family" goal consensus difficult. Some families never agree on common goals but work toward goals important to individual members or combinations of individuals. Agreement between certain family members may be considerably more likely than between others—for example, agreement between mother and father may be more likely than agreement on a goal by the sixteen-year-old son and the seven-year-old daughter.

Lack of family-member consensus on goals and goal priorities can lead to conflict. If a parent can meet a goal of a new position in a firm only by moving to another city, all family members may not agree on the goals and goal priorities. The children's objectives may be to continue in the same school system with their current friends; the other parent's goals may be to keep the family intact under one roof and, at the same time, to increase their level of living. These objectives may or may not have high priority for other family members. If the parent's personal achievement goal is accompanied by a goal to meet the family's needs, a review of the family's needs or varying career objectives will be more likely than if achievement were the primary goal.

Events

Events are pertinent unexpected or low-probability occurrences that require action. They include (1) unexpected occurrences that cause delays or adjustments in the flow of life but do not change it, and (2) unexpected occurrences that change the direction of the flow of life. Most accidents are events, since no conscious prior expectations exist, and they may bring about adjustments in the flow of life or be severe enough to cause redirection. A test of an event is a circumstance to which response is required but which is not or would not have become a goal.

An event, as used in this context, is not a social occasion but rather systems terminology for the output or event from one system that becomes the input of some other system. For example, turbulent weather or fires result from a set of circumstances involving physical systems plus, perhaps, human error (in fires or accidents). All become event demands on the human systems affected.

Many events can be unpleasant, as when a person's health or safety is threatened, when a valuable object is damaged or destroyed, or when a dwelling is burglarized.

Minor events create a need for quick managerial reactions. Having unexpected visitors or losing one's billfold requires an adjustment. The events may be pleasant, as is usually the case with visitors from out of town—after necessary adjustments are made.

Families with different values and resources vary in their recognition of events. The frequency and severity of events they experience also may vary. Observations suggest that some individuals and families do not anticipate recurrent, predictable occurrences. Other families are skillful in predicting occurrences because they are aware of the high probability of certain occurrences and manage preventively before they happen.

Families' responses to illness show differences in event recognition. Some individuals may consider the flu an event that can be handled only by medical attention; others use home care and a wait-and-see attitude.

People have different thresholds for absorbing situations without being thrown for a loss. When one event causes more than one specific response to one situation and is actually a turning point in direction, it is a crisis. A plane crash in a residential area, unpredicted and of low probability, is a crisis event.

In a crisis, the family must manage in relation to the changed situation and must react rapidly to the most pressing events. During a crisis, the family's sense of commitment may be stronger than it is in less dramatic events.

In their response, families ordinarily go through a stage of disorganization, where the impact of the event makes coping seem impossible. Gradually, capacities for facing and constructively dealing with the circumstances begin to take root, followed by acceptance of the need for and an ability to proceed with reorganization. The rate and effectiveness of recovery can vary with such factors as how family members perceive their roles, the family life cycle, family composition, and the levels of functioning prior to the crisis.

When a storm damages homes, shopping areas, and schools, actions must be taken quickly to provide shelter and a safe food and water supply. The families involved respond to events as demands, just as if they were goals. The sureness of daily living is affected, and action taken is intended to return to the previous level of organization.

In a study of tornado victims, recovery was often aided by kin. Families who had frequent interaction with kin were offered and received aid more than those who interacted less; those families who had greater damage to their homes and who had close relationships to their kin received considerably more aid than did families who had minimal damage and infrequent contact with kin.[9] Kin, friends, and neighbors play important roles in recovery from unusual crises, such as natural disasters.

Crises can be growth producing and expansive, that is, morphogenic in nature. In a family—mother (aged forty-eight), father (fifty), son (nineteen), and daughter (sixteen)—in which the mother was hospitalized for anxiety, depression, and drinking, the family entered therapy.[10] Seemingly no improvements came in the therapy sessions until the father's favorite uncle died. All family members felt bad about it but could not express themselves to the father. The session held after the father heard of his uncle's death was characterized by openness, as the therapist spoke of his difficulty in expressing his concern to the father. Family members shared the difficulty in communication; the family began to find ways to feel more comfortable with each other and even planned times to share dinner together—a real change for them. The family, in their recovery and reorganization following this crisis, grew together rather than reverting to their former plane.

DEALING WITH EVENTS

Events are demands in the family systems, occurring inside and outside the system; they are unanticipated or unforeseen, but the consequences are made tolerable through management.

Perhaps the realistic stance for a manager with respect to events is to:

1. recognize that both goal and event demands elicit managerial responses
2. be alert to situations that may precipitate an overbalance of event demands that detract from progress toward important goals
3. approach events as positively as possible to maintain flexibility in a changing world
4. avoid a feeling of management failure that hinders the exercise of control or progress toward desired goals.

Summary

Values provide the criteria and meanings that guide decisions and actions. The characteristics of values that affect *how* they give direction to decisions relate to a number of factors. Values that are influenced by and interpreted in relation to their surrounding conditions are relative ones. Their relevance in situations is determined through management processes.

Values may be experienced for their own

sake—for example, beauty; these are ultimate or intrinsic. Or values may be apparent at each part of the sequence through which higher or intrinsic values are fulfilled; such values are instrumental or extrinsic. If a meal is enjoyed intrinsically, then the menu and preparation criteria are extrinsic. Managerial activity is guided by values, either intrinsic or extrinsic.

Values evolve through managerial processes as a result of decision making in relating values (goal criteria) with resources. All decision making involves a subjective aspect (goals) and an objective or resource aspect. Decision making is the process through which the subjective and objective evaluation takes place, and the decision is a form of value. In keeping with their subjective and objective components, values have both affective and cognitive dimensions.

When values become translated into a direction or an objective to guide action, they are called goals. Management may either clarify a value orientation into a more defined goal or respond in the situation to the general direction of the value orientation. Circumstances such as the extent of demands or the amount of resources may influence whether more or less specific goals are evolved. Or the difference may be determined by a life-style preference. In any case, values underlie managerial processes, providing the criteria for decision making.

Events are identified as unexpected occurrences that are pertinent or significant enough to require managerial response. Although the possibility of events may be foreseen and some protective action (managerial) taken to minimize the effects, the timing and severity of the actual event cannot be foreseen or become a goal.

Events and goals combine as inputs to determine the demands placed on the managerial system. It is the demands that identify the nature of the response of the management system, depending on its potential. Resources that provide that potential are discussed in the next chapter.

Notes

1. Stephan Arons, "Compulsory Education," *Saturday Review* 55 (January 15, 1972): 52.
2. Richard Erdoes, "My Travels with Medicine Man John Lame Deer," *Smithsonian* 4 (May 1973): 36.
3. Robert L. Jacobson, "Most Students Are Satisfied with Their Education, Survey Indicates, but Frustrations Are Widespread," *The Chronicle of Higher Education* 31 (February 5, 1986): 1, 27–31.
4. Tom Huth, "$30,000 a Year 'Permits' Dissatisfaction," *The Washington Post,* May 13, 1973, pp. A1, A20.
5. Mortimer J. Adler, *A Guidebook to Learning for the Lifelong Pursuit of Wisdom* (New York: Macmillan, 1986), p. 113.
6. Ibid., p. 114.
7. Ibid.
8. D. W. Gotshalk, *Patterns of Good and Evil* (Urbana: University of Illinois Press, 1963), pp. 66–81.
9. Thomas E. Drabek, William H. Key, Patricia E. Erickson, and Juanita L. Crowe, "The Impact of Disaster on Kin Relationships," *Journal of Marriage and the Family* 37 (August 1975): 488.
10. Andrew L. Selig, "Crisis Theory and Family Growth," *The Family Coordinator* 25 (July 1976): 292.

5

Resources

Resources provide the means to satisfy the family system's purposes or demands; they are necessary in solving every management problem. Resources vary in kind and in their potential for meeting the complex and unique needs and interests of individuals and families.

Nature of resources

SYSTEMS CONTEXT

Demands (goals and events) enter the managerial system as information. Information likewise serves as a part of the resources input by informing the system about the nature of resources needed and available for the solution to given problems. Information in this sense is part of the process of keeping all components of the system on track. From this information base, the system builds its more comprehensive response to utilizing its various resources.

CATEGORIES

Human resources are all the means that are vested in people that can be used to meet demands; they are the continuing personal characteristics—cognitive insights, psychomotor skills, affective attributes, health, energy, and time. *Material resources* are nonhuman means for meeting goals and events; they are natural and processed consumption goods, housing, household capital, physical energy, money, and investments.

The "developing capacities" subsystem of the personal system plays a major role in the ongoing development of the human resources that an individual has available for management. These capacities are fostered within the family setting, where interpersonal exchanges beginning in childhood provide the opportunity to experience and then comprehend an increasingly differentiated scope of resource classes.[1] Stages of development are represented in Figure 5.1.

As illustrated, undifferentiated experiences of need fulfillment evolve from the caring and dependency of infancy into a separation of love and services, which grow into both giving and receiving as there is an increasing capacity to perform reciprocally or for one's self.

Fuller awareness of services leads to an extended differentiation, which includes goods. Likewise, the concept of love expands to recognize varying levels of esteem or regard (status). A broader perspective on goods develops with experience in the family and with peers, and the

FIGURE 5.1 *A schematic representation of the differentiation of resource classes. Double frames indicate newly differentiated classes.*

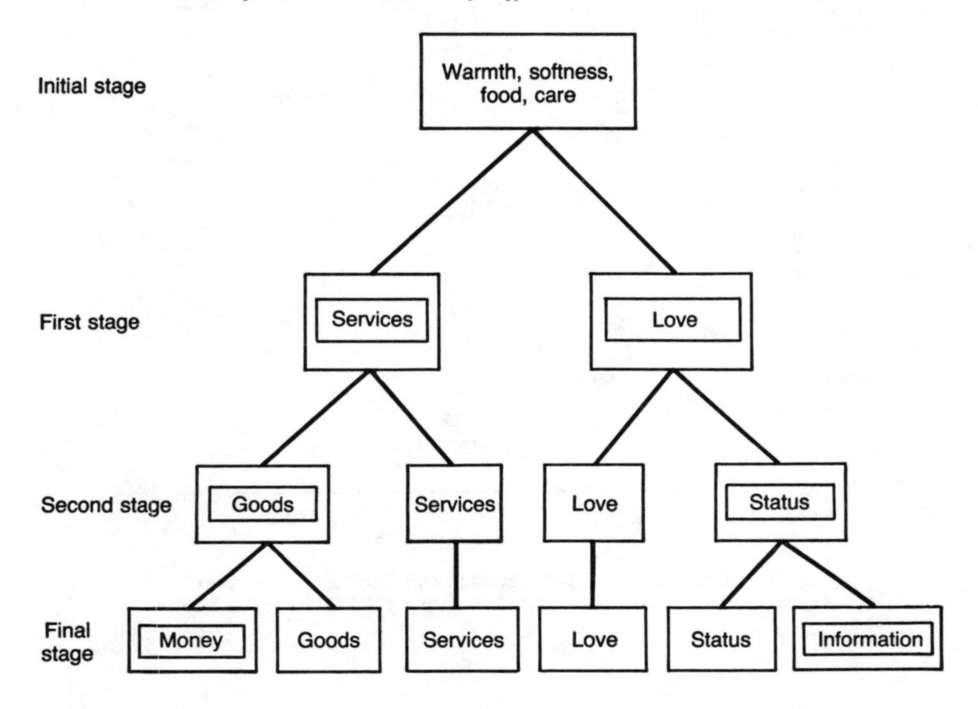

Source: From Uriel G. Foa and Edna B. Foa, *Societal Structures of the Mind,* 1974. Courtesy of Charles C Thomas, Publisher, Springfield, Illinois, p. 38.

relation of the acquisition of goods to money is identified. Likewise, broader experiences in the family and with outsiders bring continuous sources of information affecting status judgments and other matters, eventually separating status and roles from a more objective information or knowledge base.

The same authors have elaborated on these "resource exchanges" within the context of interpersonal relationships, where giving and receiving also represent value/goal fulfillment for each other. They observe that it matters very much who is involved in some exchanges (particular) and very little in others (universal). A *particularistic resource exchange,* therefore, depends for its value on the significance of the given interpersonal relationship, while a *universalistic resource exchange* does not. Some resource needs are concrete, and others are symbolic. These relationships are shown on the grid in Figure 5.2, which can be accomplished by bending the bottom line of Figure 5.1 into a circle with relative particularism represented on the vertical axis and relative concreteness on the horizontal one. It can be seen that human resources are more particularistic, and the material ones, including information, are more universal. Evidence supports this particular-to-universal ordering as a basis for satisfaction in marital exchanges, although husbands and wives differ in their interpretations.[2] It is possible that the same actions can involve both par-

FIGURE 5.2 *Configuration of resource classes*

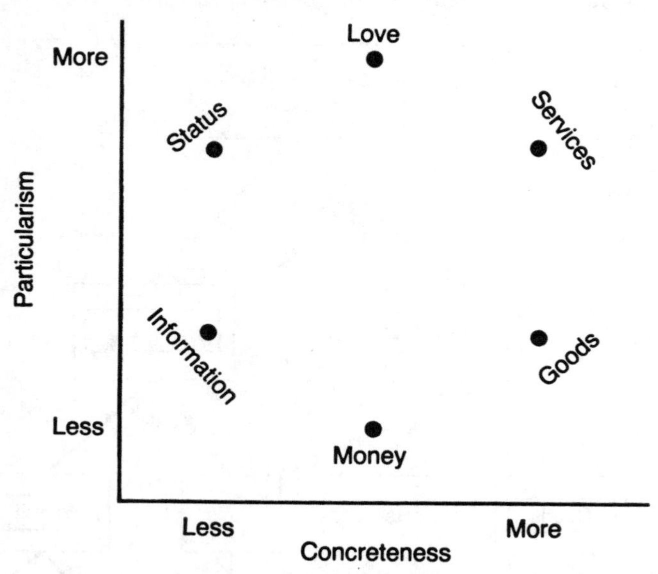

Source: Uriel G. Foa, "Interpersonal and Economic Resources," *Science* 171 (January 29, 1971): 347. Copyright 1971 by the AAAS.

ticular and universal exchanges. In such cases, the goal for the material exchange can be an expression of love or esteem. This insight into our growing ability to differentiate resources in our interpersonal exchanges will be built upon as resources are considered for their use in money contexts.

Human. Human resources or capabilities are the content of the solution to a problem, just as material resources are, but they are often less tangible and thus less measurable.

Human resources encompass the understandings, feelings, and skills (the cognitive, affective, and psychomotor elements) of human capacity. In conjunction with these, human energy and time considerations also are fundamental aspects. Health status is, of course, basic to energy levels as well as to the ability to function effectively in the cognitive, affective, and psychomotor areas.

Human and material resources on a macro level are represented by our national income and product accounts. They include what individuals and families contribute through employment and what they expend for consumption from their earnings, but economic activities within households are excluded. In recognition of the significance of this omission, there have been a number of approaches to studying household production, not only to place a value on it, but also to understand resource interactions within households, as well as the relation between market and nonmarket sectors.

In one approach to conceptualizing what needs to be represented by a household-based social accounting system, efforts have been made to provide "a coherent organization of all of the resources, measurable outcomes, and satisfactions."[3] Categories were developed through which changes in resource "stocks" and in "states of being" could be identified by obtaining information primarily on time use:

1. TK: Conventional stocks of tangible assets, such as machinery and houses.
2. KK: Stocks of abstract knowledge about the history and properties of the world, not embodied in specific individuals.
3. HK: Human capital embodied in individuals, such as their health, skills, and knowledge.
4. OK: Organizational contexts that reflect networks of relationships among the particular people populating society. Types of networks include families, associations of friends and neighbors, public associations, such as towns and state and federal governments, business organizations, and various other private voluntary organizations.
5. SK: Sociopolitical contexts which reflect the institutional arrangements for performing collective or societal activities, and also provide an environment for individual behavior in the form of legal and habitual rules for social interaction.
6. EK: Environmental stocks reflecting the physical and biological conditions of human society. Such stocks include climatological resources, environmental quality, and the availability of natural resources.[4]

The complexity of a framework through which the overall impacts of nonmarket decisions of families can be measured and understood is reflected by the above classification. The categories help convey the scope of resources and the environments affecting family decisions. While the purpose of the categories is to provide a framework for measuring the interrelations among them as reflected over time, the focus of this book is to strengthen the capacity of individuals and families *to make decisions* within their own situations that encompass these categories in ways that are enhancing to their lives.

Cognitive attributes. The cognitive domain, as noted in the discussion of values in Chapter 4, encompasses different levels of knowledge characterized as "modes of knowing"—knowing that, what, how, why, and wherefore. Knowing that something or someone possesses certain skills or attributes, knowing what is needed to meet a certain criterion, and knowing how to proceed in alternative ways are all aspects of resource considerations. As more complex or analytical situations are interpreted, higher levels of resource interactions are understood. Bringing this knowledge to bear on whys and wherefores is the part of the valuing process that gives full integrity to managerial decisions.

In today's rapidly changing environment, knowledge applied to new situations is a significant cognitive resource. Recognizing how existing knowledge relates to present situations is imperative to avoid the application of knowledge that is inappropriate to the situation. For example, highly mobile individuals or families can make better decisions about the selection of a new apartment when they apply knowledge acquired through both experience and study. The ability to analyze, synthesize, and reformulate varied insights and experiences creatively into new approaches to situations is one of the highest of human capacities: resourcefulness.

Cognitive resources are used to identify pertinent resources for a situation, to analyze alternatives in decision making, and to evaluate the realistic possibilities for meeting goals. This process of evaluation and reevaluation is the basis for resourcefulness, building the avenue through which the attributes or satisfying characteristics of more-specific resources may be applied to the meaning of the goal criteria.

Affective attributes. While affective values are more related to the goal or subjective side of the subject–object equation, affective dimensions may also serve as resources, either directly or indirectly. Affective expressions serve directly as resources in interpersonal exchanges. An expression of gratitude or love extended to someone can be the affective reinforcement needed or desired—serving as an effective resource for the recipient. Such affective support might also be accompanied by more-tangible evidences, such as assistance in a task or a gift. Such evidences can strengthen, but not replace, the anticipation of the recipient when the affective goal is primary.

Affective and other human resources are different from material ones in that they are pervasive. Skills or affection (including negative feelings) may well grow in the process and can be extended again. With material exchanges, it is assumed that something of equal value is received or given.

Affective attributes contribute to the effective or ineffective use of material and other human resources. When a sense of trust accompanies an exchange, the degree of protection can be minimized. When such trust is lacking, restraints may be placed on the conditions of the exchange or on the use of the resources exchanged. Certain resources may not be shared within families because of affective elements that exist; the interpersonal climate and openness of relationships often affect the scope of alternatives that can be considered. People may be prohibited from using certain tools because they are prized possessions; or family members may feel the skills of other family members are inadequate to meet a particular need. Economists have referred to these affective dimensions that pervade interactions as integrative influences—ones that may be either expansive or constraining in their effects.[5]

Psychomotor attributes. Psychomotor resources are physical reactions to mental stimuli. They are the capacity for producing movement and doing physical work. Manipulating equipment dials, reaching stored items, cleaning surfaces, or caring for an infant require psychomotor resources. With ever-changing equipment, products, and processes that alter the necessary skills, psychomotor resources remain important in family resource management. People with poor manipulative skills or infants in the process of maturation demonstrate the value of psychomotor resources. The effort and adaptations necessary for a physically handicapped person exemplify the significance of psychomotor resources. For the person with motor limitations, each of these tasks may be difficult and may require mechanical aids.

Cognitive and psychomotor resources are closely interrelated human resources. Receiving, processing, and storing information (cognitive skills) are a part of adapting motor skills to new situations. Using new products, whether paint, food mixes, or video disks, often requires information that differs from that used for past products. Both cognitive and psychomotor resources help accomplish a task that involves a new product.

Human capital of an individual or family is the total stock of human capacities at a point in time for affecting future resources and their use. Economists define human capital as people resources that affect future income. People investing in themselves enhance their production and consumption capabilities. For households, these capacities of its members make differences in the quality of living as well as the ability to function well in earning, spending, or other activities outside the unit. Promoting family health through nutrition and personal care contributes importantly, although education represents the largest monetary investment in human capital.

A significant part of human capital development is the unconscious learning and conscious training carried out by household members. A parent who takes time to teach a child to perform a task may contribute to the child's human capital, conceivably at a cost to the adult's development. Informal training at home, as well as formal education, can contribute much to the capacities of individuals for meeting their many demands.

Material. Material resources are natural and processed goods plus physical energy (and the monetary capacity for acquiring them) that have properties and characteristics which serve as means for meeting demands. Material goods contain attributes that, in combination, are identified with the life-style of the individuals and families who own them. Through manufacturing or other production processes, the characteristics thought to be useful to consumers are built in or added to raw materials. The material items may be purchased ready for consumption, or households may add some further processing before the goods are ready to consume. Purchasing unfinished furniture is an example of planned processing after purchasing to complete the production of an item having the desired characteristics.

Households are an important part of the production process, though too often overlooked. Most households acquire capital items for production: ranges, sanders, washers, dryers, and so forth. Capital goods and those on hand for direct consumption are part of the material resources available to meet demands.

Acquisitions are not the only ways that families can meet their goals through material resources. Durable goods may be shared through some personal arrangement or public process (as with the library), or rented (as with the garden tiller), or through obtaining the full service of an individual who owns the garden tiller and performs the tilling as well.

Publicly shared resources include a wide range of items, from energy and water to schools, streets, and fire engines. Ordinarily, community resources are those that apply to a wide range of citizen needs for which there is a public interest in distribution and control, or for which there can be more efficient arrangements in providing for allocation to citizens. The responsibility for allocating basic utilities may be delegated to private interests over which the public provides oversight, as through a public-service commission. Energy and water sources illustrate these areas of public responsibility.

RESOURCE USE AND ACCUMULATION

Resources entering the family system may be used immediately in some managerial action. Although consumption usually reduces the tangible value of available resources, the intangible satisfaction from resource use compensates for the reduction. All processes within the managerial system contribute to the *flow of resources* and involve some change in their value.

Resources may be developed or gained by the family system and kept for later use; thus, they become a part of the family's "stock" of resources. Through managerial decisions and actions, resources are added to the stock or are taken from the stock. Managerial actions inside the family may change the nature of the family's stock of resources—the plan to "do-it-yourself" and refinish a chair. The nature of the family's stock of resources changes more frequently by exchanges with other systems. When money is exchanged for music lessons, the human-resource package is expected to change. Continual shifts occur in the nature of resources that accrue to the family.

Material assets represent a stock of goods that have value. Housing and other household acquisitions represent a major part of the material assets of families. Cash or deposits in financial institutions are usually intended to be used at some future time to provide for needed consumption goods and are assets that contribute to economic security. Investments of a less liquid nature are primarily oriented to future security because they are not intended to be readily transferable into consumption items, although under conditions of need they could be liquidated. Such investments are likely to be ones that vary with the price level, and they therefore carry more risk or potential for gain due to economic fluctuations. Material resources serving both consumption and investment purposes provide the usual basis on which the economic position of families is compared, due to their measurability.

Resource stock is the sum of available means

for meeting demands at a point in time. This resource combination provides a reservoir or *stock* for use in a system's specific action.[6] For the family, this reservoir includes their *net worth*—the market value of goods owned by the family minus liabilities or obligations—and the knowledge and skills of family members.

ALTERNATIVE USES

Alternative uses for resources characterize their inherent "re-source-ability." As the term suggests, they may be used in different ways. For example, wood may be used for buildings, for heat, or for objects of art. The special qualities of given resources determine their value for the different uses to which they may be put.

Alternative uses of manufactured or highly processed items may be limited since these items are directed toward specific purposes. However, the potential for alternative uses is a general quality of more basic resources, either material or human.

The transforming of basic material resources into processed goods for consumption involves the application of knowledge, skill, energy (human and physical), and tools. What occurs is the incorporation of needed characteristics designed to be useful for particular purposes. This adaptation of resources occurs as managerial actions within the household just as it does as a part of the manufacturing process, but on a smaller scale.

Measurement of resources

To facilitate comparison and allocation of multiple resources, mechanisms that provide common bases for assessing their relative contributions are needed in management. Some decisions require precise measurements; others may be appropriately made with an intuitive sense of amounts. A family on a trip, for instance, may consider eating at a restaurant but then choose to buy hamburgers at a fast-food chain. The difference in the time and money costs for the restaurant meal may not be known when the family decides between the two alternatives, but the time uncertainty compared to the speed of the fast-food chain and the need for flexibility in getting to overnight lodgings may be overriding factors.

A complex goal, such as purchasing a condominium, may require careful comparison of (1) acceptability of living areas, (2) dollar costs, (3) the accessibility to work and shopping areas, and (4) the quality of neighborhoods. Balancing these conditions in decision making is difficult because equivalent measures of each factor are not always available.

MONEY

Because relative values of resources may be measured and reflected through price, money assists in making choices among alternative uses. Such alternatives may include selecting the most economical resource to meet a goal, directing a given resource to a higher goal priority, or utilizing the most advantageous combination of resources.

Money is both a resource and a measure of resources. To accomplish objectives, money must first be exchanged for goods and services. Considering money as a resource means that its potential claim on goods and services is recognized. As a measure of market value, money facilitates comparisons by serving as a common denominator for comparing various kinds of things.

Material goods exchanged in the marketplace have a specified money value, but human resources are not as easily evaluated. The degree of necessary skill or knowledge may be measured, but the ability to apply knowledge or other cognitive skills is not as identifiable. Tests, educational levels, and performance records help to show human potential and may be translated into money terms for the paid worker.

TIME

In the household, tests and performance records are generally not available for measuring skills. Furthermore, skills may be useful during one family life stage and minimally useful at other stages. Changes in the stock of human resources, particularly skills, are difficult to show.

Time is often the intermediate measure in assigning economic worth to human resources. "Time use is the link between tangible constraints and the achievement of ultimate psychological well-being."[7] The number of sales per week or typing speed per minute are examples of how time helps to objectively determine human resource values. Time can be an ultimate constraint for human resource use since it cannot be increased, as goods can be. Services purchased to replace the use of some human resources can increase available time. Like money, time as a measure makes possible the comparison of unlike activities on a similar basis. Where a dollar value can also be placed on time comparisons (and vice versa), choices across a broad range of alternatives can be made from a common base.

Unlike material resources, time cannot be accumulated. In an affluent society, time becomes scarcer with increasing consumption. Burenstam Linder identified conditions leading to "partial affluence" in view of time pressures to earn more money to purchase more goods, which take more time for their use, care, and maintenance.[8] Money is most constraining to poor people, while time is more often limiting to the affluent.

Energy. Some form of energy utilization or transformation is critical to most activities. How these energizing processes come about and combine to facilitate our more immediate activity may never cross our minds in the course of a day—unless there is the inconvenience of a power failure or an empty gasoline tank. Yet our energy resources provide the potential for all that transpires. We need to understand and appreciate the constant reformulation of matter and energy within the natural environment, as the various elements and life forms respond to forces seeking ecological balance.

Because energy resources are so fundamental to our lives and life-styles, questions regarding the adequacy of energy supplies are raised with more anxiety than for most other resources. This anxiety was higher in the 1970s, when oil prices were high, than during the period of lower prices in the 1980s. It is predicted that at current world consumption rates, coal deposits will last 200 years. The "life index" of the world's crude-oil reserves is estimated to be about thirty-five years, that of natural gas about fifty years. "Based on history, there is good reason to be confident that innovation in both production and conservation technologies will probably extend the benefits to be derived from the energy resources that are recognized."[9] This difficulty in estimating energy supplies represents optimism for some, since new sources may be identified, and pessimism for others, in view of what seems to be a relatively short projection in terms of human history and our past record on conservation.

Households reduced their average consumption of fuels from 1979 to 1982 by about 25 percent, from 138 to 103 million Btu's per household[10]—a significant reduction. While overall energy consumption in 1983 was similar to 1982, consumption began to increase again in 1984, as a result of lower oil prices. Of total energy consumption, residential and commercial buildings almost matched industrial use at 36 percent and 37 percent, respectively. Transportation represented 27 percent.[11]

The calorie (for human energy expenditure) and the Btu (for temperature and power needs) serve in the same way as money and time do as measures for comparing the costs of resource utilization across dissimilar items. Currently, there is considerable interest in balancing human energy needs with food consumption. It is not known whether the concurrent interest in uses of physical energy is related in the minds of individuals (although they ultimately are), but it is hoped that both continue as areas of study so that optimal decision making can be furthered.

Changing resource availability and needs

So far, this chapter has focused on the role of resources in providing varied attributes for meeting demands and on their measurability as human and material resources. The fact that decisions regarding their use are integrally related to what is valued, through the meeting of goals, has been emphasized. Different resources may contain the attributes needed to meet the criteria of a given goal. A bicycle, a car, or walking can get a student to class, but if time is limited, the car or bicycle has the advantage over walking (forgetting parking constraints for the moment). If comfort on a cold day is important, the car wins. If money cost is important, the bicycle or walking are better alternatives than the car. While such trade-offs are characteristic of resource use, decisions regarding the conditions under which they become realistic possibilities vary with the circumstances and the mix of resources.

The particular resources people have at any point in time also provide the bases on which they must build if they want either to increase the amount of resources they have or to adjust the mix to achieve their desired goals more effectively. Such shifts in amount or kind do not occur readily, as a rule. If more money is needed, it may be that earning skills need to be enhanced, which may involve night school or even giving up earnings temporarily to complete a program of study. A second job or outside employment of another family member may be alternatives, both of which reduce time for other productive or leisure activities. Ordinarily, the more limited resources provide the orientation around which the use of other resources evolve. Obtaining the best balance of resources is a matter of understanding the relation of resources both in quantity and quality to each other, to overall values and goals, and to shifting needs over time.

For any given stage of the family cycle, the combinations of resource availability and of interests and needs vary widely due to unique circumstances and individuality. For any given family, wide variations in resources and in the demands to be met also occur over the years. Recognizing these differences, it may still be helpful to visualize the effects of changing goals and resources in a general way over the life cycle.

To illustrate the different resource patterns that may occur over a lifetime, money and time representations for material and human resources are shown in Figures 5.3 and 5.4. These

FIGURE 5.3 *Wives' household work time according to age of youngest child and employment*

Source: Adapted from *Time Use: A Measure of Household Production of Family Goods and Services,* by K. E. Walker and M. E. Woods, p. 272. By permission, The American Home Economics Association, Washington, D.C., 1976.

FIGURE 5.4 *Annual income before taxes and annual expenditures of urban consumer units by age of reference person, 1984*

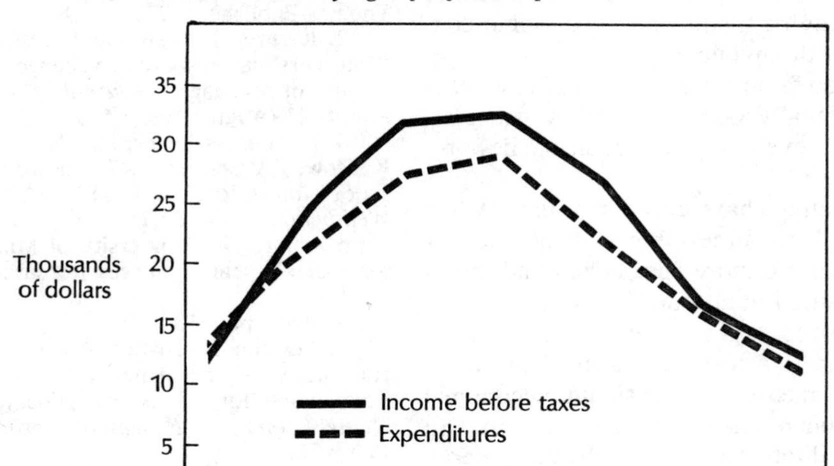

Source: U.S. Department of Labor, Bureau of Labor Statistics. "Consumer Expenditure Survey, Results from 1984," USDL 86-254 (June 22, 1986): Table 3.

profiles are drawn from studies, but as averages, they are not likely to fit individual cases precisely. Occupational profiles that reflect variations in the level of earnings and in timing of highest earnings are also factors and will be discussed in Chapter 11.

These comparisons do, however, indicate that time and money constraints as well as relative affluence can often coincide. If the lower money income stage of "under twenty-five" also accompanies the heavy time demands when the youngest child is "under one," the high demands of both time and money can coincide. Demands may exceed resources unless there are financial or other material reserves, family or social supports, or other alternatives for earning or controlling the demands. The situation illustrates the problem young families often face when money and coping skills are limited and demands are high.

Higher incomes may also accompany lower time demands for housework. But if children are born when parents are older and this coincides with income reduction for some reason, such as illness, the pressure can occur later rather than earlier. Once the pressure situation evolves, adjustment in the resource mix or the level of demand takes considerable managerial effort to reverse.

Summary

Human and material resources are the means for meeting the demands of family systems. Human resources, i.e., skills or knowledge, can be enhanced through experience or use. The total of human resources is human capital. Material resources may be acquired through the economic system, from family sharing, from neighbors, or through public programs. Human resources continue to develop over the life span. Capacities for love and related exchanges are particularistic in that there is selectivity in such exchanges. On a particularist–universal continuum, money is on the universal end because exchanges may be made with equal-value considerations with anyone.

The unit or family has a stock of resources that is continually being altered by using resources and developing or acquiring new resources.

Basic resources have alternative uses, while highly refined resources (highly processed or manufactured) are more specialized and therefore more limited in alternative uses.

Money serves as a measure of the value of resources and is a resource itself. Time is an intermediate measure in assigning economic worth to human resources. Calorie and Btu measures facilitate human and physical energy choices.

Resources need to be considered in combination because a mix of human and material resources is important in overall well-being. Differences in resource patterns occur across the life span; people should consider the potential for shifts in resource availability to avoid unduly constraining situations.

Notes

1. Uriel G. Foa, "Interpersonal and Economic Resources," *Science* 171 (January 29, 1971): 347; and Uriel G. Foa and Edna B. Foa, *Societal Structures of the Mind* (Springfield, Illinois: Charles C Thomas Publisher, 1974), p. 38.

2. Kathryn D. Rettig and Margaret M. Bubolz, "Interpersonal Resource Exchanges as Indicators of Quality of Marriage," *Journal of Marriage and the Family* 41 (August 1983): 506.

3. F. Thomas Juster, Paul N. Courant, and Greg K. Dow, "A Conceptual Framework for the Analysis of Time Allocation Data," in *Time, Goods, and Well-being,* F. T. Juster and F. P. Stafford, eds. (Ann Arbor: The University of Michigan, Institute for Social Research, Survey Research Center, 1985), p. 117.

4. Ibid., pp. 118–119.

5. Gordon E. Bivens, "The Grants Economy and Study of the American Family: A Possible Framework for Trans-Disciplinary Approaches," *Home Economics Research Journal* 5 (December 1976): 72.

6. C. West Churchman, *The Systems Approach* (New York: Delacorte Press, 1968), p. 39.

7. Juster, Courant, and Dow, "*A Conceptual Framework,*" pp. 117–118.

8. Staffan Burenstam Linder, *The Harried Leisure Class* (New York: Columbia University Press, 1970), pp. 143–144.

9. U. S. Department of Energy, Annual Report to Congress, Washington, D.C., December 1985, p. 5.

10. U.S. Department of Energy, Energy Information Administration, National Energy Conservation Surveys, *Consumption and Expenditures, April 1982 through March 1983,* Part 1, National Data, Washington, D.C. (November 1984), p. 2.

11. U.S. Department of Energy, Annual Report to Congress, pp. 7–8.

6

Decision making

Decision making is a basic process underlying all functions of family resource management. Since decisions are universal in all human endeavor, the process is fundamental to the dynamics of all social concerns and thus is not limited to management.

Many decisions of families focus on the quality of interpersonal relationships and are concerned with strengthening bonds between individual family members. Such decisions are particularistic in nature, drawing on social interaction and/or political decision-making insights, and they may find resolution in the personal system. When these or other decisions involve the utilization of means (for example, information, material goods, or money) to find an acceptable solution, they become managerial in nature—commonly involving economic decision processes. Decisions emphasizing affective dimensions relate primarily to the personal system, while cognitive dimensions involving resources provide the focus for management. It is through management that the subjective and objective elements of decisions involving both personal and economic benefits and costs are reconciled or, more positively, become mutually reinforcing.

Relationship to management

Management provides an integrated framework through which purposeful decision making is oriented and directed. The cognitive aspect of management is primary—some suggest that management is only a mental process. Management includes responsibility for action, and decisions are critical in all aspects of the system: input, throughput, and output.

It is important, therefore, to review how decision making relates to and is organized within the overall process by which individuals and families manage. The decision-making steps or process is discussed separately and in relation to factors that influence decision patterning by individuals and families.

Decision making is essentially a process of evaluation in the choice or resolution of alternatives. In the chapters on the inputs of demands and resources, the discussion centers on how values provide the criteria through which goals become formulated and needed resource attributes can be identified. Values, goals, and resources together provide the content for decision making (Table 6.1). Consideration of alternatives takes place throughout the managerial system: in the input phase (both in determining goals and in surmising available resources); in standard setting and sequencing within planning; and in checking and adjusting within the controlling phase.

Many goal-setting and standard-setting decisions with long-run implications evolve gradually. Families may become committed to certain actions that entail outcomes that were previously perceived only vaguely, if at all. As the outcomes become apparent, they are evaluated. If an outcome fails to meet the family's objectives, the family may search for other solutions or revise its goals.[1]

A family may value individual privacy over leisure by deciding on more living space in preference to a family trip. Having selected the goal, the family may then need to clarify it further through managerial planning. Considering resources, housing location, and other general factors, they may decide to add a room to the present dwelling rather than to move to a new one. This is a goal-setting contribution of management. The operational goal for management then becomes clear. Specific plans and actions for house expansion can be undertaken; that is, quantitative and qualitative standards for developing the addition can then be set and implemented.

Management components identify the nature

TABLE 6.1 *Relationships of decision making to purpose, content, and system components of management*

Component	*Management system purpose*	*Content*	*Decision-making process*
Input			
Goal demands	Provide direction to management	Nature of values; needs to be met	Identify and decide goal priorities
Resources	Provide means for meeting goals	Attributes of needed resources	Identify available, relevant resources and estimate their worth
Throughput			
Planning	Clarify goals	Goal criteria	Identify, weigh, and decide among alternative qualities and quantities (standards) in relation to alternative sequences
Standard setting	Assess resources	Resource attributes: worth and availability	
Action sequencing	Create order in sequencing activities	Task succession, interaction, and time relations	Identify and choose alternative sequences in relation to alternative standards
Implementing			
Checking	Examine standards and sequences during plan implementation	Define standards and sequences	Determine the degree of consistency with planned standards and sequences
Adjusting	Change process, standard, or sequence to achieve acceptable outcome	Known criteria, attributes, and previous planning results	Determine alternative standard or sequence
Output/feedback	Evaluate outcomes relative to goals	Relation of achieved results with identified criteria	Determine consistency of results with desired end; consider costs and benefits

of the decisions needed to accomplish given management functions. The content and purposes for decision making vary throughout the management process; in turn, content, purposes, and process are interdependent elements of all decision making. Within these aspects of management, the decision-making process remains consistent. Purpose and content determine whether the decisions relate to goal setting, planning, implementing, or analysis of input–output relations.

Importance and complexity of decision making

Predictions about choices available in the future indicate increasing variety in decision alternatives. Naisbitt suggests a megatrend of moving from either/or to multiple options.[2]

> The either/or choices in the basic areas of family and work have exploded into a multitude of highly individual arrangements and lifestyles. But the basic idea of a multiple-option society has spilled over into other important areas of our lives: religion, the arts, music, food, entertainment, and finally into the extent to which cultural, ethnic, and racial diversity are now celebrated in America.[3]

Decision making in families and for individuals is often complex. Computerization of the household has been suggested as a vehicle for promoting major assistance in decision making. However, computers are as yet unavailable to the majority of families and individuals, and those with computers lack customized software for processing the wide variety of decisions facing them.

Decision-making process

While the decision-making process may be described in various ways, it generally contains three steps: (1) recognizing that a decision is needed, (2) identifying and weighing appropriate alternatives, and (3) choosing among or resolving alternatives. This process is the basis for a rational approach to decision making.

RECOGNIZING NEED FOR A DECISION

The variations in recognizing a need for a decision are probably great, even among families that have similar goals and resources. Educational and sales programs frequently try to alert families to needs for decisions. The birth of a first child brings new risks and, often, shifts in goals. For some, this may lead to recognition of a need for a decision about insurance. In other cases, an insurance sales representative may ask about life insurance for a young mother or about educational insurance for the child. Until the representative brings the questions to the attention of the couple, consideration of the need for a decision may not have arisen.

Other informal episodes alert us to situations needing decisions. People may consult neighbors about lawn care or request their support in a campaign for better lighting in a parking lot. Some people seem to have a heightened alertness to needs for decisions. One spouse may recognize decision needs before the other is aware of a need or wants to consider a decision.

IDENTIFYING AND WEIGHING APPROPRIATE ALTERNATIVES

Before decisions can be made, alternatives need to be generated and information secured sufficient to make the decision. Individuals vary in the extent to which they (1) identify or evolve alternatives, (2) search for information about the alternatives, and (3) attempt to predict hypothetical consequences of decisions. Weighing an alternative involves gathering information on its attributes and considering its perceived consequences. The number of alternatives considered in decision making varies with the importance of the decisions and with the background or opportunity of the decision makers for generating them.

Information contributes to clarifying possible consequences of alternatives. Decisions are made under varying circumstances, with different amounts of information about alternatives and consequences. *Certainty* is complete knowledge of consequences of a decision,[4] and *uncertainty* is the lack of this knowledge or unknown outcome probabilities.[5] Knowledge of a decision's consequences can come from experience, experimentation, a search for information, or any combination of these.

Risk is the hazard or chance of a loss. "Perceived risk is a function of uncertainty with regard to the economic, functional (performance), social, and psychological outcomes (or consequences) of a decision and the importance of the decision to the decision maker."[6]

Decisions are frequently made under uncertain conditions because their outcomes cannot generally be predicted from past outcomes, due to either too meager or nonexistent information or circumstances differing significantly from those of the past.[7]

Searching for reliable, relevant information is best done when the situation surrounding the decision is clearly defined. Sometimes, specific information is unavailable for decisions; but often, readily available facts are unused. A simple example is unit pricing in the grocery store—not used by many consumers because of errors in interpretation or computation. When consumers were asked to compare two sizes of products, a large portion of them were not able to calculate the needed ratio for comparison.[8]

The number of alternatives, especially when it exceeds ten, can confuse decision makers. When the variability among alternatives in terms of attractiveness is greater, confusion is less.[9] The same study also reported that "cognitively complex" decision makers used significantly more information than "cognitively simple" decision makers.

In weighing alternatives, desired attributes are balanced against anticipated negative attributes and/or outcomes. The quality of information about a product, for example, may be more important than the quantity of information.

Decision making that includes evaluating trade-offs of both nonmoney and money factors often yields an improved understanding of the relation of anticipated costs to benefits. The case of buying a house or condominium exemplifies the information search process since it often contains money and nonmoney factors. Time and effort may be expended securing information on factors deemed important in weighing alternatives. The distance from an elementary school, the mix of age groups in the neighborhood, and the aesthetic appearance of the house and neighborhood may all be qualities important to the decision maker in weighing alternatives. Sources of information for the initial screening of houses typically are realtor multiple-listings services, newspaper advertisements, and the personal knowledge of a realtor, friends, or the decision makers. Information overload may be a decision maker's obstacle, especially if a number of properties are visited in a short period of time.

The extent of information search in a childbearing decision and in life satisfaction was the focus of a study of childless women and mothers. The study found that "greater parenting satisfaction and more favorable perceptions of parenting performance were associated with higher levels of information search. . . . For nonmothers, a higher level of reported information search was associated with lower life satisfaction."[10] These results suggest that childless women who are most happy have either experienced little conflict about their decision or have resolved conflict by avoiding investigation of the implications of their decision.[11] The extent of information search and the quality or success of the decision may thus not always be positively related.

CHOOSING OR RESOLVING AVAILABLE ALTERNATIVES

Appropriate strategies for choosing among decision alternatives vary to some extent by the certainty associated with the outcome and the risk involved. In dealing with uncertainty, one may attach subjective or objective probabilities to aid in choosing among available alternatives.

Objective probability is the ratio of the number of actual occurrences to the total number of possible occurrences of a particular situation.[12] Objective probability relates to measurable expectations building on such varied bases as past experiences, repeated experiments, or the outcome of large samples. Objective probability is used in the incorporation of mortality tables into the design of life insurance products.

Subjective probability is a measure of the decision maker's belief that a given outcome will occur.[13] Subjective probability is likely more prevalent in decisions concerning the household than is objective probability. The measure of the belief in the occurrence of the outcome may be inexact; that is, one alternative may be thought of as having a much greater likelihood than others of occurring.

Many decisions have both subjective and objective probability elements. There may be objective evidence that the fiber and construction of a carpet are durable. Individuals can also believe that the color and construction will bear up under traffic and attach a subjective probability to that belief.

A "decision tree" offers one way of visualizing alternatives and the probability of predicted outcomes. A decision tree combines choices of actions and consequences of action that are affected by "chance or uncontrollable circumstances."[14] It provides a systematic approach for examining alternatives and their consequences. The steps for making a decision tree, as suggested for business and industry, follow:

1. Identify the points of decision and alternatives available at each point.
2. Identify the points of uncertainty and the type or range of alternative outcomes at each point.
3. Gather information needed to make the analysis, especially the estimated probabilities of different events or results of action and the costs and gains of various actions.
4. Evaluate the alternatives and choose a course of action.[15]

In Figure 6.1, the tree's branches represent alternative courses of action or decisions. The example shows a person ready to graduate from college with a job opportunity in another state. The person's spouse is employed on the college campus but is willing to seek employment elsewhere. Only one decision is considered, thus yielding a single decision tree. Many decisions would require a much more complex tree.

In the example, subjective probability is used, with outcome probabilities predicted on the basis of personal perception. The goal of both spouses being satisfied is best met by the graduate's taking a job in another state using the information available in making the decision. The subjective probability of the spouse finding a job in another city is based on as much information as the couple can bring to bear without the spouse having to go to the locale and search for a job.

Decision strategies are sets of procedures for relating anticipated benefits to objectives. Decision models or strategies available to individuals and families in choosing among available alternatives include optimizing, satisficing, incremental, cybernetic, and random.[16]

Maximization as a strategy is not presented for the family context. For business and other organizations, maximization commonly is interpreted as the alternative that accrues maximum return or benefits in resource terms, considering market factors. For maximization, it is assumed that resources can be moved at will and that complete information is available.

FIGURE 6.1 *A decision tree*

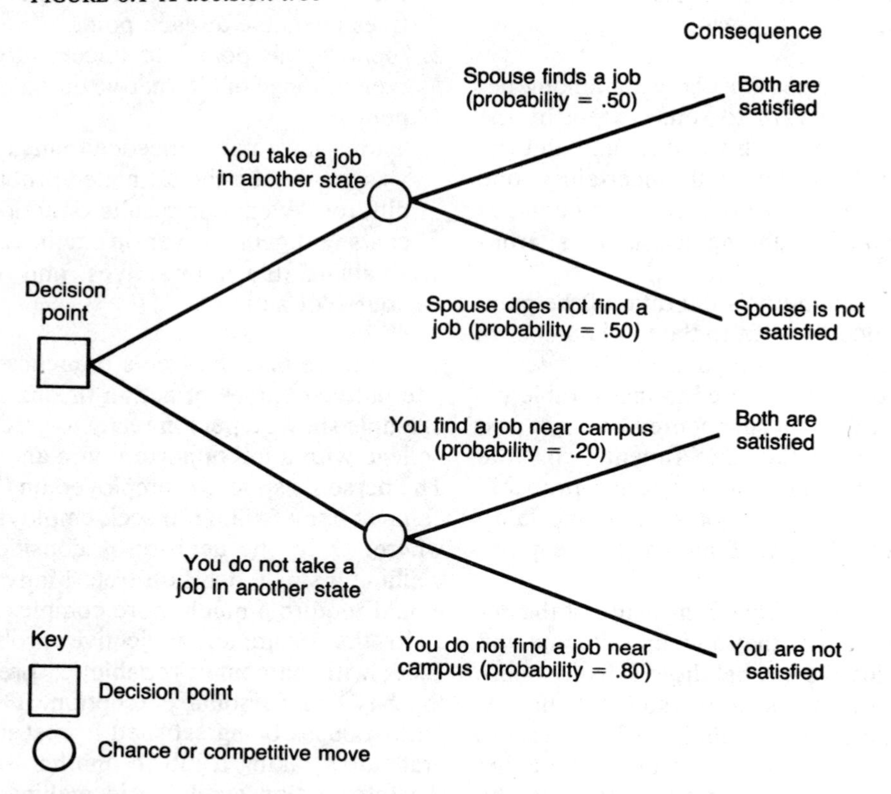

Source: Adapted from John F. Magee, "Decision Trees for Decision Making," *Harvard Business Review* 42 (July–August 1964): 127.

Questions to ask before selecting a strategy are given in Figure 6.2.

Optimizing. In the *optimizing strategy*, available solutions are sought that will "produce *as much or more* satisfaction than can any other solution. . . ."[17] Ill-structured situations and conditions surrounding decisions do not lend themselves to the optimizing strategy, while well-formed and clear conditions do. Relevant alternatives and probabilities of the desired outcome can be developed.

In the "real world" of individuals and families, well-formed and clear conditions are often missing, as is complete information. Nonoptimizing strategies are presented as having capacities to deal with uncertainty.[18] In order to deal with uncertainty, limited structure in a situation, and the cost of gathering and processing full information, nonoptimizing strategies are probably more often used than optimizing.

Satisficing. Individuals and families often simplify decision making by selecting the first alternative good enough to accomplish the anticipated outcome.[19] *Satisficing* assumes that alternatives are sought only until an acceptable aspiration level can be met.[20]

The satisficing strategy is appropriate when it provides for:

1. Coping with uncertain circumstances surrounding a decision while linking outcomes

FIGURE 6.2 *Applicability of different strategies*

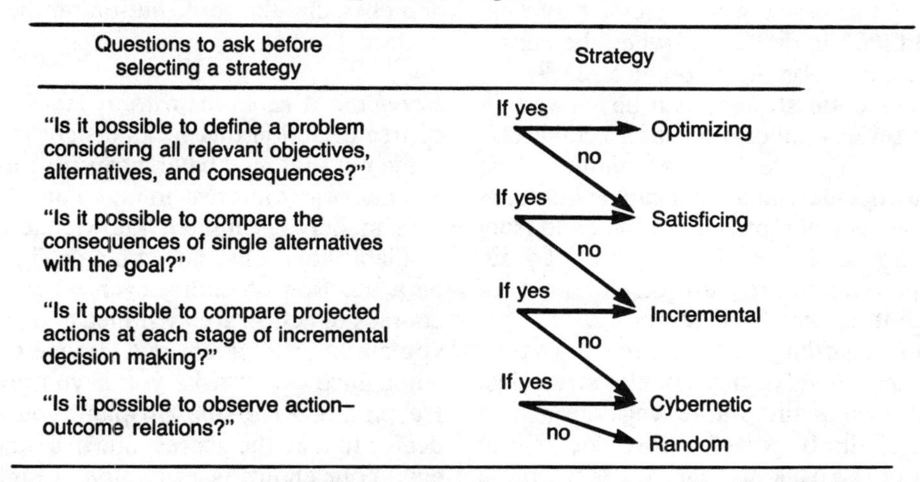

Source: Adapted and reprinted from "A Prescriptive Contingency View of Organizational Decision Making" by Ana Grandori, published in *Administrative Science Quarterly* 29 (June 1984): 209. By permission of *Administrative Science Quarterly*. Copyright © 1984, Cornell University.

closely with objectives. Uncertain circumstances may surround a woman's decision to return to the labor force. The satisficing strategy means taking the first job that adequately meets the objectives set, considering the woman's uncertain circumstances of how her children will adjust to continuous day care, how responsibilities of the household will be met, or how transportation will be arranged.

2. Further searching is not considered when an alternative within acceptable range of standards and sequences is identified. For example, when making an investment, there would be a willingness to trade off a potentially higher return for a decrease in the search time for additional information.
3. Completing the decision when differences in alternative outcomes are small, making further decision-making effort relatively unproductive. In shopping for an ice axe, when size, quality, and price of axes at several stores vary little, a decision may be made when an acceptable axe is found, rather than continuing a time-consuming, exhaustive search in another shopping area.
4. Believing that the identified alternative is near the maximum payoff.[21] For example, a patient contemplates elective but recommended surgery and sees a respected surgeon who confirms a previously suggested plan for surgery. The patient might then believe that the newly found surgeon represents nearly the best solution, or payoff, available (and thus that the satisficing strategy is appropriate) because the surgeon has a good reputation for skill and the "second opinion" has confirmed another physician's recommendation.

Incremental. The *incremental strategy* progresses toward a final solution through a series of additive stages. The anticipated end is kept in view, but each successive stage, while distinct, is also influenced by the outcome of the previous one. There is a risk-reducing premise that small decisions will avoid big effects and especially avoid extensive negative consequences that cannot be anticipated. Such an incremental strategy is appropriate when relevant alternatives are difficult to define and when the consequences of a decision are unpredictable.[22]

The incremental strategy can be viewed almost like a series of pilot projects. In child rearing, incremental strategies are common. The parents may decide that a child can be outdoors alone as long as a parent can see the child from inside the house. Later, the child may go out without a parent into the yards on either side of the house but not cross the street.

Decisions regarding the landscaping of a residential lot may involve incremental strategies. A resident may plant prairie vegetation in a small area of the backyard before deciding to plant most of the back and side yards in prairie grasses.

Decisions about acquiring peripherals for one's microcomputer are often made incrementally, as money becomes available and/or new equipment is found to satisfy current needs.

Cybernetic. A *cybernetic strategy* proceeds through trial and error, using feedback as the mechanism for correction. A cybernetic strategy is useful when even limited comparisons among alternatives are not feasible and when the only information available is that something needs to be done or is not working and the cause of the problem is not apparent, but there is some experience in identifying safe limits for evaluating progress. The decision outcomes are important in meeting the objective or returning a situation to an acceptable condition. For example, on a very warm holiday when the air conditioning fails, you may decide (by another strategy) to try to correct the problem yourself. Within the do-it-yourself approach, the effectiveness of alternatives cannot be compared without actually trying them. If one has sufficient knowledge of the problem to assess probable causes and promising solutions, another strategy becomes appropriate. The trial-and-error method includes a series of implementing decisions, such as checking the circuit breaker, checking the site glass for a shortage of coolant, and checking the reset button on the air conditioner.

Random. A *random strategy* involves taking a course of action that lacks insight into the outcome but that may have intrinsic, spontaneous, or emergency interest in a response. The decision maker has limited knowledge of past or available solutions. The choice being made may be a function of timing even when alternative courses of action are identified. For example, if you are in an accident in a strange city and the ambulance driver asks you if you prefer Grant Hospital or Riverside Hospital, you might well decide to take the nearest one in a random strategy. Your choice is a function of timing among the courses of action identified for you.

When a random decision fails to satisfy the decision maker's needs, the person may move to other strategies when faced with similar situations of limited information. When feasible, you might transfer to a hospital in your own city, where prospects are known or thought to be better for treatment. If you face a related decision, you may seek more information and move to a satisficing or rudimentary optimizing strategy.

How people make decisions

INDIVIDUAL DECISION MAKING

In addition to the rational processes just described, individuals may also use intuition in decision making. *Intuitive decision making* conceptualizes or comprehends all steps of the decision-making process without explicit interpretation of the parts. The manner in which individuals process information differs and will be discussed in this section.

Intuition yields a solution that bypasses well-defined, conscious steps of decision making. From intuition come proposals of solutions that may be consciously examined; the solution is believed to be one that will prove to be correct, and it is more than a guess.[23]

Intuitive decision making is aided by experience, but it does not necessarily result from it. The intuitive person focuses on a total conception of the problem and does not consider the elements of decision making singly. More things appear to be taken into account than can be verbalized. But there is a sense of comprehending the total situation and considering a number of alternatives simultaneously. Facts or experience may provide some insight, but an interrelating of unknowns may occur and result in a conscious sense of rightness or wrongness about some situation. Real and imagined obstacles are differentiated. Decisions as varied as a new business venture or a leisure activity may be approached through intuitive or rational processes.

Intuition may be particularly appropriate under the following circumstances:

- High level of uncertainty
- Little precedent for decision
- Limited information
- Limited time for decision
- Several plausible alternatives[24]

Individuals process information about decisions differently. *Heuristics* are procedures that provide relatively simple guidelines for decision making. Three common heuristics we will discuss are representativeness, availability, and adjusting and anchoring.[25]

Some individuals make judgments based on familiar objects or subjects. For example, in choosing a motel, experience with or knowledge about a certain motel chain may form the basis for selecting another motel in the chain.

The heuristic of availability is used by individuals who can bring to mind similar happenings. An example is the decision of a single parent to send her child to a private school. She recalls the experiences of her friends' children and selects the school where more of her friends have sent their children.

Another heuristic is adjustment and anchoring. The person starts from an anchor and adjusts to that point. For example, in decisions about options for an automobile purchase, a consumer may take as an anchor the options on the current car and then adjust upward or downward depending on price or other factors. Heuristics or simplification procedures used in decision making imply that the consumer does not start with a "clean slate" and consider all options objectively. Information stored in memory via learning experiences acts continually as a screen that both aids and simplifies decision making.

FAMILY DECISION MAKING

The three types of family decision making to be considered are consensual, accommodation, and de facto. *Consensual* decision making involves communication that concludes with all family members giving equal assent and feeling equally committed to the decision.[26] Communication yields agreement or no conflict regarding the relevant value or alternative in a situation where several interests or possibilities need to be sorted out. In the latter case, the satisficing decision strategy may be applied. The first alternative that satisfied minimum expectations of all members is the alternative agreed on by consensus.[27] For some families, consensus in decision making is rare.

For upper-middle-class white couples, low disparities and low self-defensiveness increase the likelihood of consensus decision making. Low or high disparities in education, income, sex-role preferences, self-esteem, and in mutuality (evaluations of their prior decision making), influence decision-making styles. Each of these characteristics stimulates the consensus type of decision making.[28]

Consensus as a dominant approach to decision making among some couples comes from values that were shared before marriage or from common values that have evolved throughout the relationship.

A couple with a long marriage reflects attitudes that form the basis for consensual decisions:

ED: Forty-nine years is a long time. You learn a lot about each other. You have some things in common, you develop some personal freedoms, you learn about privacy, what's valuable to each other and what both of you regard as valuable—and when you learn that, you can make good decisions, even though you fight.

SARAH ANNE: We used to talk about love, but we outgrew that. Now we know that each agreement is an act of love because every person wants to be unique and on top, and it really is very hard for two people to come together and share a world. You have to value each other a lot to give up what you have to give up to stay together. Our marriage holds up and will hold up because we have a shared sense of what is valuable. Without that, I don't know how any marriage can be sustained.[29]

The second type of decision making is *accommodation*. Agreement comes through accepting the desire of a dominant person when all the views are not reconciled.[30] Two effects of accommodated decisions are that commitment to the decision may be conditional for some group members and that the person whose desires were most closely followed in the decision dominates in its implementation.

De facto decisions tend to follow from lack of effective consideration or communication of alternatives: ". . . agreement is by the absence of dissent rather than by active assent, and more important, commitment is by the course of events rather than by acceptance."[31] For example, discussion of whether to go to the hockey game, as the sons want to do, or to go to the movies, as the rest of the family wants to do, goes on until it is past time for the start of the hockey game. De facto decision making has taken place, and the family can go only to the movie.

Decision-making patterns. Traditional decision-making patterns continue in some families, with the husband making decisions about his occupational pursuits and the wife facilitating those efforts and deciding about household operations. On the other hand, more egalitarian relationships, including more shared decision making, are emerging between spouses. As families experience changes in roles, decisions may well be made on the bases of particular skills, available time, workload, interests, and orientation to equality as opposed to specialization on the basis of gender.

In examining wives' employment decision making, "it is argued that as both wives and husbands rise in socioeconomic structure, women become less economically dependent upon their spouses, while men are socialized into an egalitarian ethic. Both factors facilitate greater influence in the area of employment decision making for married women."[32]

Recent research reveals that some decisions (such as deciding on a husband's job) are typically seen as being in the husband's realm, others (such as deciding if the wife should take a job) as in the wife's realm, and yet others (such as deciding where to go on vacation or what house to live in) as being shared. "These perceptions seem to be the products of larger cultural processes more than the husband's and wife's interaction."[33]

An examination of farm and household decision making found that many decisions were made jointly by a farm woman and another person, usually her husband.[34] Women made more of the household decisions, and men were more likely to make production decisions for the farm. "The wider the range of a woman's farm tasks, the greater the proportion of types of farm decisions she made. . . . Cross-societal research has emphasized that labor contributions are only a necessary but not [a] sufficient condition for women to have higher status and power."[35] For example, in developing countries, women may play an important part in agricultural production, but that alone does not give them higher status and power.

In a sample of low-income families, the egalitarianism of the decision-making process was identified as the most important factor in the family's remaining intact.[36] The pattern of decision making can be influential in maintaining a successful marriage relationship. Family decision-making patterns are gradually shifting from gender-based to more egalitarian strategies. The presence of children seems to be associated with more decision-making dominance by husbands. However, a study of the influence of family versus couple on decisions related to vacations reveals:

1. Husbands tend to dominate decision making about vacations in families more than in couple situations without children; joint decision making occurs more often among couples than among families with children.
2. Within families with children, children exert relatively little influence on the overall vacation decision process, although the extent of their influence varies substantially in the different elements of the decision process.[37]

An examination of the impact of the microenvironment on decision making and the managerial activities in the home environment should include features such as time pressures, mood and fatigue of participants, and distraction factors.[38]

Future decision strategies may involve more alternatives and technological assistance, such as computers, with accompanying impacts on decision patterns.

Summary

Individuals and families today are faced with increasingly complex decisions. They approach decision making differently, depending on their personal outlook and circumstances. The nature of decisions varies with components or functions to which given decisions are more directly related. Purpose, process, and control are aspects of all managerial decisions. Also, decision making within the management context is resource-related and cognitive.

Actions are preceded by some evaluation or decision-making process to resolve such questions as whether or not to act, why act, how to act, when to act, and where to act. Steps in the decision-making process include (1) the recognition that a decision is needed, (2) the identification and assessment of alternatives, and (3) the resolution or selection among alternatives.

Decision situations vary in the degree of certainty and risk surrounding them, and decision-making approaches, patterns, and processes influence the management of these differences. In the family setting, goals and preferences of members are both individual and shared. Social decision making—with its focus on the quality of interpersonal relations—interacts with economic processes in the search for optimum solutions, as does political decision making, which recognizes the degree to which family roles and policies reflect power positions in the family. Economic decision making is made more complex by the need to relate to the many choices made in relation to nonmarket as well as market interactions.

Individuals and families use decision strategies, including optimizing, satisficing, incremental, cybernetic, and random, to choose among available alternatives. Both subjective and objective probabilities are useful in making decisions with perceived risks. A "decision tree" is one form of visualizing probabilities of success that allows for examining alternatives and outcomes.

The optimizing strategy seeks to maximize the value to be received and requires identification of relevant alternatives and probabilities of the effects, outcomes, or consequences.

Satisficing is a strategy that calls for seeking

alternatives until one alternative acceptably meets the desired end. It is less exhaustive than the optimizing strategy and may not result in as advantageous a benefit-to-cost ratio.

The incremental strategy involves taking a series of smaller steps in a decision, thereby reducing the risk in a decision with major consequences.

The cybernetic strategy employs feedback and correction and is used when limited comparisons of alternatives are possible.

The random strategy is used in limited information situations. Making the choice is a function of timing rather than the attributes of identified alternatives.

Individuals process information differently, and they use procedures to simplify decision making. These heuristics include representativeness, availability, and adjustment and anchoring. In order to function effectively, individuals use methods of simplification to reduce the amount of information they consider in decision making.

Families continue to have decision-making patterns that are husband-dominant, although increasingly families seem to be moving toward an egalitarian pattern.

Intuitive decision making emanates from a holistic orientation to decision situations, where the problem is conceptualized without detailed analysis of its elements. There is a sense of rightness (or wrongness) about such choices where comprehension exceeds an ability to communicate. Evaluating the correctness of one's choices in terms of ultimate outcomes provides the bases for continued reliance on intuition.

Besides drawing on the previous processes, decisions involving the family group include those based on consensus (mutual agreement), on accommodation (yielding to the preference of a dominant member), or de facto (absence of dissent). Those based on consensus provide the opportunity for intrasystem dynamics that would strengthen cohesion, adaptability, and functionality.

Notes

1. Joan Aldous, "A Framework for the Analysis of Family Problem Solving," in *Family Problem Solving,* Joan Aldous, Thomas Condon, Reuben Hill, Murray Straus, and Irving Tallman, eds. (Hinsdale: The Dryden Press, 1971), p. 267.
2. John Naisbitt, *Megatrends* (New York: Warner Books, 1982), p. 231.
3. Ibid., p. 232.
4. Marcus Alexis and Charles Z. Wilson, *Organizational Decision Making* (Englewood Cliffs, N.J.: Prentice-Hall, 1967), pp. 149–150.
5. Ronald W. Stampfl, "Perceived Risk and Consumer Decision Making," *Journal of Consumer Studies and Home Economics* 2 (September 1978): 241.
6. Ibid., p. 235.
7. Samuel Eilon, "What Is a Decision?" *Management Science* 16 (December 1969): B–185.
8. Noel Capon and Deanna Kuhn, "Can Consumers Calculate Best Buys?" *Journal of Consumer Research* 8 (March 1983): 452.
9. Naresh K. Malhotra, "Information Load and Consumer Decision Making," *Journal of Consumer Research* 8 (March 1982): 426.
10. Carole K. Holahan, "The Relationship between Information Search in the Childbearing Decision and Life Satisfaction for Parents and Nonparents," *Family Relations* (October 1983): 534.
11. Ibid., p. 533.
12. Jess Stein, ed., *The Random House Dictionary of the English Language* (New York: Random House, 1967), p. 1146.
13. Gerald J. Hahn, "Evaluation of a Decision Based on Subjective Probability Estimates," *IEEE Transactions on Engineering Management* EM-18 (February 1971): 12.
14. John F. Magee, "Decision Trees for Decision Making," *Harvard Business Review* 42 (July–August 1964): 128.
15. Ibid., p. 130.
16. Ana Grandori, "A Prescriptive Contingency View of Organizational Decision Making," *Administrative Science Quarterly* 29 (June 1984): 192–209.
17. Russell L. Ackoff and Fred E. Emery, *On Purposeful Systems* (Chicago: Aldine-Atherton, 1972), p. 109.
18. Grandori, "A Prescriptive Contingency View," p. 192.
19. David I. Cleland and William R. King, *Management: A Systems Approach* (New York: McGraw-Hill, 1972), p. 225.
20. Herbert A. Simon, "Theories of Decision-

Making in Economics and Behavioral Science," *The American Economic Review* 49 (June 1959): 277.

21. Grandori, "A Prescriptive Contingency View," p. 196.

22. Ibid., p. 198.

23. Ackoff and Emery, *On Purposeful Systems,* p. 114.

24. Weston H. Agor, "How Top Executives Use Their Intuition to Make Important Decisions," *Business Horizons* 29 (January–February 1986): 49.

25. A. Tversky and D. Kahneman, "Judgment under Uncertainty: Heuristics and Biases," *Science* 185 (September 27, 1974): 1124–1131; see also Mary Winter, "Management as a Mental Process: Implications for Theory and Research," Paper presented to North Central Regional Committee (NCR-116) on Family Resource Management, St. Louis, Missouri, 1986. Home Economics Research Institute Journal Paper No. 367, Iowa State University.

26. Ralph H. Turner, *Family Interaction* (New York: Wiley, 1970), p. 98.

27. Harry L. Davis, "Decision Making Within the Household," *Journal of Consumer Research* 2 (March 1976): 252.

28. Wayne Hill and John Scanzoni, "An Approach for Assessing Marital Decision-Making Processes," *Journal of Marriage and the Family* 44 (November 1982): 938.

29. Gerald M. Phillips, "Consensus as Cultural Tradition: A Study of Agreements between Marital Partners," in *Emergent Issues in Human Decision Making,* Gerald M. Phillips and Julia T. Woods, eds. (Carbondale: Southern Illinois University Press, 1984), p. 119.

30. Turner, *Family Interaction,* p. 98.

31. Ibid., p. 99.

32. Mark R. Rank, "Determinants of Conjugal Influence in Wives' Employment Decision Making," *Journal of Marriage and the Family* 44 (August 1982): 591.

33. Catherine E. Ross and John Mirowsky, "The Social Construction of Reality in Marriage," *Sociological Perspectives* 27 (July 1984): 290.

34. Rachel Ann Rosenfeld, *Farm Women* (Chapel Hill: University of North Carolina Press, 1985), p. 137.

35. Ibid., p. 138.

36. Marie Withers Osmond and Patricia Yancey Martin, "A Contingency Model of Marital Organization in Low Income Families," *Journal of Marriage and the Family* 40 (May 1978): 328.

37. Pierre Filiatrault and J. R. Brent Ritchie, "Joint Purchasing Decisions: A Comparison of Influence Structure in Family and Couple Decision-Making Units," *Journal of Consumer Research* 7 (September 1980): 139.

38. Susan P. Douglas, "Examining Family Decision-Making Processes," *Advances in Consumer Research* 10 (1983): 452.

7 Planning

Planning is a process using cognitive skills to envision what is to be done. Planning is a series of decisions about future standards and/or sequences of action. "Although there is no generally accepted definition of planning, most writers agree that it involves attempts at purposeful, future-oriented decision making."[1] It is important to keep planning as a part of the whole of management in mind, even though we will discuss the components separately.

Planning, a part of the managerial system, results in design of actions in pursuit of a goal. Plans give focus and direction for accomplishing goals. Well-made plans can affect success or failure in goal achievement.

Standard setting

Standard setting is the reconciliation of resources with demands. The resulting standards then represent the operational criteria. Clarification of demands and determination of the available resources that can translate goals into purposeful, realistic actions are preliminary to standard setting. Standards have quantitative and qualitative components that indicate the capability of resources to satisfy demands. The operational criteria (standards) communicate expected outcomes from the use of resources to accomplish goals. Once standards of quality and quantity are set, they become criteria for action. The criteria emanate from the direction-oriented goals that are undergirded with values held by individuals and family members. Standards are developed for a particular set of circumstances and are situation specific. Because household and life situations may be repetitive, standards may be developed for single use or repeat use. When the specifications developed for previous or ongoing situations continue to fit, the standard-setting aspects and, indeed, the planning subsystem may be bypassed (see Figure 7.1).

DEMAND CLARIFICATION

Goals and events, as demands, are clarified and resources assessed preparatory to setting standards.[2] Demand clarification is the refinement of objectives consistent with values; both goals and events may be clarified. General goals and directions are considered, and particular goals to be sought are identified. For example, two different majors in college might be appropriate for one goal that serves a value. The clarification and selection of the major must be made before the action plan is developed. It may be

FIGURE 7.1 *Planning*

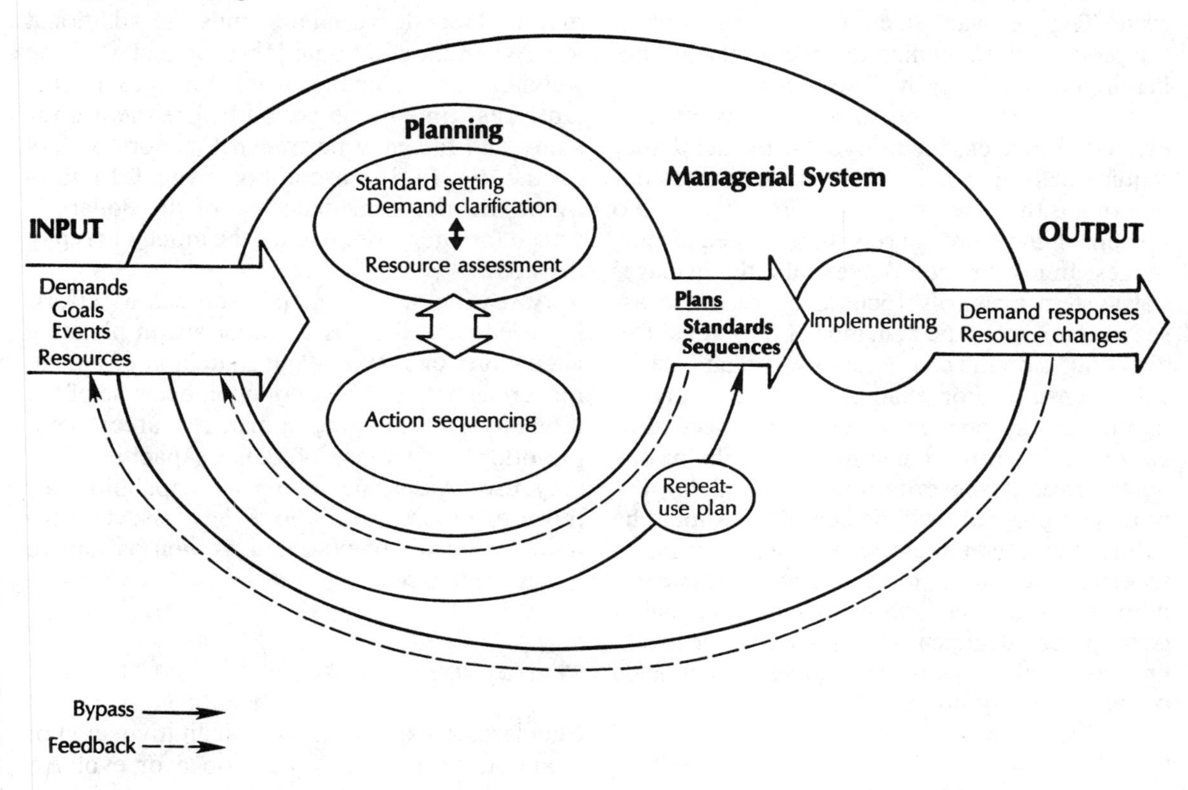

that in the process of selecting one of the two majors, you have some criteria in mind already, and you test the information about the major against the criteria. You may have resources to remain in college for four years, and one major may take you longer than the other. Goal clarification and resource assessment are both taking place, and you can move to reconciliation of resources with demands or standard setting.

Cursory or incomplete delineation of goals and problems can cause the real problem to go unaddressed. Sometimes, the problem is ignored or denied, and no goal is set. Ill-structured goals and subsequent ill-structured plans can provide a measure of direction. Some things can be accomplished through them; but with clearer goals, clearer specification of operational criteria (standards) can be set, enhancing the chances for accomplishing goals.

Goal clarification may occur before resources are assessed, so that all resource considerations are subject to meeting predetermined criteria. Goals may also be clarified concurrently with resources assessment. An example of the latter case is the advisory committee of a day-care center that values high-quality child care and strives to improve care services. The committee realizes that a number of child-care needs in the community are unmet. After learning of needs for drop-in care, sick-child care, and for after-kindergarten care, the committee assesses resources and clarifies the direction of improved child care services—broadening the scope of the center to serve the community's needs. A specific goal evolves for child care for sick children already in the program. The goal was selected and clarified during the process of examining the situation and aiming at generally improved services.

As with goals, events in some cases must be evaluated and clarified. Events, by definition, require action; that is, if the system does not determine that they require action, there is no response; they are merely unexpected occurrences. In taking action on events, the managerial system primarily focuses on resource assessment to meet the demands of the event. The event takes on the character of a goal and clarification ensues. For example, if you receive a minor cut on your leg, a decision is needed to either seek professional medical help or try home care. If the criterion is minimizing the scar, you probably will decide that it should be sutured; you then plan a sequence for getting to an emergency room, canceling conflicting commitments, etc. The continuing value and goal of good personal appearance provides the background for clarification of the event's demands on available resources.

RESOURCE ASSESSMENT

Resource assessment is the analysis of potential means to meet particular demands. Standard setting matches resources to demands and forms a basis for action in a particular situation. Standards are the ultimate output of goal clarification and resource assessment as shown in Figure 7.1.

Assessing resources begins with the recognition of available resources, and if the need arises, consideration of ways of increasing resources. In specific situations, only limited resources are effectively available. For example, in developing a plan for skiing during a winter vacation, the student must assess the financial resources that can be assigned to the ski trip. Most people, even if savings are extensive, must weigh other uses for available resources against those of the ski trip. If funds are insufficient, potential sources for additional dollars may be tapped: parents, friends, an additional job. When an additional job is considered, the weighing of resources again becomes important. Less time in the period before the trip for study and fun may be traded for more dollars for the trip. In the case of borrowing from family or friends, immediate use of the dollars is traded for later work to earn the money to repay the debt.

Assessing such human resources as effort, knowledge, and skills is important in planning almost any endeavor. Poor matching of human resources with needs is common because of the difficulty of evaluating human resources. People often have more of these capacities than they use. Assessing their own capabilities or those of others with whom they associate requires analyses of potential as well as known human resources.

STANDARDS

Standards, expressed in qualitative and/or quantitative terms, are developed or evolved. The contribution of human and material resources in meeting goals may be explored, clarified, and defined as qualitative and quantitative criteria. *Quality* is the property or image of what is desired. *Quantity* is a definitive or estimated amount of what is desired, which can be measured in absolute terms or estimated in a comparative way. When the quantity of one thing is compared with the quantity of another, as in relating prices, the comparison is meaningful if the quality is similar.

Grading is a method of making systematic judgments about the quality of a product or thing. Grading is a quality judgment and usually refers to the position of something in relation to all other items of its kind or, at least, of those known. Specific qualities for milk, eggs, and other foods are graded according to generally recognized standards. Individuals may use existing criteria to approximate grading while shopping, for example, by searching for clothing items that meet identified characteristics of construction, design, care, or warmth.

Decision-making strategies for developing standards include the optimizing strategy discussed in Chapter 6. In that strategy, options are ranked according to criteria that one has identified as being important in the situation. Qualitative characteristics may be ranked according to criteria that permit comparisons about whether one thing is better or worse than another. Ranking for standards for quantity aspects like size or distance can be accomplished relatively simply after determining the amounts or dimensions. Combining quantity and quality properties into a ranked order is a more difficult task.

Table 7.1 presents a housing plan for a senior at "Maumee University." Included in the plan is a ranking of options by qualitative and quantitative criteria that are important to the student. Wally has a friend who is open to sharing a room or apartment with him, but the friend is in a co-op program and is away during spring quarter, when they need to make a decision. Their operational criteria (standards) are given in Table 7.2. Gathering information about what is available (resource assessment) is Wally's task. With that information, he can align the criteria and the options and rank each option based on each of the multiple criteria. Table 7.2 illustrates numeric indicators that are weighted equally. If one criterion is more important than another, it may be weighted more heavily. The table indicates that the apartment is the best choice when using an optimizing strategy.

Choices such as a living arrangement may or may not be of sufficient importance to actually assign numerical ratings to factors identified as relevant. Rather, one may choose to sort through qualities and quantities—the standards—of the available options in an informal manner.

Consideration of both quality and quantity aspects is likely to bring better results. A group of families reported that they had more nearly achieved their expectations for food, clothing, housing, and furnishings when both quality and quantity were considered important than when only one or the other was emphasized.[3]

TABLE *7.1 A plan for housing for a senior at "Maumee University"*

Standard setting

Goal clarification: to secure suitable housing
  Define operational criteria or standards (see Table 7.2 for housing options)
  Decide on criteria for moving—decided to seek the lowest moving cost

Resource assessment: obtain information on housing available to meet goal/outlay (requires action sequencing)

1 Call University Housing Office to see about a dormitory suite or room
2 Check the newspapers for ads for apartments and rooming houses
3 Call the managers
4 Set up appointments in later afternoon after work, first for housing units near the campus and then, if they don't work out, beyond the campus area

Standard: choose the option on the basis of ranking how well they meet the operational criteria; choose the apartment

Action sequencing

Late spring Rent the housing unit and prepare for occupancy
Make an appointment to see manager on a weekend when apartment mate can return to campus
Look at the apartment or model and determine anything that needs to be done or furniture that is needed
Sign lease
Pay deposit

Before August 15 Call utilities to set up accounts
Agree with apartment mate about move-in date
Line up brother and his friends to help move—see if brother's friend will use his pickup truck if you pay for gas; if not, reserve a rental trailer and hitch

By September 5 Get things packed
Perhaps prepare a packing list, which then becomes a part of the planning process
Arrange for apartment mate to pick up apartment key

September 5 Moving day (Implementation)

TABLE 7.2 *Ranking of housing options by operational criteria (standards)*

Operational criteria	*Rooming house*		*Dormitory suite*		*Dormitory single room*		*Apartment*	
	Characteristic	*Rank**	*Characteristic*	*Rank**	*Characteristic*	*Rank**	*Characteristic*	*Rank**
Quantitative								
Within walking distance of campus	8 blocks from main campus	1	Near center of campus	4	Near edge of campus	3	6 blocks from campus	2
Rent $200/month or less	$200/month plus telephone	3	$215/month plus telephone	2	$245/month plus telephone	1	$150/month plus telephone**	4
Qualitative								
Maximum flexibility in meal arrangements	Share cooking facilities	1	Optional meal tickets; kitchen available for occasional use	2.5	Optional meal tickets; kitchen available for occasional use	2.5	Small kitchen	4
As quiet as possible	Not very noisy	3	A bit noisy	1	Average noise	2	Quiet	4
Prefer to room alone but willing to share a room with friend	Single	3.5	Share suite	.5	Single	3.5	Share a bedroom	1.5
Pleasant appearance with good lighting	Rather dark; one small window	1	Contemporary furniture; needs extra lamp	3	Ugly furniture in available dorm; rooms have high windows	2	Motel-modern furniture; good light	4
Connecting bath	Down the hall	1	Yes	3	Yes	3	Yes	3
Well-lighted; safe parking near housing	On-street parking	1	Safe parking lot away from dorm	3	Safe parking lot away from dorm	3	Parking space lighted only by streetlight	3
Total		14.5		19		20		25.5

* 1 = low, 4 = high; rank comparisons apply across housing options. Tie rankings between two housing options are given an average value of the two rank values that the tie replaces.

** Includes estimates of cost of electricity and gas.

Action sequencing

Planning is a way to get things together: to recognize and make interrelationships and to synthesize activities purposefully. *Action sequencing* is the ordering of parts of an activity or specifying succession among activities. Skillfully ordering the parts of an activity (arranging the steps) can improve the flow of action. For example, if the car engine is not at operating temperature when oil is changed, the engine should be run long enough to warm it up. Arranging to change the oil soon after a trip when the engine is already warmed up can thus shorten the time for the task and save gasoline as well.

Activities occur in a sequence whether or not a plan is involved—that is, by the flow of time and the necessity of one thing being done before or separately from another, activities occur in succession. Conscious sequencing is the placement of one activity in relation to another to accomplish the standards set for the activity.

Alternating between physically or cognitively heavy and light tasks and taking more rest periods were two efficient sequencing techniques used by women in a study of their time use, but work-load pressures discouraged the use of these techniques.[4]

Sequencing activities or tasks can be described as interdependent, dovetailed, or overlapped in nature. Figure 7.2 shows an example of the need for recognizing interdependent activities.

Interdependent activities are those in which full completion of one task depends on the completion of another task. Failure to complete one task would delay completing the other task; they are interdependent. Completing a term project is an example of an interdependent activity. Library references and information needs are anticipated, correspondence is completed, and interviews are conducted before starting to write. Lack of correlation of tasks may postpone completion of the project paper or force omission of information (a change in standard).

FIGURE 7.2 *Sequencing of activities*

Source: The Family Circus, by Bil Keane. Reprinted courtesy The Register and Tribune Syndicate, Inc., January 22, 1974.

Interdependent activities must often be scheduled when occupational and volunteer demands affect the lives of several members of a unit. An example is an all-adult household whose members are employed outside the home. Plans must accommodate each person's schedule for arriving at work and the anticipated times to be together in the home. If members are involved in continuing education and volunteer activities, the participation and assistance in meetings, camps, classes, and so on must also be coordinated.

Giving intermittent attention to two or more tasks until they are completed is called *dovetailing*. When you run errands in the shopping center while clothes are being washed at the laundromat, the activities are dovetailed.

Some activities are amenable to *overlapping*, or giving intermittent and/or concurrent attention to two or more activities until they are completed. Overlapping is possible because of differences in attention levels required for the tasks. Child care is probably the activity most often undertaken concurrently with other homemaking tasks.

Regular educational activities (clubs, lessons, Scouts, etc.) affect sequencing for many individuals and families. Sequence adjustments occur when there are changes in activities or school due to holidays, bad weather, fuel shortages, illness of leaders, or suspension of a student from school. Each change contributes to the frustrations of those who arrange for getting someone to the activity.

Independent tasks are those that are completed before another activity is begun. Costa Rican women are described as having a preference for independent tasks:

> They seem to wish to complete cleaning, clothing care, and food preparation activities before changing to some other type of activity. In the making of tortillas, this apparent goal was achieved. Once the homemakers began this task, they seldom changed activities until all the tortillas for the day were completed. They achieved this continuity by verbally instructing other family members to handle such chores as caring for babies, grinding corn, cutting wood, or hanging laundry to dry. The homemaker remained attentive to what was happening but did not break her physical attention to the tortilla making.[5]

Individual qualities that affect planning

Individuals may differ in their planning skills and outlook on planning because of their demographic qualities, their time orientation, foresight, and/or internal or external control differences.

DEMOGRAPHIC CHARACTERISTICS

Factors thought to affect planning include age, stage in the family life cycle (highly correlated with age), experience, and education. In a study of low-income families, education directly affected realistic standard setting;[6] education was also correlated with the extent to which small business managers made plans.[7] The education level of mothers, but not fathers, was related to an expansive style of planning among a sample of single parents.[8]

TIME ORIENTATIONS

Time orientations—the dominant reference points in life—differ for men and women, probably due to socialization differences. Men tend to "treat the present as a series of preparative moments" and they are taught "to accept the uncertainties and ambiguities associated with a future orientation as normal features of everyday behavior."[9] Women are supposed to deal with the present and men with the future. Such differences in society's expectations and in individuals affect plans. With changing socialization and consequent changes in roles, current time orientation differences and any planning differences that exist will likely change. Relatively little is known about differences in planning by men and women.

Time orientation is probably related to income levels. Carolina Maria de Jesus writes in her diary in a favela in São Paulo:

> I got out of bed at 4 a.m. and went to carry water, then went to wash clothes. I didn't make lunch. There is no rice. *This afternoon I'm going to cook beans with macaroni* [emphasis added]. The boys didn't eat anything. I'm going to lie down because I'm sleepy. It was 9 o'clock. João woke me up to open the door. Today I'm sad.[10]

The planning horizon is very short: what she will do in the afternoon. Carolina actually had a vision of leaving the favela through her writing—a long-term goal.

FORESIGHT ABILITY

Anticipation of the future is an important part of planning. The planning ability of *foresight* is an awareness of possible future events relating to a current situation.[11] Foresight has at least two facets: perceptual and conceptual.

Perceptual foresight is the ability to project to the future from the present—to explore possible alternatives and select the most effective alternatives for solving problems.[12] The scheduling of classes requires perceptual foresight—to examine alternative classes available at nonconflicting times and select those meeting requirements for a program. Perceptual foresight involves analysis of existing factual information in relation to a specific future situation.

For people preparing for a foreign assignment, perceptual foresight is the ability to examine available information about medical assistance and choose alternatives for dealing with the level of available help; to plan clothing for the climatic, cultural, and occupational demands; and to determine which household goods will meet the envisioned needs. In this case, present information is used to deal with the future in a relatively concrete manner—a characteristic of perceptual foresight.

Conceptual foresight is the ability to relate anticipated future situations to the present. Conceptual foresight involves anticipation of needs or consequences of problem situations.[13] Conceptual foresight in scheduling classes would place emphasis on the anticipated occupation or life-style and then identify courses that would contribute to it.

People with conceptual foresight can examine more abstract questions. Conceptual foresight is also the ability to alter factors in the present situation that will affect future needs.

The anticipated advantages of cultural enrichment for the children in a different country may be weighed against the predicted educational and social disadvantages.

If, for example, the children's education is thought to be inadequate in the foreign land, they may be left in the home country.

Conceptual foresight is a more abstract and idea-related concept than perceptual foresight, but the two are interrelated. Good measures of foresight are needed so that the effect of foresight ability on planning can be clearly established.

As a start in this direction, planners (having at least perceptual foresight) were more satisfied with outputs of their management in a study using data from a nationally representative sample. The results supported planning as "an integral and satisfaction-enhancing component of the management subsystem."[14]

INTERNAL–EXTERNAL CONTROL

Another individual factor that influences planning is that of internal or external control. People who believe they can control their own destiny have internal control; they also believe in the potential benefits of planning.

However, in the study of low-income families referred to earlier, greater internal control was not directly related to planning behavior;[15] husbands and wives with more internal orientation had higher incomes and higher agreement on family matters, which was associated with realistic standards.

Persons with external control perceive events as being unrelated to their own behavior or as unpredictable because of complex forces and, therefore, beyond personal control. A strong orientation to external control, such as belief in astrological power or influence, can profoundly affect people's planning. On auspicious days in the East, many weddings take place; on ordinary days, few or no weddings occur.

Attributes of plans

A good plan is clear to the person or people who will implement it, contains appropriate detail, is well defined for the activity or goal to be accomplished, has realistic standards and sequences, and can readily be adjusted to accommodate changes during implementation. The attributes *clarity, flexibility, reality,* and *complexity* are considered here in relation to plans as a whole.

CLARITY

Clarity in plans means that both specific standards and sequences have been fully developed. Specific plans are important when goals are critical, when time or money pressures are great, and when little previous experience or knowledge is available to meet a goal.

Definite plans for a specific time are more likely to be carried through to completion than are indefinite plans. The need for clarity of plans is increased whenever someone other than the planner is carrying out the plan. The plan for a bus route, for example, must be clearly stated with specified standards for times and stops, if a variety of drivers will take the route and if bus riders are to have assurance of catching the bus at the planned time.

The importance of the plan would seem to be the most rational determinant of the specificity of actions anticipated. Yet, plan specificity may not be based on importance. In discussing when and why they decided to have their first child, the wife, Debby, perceived more careful attention to owning a cat than to planning for a child.

DARYL: I don't know whether we actually gave the cat more consideration.

DEBBY: I think we did. . . . We planned the arrival of the cat specifically so we'd get him just before we moved out of the house.[16]

Clarity in plans can be important to the person who also implements the plan. Planning with specific details of standards and sequences can simplify implementing the plan because prior attention has been given to how much, how many, how long, and when, questions that must be answered at some point. For open and carefree situations, clarity in plans may enhance freedom by allowing the activity to flow unfettered, with participants making decisions as they are needed; strict interpretation of the specific details of a plan can reduce the free feeling, however. An example is informal entertaining in which clear plans can contribute greatly to the feeling of informality as long as implementation of the plan is not rigid.

The specificity of plans varies greatly; some people have the capacity to remember specific aspects of unwritten plans. Others find it helpful to write their plans down and feel accomplishment when they check off parts of the plan as they complete them.

FLEXIBILITY

The range of acceptable standards and sequences of plans indicates their degree of *flexibility*. An example of a plan that has limited flexibility is a prepayment plan for college. Payment can be made at the birth of a child and/or as the child grows up. Generally, the payment is for a specific college, and there is sometimes a clause in the plan that allows for withdrawal of the money if the child is not accepted into the school or if he or she chooses not to attend that school. But the financial loss is rather great, since many of the plans return only the principal. A more flexible plan would have money invested for the purpose of sending a child to college while keeping the plan open and flexible regarding use of the funds.

Flexibility in standards is also interrelated with flexibility in sequences. A wide range of quality and quantity aspects of standards and a wide latitude in the sequence may be acceptable.

The increasing number of women in the labor force means that often two employment schedules must be reconciled with the sequencing of household activities. When previously held schedules are met after a woman is employed outside the household, the cost may be high if the household activities are not shared. The woman working outside the home who is expected to handle child-care arrangements and to have meals prepared at the same time they were before she worked away from home experiences stress that can be alleviated only by a change in task allocation or an increase in flexibility of the sequence of tasks.

REALITY

Reality is the feasibility of achieving the chosen standards and sequences in a plan. When a task or activity is accomplished as planned, the plan is realistic. Estimating a realistic approach is, in part, clarifying probabilities for certain parts of the plan.

For example, under ordinary conditions a tank of gasoline will last during the drive from Cleveland to Cincinnati. With a strong head wind, the mileage per gallon is reduced. Under conditions existing at the time of planning, the tank will need to be refilled en route. Such estimates are mixtures of certainty and doubt about an outcome and can be expressed as an estimate of probability. A person who arrives at a .50 probability (intuitively or mathematically) that the tank will need filling before reaching Cincinnati is less likely to take a chance than the person who concludes that the probability is zero. The more factors considered (or the more dependable the gauge), the less uncertainty there is. But variable conditions make such gaming a rather common way to deal with uncertainty even though exact probabilities are not specified.

Estimating or establishing probabilities associated with accomplishments of both standards and sequences can alter plans and increase reality in plans.

COMPLEXITY

The degree of interrelationship between people and tasks determines the *complexity* of a plan. The number of people involved in a plan, the relationship of the people—employer-employee, parent-child, husband-wife, teacher-student—the scope and importance of the task, and the adequacy of resources all affect the complexity of a plan.

A simple plan is required for one person to do an uncomplicated task with adequate resources. For example, a simple plan would be to write to one's parents tonight after dinner. A more involved plan would be needed to get an organization to write a letter to a member of Congress about some legislation; an even more complex plan is necessary if a letter-writing campaign is to be conducted by an organization and it has no financial resources to allocate to the effort. Figure 7.3 illustrates the impact of persons and tasks on complexity.

SINGLE-USE AND REPEAT-USE PLANS

Single-use plans are used only once or as part of the development of a repeat-use plan. Due to the nature of the activity, single-use plans often involve detailed standards and sequences. Plans to purchase a particular house or car, to share an apartment with certain people, or to celebrate a twenty-fifth wedding anniversary are examples of plans likely to be used only once. Although many plans are created to meet special situations with no intention of reuse, plans or parts of plans once developed are a form of resource since they represent information that may be called upon to simplify related situations that arise.

Repeat-use plans employ previously developed standards and/or sequences. For recurring activities, planning is often simplified by determining a plan or procedure that can be called upon whenever a given situation arises. The recurrences may be daily or less often, but such situations permit repeat-use plans in terms of given standards or a given schedule or pattern of performance. For certain conditions, fixed standards are the most appropriate:

1. when no feasible choices or options exist, e.g., the replacement of a part for a kitchen

FIGURE 7.3 *Effect of sequences on complexity of plan*

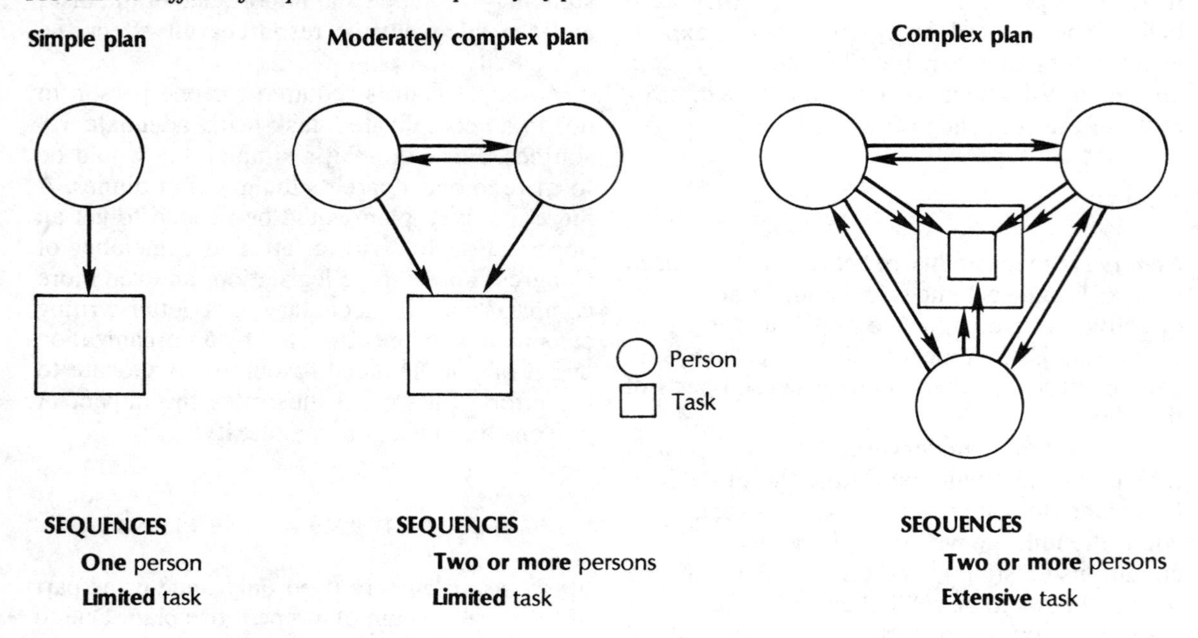

range where the range will not function without the part and parts of another manufacturer will not fit;
2. where results must conform rigidly to expectations, e.g., the formula preparation for an infant who has been having feeding problems;
3. where a plan is often repeated and only one outcome is acceptable, e.g., balancing the checkbook.

Developing sequences of action that are reused gives structure to life—in the home, in employment, and in other systems. Routines help give stability to people's lives. "When we have certain routines worked into a structure or framework, we reduce some of the element of change in our life. . . . Rhythms help us to perceive change and permanence and let us respond to the varying and enduring content of our lives."[17]

Figure 7.1 shows a repeat-use plan bypassing the planning subsystem. Plans may be reusable for a current purpose. Family rituals bring to mind sequences that vary little from year to year—celebration of Chanukah, birthday dinners, or opening Christmas presents after breakfast.

But continued use of repeat-use plans in changing situations can result in inappropriate actions because new or altered plans are often needed to deal with changed circumstances.

A bizarre, allegedly true story tells of a woman mopping her kitchen floor (she mopped it every weekday) as flood waters rose around her house! From a study of 335 wives and husbands, it was found that "an increase of one unit in the wives' perceived importance of doing household labor the 'way it was done when they were growing up,' added 32 minutes to their household day."[18] In retaining the standards imposed or developed when growing up, one bypasses the conscious reconciliation of resources with demands, substituting repeat-use plans.

Relation of plans to change and uncertainty

Plans are especially important when circumstances change the resources or demands faced by individuals and families and when uncertainty exists in relation to conditions.

"Problems and solutions are in constant flux; hence *problems do not stay solved.* Purposeful systems and their environments are constantly changing."[19] Even though problems continue largely unchanged, solutions to problems have to change to avoid being obsolete.

Examples of changed circumstances that create a need for plans follow:

Increased demands	An "extra" course requires expensive laboratory fees.
Decreased demands	An instructor reduces course requirements by one term paper.
Increased resources	An unexpected cash gift.
Decreased resources	A decrease in the hours the company will let you work.
Changed resources other than amount	A new apartment has the same total space, but a different room arrangement; or, time for studying is in small rather than large blocks because of work-schedule changes.

In each example, some different standards and sequences will need to be developed in response to the changes. The plan for the time released by an instructor deleting a term-paper requirement may be easy to develop; the matter of expensive laboratory fees may not be as easy to deal with.

Plans are needed when circumstances with the individual or family systems—particularly the personal subsystem—change. Throughout the life cycle, the dynamic nature of the family creates a need for planning: Children are born, divorce occurs, a child or spouse dies, a child goes to college—all changes calling for planning. In a study including three generations, more extensive and intensive planning was found among families in the expanding family life-cycle stage than at other stages.[20]

Decisions made at turning points in the life cycle are often central to other decisions that must be made.

DIRECTIONAL PLANNING

Although planning to meet established goals is emphasized in this book, a related approach to planning is potentially useful: *Directional planning* identifies areas of activity and preferences for action. Directional plans lead in a general way toward a long-range goal and introduce actions consistent with the general direction. Whenever actions must be taken before a situation is fully known, directional planning can be most appropriate since it has been characterized as "a set of approximations being revised in time as we learn more about ourselves and the environment."[21] In this view, goals are used to rationalize and justify actions, but recognition is given to the role of intuition and fantasy in planning.

Planning for a career is often directional in nature. A generalized focus on a career, while remaining open to opportunities and influences from the environment, gives a basis for directional planning. People and systems with directional plans may make false starts, may start down unproductive paths, and may generally be less efficient. But if they are able to deal with ambiguity, they may also be more resilient in the face of adversity and find new challenges and directions that give variety to life. Directional planning leaves many alternatives open.

CONTINGENCY PLANNING

Another way of handling uncertainty is contingency planning. A *contingency plan* specifies alternative standards and sequences of action for indefinite conditions. Disruption in a system is probably greatest and planning is frustrated most when uncertainty is high and the environment is turbulent.

Examples of contingency plans follow: *If* the landlord keeps bothering tenants about the rent, *then* they will move to other housing; *if* the landlord insists they pay rent on time and they cannot find another place for rent, *then* they'll borrow money from the new man at the neighborhood center. Simple contingency plans are often a part of everyday life—*if* the line at the cafeteria is too long, *then* that's the time to run an errand and eat later. Additional information can increase the specificity of planning and minimize uncertainty; for example, information that the lines are long at the cafeteria every Monday, Wednesday, and Friday at a certain hour enables more specific planning.

Planning in a systems perspective

Planning is part of the throughput of the managerial system. Planning differs considerably in relatively closed, relatively open, and relatively random systems. Characteristics of these systems, with an emphasis on planning, are given in Table 7.3. Individuals, groups, and families may not function exclusively as one type of system. Some may operate as almost random systems on weekends but use more regulated planning and management during the week; both are needed to give balance to their lives. A basic stability is needed for continuity of the system and enough adaptability is needed to remain viable. Even so, family systems tend toward identifiable planning approaches.

People in a group whose members use different approaches to planning may—probably will—experience some conflict or adjustment.

TABLE 7.3 *Characteristics of systems with an emphasis on planning*

		Planning		
		Standard setting		
Type of System	*Environment*	*Goal Clarification*	*Resource Assessment*	*Sequencing*
Relatively closed (Morphostatic) Tight ship	Certain	Present or unchanging goals	Little seeking or opportunity to expand resources	Low flexibility; Routines clearly established; Mechanistic
Relatively open (Morphogenic) Hang loose	Variable certainty	New goals are readily evaluated and accepted if appropriate	Vigorous seeking to expand resources	High flexibility; Adaptive
Relatively random (Spontaneous) Let it all hang out	Maximum uncertainty; Turbulent	Any activity may be taken as a goal any time	Erratic	Extreme flexibility

Source: Adapted from Doris Marie Beard, "Morphostatic and Morphogenic Planning Behavior in Families: Development of a Measurement Instrument," Ph.D. dissertation, The Ohio State University, 1975, p. 21; used with permission. Also adapted from David Kantor and William Lehr, *Inside the Family* (San Francisco: Jossey-Bass, 1975), pp. 134–142. Used with permission.

TABLE 7.4 *Examples of planning characteristics in morphostatic systems*

Prevalence of rigid standards and sequences in plans and high commitment to the current family system structure:

Parents evaluate all purchases grade-school children want to make before letting them have money.

There is a set time and day for doing most household chores that people try to avoid changing.

"Borrowing" from a fund set aside for food, taxes, etc., to buy things not in the budget is avoided.

Admission of new demands to the relatively closed system only if resources are readily available:

Plans are made for buying something only after it is obvious that the time and money are available.

Plans for spending the income tax refund are made after the exact amount of the refund is known.

People accomplish more goals if they check the means available for meeting them before deciding what they want.

Desired goals are squelched if resources seem too limited, rather than seeking new resources:

Wants beyond what people can afford are either changed to something that costs less or delayed until they can afford them.

If the children want something that the parents approve of but cannot afford, they are encouraged to choose goals to teach them to live at a level they can afford.

Once a good money plan (budget) is established, an effort is made to carry it out without being tempted by additional wants.

Resource limitations dominate the development of new alternatives to meet demands:

Money for food and time for preparation are carefully checked before expensive or fancy foods are planned for a meal with guests.

When plans are being made to purchase a car, prices of various features and models are obtained before deciding which features and models are desired.

Money is the primary consideration in selection of housing for the family.

Family or individual well-being may suffer when new demands must be met:

If a family member lost $10, he/she would do without something that is important to him/her but not to the rest of the family.

There seems to be no way to buy all the things people used to have with the current rampant inflation.

People often must settle for less than they expect because of emergencies, inflation, and the like.

Source: Adapted from Doris Marie Beard, "Morphostatic and Morphogenic Planning Behavior in Families: Development of a Measurement Instrument," Ph.D. dissertation, The Ohio State University, 1975, pp. 38–40; used with permission.

Living in a setting where deviation from meal times is unacceptable leaves the choice between accepting the schedule or eating elsewhere. Meals may be missed because of other activities or because a person is oblivious to time. Where a regular meal structure may be impossible or unacceptable, living in an apartment where an individual can plan for meals and other activities as desired may be preferred over other arrangements.

MORPHOSTATIC SYSTEMS

Planning in morphostatic systems emphasizes relatively rigid routines, specific policies, and short-term activities directed toward maintaining established standards and sequences. Examples of this "tight ship" planning in morphostatic systems are given in Table 7.4. The planning emphasizes the status quo for various reasons: preference for a simple and stable

TABLE 7.5 *Examples of planning characteristics in morphogenic systems*

Openness of system to new demands:

Most really important wants can be worked into plans.

If the children want something the parents approve of but cannot afford, the family finds a way to get it.

The children are learning to be creative in reaching goals that might at first seem impossible.

Admission of new demands to the system by attempts to increase resources:

If the refrigerator breaks and the vacation fund is the only readily available money, some way would be found to pay for both vacation and refrigerator.

There are other means of accomplishing goals when time and money are limited.

When wants cost more money than is available, attempts are made to increase income or to use something besides money to get them.

Flexibility in plans for both family and individuals:

The household routine can be easily changed to fit around unexpected opportunities and emergencies.

If a schedule is disrupted, it is fairly easy to make a new one.

Plans for use of money are frequently changed to take care of new goals.

Decentralized decision making:

Individual family members decide how much they should give to church and charity.

Family or individual well-being will suffer as little as possible when new demands must be met:

If a family member lost $10, plans would be adjusted so that no individual member would have to suffer much.

Source: Adapted from Doris Marie Beard, "Morphostatic and Morphogenic Planning Behavior in Families: Development of a Measurement Instrument," Ph.D. dissertation, The Ohio State University, 1975, pp. 40–42; used with permission.

style, limited alternatives, or perhaps because periods of stress require limits on change.

Systems that are relatively closed and morphostatic in nature have considerable structure. The following description of a relatively closed family system emphasizes the routine, stable qualities of the sequencing of activities:

> Important family events, such as getting up in the morning, mealtimes, and going to bed, tend to take place at the same time every day. Schedules for maintenance chores, field trips, appointments, and other activities determine each member's comings and goings as a train or airline schedule governs departure and arrival times. Even "free periods," in which members may do as they wish, may be rigidly scheduled. That events occur on time, and tasks get done on time, is a matter of urgency and necessity for the closed family.[22]

MORPHOGENIC SYSTEMS

Flexible and single-use plans for nonroutine, nonprogrammed activities result from planning in a morphogenic system. The "hang loose" planning works in a system that expands when new opportunities come along; current goals are reexamined (goal clarification) to determine whether a new goal should replace an existing goal. Selected planning characteristics of morphogenic systems are given in Table 7.5 This system encourages adaptive and expansive behaviors that accordingly influence planning.

Relatively open systems also have order in their sequence of activities, but they have greater flexibility than the more closed systems. An example in the business world is the growing number of offices that have flexible working times (flextime). Usually everyone must be at work during a core period; times for arriving at and departing from work are flexible in satisfying the total hours of duty.

RANDOM SYSTEMS

Planning in a relatively random system is characterized by spontaneity. Spontaneous planning is fluid and results in unstructured behaviors. The carefree nature of the random system allows interests, projects, or other people to fit the sequence of activities in a day; thus, the phrase used here to describe planning is "let it all hang out." Some families have a fluidity in their activities that reflects their leaning on intuition and inspiration. Meal times, projects, and housework are seen as one of many ways to spend time. Each member of the system seeks a daily rhythm suitable for him or her. "The random life plan is certainly not predetermined, as it is in the closed family, nor is it evolutionary as it is in the open family. Rather, it is spontaneous. If there is a plan, the plan is that events should happen of their own accord."[23] The challenge is to make the most of situations as they arise.

Application of these systems orientations and of foresight to financial planning is illustrated further in Chapter 11.

Summary

Planning is made up of standard setting and action sequencing. Clarifying goals and events and assessing resources are important parts of setting standards; through the standard-setting process, specific qualities and quantities of the standard can be set for each situation. Qualities, the desired properties or images of properties, can be used to indicate how well the standard has been met. They are relatively intangible compared with quantities, which are ordinarily measurable.

Sequencing activities has particular importance when the lives of members of a family or household are complicated by diverse occupational, volunteer, and family demands. Effective sequencing involves interdependent tasks, dovetailing tasks by giving intermittent attention, or overlapping tasks through giving them concurrent attention.

Individual characteristics and capacities affect planning. Differences in present and future time orientation affect how far ahead and how much planning is done. The nature of foresight ability varies among individuals; perceptual foresight involves analysis of factual information in dealing with the future, while conceptual foresight anticipates future consequences in relation to the present. A sense of internal control gives confidence in the potential of one's own planning. A preference for or a belief in external control may minimize the need for planning; sources of structure may be dependent on government, social norms, or other external factors, including the stars.

Plans have varying clarity, flexibility, reality, and complexity. Clarity deals with specificity of standards and sequences in the plan; flexibility, the range of acceptable standards and sequences in the plan; reality, the feasibility of achieving the chosen standards and sequences in a plan; and complexity, the degree of interrelationship between people and tasks in relation to a plan.

Single-use plans are for one-time situations; repeat-use plans are expected to be used more than once and are more likely for common activities or goals, rather than unusual ones. Alterations in resources and demands contribute to needs for changes in plans.

Directional planning is particularly appropriate when something must be done before the information regarding the activity or goal is complete. Directional planning aims in a general way toward a desired area of activity or mode of living. Today's complexity of living may, for many people, require directional planning.

Contingency planning aids in dealing with uncertainty by developing alternative approaches for meeting situations.

Planning in morphostatic (relatively closed), morphogenic (relatively open), and relatively random systems differs in the degree (low to high) to which change is encouraged in goal clarification, resource assessment, and sequencing. Whatever the type of planning, some anticipation of the future is an essential part of management.

Notes

1. Robin M. Hogarth and Spyros Makridakis, "Forecasting and Planning: An Evaluation," *Management Science* 27 (February 1981): 115.

2. Geraldine I. Olson and Doris M. Beard, "Assessing Managerial Behavior," in *The Balancing Act: Thinking Globally/Acting Locally,* ed. Sharon Y. Nickols. Proceedings of a Workshop sponsored by the Family Economics/Home Management Section of the American Home Economics Association (Washington, D.C.: American Home Economics Association, 1985): 141.

3. Virginia K. A. Sheffield, "Managerial Standard Setting and Family Resource Distribution," M.S. thesis, Iowa State University, 1976, p. 51.

4. Rosemary J. Key, "Sequencing Techniques Used in Home Production Activities," M.S. thesis, The Ohio State University, 1984, pp. 37–39.

5. Linda Nelson, "Household Time: A Cross Cultural Example," in *Women and Household Labor,* Sarah Fenstermaker Berk, ed. (Beverly Hills: Sage Publications, 1980), pp. 183, 186.

6. Jodie Johnson Brown, Mary E. Heltsley, and Richard D. Warren, "Planning in Low-Income Families: Influence of Locus of Control and Dyadic Consensus on Realistic Standard Setting," *Home Economics Research Journal* 11 (September 1982): 67–75.

7. V. K. Unni, "An Analysis of Entrepreneurial Planning," *Managerial Planning* 33 (July–August 1984): 52.

8. Cheryl Buehler and M. Janice Hogan, "Planning Styles in Single-Parent Families," *Home Economics Research Journal* 14 (June 1986): 360.

9. Thomas J. Cottle, *Perceiving Time: A Psychological Investigation with Men and Women* (New York: Wiley, 1976), p. 183.

10. Carolina Maria de Jesus, *Child of the Dark,* translated by David St. Clair (New York: New American Library, 1962), p. 128.

11. R. M. Berger, J. P. Guilford, and P. R. Christensen, "A Factor-Analytic Study of Planning Abilities," *Psychological Monographs* 71, Whole No. 435 (1957): 28.

12. Ibid., p. 15.

13. Ibid., p. 17.

14. Ramona K. Z. Heck, "A Preliminary Test of a Family Management Research Model," *Journal of Consumer Studies and Home Economics* 7 (June 1983): 132.

15. Brown, Heltsley, and Warren, "Planning in Low-Income Families," p. 74.

16. Ralph LaRossa, *Conflict and Power in Marriage, Expecting the First Child* (Beverly Hills: Sage Publications, 1977), p. 112.

17. Rose E. Steidl and Esther Crew Bratton, *Work in the Home* (New York: Wiley, 1968), p. 85.

18. Sarah Fenstermaker Berk, *The Gender Factory* (New York: Plenum Press, 1985), p. 179.

19. Russell L. Ackoff, *Redesigning the Future* (New York: Wiley, 1974), p. 31.

20. Reuben Hill, *Family Development in Three Generations* (Cambridge, Mass.: Schenkman, 1970), p. 237.

21. Michael B. McCaskey, "Goals and Direction in Personal Planning," *The Academy of Management Review* 2 (July 1977): 459. See also Michael B. McCaskey, "A Contingency Approach to Planning: Planning with goals and Planning without Goals," *The Academy of Management Journal* 17 (June 1974): 283.

22. David Kantor and William Lehr, *Inside the Family* (San Francisco: Jossey-Bass, 1975), p. 121.

23. Ibid., p. 136.

8

Implementing

Implementing is actuating plans and procedures (standards and sequences) and controlling the actions. *Actuating* is putting plans into effect, and *controlling* is checking or comparing actions with plans and, if necessary, adjusting the planned standards and sequences of the actions to increase the chances of the desired output. Facilitating conditions are situational "givens" that assist the progress or flow of the actions. Figure 8.1 depicts implementing in the setting of the managerial system of the family.

Management encompasses action and includes responsibility for the execution of plans. Plans account for the action but may or may not be executed by the people who developed them; they may be assigned to other people, to machines, or to outside agencies.

Plans *for* implementation are made and should not be confused with the action *of* implementation. Emphasis is placed on the mental process of planning and whatever overt action is necessary to bring to fruition the review of possibilities, the decision making, and any recording of standards and sequences necessary for their effective implementation. The essential dimension of planning is mental. Any written notations on plans developed are to facilitate implementation to protect significant expectations regarding outcomes.

In implementing, likewise, the managerial responsibility focuses on the mental processes involved in overseeing (and at times evolving) the plan as it unfolds through *actions* by someone or something. Actions are dynamic processes necessary to the implementation of a plan.

Actuating

Putting plans into effect, or actuating, most effectively occurs when there is high goal intensity, when the desired outcome is important to people involved, when the plan is clear and feasible, and when resources suffice to meet the needs.

The planner is significant to the actuating of plans, regardless of who or what does the action. The person who delegates responsibility to another for implementing has the responsibility for conveying the results (standards) to be attained and when they are expected to be completed. If the person is unfamiliar with the process, detailed directions may be needed. Otherwise, asking or giving approval to someone to put a plan into action—a family member, a friend, or service company—may be based on past experience or trust in the judgment of another. If people to be involved in implementing

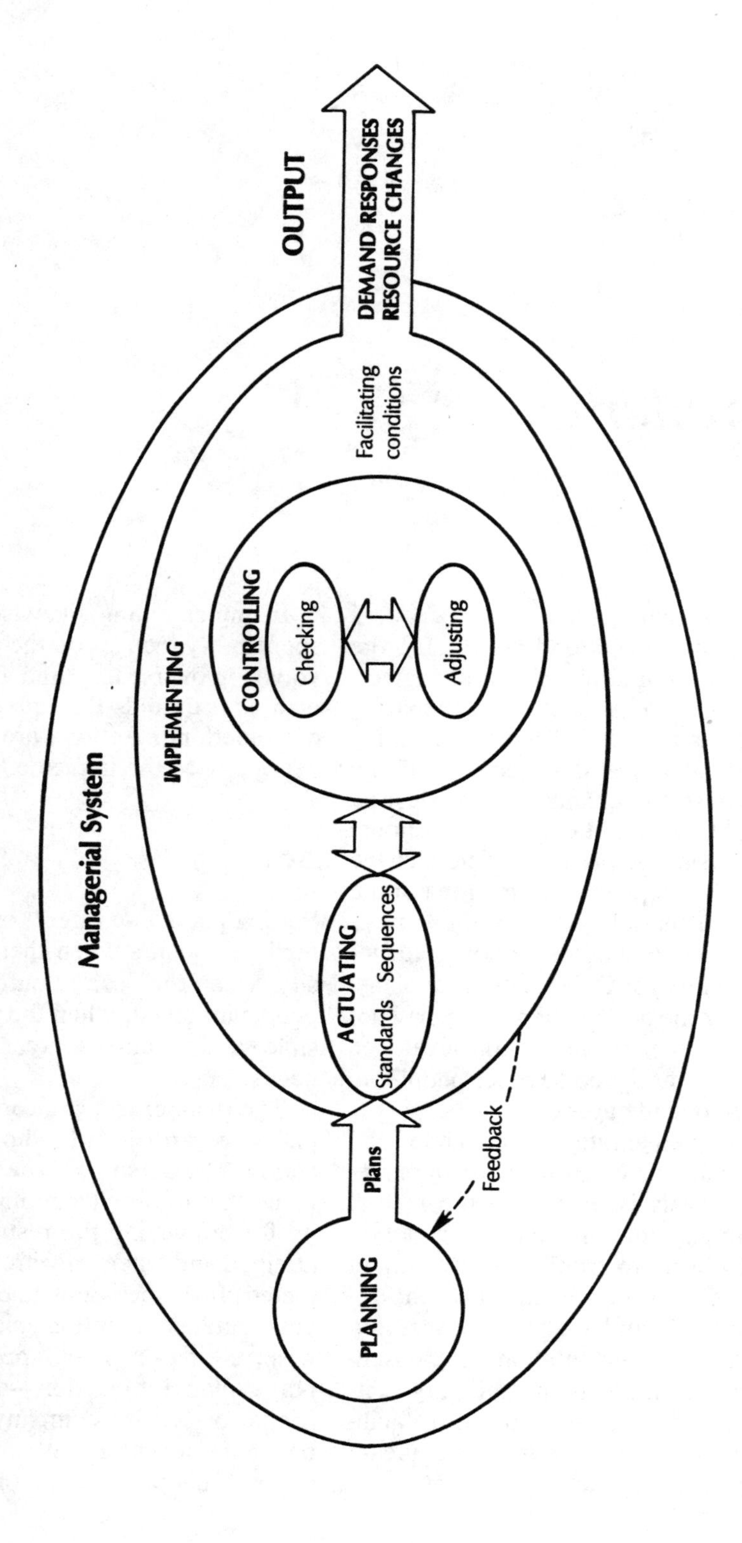

FIGURE 8.1 *Implementing*

a plan are recognized or included in the development of the plan, the chances are greatly increased that the plan will be actuated and that the results will be the ones planned.

Actuating one's own plans appears to be barely separable from controlling. This is especially true when there is little or no time lag between planning and implementing. As noted, in planning, in some cases, even planning and implementing are almost simultaneous, with constant interaction between them due to their different functions in promoting meaningful activity.

Actuating and controlling are distinct in complex plans spanning time with variable conditions. It is possible to actuate only one segment of a plan and actuate other steps at a later stage. Actuating parts of a plan may coincide with controlling other parts of a plan. In Beijing, an elaborate system of defense shelters has been designed and partially developed. The plan, providing temporary shelter for the city's millions, was first actuated long ago, but construction of each section involves actuating only that part of the plan.

Within the family system, an example of implementing segments of a plan could relate to the goal of enrolling a teenager in a vocational program. The plan is actuated with the first visits to programs to see if they meet the interests and provide the environment the teenager needs. When a program does not meet the standard and other possible programs are considered, the plan must be reactuated and controlled.

Contingency planning in the extreme means a low ratio of actuated plans to total plans made. While it is good to have alternatives where there is potential for a shift in direction or resource use, it is also a good idea to examine one's plans to see how many "needless" plans are being made. The planner may develop a sense of order through plans to meet many eventualities, with little or no commitment to execution of the plans.

Controlling

In large organizations of the private sector of the economy, management control systems "are concerned with the coordination, information processing, and resource allocation dimensions of the management process."[1] So it is with household units, although on a much smaller scale. Once it is decided what is to be accomplished within an organization, and the time frame, the effort is to coordinate the various subunits "so that, like a good orchestra, the individual parts act in harmony toward fulfillment of common purposes."[2] Control systems are evolved for monitoring progress. Within the implementing subsystem of the family resource management system, the processes for monitoring and adapting to situational factors while the plan is actuated are identified as checking and adjusting.

Checking on actions and outcomes is needed to assure progress toward reaching a goal or that the product is the desired one. Adjusting actions, or parts of the plan, either standards or sequences, may be necessary to accomplish the goal as reflected in the plan of action.

The traditional concept of control is based on a cybernetic model, with negative feedback to enable correction of any deviations. The conditions necessary for cybernetic control follow:

1. There must be a standard.
2. The accomplishments or output must be measurable.
3. When comparisons of the standard and the measured output are made and differences identified, these differences can be eliminated in subsequent rounds.[3]

The controlling process in family systems at times follows the cybernetic model, but often standards are not so explicit that the attainment can be precisely measured. Also, the opportunity to identify ranges of acceptable deviation provides useful flexibility for evaluation. The concept of cybernetic control is useful as a general idea for control, but the many nonroutine activities in a family system are not ordinarily managed in such a nondeviating fashion. In fact, as an open system, the family utilizes both positive and negative feedback in its response to the conditions that pertain while plans are actuated.

CHECKING

Checking is the component of controlling in which actions and outputs are examined for compliance with standards and sequences. Checking means that quality or quantity aspects of standards are compared to results evolving during implementation.

When a wedding dinner is being catered, the host or hostess may check to see whether the number of guests equals the number anticipated (plan). How many guests responded to the invitation is a quantitative aspect of the plan. The qualitative portion can be illustrated by whether the food, as checked by the host or hostess observing or tasting it, meets agreed-to criteria.

In a consumer purchase, such as buying a desk lamp, specific standards of quality and quantity can be established and checked for how well they are met. For example, an individual can compare whether the qualitative criteria are met by such features as style and color or whether the size is appropriate.

In addition to delegating the checking of actions to someone else, a device may be the executor of the plan, as well. Automatic appliances, for example, have built-in devices for checking such factors as temperature or dryness. Clothes to be dry-cleaned are checked for spots and decorations that need special attention and for other potential problems. After processing, the cleaner may check for general appearance, missing buttons, condition of decorations, and other qualities. A customer may also check these items or may rely on the dry-cleaning establishment and transfer the checking to it.

Sufficient checking to assure the meeting of desired standards and sequences can improve implementation. Insufficient checking can result in time spent trying to restore or regain the original status to start over. The office manager who says, "If only you had asked, I would have explained what I wanted" may well need to improve checking. Another clue of inadequate checking is the worker who suggests to the manager that "if you'd stop by to see how we're doing before we are through with the job, we'd be sure we were doing it the way you want it done." In the family situation, it may be difficult for the parent employed outside the home to check on how a child is carrying out an agreed-upon plan.

Too-frequent checking can create resentment by the person carrying out a plan and lost time for the manager. A strong interest may contribute to checking too frequently. A child learning to carry out a task is easily discouraged by constant checking; yet with too little checking, results of the effort may not conform to desired standards. Achieving a balance in the amount of checking may be rather delicate, as well as complex.

The complexity of shopping is illustrated by a study that focused on how consumers might fare by applying shopping strategies to the purchase of nineteen items commonly purchased in supermarkets. Results of the strategies were found to depend on how consumers valued their time in relation to their money. The strategies included unit pricing (least cost per unit), buying largest sizes (assuming size provided a unit-price advantage), buying generic items or store brands (assuming a price advantage over name brands), buying sale items, or buying preferred name brand in size with lowest per-unit price. Results indicated that shopping strategies were affected by how they valued their time, characteristics of their store, and comparative shopping expertise.[4] "Although unit pricing . . .

does successfully reduce costs, it is the most time intensive. Almost the same dollar savings can be realized by a less time-consuming strategy, namely buying generic and private label products."[5]

Approaches to checking may vary for a number of reasons—gender and time, among others. For grocery shopping, one study found less checking behavior for men than for women (see Figure 8.2).

ADJUSTING

Adjusting is changing a planned standard or sequence or changing the underlying process in order to increase the chances of the desired output. Adjusting may occur after checking has identified deviations from planned behavior. Changes or adjustments in both sequences and standards may require a new plan, with resulting adaptive or expansive behavior leading to altered expectations.

Not finding a garment, after looking for certain qualities relating to the design of the garment and the weave and fiber content of the fabric, may mean that a new plan has to be developed. A recognition that a higher price will need to be paid, that some compromise on features at the anticipated price is needed, or that time may need to be found to make the item oneself is inevitable—all possible adaptive behaviors.

Many plans must be adjusted in the real world. Plans for a weekend visit may have to be altered near the time for departure when the person to be visited becomes ill. The same plan for activities relating to the visit while there in terms of both standards and sequences may work on another weekend, but the time of implementing the plan is postponed (adjusted).

Within patterns for regular household tasks,

FIGURE 8.2 *Supermarkets and men*

Supermarkets and Men

As more women work, more men are doing the grocery shopping. Forty percent of supermarket shoppers are men, according to Edward McLaughlin, a food marketing professor at Cornell University. Males shop differently from females, spending less time in the store, spending less money, using lists less often, paying less attention to specials and sales, and doing less comparative shopping. Men also read food ads, check expiration dates, and read nutritional labels less often than women. Shopping habits of professional women resemble those of men more than those of women homemakers.

Source: "Supermarkets and Men," *The Futurist* 20 (March–April 1986): 4. Reprinted, with permission, from THE FUTURIST, published by the World Future Society, 4916 St. Elmo Ave., Bethesda, Md. 20814.

such as food shopping, variations to meet special needs and interests can often be accommodated. For example, food shopping for special items for a family birthday and exercising constraints in purchases if funds are short prior to payday illustrate the potential to adjust standards within a repeat-use plan for sequencing.

Successful dieting for most people requires establishing a plan from which there is minimal deviation calorie-wise and adequate variation in how needed nutrients are provided to maintain interest. One dieter who reduced his weight from 492 to 230 pounds and has maintained it for fourteen months commented that the process "was anything but a piece of cake. . . . Every now and then, I'll have a steak . . . but I won't go back to fried foods."[6] The aspect of the plan that was a particular "drawback" was the need to replenish his wardrobe every few months. Were these changes, adjustments, or new plans?

Apparently, the dieting plan allowed for occasional deviation. So long as the plan toward the goal of weight loss or maintenance was adhered to, there was no fundamental adjustment. The need to make more frequent changes in the wardrobe was a major adjustment. The major impact was apparently on the clothing budget as an accelerated replacement sequence was needed. Although not indicated, change that also occurred in the quality and quantity of the wardrobe would mean that a new clothing plan was called for.

Inadequate information during the planning process may create a need for adjusting a plan. A plan to look for a radio at a downtown shop in conjunction with other errands must be adjusted when, upon arrival at the shop location, there is a notice that it has moved to a suburban shopping center.

The adjustment of plans and actions is often accepted as a necessary and even enjoyable part of life. The extent of adjustments and the reactions to them are likely to depend on the particular situation and how critical it is to meet given goals or to conserve resources. Beyond such commitments, expansive or adaptive behavior to accomplish altered and new expectations probably depends on both the personality of individuals and the orientation of the family systems they comprise.

Facilitating conditions

Facilitating conditions are not accounted for in planning, but they contribute to the progress or flow of actions. These conditions are primarily aspects of the environment surrounding the implementation of plans. *Facilitating conditions* are situation characteristics that promote the flow of actions. They are not considered as resources to be included as a part of the cost of a specific plan. Probably the most readily recognized facilitating condition is a well-arranged work area, the supporting "facilities."

Other conditions that facilitate the progress or flow of actions include avoidance of known distractions in the environment even though introducing facilitating conditions usually represents a separate plan that, when complemented, facilitates later activity. Padding a noisy floor may be such an item, even though it has no direct relation to the work being done in the area.

Ease in communication is also a part of the situational climate that can facilitate tasks. When such conditions are missing, the underlying facilitating effects become apparent. Sometimes, people are not comfortable doing tasks around others who can only imagine the task being done "their" way. Finding a time when neither affects the other is in itself a plan. When achieved, however, the plan contributes a facilitating condition for performing the tasks otherwise taking place under constraining circumstances.

The natural environment facilitates some tasks. For instance, in applying a sealer to a blacktop driveway, the right weather and temperature facilitate easy spreading and quick drying. Facilitating conditions affect ease of execution of a plan, but not the determination of the standards and sequences within the plan.

Well-designed equipment in good working order may be part of facilitating conditions. In low-income homes, household equipment often functions poorly or is not available. The purchase of labor-saving equipment, such as microwave ovens and dishwashers, is not determined by a wife's employment or the recency of her entry into the labor force, when income and stage in the life cycle are held constant.[7] Further, working women "do not seem to use frozen foods or mail order catalogues any more frequently than do nonworking wives in the same income or life-cycle group."[8] Working wives prepare fewer meals. The lack of definitive relationships between time pressures and having facilitating conditions is both interesting and confusing.

Improving kitchen storage facilities through arrangement of items where first used, and where easy to see and easy to grasp, can increase the flow of work and bring feelings of better organization.[9] Making such improvements involves planning. Once completed, they are part of the facilitating conditions. With improved storage space, the time spent on tasks may be lessened little, if any, but the increased flow of work can make changes in storage very desirable. Time is an inadequate measure of ease or flow of work.

When a young parent plans to shop for groceries, leaving the children at home with the other parent and setting out with a full grocery list may make shopping flow more smoothly. The standards and sequences of the plan for purchasing are not altered, but the conditions improve the progress or flow of actions. Such situations can be anticipated when planning.

Factors that affect implementing

Individuals, families, environments, and qualities associated with tasks affect implementing. The individual probably has the most effect, and so the way in which the individual affects implementation of plans introduces the discussion.

INDIVIDUAL CHARACTERISTICS

The ability of people to focus clearly on what it is they want and then to plan to achieve those wants improves the possibility of success through implementing. A common method writers propose to make the most of one's time is to plan realistically, set priorities, and then write down the items in order of importance as a reminder to avoid putting off important but less interesting jobs. It is easy to implement minor plans that give people a sense of accomplishment (e.g., straightening the living room, washing the car) and to postpone those plans that lead to lifetime goals.

Some personalities may not want to control their lives and their time use. The artist is stereotyped as a creative and, to some extent, impulsive person, without order and routine. But when actions in pursuit of important goals are examined, the artist stereotype does not really fit. The steady painting, practicing, or drilling in technique to create desired effects may demonstrate a strong controlling emphasis. Personality traits related to control are responsibility, tolerance, intellectual efficiency, and flexibility.[10]

An individual's orientation to a situation can affect task performance. Individuals who are in situations in which personal competence can affect the outcome tend to perform more adequately than when the situation is less controllable.[11] People in public housing may feel that they have little or no opportunity to affect outcomes, and they may perform less and less effectively over the years.

There is increasing indication that the possibility of meeting the impacts of life events without deleterious effects is improved when there is a sense of having some control over their occurrence. In a study of a group of psychiatric patients, the results showed that their perceptions about life occurrences have more to do with the nature of those occurrences than with the individual's personal disposition. The implication drawn was that accepting rather than trying to modify a person's fatalistic attitudes and focusing attention on promoting adaptive behavior might provide more effective support.[12] Recognizing the necessity for professional judgments in individual cases, education that helps to anticipate life events and to develop adaptive skills has potential for the prevention of problems.

Health understandably has direct effects on both the need for adjustments and perceptions about capacities for making them. A study of organizing, which included checking, adjusting, facilitating, and sequencing, found a relationship between health and the homemaker's concept of her organizing ability.[13]

FAMILY CHARACTERISTICS

Individuals can implement plans with greater certainty than families or small groups. Because individuals within a group have different interests and goals, they may associate different levels of importance to implementing plans. In households that are relatively closed in nature, differences in goals and interests to be pursued may be minimized in order to keep progressing toward agreed-upon goals.

As in organizational settings, the nature of the tasks and the make-up of the personnel (family members) may affect the emphasis given to control. If there is goal compatibility within the group, it is recognized that desired ends will be pursued, and there is tolerance for imprecise measurement and evaluation of performance. On the other hand, if diverse goals are tolerated but given ends are needed, a more precise performance evaluation system is needed to which all can relate if control is to occur.[14]

Families that operate primarily as open systems may encourage individual differences and then have to find ways of getting together:

> At any point in the day, the four Clouds could be doing different things in different parts of town: Oscar (architect) meeting with a client, Muriel working on a terminal hospital ward, twelve-year-old Peter printing some photographs in a darkroom, and nine-year-old Susanna dressing up in costumes at a friend's. Partly as a strategy to bring themselves and their various jobs, hobbies, and activities together, the Clouds have purchased a farm jointly with another professional family, whose parents and children they consider part of their own "extended family."[15]

Implementing plans in such a setting is complex:

> Oscar's work pattern is one of taking it somewhat easy on a project and then launching a big, all-night push as his deadline nears. Muriel is also frequently behind schedule, whether she is cooking dinner, meeting her ride to work in the morning, or buying gifts for birthdays and Christmas. Yet somehow all these tasks are eventually done before it is too late.[16]

Family-related variables that can make a difference in implementing plans are family life cycle, ages of the children, and family size—all interrelated factors. Having preschool children present may make some household tasks more difficult to control, but this situation may or may not be prominent in a person's analysis of the job to be done. Some parents try to accomplish certain plans while the children are asleep, while others seem to carry on oblivious to interruptions.

The complexity of implementing plans in a family setting in which both spouses are employed is shown in the following scene as the mother arrives home:

> There are cereal bowls all over the table and I forgot to put the milk away. The dog sobs with joy to see us. What is there in the freezer that will melt in time for dinner? I put the wash in the dryer

and turn it on. Another section of the day begins, and miles to go before I sleep.

In five minutes, they'll be home, all of them, a solid block of noise saying, "Mom, listen I have to have a new gym suit and I have to have it by tomorrow, shut up, *I'm* talking, my teacher *said*—" . . . "and I hate school and I'm never going back!" "Can I have a cookie? Can Rob come over and play? Can you walk him over? Can I call him?" "One hundred on the spelling test and I was the only one in the room!" "Look, I made it in Art, you're not *looking*!"[17]

Work schedules were found, in general, to be nondisruptive among dual-career families whose schedules were typically regular. Nor was there any apparent effect on quality of family life due either to the number of hours of work or how they were scheduled. The dynamics within the work schedules revealed some sex-specific and traditional patterns, however. "Men depend on their wives to find time for home and children more than wives depend on their husbands. . . . Wives continue to assume primary responsibility for domestic tasks and tend to see greater difficulties associated with the couple's work schedule."[18]

ENVIRONMENT-RELATED CHARACTERISTICS

The environment affects the system's performance. The macroenvironment includes the human-made and natural space and the biological contents of the surroundings; much of this environment is outside the family's control. More controllable is the microenvironment, the immediate surroundings of the family—its physical setting, the family members, the things directly impinging on the family. Inclement weather may interrupt or postpone activities, presenting problems in controlling and causing plan adjustments. Outdoor cooking, as practiced in many areas of India, is subject to weather disturbances such as dust storms.

The stage in the family life cycle may well influence the impact of weather on implementing activities. Families with young children may be particularly affected by inclement weather when the children remain indoors. The time set aside for relatively uninterrupted work is "lost," and work may become more difficult or "negatively facilitated."

TASK CHARACTERISTICS

Young homemakers who were asked about tasks with high and low cognitive requirements—attention, judgment, and planning—reported what made the tasks more or less difficult. Tasks that were ranked as the most liked, most complicated, and most difficult were almost always the highly cognitive tasks; those ranked as the least complicated and the least difficult were nearly always the low cognitive tasks and were very often the least liked.[19]

Complicated tasks need more controlling and greater attention to reach the desired standard. Food preparation and child care are tasks with reportedly high cognitive requirements. The complexity of food and meal preparation probably varies widely among families; and for many, a concern about meals and nutrition contributes to the need for controlling plans.

A mother previously employed outside the home and now doing freelance work at home states:

> I find it very hard to work well with fragments of time, and almost impossible to think of more than one thing at a time. Paid work, with its organized chunks of time, fits my habit of mind, and makes me turn my lazy side to good use. Juggling the fragments of several projects, committees, housework leads to just one end: procrastination.[20]

Task discontinuity is the feature of household work that the mother found frustrating; apparently, she was unable to sequence adequately or control plans she had made.

Implementing in a systems perspective

Characteristics of implementing in relatively closed, open, and random systems are summarized in Table 8.1.

MORPHOSTATIC SYSTEMS

Relatively closed, or *morphostatic,* systems are characterized by correction of actions that deviate from the plan, rather than adjusting the plan. These systems are deviation correcting; that is, if the standards and sequences as planned are not being met, the tendency is to confirm the original plan and correct the deviation. Corrective measures are taken to align the actions with the plan or to adjust the plan so that the output will coincide as nearly as possible with the original demand. If the correction is not possible, the other alternative is to reject the outcome and stop the actions.

Impersonal rules or regulations are the primary controlling mechanisms in a morphostatic system.[21] In a state office building, lights may be turned off by area at specified times through time-control devices. Controlling is rather precise in a relatively closed system, and it may be mechanical. Checking is frequent in a relatively closed system, with deviations from expectations being readily corrected.

For an individual's or family's money management, employer withholding from paychecks can be a rigid controlling tool. Withholding may be used for taxes, charitable contributions, retirement, health insurance, or purchase of shares of stocks or savings bonds. Some employers allow pay deductions to credit unions to discharge consumer credit obligations. Families often finance their children's college education by exercising control of their financial situation through the precollege years by following a contractual or self-enforced savings plan.

MORPHOGENIC SYSTEMS

The response to feedback in relatively open, or *morphogenic,* systems produces change. There is openness to adaptive plans and to accepting altered outcomes. When standards and sequences are not being met, the outcome is examined, and the changed outcome may be

TABLE 8.1 *Characteristics of systems with an emphasis on implementing*

Type of system	*Environment*	*Implementing*
Relatively closed (Morphostatic) Tight ship	Certain	Response to feedback—deviation correcting; change resistant. Control emphasizes maintaining identified standards or regulations and is continuous.
Relatively open (Morphogenic) Hang loose	Variable certainty	Response to feedback—deviation amplifying; change generating. Control is through personal contacts, suggestions, or persuasion; occurs infrequently or at "milestones."
Relatively random (Spontaneous) Let it all hang out	Maximum uncertainty	Unstructured.

Source: Adapted from David Kantor and William Lehr, *Inside the Family* (San Francisco: Jossey-Bass, 1975), pp. 134–142. Used with permission. Also from *Contingency Views of Organization and Management* by Fremont E. Kast and James E. Rosenzweig. © 1973, Science Research Associates, Inc., p. 318. Adapted and reprinted by permission of the publisher.

found more or less desirable than the planned outcome.

Controlling in an open and adaptive system is often through personal contacts, suggestions, or persuasion.[22] In a family setting, a parent may stop by a child's room and remind him or her that it's time to go to bed and turn out the lights.

Controlling occurs at "milestones" or infrequent critical points in open systems. Infrequent checking and adjusting allow for expansive behavior in such systems. For example, a father may tell a daughter that it is time to clean her room and that he will come to see it when she is through. Although the room's general appearance may not meet the standards the father expects, some special feature of the cleaning (such as rearranging clothing storage for better access) may be far more creative than the father imagined. The original plan with its standards and sequences (assuming those envisioned by the father were understood by the daughter) may then be abandoned, and the unexpected outcome accepted and appreciated as a deviation-amplifying effect. Information about both acceptable deviation of actions from a plan and a rapidly changing environment may lead to a far greater variety of actions than was previously projected. With a repeat-use plan, for example, the effect may be a relaxation of formerly stringent standards or a change in some aspect of the sequence. In other cases, entirely revised standards and sequences may be needed for a better fit with the situation.

The many decisions that lead to a wife's employment outside the home illustrate change, which can be both expansive and realistic. For example, a family with five children had the goal that the husband would earn money to support the family and the wife would care for the children and all household matters. Their lives were planned around this goal. When they checked the family expenses against the anticipated income, they found that some change was necessary. Reducing expenses (corrective action) no longer seemed possible, and the couple decided the wife should work outside the home. After her employment, the husband gradually changed his standards and sequences by helping with child care and other household matters. In this situation, deviations led to new plans more consistent with the resources and demands.

RANDOM SYSTEMS

Feedback to controlling from actions in relatively *random systems* leads to no identifiable response. Thus, implementing is unstructured. The uncertainty in the environment of systems that "let it all hang out" contributes to the lack of pattern in implementing. The absence of specification in plans that are created spontaneously also contributes to the indefinite role of implementing.

Actions probably dominate random systems far more than controlling; perhaps a relatively random system bypasses controlling and in effect moves from a spontaneous plan to actions with little or no checking and adjusting in relation to the plan.

Diversity, creativity, and originality are important ideals in the random-type family system and careful control of actions is in opposition to these ideals. "The reasoning process is dominated by personal intuition and inspiration," which also stands in opposition to checking and adjusting actions in relation to a plan.[23]

Summary

Implementing is putting plans into effect. Actions involved in implementation may be undertaken by the planner or by another person, machine, or company. Checking the actions against the plan and adjusting the standards and sequences or the actions themselves make up the controlling aspect of implementing.

Facilitating conditions assist the progress or

flow of actions; but once established, they are not an integral part of planning.

Implementing is affected by characteristics of the individual: personality, health, and employment. Family, environmental, and task qualities can affect implementing as well. Implementing varies with the type of family system: relatively closed, open, or random. The response to information about deviation of actions from a plan is (1) correction in the relatively closed system, (2) change generating in the relatively open system, and (3) indefinite in the relatively random system.

Notes

1. Joseph A. Maciariello, *Management Control Systems* (Englewood Cliffs, N.J.: Prentice-Hall, 1984), p. 2.
2. Ibid., p. 4.
3. Geert Hofstede, "The Poverty of Management Control Philosophy," *Academy of Management Review* 3 (July 1978): 451–452.
4. Rosemary Walker and Brenda Cude, "In-Store Shopping Strategies: Time and Money Costs in the Supermarket," *The Journal of Consumer Affairs* 17 (Winter 1983): 356–369.
5. Ibid., p. 368.
6. "Cutting the Waist, Trimming the Fat," *Ebony* 40 (October 1985): 52–56.
7. Myra A. Strober and Charles B. Weinberg, "Strategies Used by Working and Nonworking Wives to Reduce Time Pressures," *Journal of Consumer Research* 6 (March 1980): 346.
8. Ibid., p. 347.
9. Rose E. Steidl and Esther Crew Bratton, *Work in the Home* (New York: Wiley, 1968), p. 277.
10. Sarah Jane Smith, "Personality Traits, Values, Expectations, and Managerial Behavior," M.S. thesis, The Pennsylvania State University, 1971, pp. 29–30, 43–44.
11. Herbert M. Lefcourt, "Belief in Personal Control: Research and Implications," *Journal of Individual Psychology* 22 (November 1966): 188.
12. Mary E. Jackson and Richard C. Tessler, "Perceived Control Over Life Events: Antecedents and Consequences in a Discharged Hospital Sample," *Social Science Research* 13 (September 1984): 287, 298.
13. Nancy Ann Barclay, "Organization of Household Activities by Home Managers," Ph.D. dissertation, The Ohio State University, 1970, p. 50.
14. Kathleen M. Eisenhardt, "Control: Organizational and Economic Approaches," *Management Science* 31 (February 1985): 135.
15. David Kantor and William Lehr, *Inside the Family* (San Francisco: Jossey-Bass, 1975): p. 131.
16. Ibid.
17. Barbara Holland, "The Day's Work," *Ms.* 6 (August 1977): 79.
18. Paul W. Kingston and Steven L. Nock, "Consequences of the Family Work Day," *Journal of Marriage and the Family* 47 (August 1985): 628.
19. Rose E. Steidl, "Difficulty Factors in Homemaking Tasks: Implications for Environmental Design," *Human Factors* 14 (October 1972): 480.
20. Sidney Cornelia Callahan, *The Working Mother* (New York: Macmillan, 1971), p. 178.
21. Fremont E. Kast and James E. Rosenzweig, *Contingency Views of Organization and Management* (Chicago: Science Research Associates, 1973), p. 318.
22. Ibid.
23. Kantor and Lehr, *Inside the Family,* p. 149.

9
Communicating

"Communication is ultimately the source of any family's viability, for it is what binds the system together. When communication goes astray, the boundaries are weakened; when communication ceases, the system no longer exists."[1] *Communication* is using messages to engender meaning in the minds of others. *Messages* flow from a sender to a receiver by such means as words, tone, body postures, gestures, eyes, or other stimuli.[2]

The communication cycle and communication skills

For effective communication, the sender gives a clear and congruent message, and the receiver must (1) receive or experience the full message, (2) understand, verify, and draw conclusions from the message, (3) relate the message to past experiences or generalize about the message, and (4) reply or respond to the message with appropriate behavior. Evidence of whether the receiver is getting the message is received by the communicator or sender as feedback. The receiver's response to the message is output from the receiver that returns to the communicator as input. This is the communication cycle of an open system[3] (see Figure 9.1).

One requirement of the communication cycle is to receive the message fully. *Interference* with receiving the message in a complete form is "anything that distorts the information transmitted to the receiver or distracts him or her from receiving it."[4] Sometimes, there is a low signal-to-noise ratio, that is, many extraneous or distracting factors that interfere with the reception of the information. The interference may be technical: It is simply not possible to hear the message because of a loud stereo, for example. Or it may be semantic: a person does not assign the same meaning to a message that the sender intends. The receiver must also be a good listener in order to receive the message accurately.

Listening can be developed as a skill, whether the listening is serious, social, conversational, appreciative (plays, radio, TV, records), or courteous (as when one listens because the speaker rather than the content is of interest). Circumstances commonly related to listening problems follow:[5]

1. Viewing a topic as uninteresting, and therefore "turning off" the speaker. Classroom instruction or a grandparent's story of the depression may be so uninteresting as to obscure other reasons for hearing the message.
2. Considering a speaker's features more than the message content. A child may be so em-

FIGURE 9.1 *Communication in an open system*

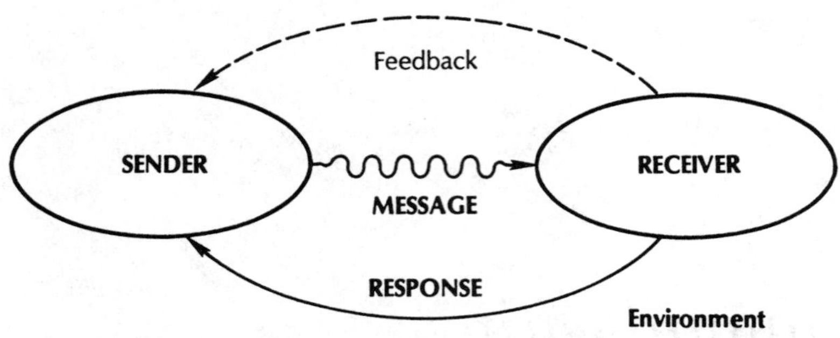

Note: Feedback may occur while the message is in progress or as part of the receiver's response.

barrassed by the parents' appearance, when they come to visit school, that the child cannot listen to the exchange between the teacher and parents.

3. Not agreeing with or liking the sender's message. The remainder of the message may be lost while the listener works on a rebuttal.
4. Faking attention or pretending to listen when really thinking about something else. Vocal sounds or body motions that imply listening may give the sender misleading feedback.

These listening problems may lead to responses that focus on the receiver rather than the message of the sender. Partners who tend to emphasize their own position, rather than giving attention to the other's position, limit effective listening. When each can respect or interpret the views of the other, effective listening has occurred in both directions.

Communication among individuals may employ verbal or nonverbal expressions, each conveyed by various means. Nonverbal communication includes body movements and the use of space.[6] Nonverbal hugs or pats or ruffling of hair may convey particular messages of feeling in a family or group.

Congruence between verbal and nonverbal communication is an important part of positive communication skills. *Leveling* is a term that is used to describe the congruence in all parts of the message: words, facial expressions, tone of voice, and body position.[7] Leveling is obvious to the receiver—words of praise spoken in a depreciating tone are easily detected as not being "on the level."

Communication barriers may develop in families and the barriers may form boundaries of subsystems within the family. These barriers (boundaries), which prevent messages from getting through, can occur when two siblings take sides against another and form a temporarily separate system. Or grown children may break away from their parental system when serious conflicts occur because impermeable boundaries between the generations have been permitted to develop.

Adjustments to life-cycle changes provide constant potential for development of communication barriers because each member is moving through his or her own life changes. Making these individual transitions, as well as recognizing and considering the transitions of others, introduces ongoing communication challenges. Changing demands that follow from life-cycle transitions and affect individual family members differently are unique to family systems. Continuing efforts to keep channels open are needed to minimize interference and the development of communication barriers.

Positive and negative communication qualities and skills are given in Table 9.1. If you

TABLE 9.1 *Positive and negative communication qualities and skills*

Positive	*Negative*
Clear, congruent messages	Incongruent, garbled messages
Empathy or receptivity for senders or receivers	Lack of empathy or receptivity for senders or receivers
Supportive statements	Negative statements
Relates or adapts to situation	Oblivious or unsympathetic to situation
Appreciates or recognizes the other person's worth	Fails to recognize the other person's concept of self or worth
Listens attentively	Lack of attention

currently perceive low effectiveness in communication, try to identify where your skills might be improved. Do you recognize the communicator as an individual with a set of beliefs and behaviors, not just as a sender? Are you missing important clues in the situation that might help you relate more appropriately?

Communication in the family system

Communication is transactional in nature, that is, "when people communicate, they have a mutual impact on each other."[8] Interpersonal communication is an interdependent or mutual process between two or among more people in a small group, such as a family system. Each influences the communicator relationship. Communication facilitates the intrasystem dynamics of cohesion, adaptability, and functionality, which are sources of strength. Family interaction occurs particularly in social times, eating together, and during care of family members, and it is no surprise that they interact more on weekends and during vacations.[9]

Communication can be a managerial tool for enhancing prospects of meeting goals of the system. Communication helps to shape the ability of family members to function, to manage their lives. As defined in Chapter 2, functionality is the ability of family members to use their human and material resources to anticipate and meet demands. The exchange of fully understood messages is essential for sharpening goals, for clarifying standards involving more than one person, for conveying plans, and for discussing satisfaction or dissatisfaction with outcomes.

Whether common interests evolve from effective interpersonal communication or promote it, communication in well-adjusted families has positive and mutual bases. Transactions in normal compared to pathological families are likely to be more harmonious, more task-oriented, and more satisfying for individual members. Less time is required to decide about common activities, and common decisions often fulfill personal wishes.[10]

Families in existence for several years "know" from past experience what the other family members have in mind from the signals they send. Perhaps many years of building understanding and meeting common problems alter verbal communication.

Within the family system, interpersonal communication is bound up with symbolic meanings.

> After you have functioned within a family system, you begin to become comfortable with your ability to handle the symbols, mainly because you are able to interpret the symbols on all levels and feel

that you really understand them. As a child, when you heard your mother yell "Johnny" or "Sara" or "Elizabeth-Marie," you were able to tell from her tone of voice just what to expect. Today, you can . . . hear your younger sister say, "I just hate that Ernie Johnson" and know that she's really falling in love.[11]

MORPHOGENIC SYSTEMS

Communication in families functioning as morphogenic systems is described as supporting "authentic interaction" between family members, as given in Table 9.2. Verbal and nonverbal messages are consistent, clear in meaning, and include "spontaneous affective expressions." Spontaneous affective expressions could be a pat on the shoulder, a quick kiss, or a special hug. An example of communication within a morphogenic family system follows:

> During dinner, Mr. Cloud looks across the table and says, "Peter, I'm afraid I've got a bone to pick with you." "What's that?" "The mess from your mice is getting out of hand. I almost broke my neck in the hallway outside your room this afternoon. When we agreed to let you keep those mice, it was on the condition that you clean their cages." "I do clean them," Peter counters, "once a week." "Well, it's not enough," Father says. "Their excrement's piling up on the floor." "That's because they're getting out of their cages," Peter replies. "Because you've got too many mice," says Father. "No, because you won't give me the money to buy new cages." "Wait a minute," interjects Mrs. Cloud. "Dad's right, Peter. Something's got to be done about the mess. But Peter's got a point, too, Dad. Those cages are falling apart." "I'm glad somebody believes me," Peter remarks. "We can't afford new cages," says Father. "Well, what about the two of you getting together to repair the ones that are in there now? That might solve both your problems," says Mother. "On one condition," agrees Father. "You agree to clean them twice a week." "Agreed," says Peter.[12]

Open communication and authentic integration are illustrated by the example. The conversation conveys exchanges that are more than moderately clear and certainly direct. The family system is acting in a morphogenic fashion in that the process leads to a resolve to work together on repairing the cages and provides a solution that is expansive in nature.

TABLE 9.2 *Communicating in family systems*

Type of system	*Communication style*
Morphostatic	
Relatively closed	Predictable
Resistant to change	Rigid
Status quo controls	Ritualistic
Less impermeable boundaries	
Morphogenic	
Permeable external boundaries	Open interaction
Flexible internal boundaries	Spontaneous affective expression
Responsive to change	Moderate clarity
	Congruent and direct
Random	
Unstable boundaries	Unpredictable, chaotic
Lack of structure	Fragmented messages
	Avoidance of blame

Source: Adapted from Evelyn Sieburg, *Family Communication, An Integrated Systems Approach* (New York: Gardner Press, 1985) pp. 232, 235, and Fremont E. Kast and James E. Rosenzweig, *Contingency Views of Organization and Management* (Chicago: Science Research Associates, 1973) p. 318.

MORPHOSTATIC SYSTEMS

Families that operate in a morphostatic fashion are suggested as having communication styles that are predictable, rigid, ritualistic, and that focus on decisions and instructions.

The Budge family responds in a somewhat morphostatic fashion to the possibility of a change in plans for a Saturday morning:

> Peter Budge, the older of the Budges' two teenage sons, receives a telephone call from Joe Carter, a friend who invites him to join the Carter family for a weekend of camping in the mountains. Peter says, "It sounds great, but I have to ask my parents. I'll call you back." "O.K., but hurry," replies his friend. "Mom, can I go camping with the Carters?" asks Peter. "It's all right with me," replies his Mother, "but isn't your father expecting you to help him plant some trees in the yard?" Moments later, Father comes striding into the kitchen. "Dad, I've just been invited to go camping with the Carters. Can I?" The enthusiastic expression that has been on Father's face disappears. "I thought we were gonna do some work together today," he remarks. "Yeah, I know I promised," Peter replies, "but I didn't know Joe was gonna call." Father agrees to let Peter go. He says, "If you really want to go, Gordy and I can plant the trees by ourselves." "You don't mind too much if I go, do you, Gordy?" asks Peter. "No, not too much," answers Gordy. On the way back to the phone, Peter passes his mother, who says, "You know, I think they really want you to stay." "Yeah, I know," says Peter, who proceeds to call the Carters and tell them he can't go. Later that morning, as they are planting an apple tree in the front yard, Mr. Budge says to his son, "Peter, I know it was hard to do, but I think you showed a lot of maturity in keeping your promise to me." "Yeah," says Gordy, "I'm glad you decided to stay."[13]

The maintenance of the status quo is evident in the communication in this family. The nonverbal message conveyed by the father and by Gordy is one of disappointment if their plans are changed, even though their words are to the contrary. In the end, Peter's interest in preserving family cohesion prevails. There is some lack of congruence, although the communication does not fully approach the rigidity and ritualistic nature of morphostatic communication described in Table 9.2.

RANDOM SYSTEMS

In the case of systems that function in a more random fashion, messages are unpredictable and fragmented and emphasis is placed on the "avoidance of blame."

Communication in a random-type family is illustrated in the following sketch about such a family:

> "The bathroom door handle is off again," shouts Maria Canwin. "Teddy, will you fix it?" she calls to her nine-year-old son. "I'll do it," her husband Herbert volunteers. "That's what you said last week," retorts Mrs. Canwin. "I'm sorry, dear, I put it on the repair list, but I can't seem to find the list," he replies. . . . An old college chum, phoning from the airport on a layover, has just been stampeded into coming over. "We'll save dinner for you," Maria says, hanging up. "No, you won't. You've burned the fish again," Herbert remarks, snorting under his breath. A shrieking Teddy, leaping from the stairs to a chair and onto his father's back in an impossible acrobatic sequence, shouts, "I heard that, skunkhead." Enter Melissa, trying to peel her brother off her father's back. "Get off, jerk." She also tries simultaneously to pry her parents apart from a cluttered and obviously too energetic embrace. "Leave him alone, Mom. I want him now. You can have him later." Meanwhile, Teddy shouts, "Put up your dukes, Herby!" "Stop it," roars Maria, suddenly overcome with the chaos. Sound and motion come to an instant stop. The three onlookers check in with each other: does she mean it? "One of you three children can set the table. We're having a guest."[14]

Communication is marked in this random-type family system by the fragmented messages, the unpredictable responses, and the chaotic nature of the messages. Early in the sequence, there is an avoidance of blame: "I put it on the repair list, but I can't seem to find the list."

ROLE OF RULES IN COMMUNICATION

Families that are predominantly morphostatic or morphogenic in nature have rules, implicit or explicit, that give stability and continuity to the operation of the family.

> Rules define patterns in the use of language, of space, and of time. . . . They dictate the assignment of formal and informal roles and prescribe the various behaviors attached to different roles. . . . Without such a set of rules, life in a family would be chaotic, as each situation would be novel, and would require new planning and decision making."[15]

Many rules involve appropriate use of language and a time frame for its use, such as: whether it is acceptable to talk during a certain television program, whether the children are encouraged to talk at meals, whether husband and wife talk before breakfast, and the amount of physical contact between spouses or other members of the family on particular occasions.[16]

Changes in rules may be difficult in predominantly morphostatic families—that is, they are not subject to discussion and change—while in morphogenic families, even long-standing rules may be subject to examination.

Rules differ from standards in that they have a relation to power that is not necessarily the case with standards for specific plans. Standards can evolve into rules, but often rules develop with less conscious design than do standards.

Output or outcome of communication

Satisfaction with communication among couples has been studied, and it was found that husbands generally have a higher level of satisfaction with marital communication than wives, as shown in Figure 9.2. According to the study, the degree of marital communication was evidenced in the following ways:

> . . . comfort felt by both partners in being able to share important emotions and beliefs with each other, the perception of a partner's way of giving and receiving information, and the . . . perception of how adequately they communicate with each other. High scores reflect the couple's awareness and satisfaction with the level and type of communication in their relationship. Low scores reflect a lack of satisfaction with their communication; they indicate that the couple may need to work on improving their communication skills.[17]

Another study indicated that satisfaction with communication relates to the agreement between spouses on various aspects of marital relationships, such as finances, household tasks, and decision making, and to a feeling of being understood by the spouse.[18]

Communication is important in the perceptions that guide conflict behavior. Poor communication does not cause conflict, but it can contribute to conflict because accurate messages are neither sent nor received. When people perceive incompatibility in goals or interests or interference in meeting goals, conflict may occur.[19]

From a study of marital conflict resolution, wives as well as husbands use influence as the most frequent strategy in dealing with conflict. This may reflect a trend toward greater spousal equality, although the research indicates that husbands retain a power position.[20]

Intersystem communication

Communication between social systems is important to the family because of its involvement

FIGURE 9.2 *Marital communication*

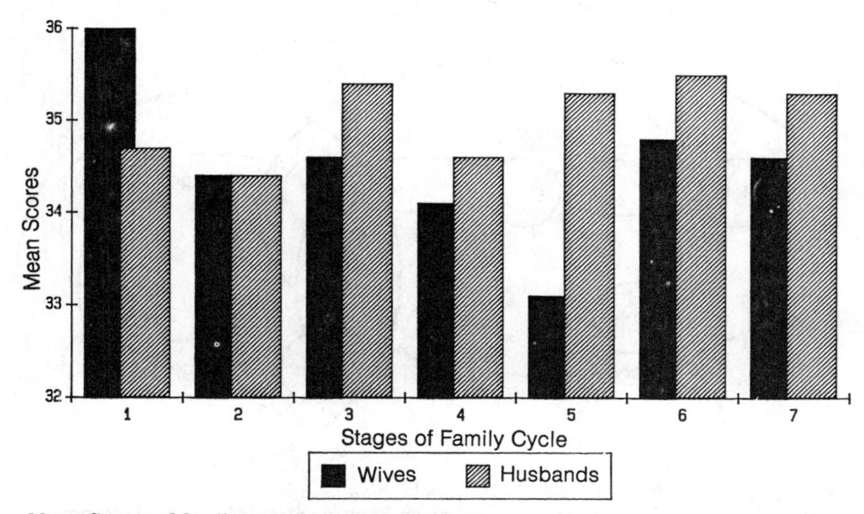

Note: Stages of family cycle defined in Table 13.1.
Source: David H. Olson, Hamilton I. McCubbin, Howard L. Barnes, Andrea S. Larsen, Marla J. Muxen, and Marc A. Wilson, "Marital and Family Strengths," in *Families* (Beverly Hills: Sage Publications, 1983), p. 104. Copyright © 1983 by Sage Publications, Inc. Reprinted by permission of the publisher. (Graph supplied by author.)

in complex, overlapping social structures (Figure 9.3). The illustration shows one person in two systems. An example is a man who is both a teacher in a county school system (oval, left) and a husband and father in the family system circle, right). Individual roles are shown as the systems' components, an approach to the managerial and personal functions of family subsystems already discussed. *Linkages* develop between people with different roles in the system, as shown in Figure 9.3. Some people and systems develop linkages or fixed interaction patterns forming bonds among the systems.[21]

Communication, whether interpersonal or between social systems, involves an interface, the common boundary of two systems. The interface between systems exists "whether the two are interrelated or not, whether they are in conflict or not, and whether or not messages are passing between them."[22] Interface barriers affect communication between systems. Examples of barriers at the interface of systems include regulations, hostility, financial requirements, and physical conditions.

The interface between families and other systems varies widely with the family. To a low-income family, a bank or a savings and loan institution may seem to be inaccessible with an almost impenetrable boundary. A higher-income family is not likely to sense such a limitation.

Summary

Communication, an important facilitator in the family system, is transactional in nature and is characterized by feedback from the receiver to the sender.

Listening attentively is essential for fully receiving messages. Interpersonal communication includes both verbal and nonverbal messages. Leveling, or agreement in all parts of a message—expression, body posture, and tone of voice—promotes effective communication.

FIGURE 9.3 *Communication linkages between roles within systems and between systems*

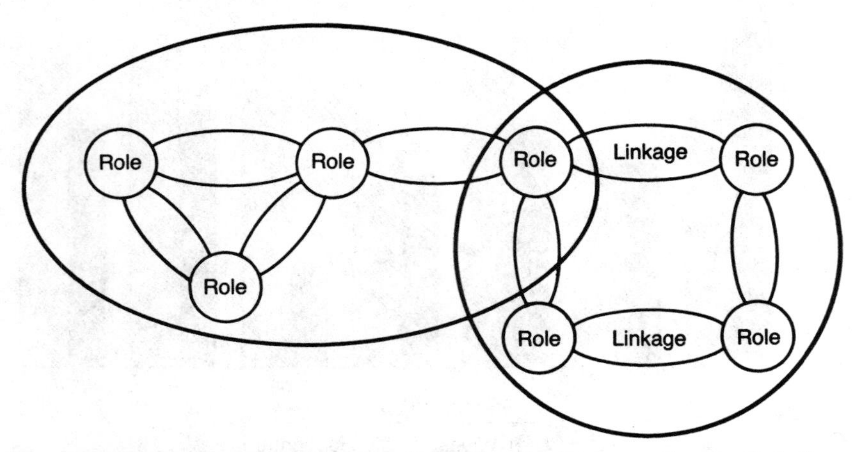

Source: Adapted from Ronald G. Havelock, *Planning for Innovation,* Institute for Social Research, The University of Michigan, Ann Arbor, 1969, pp. 1–3. Reprinted with permission of the publisher, Center for Research on the Utilization of Scientific Knowledge, Institute for Social Research, The University of Michigan, Ann Arbor.

Other positive communication practices and skills include empathy, supportive statements, and appreciation of other persons' worth.

Communication styles differ in morphostatic, morphogenic, and random types of family systems. Communication in predominantly morphostatic families is somewhat predictable, rigid, and ritualistic; in morphogenic families, communication is congruent, open, clear, and often spontaneously affectionate; in random family systems, communications frequently involve fragmented messages and occur in a somewhat unpredictable manner.

In relatively open systems, exchanges center on information, advice, or counsel; in relatively closed systems, the emphasis is on decision and instructions. In managerial activities, communication facilitates demand (especially goal) clarification, plan formation and implementation, and review and consideration of the effectiveness of outcomes.

Because of complex multiple roles, people and systems may be linked by interaction patterns that form bonds among different but related systems. Discrepancies between communicators in age, status, values, and language are potential communication barriers within the family system. Accurate communication messages help deal with and, in some cases, reduce potential conflict situations that may arise. Over the life cycle, husbands somewhat more than wives are satisfied with a more ritualistic communication pattern. Families interact at meals, during social periods, and in the care of individual family members, in particular. Communication binds the family system together.

Notes

1. Evelyn Sieburg, *Family Communication, An Integrated Systems Approach* (New York: Gardner Press, 1985), p. 33.

2. James C. McCroskey, Carol E. Larson, and Mark L. Knapp, *An Introduction to Interpersonal Communication* (Englewood Cliffs, N.J.: Prentice-Hall, 1971), pp. 3–4.

3. Richard Bandler, John Grinder, and Virginia

Satir, *Changing with Families,* Vol. 1 (Palo Alto: Science and Behavior Books, 1976), p. 118.

4. Stewart L. Tubbs and Sylvia Moss, *Human Communication* (New York: Random House, 1983), p. 36.

5. Freda S. Sathre, Ray W. Olson, and Clarissa I. Whitney, *Let's Talk* (Glenview, Ill.: Scott, Foresman, 1973), pp. 21, 23.

6. Edward T. Hall, *The Hidden Dimension* (Garden City, N.Y.: Doubleday, 1966).

7. Virginia Satir, *Peoplemaking* (Palo Alto: Science and Behavior Books, 1972), p. 72.

8. Kathleen M. Galvin and Bernard J. Brommel, *Family Communication Cohesion and Change* (Glenview, Ill.: Scott, Foresman, 1982), p. 6.

9. Alice J. Davey and Beatrice Paolucci, "Family Interaction: A Study of Shared Time and Activities," *Family Relations* 29 (January 1980): 43–49.

10. Haris D. Katakis, "The Systems Approach in the Study of Family Interaction," *International Journal of Social Psychiatry* 22 (Summer 1976): 101–102.

11. Galvin and Brommel, *Family Communication,* p. 10.

12. David Kantor and William Lehr, *Inside the Family* (San Francisco: Jossey-Bass, 1975), p. 130.

13. Ibid., p. 64.

14. Ibid., p. 138.

15. Ann Hartman and Joan Laird, *Family-Centered Social Work Practices* (New York: Free Press, 1983), pp. 96–97.

16. Irene F. Goodman, "Television's Role in Family Interaction," *Journal of Family Issues* 4 (June 1983): 411.

17. David H. Olson, Hamilton I. McCubbin, Howard L. Barnes, Andrea S. Larsen, Marla J. Muxen, and Marc A. Wilson, *Families: What Makes Them Work* (Beverly Hills: Sage Publications, 1983), p. 105.

18. Agaitha Allen and Theresa Thompson, "Agreement, Understanding, Realization, and Feeling Understood as Predictors of Communicative Satisfaction in Marital Dyads," *Journal of Marriage and the Family* 46 (November 1984): 915–921.

19. Joseph P. Folger and Marshall Scott Poole, *Communication* (Glenview, Ill.: Scott, Foresman, 1984), p. 4.

20. David C. Bell. Janet Saltzman Chafetz, and Lori Heggem Horn, "Marital Conflict Resolution," *Journal of Family Issues* 3 (March 1982): 130.

21. Ronald G. Havelock, *Planning for Innovation* (Ann Arbor: The University of Michigan, Institute for Social Research, 1969), pp. 2–14.

22. Ibid., pp. 2–9.

10

Output and input–output relations

To judge the effectiveness of a system, people can compare actual outputs with the anticipated outcomes of met demands and changed resources. The more consistent the outputs are with what was anticipated (goals), the more effective the management system. Anticipated outcomes are translated into expected outcomes through planning and into actual outcomes through implementing. Actual outcomes represent the degree to which anticipated and expected outcomes are achieved. Unexpected outcomes—those that exceed anticipations or yield more interesting effects than expected—may contribute to system growth; or deviations from what was expected can be costly if the goals fall short of what was anticipated or if resources were ineffectively used.

As part of a purposeful social system, household members do more than respond mechanically to the stimuli of goals when they manage.[1] Numerous decisions accompany the management processes as they are initiated by a goal and brought to fruition. And these decisions are continually monitored through feedback in terms of their relation to the system's demands. To understand the effectiveness of a goal-directed management system, outputs, as such, and their relationship to inputs must be examined.

Output

Managerial action is stimulated by the system's demands. The system's response is reflected in terms of the outputs to which the action has been directed: the translating of demands into met demands and the accompanying changed resources.

As a subsystem of the individual household or family, the output may be conveyed to the system's internal environment—as with the preparation and consumption of a meal—or be conveyed to the system's external environment, as with the mailing of a letter. The meal and letter can be assumed to be tasks initiated intentionally as goals. Output that results from a disastrous event also flows to the internal and external environments.

DEMAND RESPONSES

Demand responses are the output from managerial actions relating to values and satisfaction. The nature of the satisfaction is affected or determined by the source and purpose of the demands, goals, or events and by the planning and implementing processes involved in fulfilling them.

Goal related. As indicated earlier, goals may give either specific or general direction to planning. Specific goals can provide the satisfaction of achieving a desired end, which is clearly recognizable. When goals are met through a relatively closed (morphostatic) planning and implementing mode, the satisfaction that comes from completing a task—that is, reaching closure—is a likely result. There may be, in addition, a sense of being in control of the outcome of a well-defined goal or segment of a task.

All evaluations of outcomes may not be positive. Satisfaction may be viewed as falling somewhat on a continuum with negative, neutral, and positive positions on the scale. The more affectively charged activities will likely result in higher or lower levels of positive or negative satisfaction. Some goals are undertaken of necessity or obligation due to unfortunate or undesirable circumstances. If effectively carried out, there can be positive relief or satisfaction that the job was responsibly done even though there were personal feelings of loss or regret. A case in point could be the settling of an estate.

Satisfaction with any given managerial activity is couched within a general sense of one's satisfaction with some area of life. Evaluation of the specific situation is probably not isolated from the broader circumstances but in fact carries overtones that relate to whether we are closer to or further from some life goal compared to the situational one. Even so, people tend to respond positively to questions regarding satisfaction with most aspects of their lives.[2] Among groups within the population, however, there are differences in the degree of satisfaction felt. Older and lower-income groups reflect lower scores than those younger or more affluent, for example.[3]

The meaning or significance of the output may be viewed, also, from another perspective: a more open, or morphogenic, approach to planning and implementing. The goals may be more general or "directional," rather than specific. McCaskey observes:

> [While] a goal is generally assumed to be an end-state, the terminal point of a planning process, underlying a goal is often a desire for a longer-term *process* rather than a desire for an end-state itself; . . . most people do not merely want to get the job or get married. What they seek is a living relationship, rather than a terminal state. . . . Moving in a particular direction can be satisfying in itself, and journeying is often more important than the destination.[4]

Individuals probably gain satisfaction from tasks both through the process of their accomplishment and from their completion. Part of the difference is in interests and part in the nature of the tasks or activities themselves. Repetitive tasks may lead to a greater pleasure in completion than the process of accomplishing them. The same task, undertaken occasionally, might yield to the same person greater or equal return in the doing than in the completion. Still, people's styles for approaching planning and implementing activities tend to differ in terms of their specificity or generality, their focus on outcomes or process, and their openness to change. Conditions in the situation—for example, availability of resources or role expectations—may promote a more specific and controlled approach compared to a more general and open one. A recent study of managerial behavior of families with preschool children indicated "that socio-economic/demographic characteristics may not be as important to the effectiveness of managerial behaviour as family composition."[5]

Whether the satisfactions from output follow from goals providing specific or general direction to the system, the satisfactions reflect back on goals generated within the family system—influenced often by factors both within and outside the family. For example, the goal to fix up the basement by using their own time and skills may be motivated by the family's pleasure in sharing projects as well as by wanting more living space or needing a place for the children to entertain friends. The shared meanings and satisfactions developed during the project and at its completion are likely to contribute to the family's sense of cohesiveness.

If the family's motivation to finish the basement was also prompted by a desire to improve the value of the house, their ability to look ahead and to use their resources in anticipation of future advantage does not just bring the satisfaction of a met demand: Their overall functionality has broadened their alternatives for today's living as well as their options for the future. If the family finished the basement to provide extra room to care for a family member's impaired health following an accident, the satisfaction of finding a way to meet an event, which has now become a goal, also accrues to the family through intrasystem dynamics as increased capacity for adaptiveness.

The personal system has a major influence on the nature of the satisfaction from the goal-related activity of the management system. Families characterized as healthy in terms of their positive, flexible, affective, realistic, and shared relationships have been found to perceive or assess their competence in much the same way as others do.[6] The reality with which families perceive how satisfactorily their demands are met varies with the circumstances, of course. Interrelationships between the personal and managerial subsystems of the family are illustrated by a study of middle-income mothers who reported more satisfaction with the organization of their household work when they also perceived higher marital agreement.[7] This cohesion is reinforced and strengthened by positive work activity through the additional satisfaction derived.

The above illustration indicates a number of things. The nature of the goal affects the meanings associated with the satisfaction from meeting the demand. These meanings follow from the ongoing interplay between the personal and managerial systems. From these interactions, contributions evolve that strengthen (or reduce) the family bonds in the form of cohesion, the capacity of family members to respond adaptively, and/or the general ability of the family to function effectively in its personal and managerial relationships and activities to carry out its roles and responsibilities. As was indicated in our discussion of the family system, the dynamics of these interrelated intrasystem processes depend on how well they are facilitated by communication among family members. Given situations may contribute positively or negatively to the level of cohesiveness, adaptability, or functionality, which have been cited as important bases for a family's viability. Sensitivity to these effects can make a difference over time.

Societal rules and regulations are a common form of met demands that have external effects. Certain demands may be met with a recognition of their necessity and simple compliance, while the purpose of others may be strongly supported or opposed, as is often the case with taxes. The meaning attached to meeting these demands is sometimes foreshadowed at an earlier date when, for example, a family worked either to help bring the levy to a vote or to defeat its passage.

Events. The response to an unforeseen occurrence may be positive depending upon the nature of the event and the accompanying expectations. The response to events may be retained within the system or become related to the external environment. Output that results from a disastrous event, such as a flood, is an example of internal and external output. The human resources used to clean up the silt and repair the damage to the family dwelling are internal to the family system. The money spent for materials to repair the flood damage, the human resources used to care for strangers or help neighbors with their housing, and the concern expressed are external outputs.

RESOURCE CHANGES

Resource changes are the output from managerial actions relating to the composition of the stock of human and/or material means. Whether the outcomes or demand responses follow from goal directions that are specific or more directional in terms of a long-range goal or a determining life-style, resources are utilized. Managerial decisions and actions underlie the household's resource flow, with the result that the stock of resources has been affected. Efforts to help children develop their skills in problem solving, in relating to other children, in music, or in making a presentation contribute to accruing capacities—their human resources. While the process probably requires some attention, time, money, and energy, the increments to the growth of their children (and possibly to that of the parents as well) provide an illustration of an effective trade-off between the personal and managerial systems of the family. In addition, the intrasystem dynamics have been affected if the general sense of cohesiveness, adaptability, and/or functionality has changed.

A change in material resources brought about by their utilization in implementing a plan represents a shift in the stock of available means for meeting demands, whether the effect of the resource use has occurred within the household or through interchange with the external environment.

The following list shows the direction of change in the amount of available resources resulting from managerial activities:

exchanging (no change)
consuming (decreases)
protecting (decreases)
transferring (decreases)
producing (increases)
saving/investing (increases)

Exchanging. This involves interchanges of equal values and therefore affects the makeup, but not necessarily the value, of the household resource inventory. Such exchanges may occur within the family system and between the family and other systems; they may or may not involve money, although money is likely to figure in facilitating exchanges external to the family system.

Looking first at tangible resources, universal in the Foa and Foa model (see Chapter 5), output from many household managerial activities results in shifts in the resource inventory of individuals or household members who either share resources or who have understood rights of use and disposition. A father may purchase his son's car when the son cannot take it to college. For the father, the internal exchange of money for the car affects the composition of his total inventory, but supposedly not its total value if the internal exchange was comparable to market prices. The father has more goods and less money; the son has more money and less goods. Was this also an opportunity for an exchange of interpersonal support and regard? If so, this would be a situation where both universal and particularistic dimensions were involved in the same exchange situation: father to son—money and affection; son to father—car and appreciation. It would seem that a high portion of exchanges within the family and among friends would have both particularistic and universal aspects, having implications for affective capacities in the personal system and shifts in the stock of tangible (universal) resources.

Exchanges of tangible (universal) resources inside or outside the system need not involve money. An exchange of garden tools by neighbors can be mutually beneficial. The common expectation is that an exchange will change the inventory make up but not its value, even though the new acquisition has preferred attributes over the exchanged one. If an unneeded radio is sold, the seller finds the money more desirable than the radio. When the individual spends the money for new records, he or she obviously wanted them more than the radio or the money.

Exchanges of resources often precede other managerial activities in order to acquire the more appropriate resources needed. External exchanges involve outputs from the household in return for outputs from another system. In each case, the output of one system has become the other's input. Household purchases, made in response to various demands placed on the household, contribute to the determination of market demand: the quantity of a product or service that will be taken at a price. With meat choices, for example, a decision to buy a chicken is part of the reflected demand for that product—an input to the retailer as a result of household output.

Time-related exchanges, such as services, are harder to measure than material resources because time is not exchanged; it is used in exchange for something. It cannot be held or accumulated as can material resources. These difficulties have alerted both economists and home economists to the need to account more adequately for the time factor in interpreting exchanges. For individuals and families, such realities are a part of daily living—and managing.

A person who exchanges skills and time for pay finds the money more useful than if the time and skills were used in another way. Exchange relationships are not easily weighed if the value of each good or service is not readily measured in market terms. The total impact of returns from outside productive work, the consumption level, and the demands of household work must all be evaluated in order for households to maximize their work and consumption potential. If income and consumption increase in relation to outside employment, time demands then increase for consumption and household maintenance, leading to inclinations to decrease total work.[8] Time-related choices are complex and affect the various aspects of resources and their allocation.

Consuming. Consuming reduces available tangible resources by the amount of their market value contributing utility value (a demand response) in return. *Utility* is the satisfaction or the intrinsic or extrinsic values derived from resources as they contribute to meeting demands. For example, consuming one unit of an item gives a certain amount of satisfaction or utility; consuming more units yields more total utility but (eventually) less utility per unit. *Marginal utility* is the consumer's added satisfaction from the last unit used. When satisfaction from the last dollar spent across all categories is equal, consumers experience the most total satisfaction.

Table 10.1 shows that—assuming equal satisfaction from expenditures at the margin—the sources of consumer satisfaction shifted among various categories over a ten-year period. In 1972–73, expenditures represented 76 percent of income before taxes, compared to 83 percent in 1982–83—with accompanying implications for savings (see Chapter 12). Expenditures doubled, while increases in income before taxes rose 85 percent over the decade. Increasing percentages of expenditures were made to food away from home, housing (especially shelter and utilities), transportation (vehicle-related), entertainment, reading and education, and alcohol. Decreasing shares for other categories were led by apparel and services and cash contributions. While increases in expenditures can often be traced to price increases, this was not always the case. For example, expenditure increases did not match price rises for food at home; fuels, utilities, and public services; household operations; apparel and services; transportation; and health care. Expenditures exceeded price rises for food away from home, alcohol, entertainment, and house furnishings and equipment. Life-style changes are probably reflected in the expenditure patterns, even though the composition of consumer units also contributed.

Protecting. Through *protecting*, people can minimize their potential economic losses at the cost of risk sharing. Insurance protection is the resource counterpart to protection against the effects of unforeseen contingencies (event demands). The output or resource allocation is for the private-policy premium payment or the required contribution to a governmental insurance program. The accompanying response demand is the expectation of minimizing

TABLE 10.1 *Average annual income before taxes and expenditures of urban consumer units*

Component	*1972–73*		*1982–83*	
	Dollars	*Percent*	*Dollars*	*Percent*
Income before taxes	12,388		23,027	
Total expenditures	9,421[a]	100.0	19,128	100.0
Food, total	1,675	17.8	3,175	16.6
Food at home	1,313	13.9	2,238	11.7
Food away from home	362	3.8	937	4.9
Housing, total	2,638	28.0	5,869	30.7
Shelter	1,507	16.0	3,309	17.3
Fuels, utilities, and public services	581	6.2	1,512	7.9
Household operations	138	1.5	275	1.4
House furnishings and equipment	411	4.4	773	4.0
Apparel and services	732	7.8	1,039	5.4
Transportation, total	1,762	18.7	3,766	19.7
Vehicles and expenses	1,653	17.5	3,535	18.5
Public transportation	110	1.2	231	1.2
Health care	432	4.6	834	4.4
Entertainment	389	4.1	879	4.6
Personal care	106	1.1	178	1.0
Reading and education	176	1.9	385	2.0
Cash contributions	372	3.9	586	3.1
Personal insurance, pensions	818	8.7	1,651	8.6
Alcohol	89	1.0	286	1.5
Tobacco	131	1.4	208	1.1
Miscellaneous	102	1.1	274	1.4

[a] Expenditure categories for 1972–73 were adjusted to correspond with 1982–83 definitions; estimates for 1982–83 exclude students.
Source: Raymond Gieseman and John Rogers, "Consumer Expenditures: Results from the Dairy and Interview Surveys," *Monthly Labor Review* 109 (June 1986): 17.

economic risks by sharing potential losses through insurance. In addition to risk sharing, other approaches to protection include health practices and care of property. These approaches are of fundamental importance as avenues for reducing risk-sharing costs as well as other losses that cannot be compensated economically.

If no contingency arises, the resources are reduced by the amount of the premiums. The sense of security in having protected life, health, job, or property is a form of consumption. If the contingency arises, insurance is expected to replace part or all of the economic loss. The cost of insurance coverage reduces resources, but it avoids extreme resource losses when contingencies do arise.

Transferring. While a one-way transfer of resources may occur between people within the household, it is through *transferring* to users outside the household—gifts, contributions, taxes, and so on—that a reduction in the value of available resources of a household unit occurs. These alternatives to consumption are voluntary or mandatory commitments to individuals or to society. Individuals also benefit by transfers made, in turn, to them from publicly or privately supported community services.

For both families and individuals, obligatory tax outlays are balanced to some extent by such services as public education, recreation facilities, and police and fire protection. Voluntary transfers include support of community organizations and services, for which contributors may or may not have consumption opportunities. An example is the support for neighborhood settlement houses, which are not in the individual's neighborhood but are designed for special area needs. Such contributions reduce individual assets and tend to increase social resources.

Gifts to individuals represent another form of transfer. Where material resources are given, a decrease in available resources usually means a commensurate reduction in consumption opportunities, although personal sharing may well balance out. Extensions of support to others can yield a different, less tangible return. Reference was made in Chapter 5 to the integrative effects of transfers of affective resources.

Gifts to individuals may be in the form of services, such as in times of severe illness. According to one study, relatives, friends, and neighbors gave help, while institutional and professional services, other than those of the physician, were used minimally.[9]

Transfers must be external to the household to reduce resources. A money gift to children within the household merely shifts the opportunity to make decisions about money use from adults to children and does not alter the system's total available resources.

Producing. Producing is creating added resources or utilities from existing resources. Earnings outside the home and household production are examples of productive output. Most resources of families and individuals result from their productive activities.

Productive output that is internal to the household can occur in ordinary ways, as when a household member assembles a set of shelves for the living room, paints a room, bakes a cake, or launders clothes. Value is added to products or services are performed that add utility in using or consuming. The basic materials are usually obtained through a market exchange, but either the form, location, or function of the materials is changed by productive processes to make them more useful. Management is the fundamental process that can influence the effectiveness of household production.

Household members contribute their time, abilities, and other resources in exchange for earning wages, salaries, or self-employment profits. Earnings from productive activity outside the household represent the contribution made to the "value added" to the Gross National Product by a business or industry's output that then becomes an input of income to the household. Some larger purpose or higher value behind the goal to earn can be assumed: increasing security, meeting personal needs, providing for others.

Saving/Investing. Saving (or dissaving) and investment behavior adjust the availability of resources over time. Families save in various ways and for various reasons, commonly in an effort to spread their earnings over their life cycle advantageously in terms of their needs for consumption.

A family may set money aside in savings accounts, bonds, and so on, for later spending—perhaps in ten weeks or ten years—with the expectation that delayed consumption will bring greater total satisfaction. Or desired items may cost more than current resources allow at the moment. Or the family may anticipate greater needs than future earnings are likely to cover when the needs occur. Uncertainties about unforeseeable contingencies may also motivate savings. Accumulated assets, including human capital, are part of the output that reflects such family choices.

A family's stock of resources, minus credit obligations, represents the family's *net worth.* It includes assets of lower liquidity, such as housing, and assets readily available or of high liquidity, such as cash on hand or in a checking account. All assets are output from the standpoint that the family had to make some decision or take some action in relation to resource use in order to meet a demand, as with housing, recreation equipment, or money put in a bank for a rainy day. Current flexibility may be reduced in favor of anticipated longer-term gains, as when a self-employed family needs to increase its capital by reducing its consumption in order to operate the business. Often such families feel "pinched," even though they have greater total assets than most families.

Although the term "savings" is often used to refer to all assets of low and high liquidity, investing is identified here with assets of low liquidity and savings with high-liquidity assets. From this perspective, *savings* characteristically maintain a fixed-dollar value and provide a relatively secure source of income, even though interest rates fluctuate with economic conditions. An *investment,* on the other hand, is an asset that varies with economic conditions both in dollar value and in earnings. Investing is a means of maintaining relative asset value during changing prices, an opportunity to hedge inflation and/or to increase total resources while, at the same time, assuming risks of declines in asset value should the reverse trend in economic conditions occur.

Income-producing assets, such as investments, may not be as readily available for short-term needs as are the more liquid savings, but they may be used as security for borrowing. This capability, combined with total available resources (including the negative side, debts), makes the net-worth concept most useful for analyzing household savings in a systems framework.

Dissaving is the output from borrowing that allows the use of anticipated future income for current needs and wants. Credit use is a way of life for many families. In 1985, consumer installment credit outstanding was 19 percent of disposable personal income.[10] This means that, on the average, for every five dollars of income after taxes, families and consumers extended their consumption, at least for the short run, by one dollar through credit. More than one-third of this installment credit was incurred to purchase an automobile. A 19-percent level of short-term credit in relation to disposable income is relatively high, causing some economists to wonder how high such commitments can go without affecting the confidence level on the part of lenders in the ability of consumers to meet their obligations.

Families who pay for all their charge-card purchases each month are using the cards as a convenience, in lieu of carrying cash or writing checks, rather than as a source of credit. An alternative to keeping current on charge accounts is the use of automated teller machines (ATMs) to withdraw cash directly from an account. In a 1984 study, 42 percent of the families surveyed owned an ATM card—more at higher incomes and fewer at lower incomes. Although all families having ATMs did not use them, those who did tended to make a higher portion of their expenditures with cash—especially higher-income families.[11] Short-term credit is ordinarily used to extend resources beyond current income for a limited period, committing future income.

Families who get into a process of taking on new obligations as older ones are paid off may be acquiring a habit of dissaving: living beyond their means. If income increases, the costs of the credit may seem inconsequential. A problem occurs when there are contingencies—such as one's job being at risk—that make the costs and payments problematical. For longer-term credit, there usually is collateral to protect the lender's interests—which also protects the borrower, particularly when prices are rising and the house or other item also increases in value. Difficulties arise when prices are going down. At times, not only the value of the collateral but the means of payment, earning power, may also be at risk.

Input–output relations

GENERAL

It was indicated in Chapter 3 that although inputs and outputs of open systems can be reduced to the common denominators of information, matter, and energy, these broad terms do not characterize the inputs in their relation to particular systems. Demands and resources are the terms that indicate their special relation as basic inputs to the family resource management system.

The idea of energy exchange helps people to understand the circuitous influences of input on output and of output on input for the maintenance of a system. How well the actual outcome from planning and implementing activities coincides with the desired outcome or goals is a measure of management success. Each activity has some cost or energy expenditure. This cost of transforming resources is ordinarily assumed to yield a more worthwhile product or result than was the case with the initial resources. Management outputs occur through internal system processes.

The sources of inputs for any system, on the other hand, are the outputs of its own or other systems. Inputs "reenergize" the system for continued activity. Exchanges of an open system with its environment renew the resources necessary to keep the system viable.[12]

The reciprocal input–output relation may be illustrated for any purpose to which the managerial system responds. Output from a goal to paint the house is an expenditure for the desired color and type of paint. The purchase occurs in the environment external to the household, contributing to the market demand for paint and further generating production and income through economic processes. The paint, as an acquisition, becomes input. When the paint is applied, the house value may increase (an external outcome) or it may be enjoyed more (an internal outcome). The paint job also may stimulate the owner or neighbors to make other housing improvements, thus enhancing the neighborhood's appearance.

Open systems must regenerate themselves to survive. A system may move to disorganization or death by a process called *entropy*. Chronic illness, apathy, compulsive spending, and divorce are evidences of the entropic process that can affect families. However, open systems can build up a base of human and material resources to carry them through crises. *Negative entropy* takes place when there is a positive balance of resources entering a system compared with those expended. Families that strive to get ahead exemplify the tendency of open systems to maximize this relation.[13]

Effective management is one of the most important tools for countering the entropic process of individual and family systems. Some means used to reverse entropic influences are developing a positive value system, increasing flexibility, improving skills and abilities, and acquiring financial reserves. These same means may also forestall the effects of potential catastrophic events or a gradual depletion of resources.

Ongoing systems typically develop a self-perpetuating pattern of input–output activity. Meals provide a format for transforming income into food, and food into good health and high physical energy for earning income. Mealtime may also provide an opportunity to communicate goals for the day, schedule activities, share experiences, or change plans, although the needed basic patterning can be provided in other ways. Recurrent activities are characteristic of and useful to system survival, but undue dependence on them may stifle responses to changing situations. Families that experience reduced income often retain spending habits that were established before the decline. When input shifts, output will eventually have to change.

The interdependent roles of input and output keep the system "energized," meaningfully patterned, and adequately responsive. The feedback mechanism helps to clarify input–output relations.

FEEDBACK

Feedback is the portion of output that reenters as input to affect succeeding output. While output as met demands and as used resources is both the experience and the effect of management, feedback is the monitoring or reprocessing of the output. Feedback involves the system's evaluation of its own output, including its perception about how the output is received by other systems, compared to the intended responses. Feedback helps maintain the dynamic character of an open system; it is an information source for evaluating activities in pursuit of goals and for adapting to changing conditions.

The positive or negative nature of responses to feedback from overall system output promotes either continuity or change in the system. *Positive feedback* accepts deviations from expected effects and promotes rather than inhibits change. Difference between expected and actual outcomes are acknowledged with actions that support the deviation. An increase in or continuation of the deviation is favored, which is really a change in goal. Positive feedback is expansive in nature; for example, when a student finds that one required course cannot be scheduled during the last term at the university, reconsideration may be given to goals. A decision to stay two extra terms and graduate with a double major could result.

Negative feedback processes note a difference between actual and desired output and influences the system to reduce the deviation so that the output stays within the limits established by goals.[14] Negative feedback is a monitoring function that may be used critically or defensively.

Purchasing behavior may illustrate negative feedback. Consider an evaluation on the part of a consumer that the trial of a new item, purchased as an alternative to a known and liked one that was out of stock, did not fulfill expectations and would not be purchased again. Returning to the former item is negative-feedback action.

In Figure 2.4, feedback lines within the family system extend from the output of individual systems to their input arrows. Where two-way arrows are shown, as between personal and managerial systems, internal feedback also occurs. Feedback from the external output of the family system back to its input shows the alertness of the system to the indications of its own actions in taking advantage of information that may affect future system processes.

In interpreting feedback, it is important to remember that it relates only to the system's own output. Output from family system "A" also enters other systems as input and is processed by them. Then, any output from another system that becomes input to system "A" is a system exchange rather than feedback from family system "A's" output. Sometimes you hear people say that they have not received any feedback from their communication to a group or from an activity. Technically, that is not an appropriate use of "feedback." As one systems analyst has observed: "Ordinary language sometimes used *positive* and *negative feedback* to refer to praise and criticism, respectively. That usage is unrelated to the system view and will be carefully eschewed by those who wish to appear sophisticated about system theory!"[15]

The feedback information sources for the family system are both internal and external. The information returning from external systems as a result of the family's own managerial output can be direct or diffuse. For example, forgetting to sign a check in payment of a household service will result in immediate, direct information about the oversight (negative feedback): the check is not acknowledged by the recipient until it is signed. Being delayed in shopping at a usual time and finding that the store is less crowded at a later hour can lead to a changed standing plan in favor of the new time (positive feedback).

Intersystem effects may accrue from consumers' own feedback responses. Acceptance or rejection of products is reflected in output supportive or not to retailers' offerings. Retailers' responses to these effects on their input–output feedback relationship may be to accept or reject future deliveries from manufacturers or processors. The resulting intersystem exchanges and intrasystem evaluations contribute to product change more in keeping with consumer expectations or to increased production of successful goods and services. Under these circumstances, the purchaser is encouraged to change purchases as an effective way of dealing with unsatisfactory products.

Information from external and internal experiences and situations combines to promote continuity along previously satisfactory lines or to seek new objectives and approaches. Feedback from managerial output to the personal system helps reinforce or redirect value orientations. The feedback thus influences the nature of the goals, which in turn become input to the managerial system.

Negative feedback helps maintain a "status quo," morphostatic response, and positive feedback represents an openness to change—morphogenic response. Table 10.2 illustrates examples of feedback responses.

In Table 10.2, the nature of subsystem feedback is illustrated without exhausting the possible considerations. Many other factors could be considered and could provide further insight into personal and managerial system interactions—parental preferences, for example, or the nature of alternative field work opportunities during the year. Each situation has its balance of personal and managerial conditions that makes it unique in weighing priorities from feedback information returning from output outside the system as input to the system. In Table 10.2, personal relations and economic factors were major considerations for continuing the plan for summer work. Educational priorities were upheld in the option favoring summer field work. Depending on priorities and special situations, either option could be a preferred and good solution. Where a change in earlier priorities and plans occurred and where a negative feedback force is overriding, an adjustment back to the previous expectation may well be warranted.

Evaluation has been used in the systems approach as integral to decision making, and it occurs throughout management in planning and implementing plans. Feedback relates to the knowledge of results both as the activity progresses and after it occurs.[16]

The feedback that occurs within the management system helps to identify the internal shifts that must be made during the course of action. The feedback that takes place between management subsystems is likely to differ for plans and actions that relate to the more specific compared to the more general goals. For more specific plans, the feedback response from implementing is likely to be limited to checking and oriented to maintaining the anticipated results. For less specific goals providing general direction, the plans are also less likely to be detailed, so they are more prone to adjustment in implementing or open to reorientation in process.

Feedback may flow from output to reenter the managerial system directly, or it may go by way of the external environment as input back into the family system. Through positive or negative feedback processes, the output to the management system through the personal system may differ from earlier output. Values, for example, may be reinforced or altered and affect goals accordingly. Feedback complements the overall purpose of the system and is essential to an open, ongoing, adaptive social system

TABLE 10.2 *Examples of feedback responses*

Alternative	*Possible subsystem feedback responses*	
	Positive	*Negative*
1. *Choose field work*		
Personal subsystem	Satisfaction as growing interest in program of work takes priority.	Uncertainty as school pressures mount and realization of extent that friends will be missed becomes clear.
Managerial subsystem	Satisfaction with easier scheduling of remaining program to graduate. Job opportunities can be investigated and program completed more confidently with better knowledge of job opportunities.	Growing preference to meet school expenses without additional parental support, which may mean part-time job during school.
2. *Choose resort work*		
Personal subsystem	Enjoyment of one last summer with friends—knowing their degree programs will also be completed next year and they are counting on your being there.	Some qualms at postponing graduating even though common sense says a few months will not be that significant in long run.
Managerial subsystem	Relief in having a break in study program and easier planning for expenses next year. Commitment to make field experience more meaningful at end of program with full academic background.	Uncertainty in how to proceed toward job placement without experience in area of interest.

in maintaining adequate stability in situations that require dynamic responses. Capability to correct internal deviations during an activity is important, but more is required. Feedback permits output to affect directly the underlying purposes of a system, through learning, goal-seeking, expanding the system organization, and generally supporting continuation of the system.[17] Feedback makes a system "whole" by emphasizing its purposefulness as the system responds to the surroundings and keeps elements of continuity and adaptiveness intact.

Summary

Much can be surmised about the effectiveness of any system by observing how well the goals or anticipated outcomes coincide with the outputs. While the managerial processes may not be understood, it can be ascertained whether the goals of the system are being promoted. Satisfactions (which may also be negative) occur as a part of management decisions and activity throughout the process and also in comparing the goals as met demands.

Resources are not only a source of utility or satisfaction but also are reallocated or utilized. Exchanging is where the shift in available resources does not alter the value of the resource stock. However, the available resources will be reduced by consuming, protecting, and transferring. Producing and saving/investing contribute to increases in total resources held. The net worth of families is dependent on the level of assets held minus their credit obligations.

Input–output relations are monitored

through feedback. Negative feedback promotes a system's stability, and positive feedback represents growth or change in possibilities.

Notes

1. Russell L. Ackoff and Fred E. Emery, *On Purposeful Systems* (Chicago: Aldine-Atherton, 1972), p. 6.

2. Mary Winter and Earl W. Morris, "Used Resources, Met Demands, and Satisfaction," paper presented to North Central Regional Committee (NCR-116) on Family Resource Management, Columbus, Ohio, 1982.

3. Angus Campbell, Philip E. Converse, and Willard L. Rodgers, *The Quality of American Life* (New York: Russell Sage Foundation, 1976), pp. 52–54.

4. Michael B. McCaskey, "Goals and Direction in Personal Planning," *The Academy of Management Review* 2 (July 1977): 456.

5. M. E. Garrison and Mary Winter, "The Managerial Behaviour of Families with Preschool Children," *Journal of Consumer Studies and Home Economics* 10 (September 1986): 258.

6. Jerry M. Lewis, W. Robert Beavers, John T. Gossett, and Virginia Austin Phillips, *No Single Thread* (New York: Brunner/Mazel, 1976), p. 213.

7. E. Carolyn Ater and Ruth E. Deacon, "Interaction of Family Relationship Qualities and Managerial Components," *Journal of Marriage and the Family* 34 (May 1972): 260.

8. Staffan Burenstam Linder, *The Harried Leisure Class* (New York: Columbia University Press, 1970), p. 33.

9. Sydney H. Croog, Alberta Lipson, and Sol Levine, "Help Patterns in Severe Illness: The Roles of Kin Network, Non-Family Resources, and Institutions," *Journal of Marriage and the Family* 34 (February 1972): 34–35.

10. "Domestic Financial and Nonfinancial Statistics," *Federal Reserve Bulletin* 72 (June 1986): A40, A52.

11. Robert B. Avery, Gregory E. Elliehausen, Arthur B. Kennickell, and Paul A. Spindt, "The Use of Cash and Transaction Accounts by American Families," *Federal Reserve Bulletin* 72 (February 1986): 95.

12. D. Katz and R. L. Kahn, *The Social Psychology of Organizations* (New York: Wiley, 1966), p. 89.

13. Ibid., pp. 94–95.

14. Walter Buckley, *Sociology and Modern Systems Theory* (Englewood Cliffs, N.J.: Prentice-Hall, 1967), p. 53.

15. Alfred Kuhn and Robert D. Beam, *The Logic of Organization* (San Francisco: Jossey-Bass, 1982), p. 50.

16. John Annett, *Feedback and Human Behavior* (Baltimore: Penguin Books, 1969), p. 29. See also Irma H. Gross, Elizabeth W. Crandall, and Marjorie M. Knoll, *Management for Modern Families* (New York: Appleton-Century-Crofts, 1973), p. 263.

17. Buckley, *Sociology and Modern Systems Theory*, p. 70.

Part Two

Applications to resources

11

Financial management

The purpose of this chapter is to provide an overview of the relation of management to family finances, not to provide background on the potential contributions of specific spending, saving, or credit alternatives. To do so would require more information on financial institutions than is possible in this book, which is devoted to the application of managerial processes underlying specific choices in families' acquisition and utilization of their money resources. Because a number of books on personal finance approach the subject from the perspective of the products offered by the financial institution as a business, this chapter might provide an introductory orientation to the course from the family financial perspective. Other resources of individuals and families, such as time and human capacities (physical health, knowledge, and skills), are important and often underrated. They affect how money is obtained and used in fundamental ways. These interactions will be recognized in this chapter, as well as in Chapter 12, Work and Family.

Because families' options have increasingly focused on money as the economy has grown, attention needs to be directed to its role in management. Money is the avenue by which increasing interdependence with the general economy has occurred. Money performs a number of functions:

1. It provides a basis for value comparisons;
2. It serves as a mechanism for exchanges with the general economy;
3. It can be held as a claim against resource needs in the future;
4. It provides a medium for making interchanges and transfers with government, institutions, private groups, and individuals.

The role of money is strategic as individuals and families make their daily financial decisions. An understanding of this role is important in addressing questions relating to economic well-being, for example: how attitudes about money relate to economic "success"; the relation of economic conditions to income and its use; the relation of life stages to earning potential; and how earnings are distributed over the life cycle to meet life needs. These and other topics will be covered in the following sections relating to input, throughput, and output aspects of financial management within a system's context.

Input

GOALS AND ASPIRATIONS

An individual family's goals or aspirations are complex distillations of basic values that address many facets of the lives of its members: the needs and interests of each person in the family; the expectations and achievements of those with whom it relates in the microenvironment; and the economic conditions, uncertainties, and opportunities experienced and anticipated through macroenvironmental interactions. Studies have not yet explained how these factors interrelate to affect financial goals. Part of the reason for a lack of explanation is that financial objectives are well integrated by families into their overall goals. Even so, a focus on the financial aspect can be useful to the whole.

Similar feelings of satisfaction or economic well-being are thought by some observers to accompany fulfilled aspirations regardless of the level of available resources; others believe that met aspirations are not as fulfilling at lower economic levels as they are at higher economic levels. Many observers agree that the gap between economic goals and accomplishments affects perceptions of economic well-being and provides motivation for closing the gap.

How perceptions of economic well-being evolve is recognized as an important area of study.[1] One group of families having large differences between their present and expected levels of living were found to judge their present well-being as low, a circumstance reflected especially by the younger and future- or achievement-oriented families.[2] Information on how families in various circumstances perceive their adequacy of resources could be helpful not only to educators but also to families in analyzing the reality of their goals in relation to their resources.[3]

Complex interactions of situations and judgments about them help shape financial goals. Information from cross-sectional surveys, which identify how individuals compare at given points in time, is like taking snapshots of the population. Insights from cross-sectional surveys are turning out to be quite different from longitudinal (year-to-year) studies of the same families, which only recently are accumulating to provide such data. At given points in time, "the most successful people . . . appear to be highly motivated, oriented toward the future, and imbued with a sense of control over life's events."[4] The question is whether such attitudes are the cause or the result of success. The Panel Study of Income Dynamics (Panel Study), conducted by the Survey Research Center of the University of Michigan, contains collected information from a continuing sample of over 5,000 families since 1968. Data have been obtained on the additional measures of achievement motivation, personal efficacy or sense of control, and orientation to the future each year. In analyzing these measures in terms of whether those who held positive attitudes at the beginning of the study fared better than those who did not, researchers state, "We find almost no evidence that initial attitudes affect subsequent economic success."[5] In interpreting these differences in the implications of attitudes from studies of families at given points in time compared to studies over time, it is important to remember that attitudes as general orientations or dispositions toward certain modes of behavior are not the same thing as goals. A number of different specific goals may satisfy general values or attitudes. For a full picture, the relation of financial values or attitudes to others that are held needs to be known.

From the longitudinal study, the overriding factor that affected the economic status of the families was family composition—improved for women and children if female heads married over the survey period, worsened if wives were widowed or divorced. The fact that half of the families had a different head eleven years after the beginning of the study indicates the importance of intervening situations. Situational factors are clearly important to long-run achievements. Overall values and goals may both give direction to these changing conditions as well as provide the basis for adapting goals to changing insights and circumstances. Goals are reality-bound, giving direction to the nature of managerial activity to follow.

Standard of living is the quantity and quality of goods and services that an individual or group desires, while the *level of living* refers to the goods and services currently achieved. Desired and actual living levels may have different relations to motivation and perceptions of economic well-being. For many lower-status families, a gap between what they have and what they consider adequate can be more thwarting than challenging, while the reverse is true for families of average or higher status. Higher-income and higher-status people have greater resource availability to take corrective measures to seek fulfilling experiences.

ECONOMIC RISKS

Arriving at a realistic relationship between financial goals and needed resources is complicated by uncertainties and risks regarding the future. From a family economic perspective, Kyrk divided risks into general economic and personal categories.[6] Building on Kyrk's classifications, general economic risks are defined as those conditions in the economy beyond individual control. They affect large segments of the population and are caused by such pervasive conditions as price changes, including interest rates, and unemployment. Personal economic risks reflect hazards of individual events and are independent of general economic conditions.

From the Panel Study cited earlier, we have information on the frequency with which adverse economic events occurred to married men over the eleven-year period 1968–78 (Table 11.1). From the information comparing selected age groupings, it is apparent that a higher proportion of younger as compared to older men experienced at least one occurrence of divorce, major unemployment, involuntary job change, or involuntary residential move. On the other hand, more older than younger men experienced becoming widowed or disabled or having a major decrease in family income. Work loss due to illness affected a higher proportion of men in their middle years than it did those younger or older. For all age groups, about one-fourth of the men experienced either no undesirable events or four or more. About half experienced one to three such events.[7]

Upon analysis of factors associated with the incidence of events, it was found that men with college degrees experienced one less event, on average, than men having an eighth-grade education—an effect not altered by differences in age or income. Apparently, schooling introduces skills or other characteristics that make better-educated people more successful at avoiding undesirable life events.[8]

Risks are minimized by Social Security, welfare, and other governmental and private insurance and support programs. Where individuals contribute or receive fringe benefits, the conditions whereby risks are covered are known and provide a base on which to build. Other programs are available in case contingencies cannot be met by individuals and families. With all available support taken into account, there is still a great need for families to consider how their particular risks and uncertainties can best be met.

In financial-management terminology, personal economic risks make people vulnerable to events that have potentially costly effects on resources: property losses, disability and illness expenses, premature retirement, and premature death. Through financial management, the risks of such events can be minimized. The nonfinancial demands on the family's time, energy, attention, and concern from such contingencies

TABLE 11.1 *Frequency of undesirable life events, by age, 1968–1978 (married men in 1968)*

Events, 1968–1978	*Percentage in age groups*			
	Under 30	*40–49*	*60–69*	*All age groups*
At least 1 occurrence of:				
Becoming widowed	0	4	15	5
Becoming divorced	18	6	4	9
Major unemployment	37	24	9	29
Involuntary job change	33	23	4	22
Work loss due to illness	22	38	14	28
Becoming disabled	17	27	53	30
Involuntary residential move	25	8	7	13
Major decrease in family income	15	13	23	16
Total number of undesirable events:				
0	27	19	25	27
1–3	44	44	64	48
4 or more	29	27	11	25

Source: Greg J. Duncan and James N. Morgan, "An Overview of Family Economic Mobility," in Greg J. Duncan et al., *Years of Poverty, Years of Plenty: The Changing Economic Fortunes of American Workers and Familes* (Ann Arbor: The University of Michigan, Institute for Social Research, 1984), p. 27. Reprinted by permission of the Institute for Social Research.

might also be lessened. By financial management, anticipating or meeting the nonfinancial demands involves broader management and personal subsystem consideration.

Some known situations can become eventlike. Though the birth of *one* child is anticipated, the birth of quintuplets has to be a challenging time. Such was the case when five youngsters joined the Sidney and Suzanne Gaither family in Indianapolis in 1983. The mother observed that when the quints were born, the cost of caring for them for two years was estimated to be $80,000. Having survived that period, the parents note that organization and cooperation have been the keys. Gifts and volunteer help have contributed to the housing and care, making it possible for both parents to work. According to Suzanne, "Sidney and I both work, so we're able to make ends meet. But it's still rough, because the older the quints get, the greater the expense. Right now, they're eating more and outgrowing their clothes faster."[9] Such "events" carry long-term commitments that are both rewarding and financially awesome.

Premature retirement carries the unanticipated possibility of resources inadequate for the demands of the situation. Planned retirement is not an "event," although it carries the uncertainty that resources will fully satisfy demands. Premature death, as a financial event, transfers financial responsibilities to dependents, but plans can be made to reduce its financial effects. Families with very limited resources have little opportunity to put any plan into effect because current expenditures equal or exceed their current incomes.

Shifting financial risks from events to anticipated contingencies is part of financial management's role to promote financial security. A capacity to meet emergencies also contributes to an overall assurance that consumption levels can be maintained and that gains will be protected. The availability of alternative resources to meet event demands is the predominant variable of financial security.

INCOME TRENDS AND PATTERNS

Family financial resources come mostly from the family's earned income. In 1985, the U.S. median family income was $27,735 as can be seen in Table 11.2.

Because prices almost doubled between 1975 and 1985, the higher 1985 incomes had about the same buying power of 1975 incomes. This is shown in two ways in Table 11.2. The median family income in current dollars was $13,719 in 1975 and $27,735 in 1985 ("current dollars" means the actual dollars received for the given year). Adjusting for price level changes, the $13,719 was equivalent to $27,438 in 1985 dollars. The doubling in prices is shown by the Consumer Price Index (CPI) columns, which reflect price changes in items typically purchased by urban consumers. The CPI has historically been related to the prices of a base year. From the index of 100 for 1967, prices increased to an index of 161.2 by 1975—meaning that it took $1.61 in 1975 to buy what could have been obtained for $1.00 in 1967. By 1985, the index had risen to 322.2. The CPI column for 1985 = 100 shows the relative purchasing power when the index is converted to 1985 prices as the basis for comparison. Thus, for 50 cents one could have bought in 1975 what it would have taken $1.00 to purchase in 1985. Since 1970, families have not, in general, been able to realize the improvements in their real incomes that occurred in the 1950s and 1960s, when incomes rose relatively faster than prices. The price index has remained relatively stable since 1985, so incomes have not been eroded in the recent past to the extent that they had been somewhat earlier.

In 1984, families at the median income point had 1.7 earners, on the average. Families receiving higher incomes generally had more earners contributing to that income (except at

TABLE 11.2 *Median family income, in current and constant purchasing power, 1955–1985 (5-year increments to 1980)*

	Median family income		*Consumer price index*	
Year	*Current dollars*	*1985 dollars*	*1967 = 100*	*1985 = 100*
1955	4,418	17,743	80.2	24.9
1960	5,620	20,436	88.7	27.5
1965	6,957	23,744	94.5	29.3
1970	9,867	27,322	116.3	36.1
1975	13,719	27,438	161.2	50.0
1980	21,023	27,445	246.8	76.6
1981	23,388	27,678	272.4	84.5
1982	23,433	26,124	289.1	89.7
1983	24,674	26,648	298.4	92.6
1984	26,433	27,363	311.1	96.6
1985	27,735	27,735	322.2	100.0

Sources: U.S. Department of Commerce, Bureau of the Census, *Statistical Abstract of the U.S. for 1987,* 107th ed., p. 463; Current Population Reports, "Money Income of Households, Families and Persons in the United States: 1984," Series P-60, No. 151, p. 29; and Current Population Reports, "Money Income and Poverty Status of Families and Persons in the United States: 1985," Series P-60, No. 154, p. 2 (Washington, D.C.: U.S. Government Printing Office, 1986).

very high levels). Families with earnings of $50,000 or more in 1984 had 2.3 or more earners.[10] There is a cost, of course, to earning outside the house in terms of both employment expenses and the foregone goods and services that would otherwise have been produced at home. The nature of employment and its distance affect travel, food, and clothing costs, but another major cost when there are young children is child care. It has been observed that, depending on the number of children and other circumstances, "The value of housework is so great that when the wife joins the labor force, the loss of her home production is almost equal to her increased money earnings."[11] A significant part of goods and services produced at home is meal preparation. In taking a "value added" approach to estimating the contribution of meal preparation in finishing convenience foods or making more basic transformations in preparing raw foods for consumption, the mean net value added weekly was calculated using data from the 1977–78 U.S. Department of Agriculture Household Food Consumption Survey. The mean net value added when the female householder or spouse was employed outside the home was $31.25; it was $51.25 when she was not.[12] A wife seeking outside employment in 1977 would have needed to charge the $2,665 difference—$20 weekly or $1,040 of her earnings for the year (if her contribution to her family's meals is average)—to cover the value of her meal preparation alone. At 1986 food prices, earnings would have needed to be $1,700 to cover the difference.

Although incomes have changed over the past three decades, the share of the aggregated income received by families does not reflect a more equitable distribution (Figure 11.1). The share received by the upper range of families shows some increase, with declines occurring at the lower rather than the middle level. For example, the 20 percent of families with the highest incomes received 41.3 percent of total incomes in 1985, compared to 43.5 percent in 1985. What are some differences in the composition of lower- and higher-income families? Lower-income families have younger and older household heads, more nonwhite and female heads of households, smaller families, more members in service and operative occupations, fewer earners with full-time jobs, and less schooling.[13] Higher-income families are likely to have heads who have other income in addition to earnings, who are managers or self-employed professionals, are in financial or real-estate occupations, have completed some graduate-level work, and have a spouse who is not employed.[14]

General reference to the net worth (assets minus debts) of families is made at this point since such resources are available to families in their financial management. According to the 1983 Survey of Consumer Finances, the *mean* net worth of all families was $66,050, compared to a *median* net worth of $24,574 (Table 11.3). As could be expected, the level of net worth increased with income, age, and education. Net worth was also higher for homeowners than for renters. The significantly lower levels of median net worth indicate the effects on mean incomes of the skewed distributions toward the upper levels in each of the categories. Wealth was more heavily concentrated in a smaller number of families than was income. Two percent of the families reporting the highest incomes received 14 percent of the total income, while the 2 percent having the highest net worth held 28 percent of the total. At the same time, "almost 20 percent of the survey families had a zero or negative net worth."[15] Further, a special sample of high-income families ($50,000 or more) showed that gifts and inheritances representing more than half of their assets were not a factor for families reporting net worth under $50,000 but were for families with higher net worths. The report observed:

> Unlike the population as a whole, high-income families whose wealth is from gifts and inheritance are significantly more likely to have very

FIGURE 11.1 *Distribution of incomes to families by size and share: 1955, 1965, 1975, 1985*

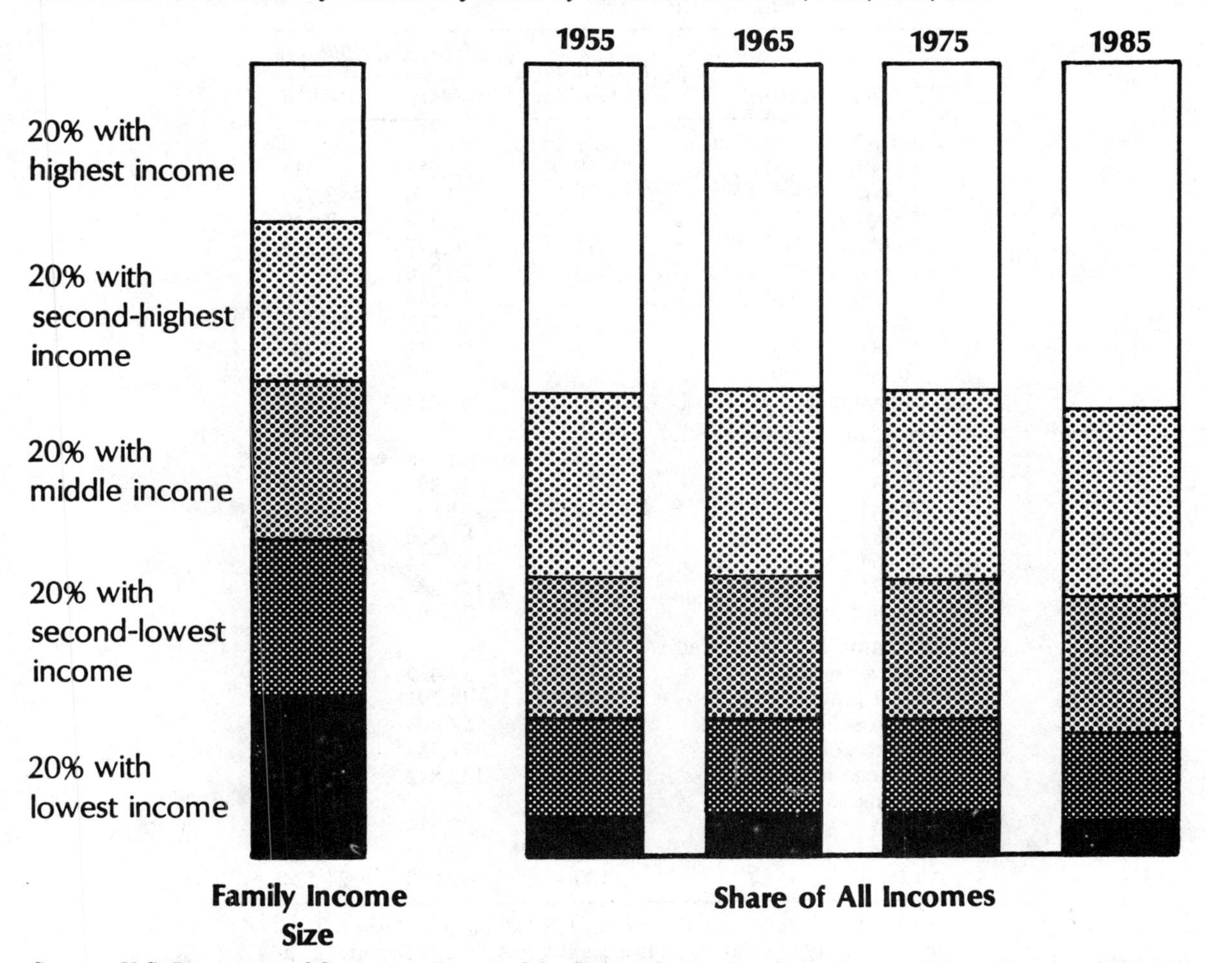

Sources: U.S. Department of Commerce, Bureau of the Census, Current Population Reports, "Money Income of Households, Families and Persons in the United States: 1984," Series P-60, No. 151, p. 38; and "Money Income and Poverty Status of Families and Persons in the United States: 1985," Series P-60, No. 154, p. 11 (Washington, D.C.: U.S. Government Printing Office, 1986).

high levels of net worth than those who accumulate their wealth through saving. . . . High-income families whose assets are derived mostly from saving have the largest part of their portfolios in business assets. In contrast, high-income families whose assets are mostly from gifts and inheritances have greater amounts of liquid and other financial assets.[16]

High-income families were also found to be more willing than the general population to take financial risk.[17]

Different occupational income patterns over the working cycle are an important factor to take into account. Both the potential income level and the point at which incomes begin to

TABLE 11.3 *Mean and median net worth, by selected family characteristics, 1983*

Characteristic	Percentage of families	Net worth (dollars) Mean	Net worth (dollars) Median
Family income (dollars)			
Less than 5,000	9	12,051	514
5,000–7,499	8	20,146	2,725
7,500–9,999	7	27,832	2,140
10,000–14,999	14	36,277	11,575
15,000–19,999	13	36,816	15,383
20,000–24,999	11	45,564	22,820
25,000–29,999	9	60,513	28,876
30,000–39,999	13	69,083	45,981
40,000–49,999	7	95,658	63,941
50,000 and more	10	262,254	130,851
Age of family head (years)			
Under 25	8	4,218	5
25–34	23	20,391	3,654
35–44	19	51,893	28,721
45–54	16	81,350	43,797
55–64	15	119,714	55,587
65–74	12	125,284	50,181
75 and over	7	72,985	35,939
Education of family head			
0–8 grades	16	37,419	16,152
9–11 grades	13	40,791	12,489
High school diploma	32	52,968	23,671
Some college	20	71,754	20,418
College degree	19	122,842	54,805
Housing status			
Own	64	97,239	50,125
Rent or other	36	10,603	15
All families	100	66,050	24,574

Source: Robert B. Avery, Gregory E. Elliehausen, and Glenn B. Canner "Summary of Consumer Finances, 1983: A Second Report," *Federal Reserve Bulletin* 70 (December 1984): 863.

decline vary by occupation (Figure 11.2). In general, the lower-income occupations tend to reach peak earnings earlier than do higher-income occupations. This difference may not be adequately considered by young families as they review life goals. An income that rises relatively fast but peaks early may have contributed to unrealistic anticipation in the early years.

In the past, women's earnings have not shown as much of a cycle as men's. A clearer cycle should appear as more women are now employed throughout their lives.

Besides sex differences, there are variations related to education, experience, location, and other situational factors. The general patterns, however, provide a basis for planning. Individual families may adjust by the husband and/or the wife seeking education to prepare for a job that will provide their preferred income; others may adjust their expectations by choosing alternative living patterns.

FIGURE 11.2 *Median income of year-round, full-time workers, by age and sex, 1985*

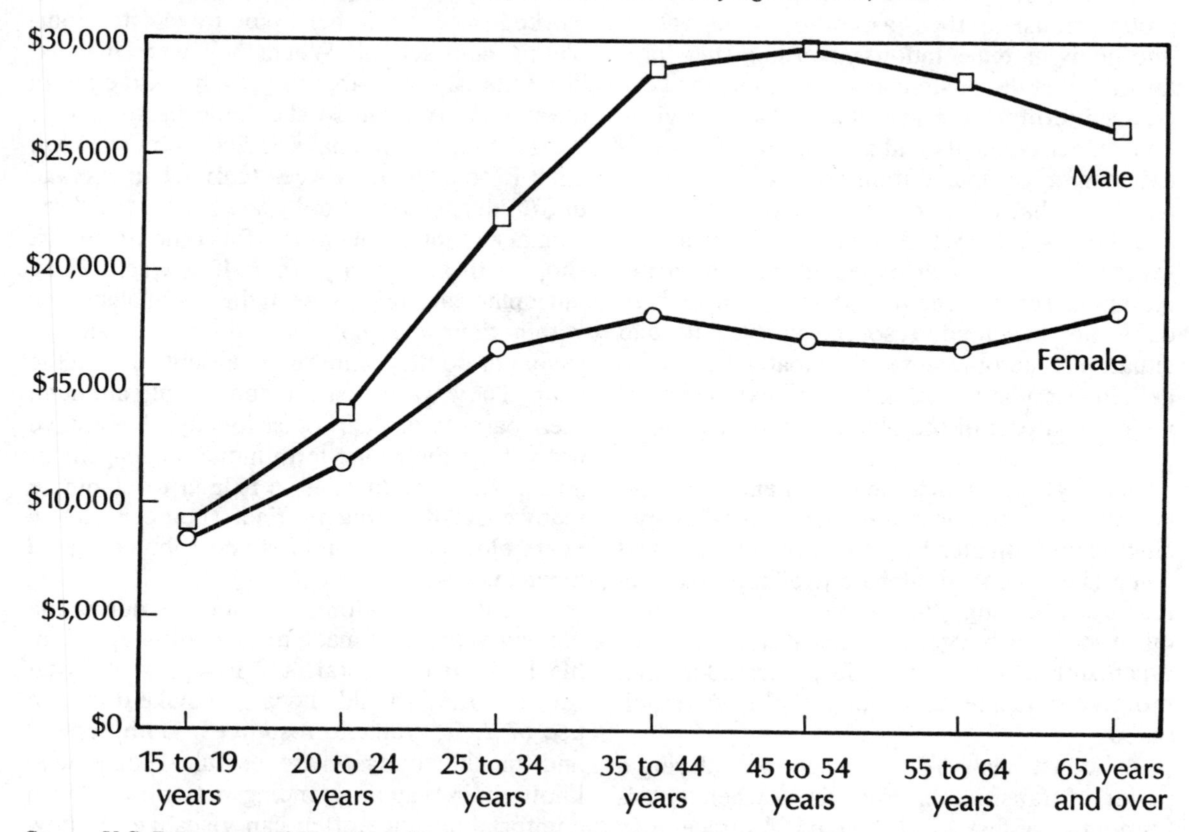

Source: U.S. Department of Commerce, Bureau of the Census, Current Population Reports, "Money Income and Poverty Status of Families and Persons in the United States: 1985," Series P-60, No. 154 (Washington, D.C.: U.S. Government Printing Office, 1986), pp. 13–14.

Throughput

Goals, resources, and managerial actions may vary with individual problems, but the basic managerial functions remain the same. The family's organization patterns and the nature of its income flow contribute to planning and implementing; they are discussed along with the related processes of budgeting and record keeping.

Most people develop a life-style consistent with their financial means, whether by trial and error or by design. For people to have a sense of financial well-being, ways of handling affairs must have evolved that seem adequate to get along and/or to get ahead. The methods may be partly unconscious and supplemental to more-formal planning activities, serving to facilitate resource use to achieve desired ends.

PLANNING

The planning and implementing functions of management translate individual aspirations and resources into spending and saving patterns. Individuals living alone, families, and groups translate their aspirations and values into goals or expectations regarding their preferred life-style. A standard of living is the generalized term for the varied goods and services that reflect the goals and aspirations of individuals and/or groups. Within groups, there is often much that is shared in terms of aspirations and goals—hence the common reference to standards as a social expectation. But in the individual sense, even though many social standards are accepted, resource constraints and situational factors, more often than not, require defining standards within the context of the situation as a part of the planning process.

Budgeting. In financial management, a *budget* is a plan—mental or written and general or specific—that indicates how (quality/quantity) and when (sequence) to allocate available financial resources among various needs and wants. Once made, a budget is a repeat-use plan with organizing features and built-in reminders that promote implementation of the plan as anticipated.

A budget has particular usefulness during a period of transition or other times when a basis for control of finances is needed. A budget may provide highly detailed and complete plans for action. But it does not ordinarily do so. Often a budget simply identifies the resources that are expected to be available in a time period and amounts expected to be allocated. Such a budget provides only broad outlines; it may tell how much can be spent for food, but not the quantities and qualities of individual items. Allocation of amounts to each category does not help to sequence the total over the year or allow for periods of greater or lesser need.

A budget is a preliminary plan that defines the inputs to which major attention will be given during the budget period. This is part of the quantitative aspect of standard setting.

For example, consider the situation of John and Jody Willis who are in their first year of marriage. John is a college junior, and Jody worked one year in her home town after completing high school. When they were married last June, she was able to get a half-time job in the university town so she could begin college classes too. Her job pays $5,800. John works in a lab 15 to 20 hours a week (earning an average of $75) during the school year. During the three summer months, he works full time at a print shop in the same city for $340 a week. They must plan carefully to reach their goal of staying within their income. They do not expect to save, nor do they want to incur debts during the year. They want to be independent, although their parents do help occasionally. They have not yet set their long-term money management goals. Their wedding gifts helped to eliminate many costs of getting married. Their car is a few years old, but it is paid for and John is a good mechanic.

To try to stay within their income during the coming year, they made an overall budget (Table 11.4). It is general, and it represents what they feel they should allocate to make optimum use of their available resources. Both general and specific budgets are useful. People who know their regular spending patterns within a comfortable range often can visualize the flow as they take stock of special needs for the year. People with different wants who are sharing the same resources may need to project spending by convenient time periods, such as per month or per pay period, to clarify possibilities. This procedure can also evolve into a realistic overall summary.

Also shown in Table 11.4 are anticipated allocations throughout the school year for items budgeted. The Willises would need a reserve of over $1,200 by the middle of the school year (early in the calendar year), particularly for tuition. With little time to accumulate savings before marriage and with the wedding expenses, they do not have cash savings. Their parents may advance the needed funds, credit may be available, or some adjustment may be possible

TABLE 11.4 *John and Jody Willis's first annual budget and anticipated money flow by month, July through June*[a]

Category	*Annual budget*	*July*	*Aug.*	*Sept.*	*Oct.*	*Nov.*	*Dec.*	*Jan.*	*Feb.*	*March*	*April*	*May*	*June*
							Dollars						
Income (after taxes)													
Husband	6,630	1,360	1,360	300	300	300	150	300	300	300	300	300	1,360
Wife	5,800	484	483	483	484	483	483	484	483	483	484	483	483
Total	12,430	1,844	1,843	783	784	783	633	784	783	783	784	783	1,843
Expenses													
Food	2,400	198	198	192	198	192	225	198	179	218	192	198	212
Rent, utilities	3,780	315	315	315	315	315	315	315	315	315	315	315	315
Transportation	2,000	80	80	600	80	80	80	80	80	600	80	80	80
Clothing	600	70	0	125	20	60	120	20	25	20	120	20	0
Medical care	200	10	20	60	10	20	10	20	10	10	10	10	10
Reading, recreation	170	10	10	20	20	10	20	10	10	20	20	10	10
Personal, other	180	15	15	15	15	15	15	15	15	15	15	15	15
Gifts, insurance	500	20	100	20	20	20	100	20	100	20	20	20	40
College	2,600	0	1,200	100	0	0	0	1,200	100	0	0	0	0
Total	12,430	718	1,938	1,447	678	712	885	1,878	834	1,218	772	668	682
Monthly net		1,126	–95	–664	106	71	–252	–1,094	–51	–435	12	115	1,161
Accumulated net		1,126	1,031	367	473	544	292	–802	–853	–1,288	–1,276	–1,161	0

[a] To conserve space, a monthly comparison is used. Weekly and biweekly pay periods could make an easier comparison.

in their food and housing allocations. The food budget allows expenditures between the low-cost and moderate plans, assuming that most meals are prepared at home.[18] Even with possible adjustments, additional resources are required now for next semester's tuition. Health services and minimal insurance are available through their school. John continues a life insurance policy that his parents started for him.

All planning is an effort to improve the possibility of achieving the desired purposes. The significance of the goals in relation to available resources dictates the form and amount of budgeting detail most likely to facilitate financial management. Sequencing of allocations by projecting income and outflow through the year helps to make the overall guidelines of an annual budget workable. For John and Jody, a major question would be their ability to repay funds advanced during the years, as planned. Extending the overall budget into a "flow chart" also helps identify vulnerable periods during the year. Except for the summer months, John and Jody would have real problems if an unexpected expense, such as a major car repair, occurred. A new budget would have to be developed in such a case.

Income and many other factors influence the planning and controlling of expenditures. Compared with middle-income earners, people with low incomes may have difficulty in planning expenditures because they continually have to adjust expenditures to make ends meet. High-income families may function well with a very generalized plan for expenditures.

In order to set up a budget as detailed as the one in Table 11.4, the Willises would at least have to arrive at general standards for their needs in specific categories. For example, perhaps they decide that the clothing allowance should allow for two pairs of shoes for each of them, a jacket for John, a dress for Jody, and miscellaneous small articles. From this point, plans for actual purchases may readily develop because the specific standard setting and sequencing alternatives and decisions can be realistically made.

A change in due dates can sometimes be arranged if a more convenient due date for fixed commitments, such as insurance, would make it easier to meet payments. When expenditures settle into a satisfactory pattern, a flow chart that registers due dates and amounts for major commitments often provides an adequate planning tool. The sequencing of fixed commitments can be studied for their relation to income. Major outlays also need periodic review as to whether the benefits are in line with the personal qualitative and quantitative standards they were planned to meet. Besides providing a summary for review, a chart showing fixed commitments can also become a reminder for and record of payment.

Individual family expenditures should be expected to differ from the *average* expenditures of families because resources, values, and situations differ. Prepared budgets or information from expenditure surveys can be useful to individuals for comparison. The table from a recent national survey (Table 11.5) clearly reflects the impacts of age, number of earners, number of persons living in the unit, home ownership, and race on both income and expenditures.

The relation of income to age shows it increasing gradually until the middle years, when income, on average, declines. The average size of household shows a pattern similar to income: increasing and then decreasing. Among two or more person units, a higher portion of income is spent when there is only one earner. Families who rent are more likely to have lower incomes and to be younger than home owners. Although similar in age, black families' incomes and expenditures were considerably lower than those of white and other races. We can gain insights from these and other comparisons that suggest the differences among groups of consumer units with varying circumstances. So it is with individuals and families: Their particular goals and

TABLE 11.5 *Comparisons of factors affecting average annual income and expenditures of urban consumer units, 1984*

Factor	*Comparison*							
*Age**	*All units*	*Under 25*	*25–34*	*35–44*	*45–54*	*55–64*	*65–74*	*75 and over*
Income	$24,578	$12,579	$24,652	$32,058	$32,285	$26,989	$16,815	$12,442
Expenditures	21,788	13,178	21,506	27,702	28,623	23,000	15,873	11,196
Number of persons	2.6	1.8	2.7	3.4	3.1	2.5	1.9	1.5
Number of persons	*All units*	*One*	*Two*	*Three*	*Four*	*Five*	*Six or more*	
Income	24,578	14,740	24,947	28,660	31,370	33,194	30,933	
Expenditures	21,788	13,220	21,351	25,955	28,421	29,546	28,032	
Age*	46.2	47.1	52.2	43.3	39.8	41.7	43.4	
		One-person units		*Two-or-more-person units*				
Number of earners	*All units*	*No earner*	*Earner*	*No earner*	*1 earner*	*2 earners*	*3 earners*	
Income	24,578	8,337	17,938	12,188	23,534	31,847	40,231	
Expenditures	21,788	8,746	15,605	13,246	21,957	27,348	34,854	
Age*	46.2	68.2	35.7	62.0	46.8	40.2	47.4	
		Housing tenure			*Race**			
Housing Tenure/Race	*All Units*	*Home owner*	*Renter*		*White/Other*	*Black*		
Income	24,578	29,953	16,511		25,566	16,046		
Expenditure	21,788	26,002	15,339		22,659	14,395		
Age*	46.2	50.9	39.1		46.4	45.0		
Percent home owner	60	100	—		63	42		

* Refers to reference person, the one first mentioned by respondent as owner or renter of the home

Source: U.S. Department of Labor, Bureau of Labor Statistics, "Consumer Expenditure Survey, Results from 1984," *News,* USDL 86-258 (June 22, 1986), Tables 3, 4, 7, 8.

circumstances are primary in determining how financial resources are used.

Long-range planning. How can resource projections be made to cover the family life cycle? They can be only tentative, but trying to project into the future can help forecast major periods of opportunity and pressure. Planning to take advantage of opportunities and strengths and to try to reduce uncertainties and risks, while difficult, can help keep people less vulnerable to passing fads—as well as to event demands.

While projecting goals and resources is not possible with specificity, consideration of some "what if" situations can be useful in evolving long-term directions (Table 11.6). The many-faceted question might be addressed to young couples. Their responses have, in turn, been related to discussion in the planning chapter about approaches to planning and the nature of foresight. Unknown aspects could alter the planning orientation. Individuals can also use such conjecture in clarifying their own position.

As indicated, the foregoing situations are illustrative and tentative in their implications. The planning chapter made clear that although individuals may seem to be more open or closed in their general response to change, their responses to given situations may be otherwise. Periods of transition, pressures, frustrating days, boredom, or a special combination of factors may promote a more open reaction on the part of a person whose ordinary preference is toward regularity and consistency. People whose general orientation is to be responsive and open to change also find too many loose ends at times and need to "close in" for a while. Even so, decisions related to conditions that have ongoing impacts on long-range goals and styles of living are the more critical ones. Learning to foresee or anticipate reactions to situations and to effects of decisions with a degree of dependability is fundamental to effective planning, particularly in terms of a long-range perspective.

For its implication for financial management, recognition also needs to be given to the other possibility of seeking morphostatic, morphogenic, and random areas of response at a given point in time. If a person's earning situation is controlled, the opportunity to "randomize" free time is a needed balance for many people. The opposite case of wanting something consistent off the job when its demands are varied may also be true. In financial planning, these varied responses need to be recognized for their interrelationships. A random decision to buy a car on credit may introduce a need for morphostatic responses for a period of time. Unless "space" is built into the planning for such random opportunities, problems may be raised in other areas of managing. If finances are tight, an individual's randomness may need to be in the time-use area, or vice versa.

Nature of income flow. Whether planning for the long or short run, stability, frequency, and amount of income are important factors affecting its availability, its flow. A stable income allows either long-term or short-term planning, while a fluctuating income requires a relatively longer planning period. During a year, two families may receive the same total income: one, stable in amount and timing, and the other, fluctuating. The fluctuating income requires careful planning since current spending cannot be directly related to current income. Where the income is steady, however, a balance between them can be drawn more readily.

Income frequency is the line between pay periods. The requirement of financial expenditures is more highly related to the payday when the time between pay periods is short than when long: That is, a higher portion of expenditures cluster around payday.[19] Food, household operation, personal, and total expenditures are especially oriented to payday.

Wage contracts increasingly emphasize weekly pay periods; apparently families find planning and controlling expenditures easier with short pay periods. If wages are received more than once a month, portioning the income

TABLE 11.6 *Illustrative long-range planning questions and orientations of responses*

Question: What would be your reaction upon learning that the usual pattern for your anticipated major income source is:	*Response having goal clarification and/or resource assessment relation*	*Implied nature of planning system orientation*
1. Regular, but peaks early at midlevel, e.g., clerical, draftsman	a. Have our children early	a. Conceptual foresight
	b. Develop a specific planning/saving plan, including investments	b. Perceptual foresight
	c. Make a change: start own business as soon as possible	c. Morphogenic if goal related; otherwise, possibly random
	d. Reinforce income later with second family earner	d. Morphogenic
	e. Grateful for the security of regular income	e. Morphostatic
	f. Take advantage of ways to improve in job—maybe qualify for supervisory role	f. Morphogenic; conceptual foresight
2. Fluctuating, but averages well, e.g., sales (commission), building trade	a. Take the bad with the good	a. Random; short run
	b. Need second earner in stable job for balance	b. Morphogenic/morphostatic
	c. Use credit for hard times; build equity during good times	c. Morphogenic; conceptual foresight
	d. Plan spending on basis of average income	d. Perceptual foresight
3. Slow at first, peaks later, but at above-average level, e.g., professional, self-employed	a. Live simply now; too busy, anyway	a. Morphogenic; perceptual foresight
	b. Can do better for children if wait awhile to have them	b. Conceptual foresight
	c. Costs and delays aren't worth it	c. Conceptual foresight or morphostatic—conceptual if based on recognition that basic goals would be frustrated by long-range demands; morphostatic if preference is for more stability

over the month limits the money available in any pay period and thus simplifies control. With pay periods up to a month apart, large obligations are more likely to be assumed near payday.[20]

The amount of income is a major factor affecting planning and control of finances. While younger and lower-income families may reflect less satisfaction with outcomes, they generally do more planning.[21] The combination of very low incomes and larger families tends, on the other hand, to deter planning and controlling.[22] Planning becomes problematical at the point where many demands meet too few resources. Higher income permits discretionary choices and permits a future orientation to spending.

Budgeting for either the short or long range may be unsuccessful, either because the estimates are unrealistic or because the expense totals carry no sense of commitment or understanding about how the overall guidelines can be used in daily spending decisions. Tying plans to important goals can increase a commitment; this is often the effect of purchasing on credit. A credit obligation may provide the commitment that a plan to save for the item would not provide. When credit is used in this way, the item needs to be worth the additional expense.

Making plans for spending and staying with them is a problem of commitment as well as knowledge of the process—not unlike dieting. Many people first begin serious budgeting during a transition period or a time of emergency when changed spending patterns are necessary. Expecting that an overall budget for a year or a month will magically become an effective plan for handling daily financial affairs is even more problematic for the person or family beginning to budget expenses. Long-term or general budgeting cannot be expected to provide details for day-to-day action; more detailed planning is needed to define the standards and sequences of a specific plan. The effort involved in keeping appropriate records is often worthwhile in providing the evidence needed for realistic planning.

Methods of handling risks—occupation/education. People may prepare themselves for varied employment-income patterns; stable employment may provide either a steady or a fluctuating income. Salaried professional positions provide a steadier income than does self-employment, but self-employed people tend to have more opportunities to increase their gains in an expanding economy. The same opportunity to realize greater gains under favorable economic conditions (when risk is assumed) applies to wage earners. Earners in more stable occupations, such as transportation and public utilities, do not receive increments as readily in expansion periods as do construction workers; nor do reductions and job losses occur as soon during recessions. Individuals can choose to increase or lessen the risks, thereby affecting their alternatives accordingly. Some individuals accept more risks for the challenges and the potential for a greater gain that may evolve. One way individuals can decrease their risk of unemployment, in spite of vulnerability to economic conditions, is to obtain an educational background that is flexible enough to allow movement to new occupational opportunities.

—Health and safety practices. Health and safety practices may help people avoid undue personal risks. Risk can be reduced, but it is nearly impossible to eliminate. Fires and accidents in homes continue to be high. Insurance protection provides for sharing risks of economic loss. If a contingency occurs, the individual's economic loss is minimized, while those who do not experience the loss share its cost; if the contingency does not occur, the nominal cost of sharing has purchased protection and an increased sense of security.

—Private and social insurance. In recent decades, responsibility for protection is shared among individuals and families, employers, and society. Government, employer, and various group programs have broadened their benefit packages to the extent that personally initiated protection by employees becomes supplemental. Dependents are frequently included in health, liability, and other insurance plans. With such assistance in basic areas, individuals and families are generally more able to protect themselves from the impact of a major financial loss from some occurrences than was the case in the past. However, with the mobility that occurs from region to region with the same employer or among different employers, it behooves most families to consider the nature of protection needed and available as shifts are contemplated. Otherwise, gaps in major risk areas can occur.

The prepaid Social Security programs, which provide income and health benefits to employees or their survivors upon their retirement or disability, are broad-based forms of insurance. Beneficiaries are taxed, but the benefits are set by law and are not necessarily commensurate with taxes. The rate for employees, to be matched by employers, for the Old-Age, Survivors, and Disability Insurance (OASDI) is projected to increase regularly from 5.7 percent on maximum earnings of $43,800 in 1987. Added to the OASDI tax is a 1.45 percent health insurance tax, bringing the total to 7.15 percent. The maximum tax on $43,800 for 1987 was $3,131.70. Paying at the same rate, the average earner paid $1,250 in Social Security taxes in 1986. Increases in benefits to match rises in prices help to alleviate anxieties of retired and disabled people who have seen their fixed income eroded by rising prices.

The Social Security System continues to evolve. Amendments have addressed the benefit and tax structures and adjusted special features, such as not reducing benefits of surviving spouses who remarry. Also, beneficiaries over 65 have been allowed higher earnings ($8,160 for retired workers over 65 in 1987). Lower-income workers receive higher proportions of their previous year's earnings at retirement than those with higher incomes.

A question of interest over the fifty-year experience with Social Security is how the program would affect individual plans for retirement. Over the twenty-two years from 1962 to 1984, the percentage of persons sixty-five and over receiving income from assets increased to 68 from 54 (Table 11.7). The share that asset income represented of the total incomes of persons sixty-five and over increased to 28 percent from 16 percent. The share that earnings represented of total income decreased comparably, to 16 percent from 28 percent. Private pensions more than doubled in the percent receiving them, but remained small as a percent of total retirement income. Now that most retirees are covered by Social Security, it seems that it provides the basic support supplemented by other pensions and savings and less by earnings.

—*Public assistance*. The public-assistance aspects of Social Security are welfare programs, noncontributory by beneficiaries, to benefit those with inadequate resources who can establish their qualification for assistance.

TABLE 11.7 *Sources of income of persons 65 and older, 1962 and 1984*

Income source	*Percent receiving*		*Percent of total income*	
	1962	*1984*	*1962*	*1984*
Social Security	69	91	31	38
Private pensions	9	24	3	6
Government employee pensions	5	14	6	7
Assets	54	68	16	28
Earnings	36	21	28	16

Source: Melinda Upp, "Fast Facts and Figures about Social Security," *Social Security Bulletin* 49 (June 1986): 7.

Both the states and the federal government interact to support and administer such assistance. Local governments and agencies also provide supplemental services.

As broad plans for minimizing major risks continue to evolve, coverage for risks that occur less frequently may be omitted. Otherwise, insuring of risks by families may unknowingly be duplicated. The individual must be alert in order to have the best possible coverage for the insurance expenditure.

—*Consumer credit*. Consumer credit provides the opportunity to alter the timing of resource use—for a price. Consumer credit allows people to acquire money, goods, or services by undertaking an obligation to repay from future income. The total available resources are not increased in the long run. In fact, they are decreased to the extent of the finance charges. Credit adds flexibility to financial management and adds a sense of security for some families. The advantages include the possibility of meeting emergency expenses when no other means are available; the use of durable goods while loan payments are being made; the opportunity to buy on sale or when other advantageous situations arise; and the opportunity to repay the debt in cheaper, inflated money during times of rising prices. Using credit depends on its availability according to an individual's credit rating and on the willingness of an individual or family to pay the cost of credit.

A consumer credit obligation is a short-term transaction, but it can be used over long periods of time. If people build their credit obligations up to $1,000 and maintain them there by the continual replacement of old obligations as they are paid off with new ones, in effect they increase their available resources by this amount. A number of families do this successfully and consider the costs worthwhile. Others get in the habit of such borrowing and find themselves seriously overextended before they realize it. Each family should question whether the continual use of its available credit for current consumption is worth the flexibility sacrificed for meeting emergencies.

A related aspect of coping with emergencies is the decision to use credit to finance major purchases even though there are available assets. One rationale often given is that savings are protected for emergency use and the commitment to repay the obligation will be honored, while an individual's own commitment to replenish savings may not be fulfilled. An assumption that better service accompanies credit use is not generally a safe one.

The amount of consumer credit held has increased steadily over the years (Figure 11.3).

FIGURE 11.3 *Consumer credit, 1970 to 1984*

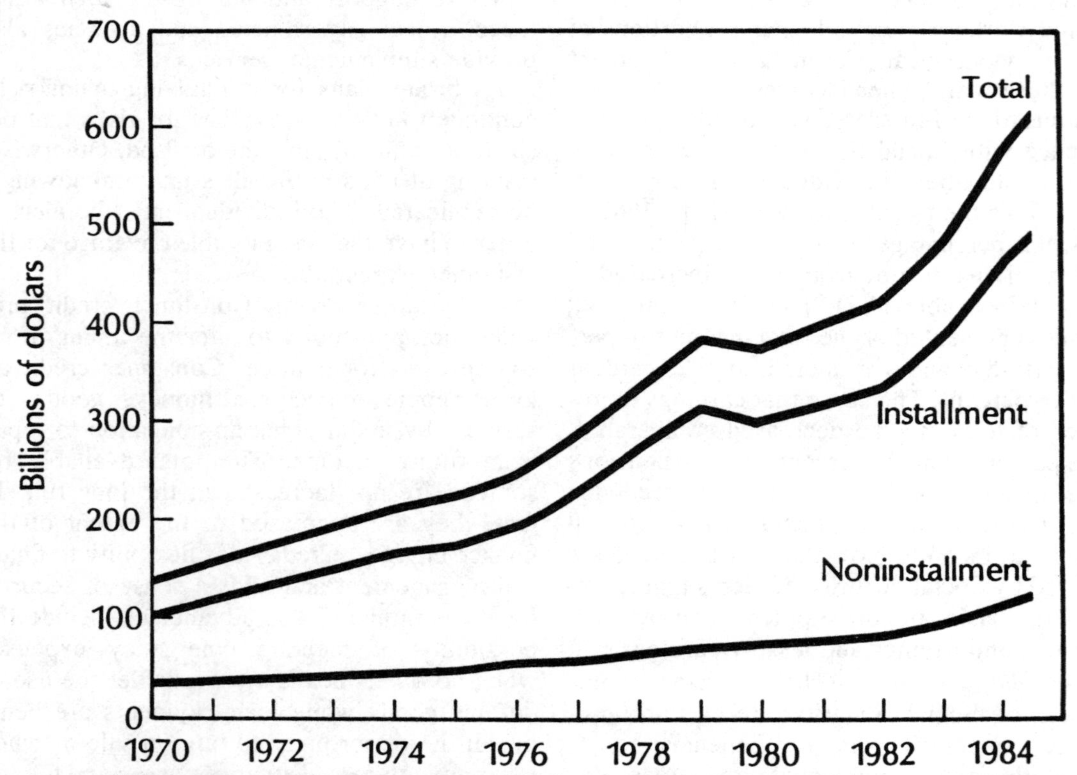

Sources: U.S. Department of Commerce, Bureau of the Census, *Statistical Abstract of the U.S., 1985,* 105th ed., p. 502; and *Statistical Abstract of the U.S., 1986,* 106th ed., p. 502 (Washington, D.C.: U.S. Government Printing Office).

TABLE 11.8 *Ratio of monthly installment debt payment in 1983 to family income before taxes in 1982*

Family characteristic	Ratio of installment debt to income				
	No debt	*1–9 percent*	*10–19 percent*	*20 percent or more*	*Total*
Family income (dollars)					
Less than 5,000	84	3	3	10	100
5,000–7,499	79	7	4	10	100
7,500–9,999	65	14	12	9	100
10,000–14,999	66	14	13	7	100
15,000–19,999	56	21	17	6	100
20,000–24,999	51	27	18	5	100
25,000–29,999	50	31	16	3	100
30,000–39,999	44	45	10	1	100
40,000–49,999	42	47	9	2	100
50,000 and more	53	39	8	1	100
Age of family head (years)					
Under 25	55	21	16	9	100
25–34	45	34	15	7	100
35–44	45	36	14	6	100
45–54	51	31	12	5	100
55–64	68	18	9	4	100
65–74	86	7	4	3	100
75 and over	94	2	2	2	100
All families	59	25	11	5	100

Source: Robert B. Avery, Gregory E. Elliehausen, and Glenn B. Canner, "Survey of Consumer Finances, 1983: A Second Report," *Federal Reserve Bulletin* 70 (December 1984): 860.

Installment credit for which there is an identified interest charge and repayment period has represented about 80 percent of total consumer debt in recent years. Of all installment credit, automobile purchases comprise about 36 percent.

How does this aggregate information relate to the situation of families? According to the 1983 Survey of Consumer Finances, 59 percent of all families reported no installment debt (Table 11.8). The percentage of families with ratios of less than 10 percent of their income committed increased with income—such debt probably being a matter of convenience. Families in the 10–19-percent range of debt to income were relatively evenly distributed through the middle-income ranges and employment years. About 10 percent of lower-income and younger families reported installment debt-to-income ratios above 20 percent. These are the families with both need and limited flexibility—and, therefore, vulnerability.

Filings for personal bankruptcy have increased in both the United States and Canada in recent years. A researcher studying a sample of Canadian families to identify characteristics associated with bankruptcy found that young families getting into financial difficulties "were borrowing too much too soon, were unable to handle their finances effectively, and found relief by declaring bankruptcy."[23] Besides overextension of credit, other complicating circumstances were unemployment, marital difficulties, and illness. Lack of understanding of the credit system and money management skills led the researcher to observe that "opportunities should be made available for people to learn the skills to manage finances in today's cashless and complex society to prevent crisis in the families of the future."[24]

—*Material assets*. Material assets are the owned resources that can be assigned an economic value and that may be used for protection, exchange, consumption, or investment/production. Their availability can simplify management of unforeseen events. Such assets may be part of a plan to provide the necessary resources to meet contingencies, especially those that cannot be insured against. Liquid assets, which can be readily converted into cash, can provide the needed quick response to a current need as well as provide security against future contingencies. However, resources may not need to be readily available to relieve the emergency situation. Equity in a tangible asset, such as housing or life insurance cash values, can also be used to obtain credit in emergency situations.

More low-income than high-income families are without liquid assets, life insurance, or equity in their homes. Although younger family heads are almost as likely to have some savings as older family heads, the median amount is much lower. The importance of savings in a family's total plan varies with the life-cycle stage and with its vulnerability to unforeseen situations.

The uncertainty that changes in the price level bring was discussed in relation to incomes earlier in the chapter. Protecting against price effects in the use of that income has become more and more problematical. When prices rise in such major categories as food, housing, transportation, and medical care, the impacts on expenditures are critical. Recent changes in both prices and interest rates, along with sluggish incomes, have affected purchases of larger items, such as houses and cars. Even so, families and lenders have been creative in evolving new forms of ownership arrangements. Ownership is a usual approach to try to protect resources when the price level is rising, because the value of goods increases in relation to the value of money. To hold their relative economic position, people who expect prices to rise or who want to protect themselves in this event seek places for their resources that take advantage of the increasing value of goods compared with money: stocks, real estate, and consumer durables that rise in value with the rise in prices. Variations in the traditional relationships of stocks, real estate, and durable goods to prices are reminders that the special economic conditions that prevail at any given time need to be recognized.

Money may be borrowed with the expectation that the cost will be less now than later. A higher future price to be paid for durable goods is considered a primary justification for borrowing now; repayment of a loan in the future with cheaper dollars is an additional incentive. However, if prices are expected to decline, the argument is reversed; dollars buy more as time passes. Renting items is advantageous if they can be purchased later with enough fewer dollars to justify the extra costs of rental.

Having savings in fixed-dollar accounts or in such investments as bonds, interest accounts, life insurance equity, and annuities is usually desirable in times of price decline. Loaned money is expected to be repaid with more valuable dollars. The preponderance of funds is concentrated less on goods and more on dollars and their increasing purchasing power. Even during a period of rising prices, some assets in a safe and liquid fixed-dollar account provide the flexibility often needed for emergencies or to protect other investments.

People often wish to protect themselves from the extreme effects of both rising and falling prices and so choose to have items on both sides of the balance. Owning a house and having a savings account is an example of hedging against future price changes in either direction.

Seeking the help of competent financial planners is advisable. They can help clarify retirement and other financial goals, advise regarding investments, interpret appropriate tax considerations/advantages, and insure adequate protection against risks. Advisers commonly relate financial planning to a pyramid, building first on a solid foundation (Figure 11.4). Each person's pyramid will be unique because his or her needs and orientations to security versus risk vary.

Financial management to minimize the effects of changing prices involves awareness of general trends and a degree of maneuverability, because actual situations usually have some aspects that deviate from the typical case. Flexibility also helps in other risk areas of financial management. Management opportunities for minimizing risks depend heavily on inputs—an awareness of risk potential, evolving goals to reduce their effects, and the availability of resources to do so.

Record keeping. From a managerial perspective, records are a tool for the exercise of control. Records provide tangible evidence for checking the allocation of expenditures according to plan. For many families, records are kept to provide information they otherwise might not keep in order to document allowable tax deductions. Keeping records to control tax payments is a bona fide reason that often provides insight into the overall financial situation that is managerially as useful as the tax information. For example, mileage records on a car can help determine whether the allowable or actual mileage rate is advantageous for figuring the gasoline tax. Even though it turns out that the allowable deduction is advantageous, the records could also be a basis for deciding to keep the car because it is relatively inexpensive to operate, rather than trade it in as had been anticipated.

Useful records for overall planning include those on major assets acquired, income and current consumption expenditures, credit obligations, health expenditures, and charitable contributions. Informal records—like checkbook summaries, which show cash on hand and chronological payments—are probably less useful for planning future allocation of resources than are other classified records.

Allocating to children. A special aspect of financial planning within families relates to how allocations are made to children. This has importance to children because the setting provides an opportunity to learn about money management. Whatever the method, providing experience in the use of money is central. Several patterns by which children receive funds can be observed: allowances, money doled out as needed, and payment for work done around the house or for others. The methods may or may not contribute to children's understanding of financial management. Each method has particular advantages. An allowance helps younger children learn to assume responsibility for certain decisions and planning within definite resource limits. Where family incomes are regular, allowances fit into the family routines—a factor that has probably influenced their use.

The dole method, if used advantageously, can be mutually beneficial in helping the child to gain insight into the family's finances. Doling should then be related to the family's ability to provide money, with amounts varying accordingly. Younger children "on the dole" particularly need assistance in their decisions regarding spending or saving, if no experience with allowances is provided. Teenagers are more likely to receive money for special purposes, often supplemented by earnings from work at home or for others.

Paying children for work at home is another way to distribute funds to them. Many parents feel that children should do some jobs around the house for no pay, payment being reserved for special contributions. Some children feel they are expected to do too much without pay.[25]

Where children's work at home makes it possible for both parents to earn, some sharing of the income may be considered by some parents as part of the team effort. Hopefully, such an approach contributes an appreciation of the value of the work at home. Whether pay for work contributes to an understanding of financial management depends, in part, on how the earnings relate to total family welfare. The pur-

FIGURE 11.4 *Building a long-range financial plan*

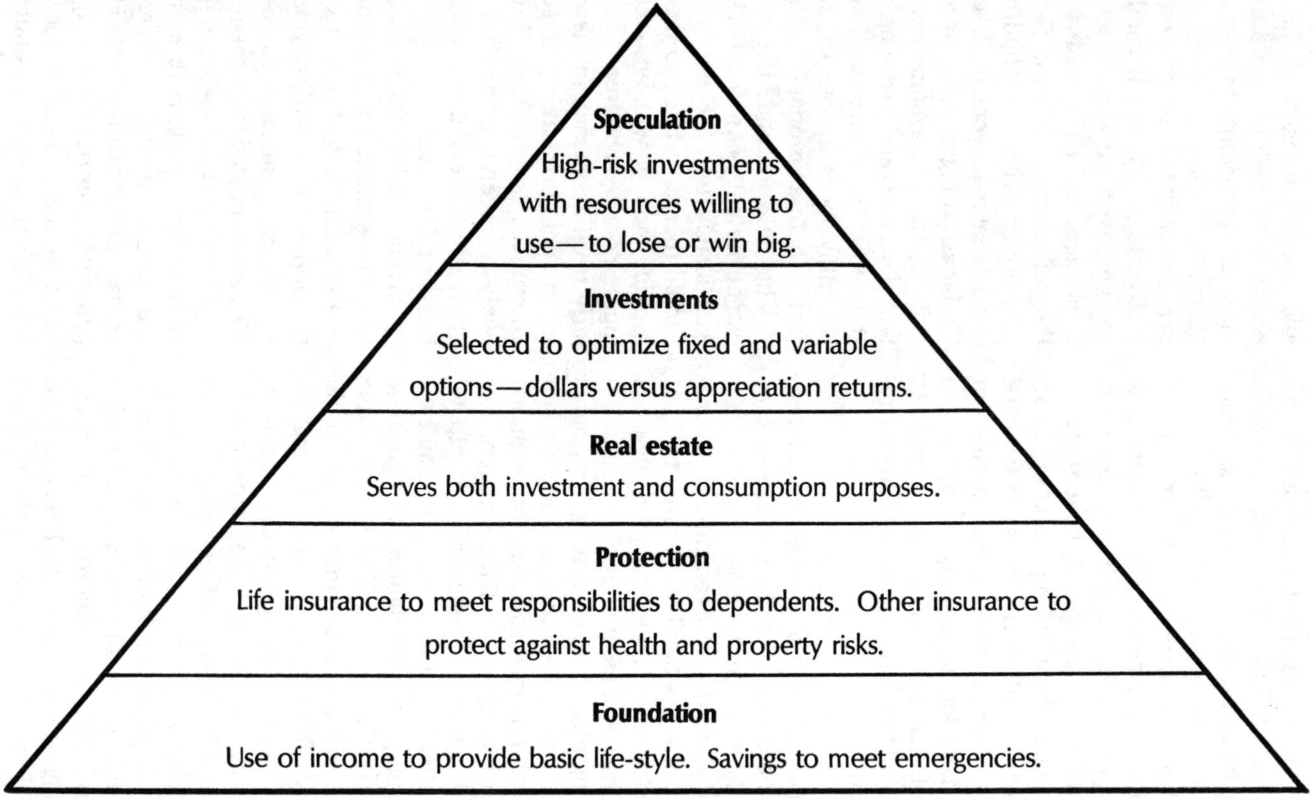

Speculation
High-risk investments with resources willing to use—to lose or win big.

Investments
Selected to optimize fixed and variable options—dollars versus appreciation returns.

Real estate
Serves both investment and consumption purposes.

Protection
Life insurance to meet responsibilities to dependents. Other insurance to protect against health and property risks.

Foundation
Use of income to provide basic life-style. Savings to meet emergencies.

poses for which they are to be used are also important understandings, as with the other methods. Learning to assume responsibility for meeting needs is another important aspect—placing spending and saving for fundamentals into a meaningful balance with today's special interest.

IMPLEMENTING

Planning is only part of financial management. Implementing provides the test situation for plans as the action is carried out.

As was discussed in the last section, budgets are plans for future expenditures. They also can be used to control spending.

Use of records. The most direct form of record keeping is the combined budget and record. Table 11.9 can easily become such a form. Space can be allotted to enter individual expenditure items for each category. Actual monthly totals can be compared with planned expenditures, and a monthly net figure can be calculated. If the net amount is close to the planned amount, small variations from the planned expenditures (part of the standard) are probably unimportant. If, when checking planned and actual expenditures, people find that the difference is significant, they may need to make some adjustments or keep closer control of expenditures. Inexperienced people or anyone who is in a period of stress or transition can benefit from developing a plan for spending (a budget) and from following through by checking actual expenditures against it.

A plan for meeting fixed commitments may also become the actual record (Table 11.9). The amounts to be allocated are knowns, and the due-date schedule is essentially a reminder of sequence. When their obligations are actually paid, plans can become a record if any changes in the amount and date of payment are noted. The fixed commitments of Martin and Rose Gomez claim about 40 percent of their income. February and April are particularly heavy months for which to plan, coming so soon after end-of-the-year expenses. They might find it worthwhile to readjust due dates to help equalize committed amounts throughout the year.

Resource allocation by fixed commitment may direct resources to important uses and avoid dissipating uncommitted funds for less important uses. When fixed obligations limit the leeway to absorb emergencies, however, the risk of this approach may outweigh its advantages. The degree of patterning that is most effective for helping to direct resource allocation will vary with each family.

In addition to helping to control plans for expenditures, records can also play an important role in planning by providing information useful for making future plans. The reason for the keeping of records will determine their type, categories, specificity, and accuracy. Traditional categories for recording resource activity have been food, clothing, housing, and other types of goods and services, plus assets and credit use. Although food items are generally intended to satisfy hunger and provide nourishment, different underlying purposes may affect the kind of food purchased. Some foods have recreational, psychological, or social purposes in addition to the physiological needs. Trying to record in relation to a specific category is complicated by the variety of purposes for which many purchases are made.

Organization patterns. Patterns or standing plans "facilitate" financial planning and implementing by specifying roles and/or procedures. Organization thus assists actions in financial affairs, influencing how allocations are made and when spending is done.

Effectiveness seems to depend more on the procedure than on who follows it. The one serving as the family's financial manager may submit proposals or plans for spending to the other and then implement them after mutual decisions are made. Successful responsibility for a role depends on interests, experience, work sched-

TABLE 11.9 *Fixed-dollar commitments by Martin and Rose Gomez[a] by months*

Commitment	*Jan.*	*Feb.*	*March*	*April[b]*	*May*	*June*	*July*	*Aug.*	*Sept.*	*Oct.*	*Nov.*	*Dec.*	*Year*
Mortgage													
Date due/paid	31/26	28/26	31/29	30/29	31/	30/	31/	31/	30/	31/	30/	31/	
Amount	$290	290	290	290	290	290	290	290	290	290	290	290	3480
Real-estate taxes													
Date due/paid	/	15/12	/	/	/	/	/	15/	/	/	/	/	
Amount		410						410					820
Insurance													
Date due/paid	/	/	/	/	/	8/	/	/	/	/	/	/	
Amount						120						120	240
Utilities[c]													
Date due/paid	20/15	20/15	20/15	20/19	20/	20/	20/	20/	20/	20/	20/	20/	
Amount	110	110	110	110	110	110	110	110	110	110	110	110	1320
Life insurance													
Husband													
Date due/paid	/	/	/	5/1	/	/	/	/	/	5/	/	/	
Amount				260						260			520
Wife													
Date due/paid	10/8	/	/	/	/	/	10/	/	/	/	/	/	
Amount	95						95						190
Mann's Auto Mart													
Date due/paid	20/15	20/15	20/15	20/19	20/	20/	/	/	/	/	/	/	
Amount	200	200	200	200	200	200							1200
Sanchez' Department Store													
Date due/paid	10/8	10/8	10/9	10/9	10/	10/	10/	10/	10/	10/	10/	10/	
Amount due/paid	55/80	55/30	55/40	55/65	55/	55/	55/	55/	55/	55/	55/	55/	660
Church													
Date due/paid	1/7	1/4	1/4	1/1	1/	1/	1/	1/	1/	1/	1/	1/	
Amount	60	60	60	70	60	60	60	60	60	70	60	70	750
United Way													
Date due/paid	31/26	/	/	30/29	/	/	31/	/	/	31/	/	/	
Amount	35			35			35			35			140
Fixed commitments:													
Total	835	1125	715	1020	715	835	645	925	515	820	515	645	9320

[a] 3 children, ages 4, 7, and 9
[b] Payments illustrated through April only
[c] Budget plan is used with cost estimated across the year, omitting seasonal variations.

ules, and so on, rather than on traditional allocation of roles—that is, the man making the decisions about large purchases, such as automobiles. Determining organization patterns is a major part of financial planning, especially for young couples.

Delegating responsibilities for meeting common financial goals assumes some prior consensus or knowledge. It does not necessarily mean that others are not involved in choices. Responsibility may be assumed for any aspect of the choice or for complete implementation, and the extent of role assumption may depend on the degree of consensus that has evolved. When greater consensus develops with time, less extensive planning is needed. Thus, in early marriage, planning and consensus are related to a high degree, but later there is apparently a tendency toward less-detailed planning with high consensus.[26]

Output

DEMAND RESPONSES

The expected outcome of financial management is to respond to those demands that focus on the use of money as effectively as possible. On the demand side, the degree to which expected results have been achieved is reflected in the sense of satisfaction and fulfillment that has accompanied the scope of decisions and actions relating to allocation of available funds—such as contributing to causes, providing for personal enrichment experiences, purchasing and consuming goods and services, protecting against or meeting crises, and providing for the anticipated wants and needs of the future. The feedback from financial activities provides the managerial information needed to clarify whether the results relating to ongoing needs are making the desired progress or whether directions should be reoriented.

RESOURCE CHANGES

On the resources side, results are summarized by how well money has been utilized in combination with other resources to provide for the present and future. For most families, day-to-day living expenses and accompanying short-term benefits use most current resources. In addition, increments to available resources occur through increasing human capital and net worth.

Human capital. The growth of the individuals involved in the process of financial management represents an important outcome: their ability to identify the meaningful issues and to cope with them effectively. Increased managerial skill is part of that. Included also are the increased knowledge and capacities for earning and for performing effectively in the various roles at home and in society that are both desired and required. All of these results are represented by human capital changes.

Human capital assets, such as education and health, have long been recognized for their actual and potential contributions to the productivity of individuals and, therefore, to family income. Higher income permits more discretionary spending. Families with highly educated adults spend more than the average amount of money on formal and informal education—a fact that reinforces evidence of an interaction between opportunity and choice.

Net worth. Net worth is the balance between the value of assets and liabilities. The specific assets and liabilities of a family can change considerably, as when a home is purchased, without making large changes in net worth (see Table 11.10).

Bankruptcy may result when net worth is seriously out of balance on the negative side, that is, when liabilities are extended beyond the ability to recover. Spending beyond the capacity to pay or attitudes that reflect limited responsibility toward payment can lead to bankruptcy.

TABLE 11.10 *End-of-year net worth statements for John and Jody Willis*

Item	Marriage year: Sixth (end)		Marriage year: Seventh (end)	
Assets				
Cash on hand	$2,000		$ 560	
Automobile	1,200		1,100	
Durable household goods				
TV/VCR	350		625	
Camera	90		80	
Furniture	900		2,100	
Lawn mower	0		80	
Appliances	0		1,460	
House	0		40,000	
Cash value life insurance	460		580	
Savings accounts	2,240		0	
Other investments	0		0	
Accounts receivable	0		0	
Total		$7,240		$46,585
Liabilities				
Mortgage	0		$32,000	
Charge accounts				
Sofa	0		420	
Range, refrigerator	0		1,020	
Other accounts payable	240		$ 4,000	
Total		240		$37,440
Balance		$7,000		$ 9,145

Catastrophic events or other situations serving as the "last straw" on top of a tight financial condition are leading causes of bankruptcy, however.

Summary

A large part of a family's total management revolves around financial matters. Sources and levels of income are aspects of resource inputs on which the achievement of financial goals and aspirations depend. An individual's or a family's economic aspirations may be relatively high or low for many reasons. At any aspiration level, the sense of economic well-being varies widely—in part, because of the degree to which resources are adequate for meeting goals. Younger families may have a wider gap between their level of achievement and their intentions and, therefore, have a lower sense of economic welfare than other age groups. But other factors may increase the width of the tolerable gap. According to a study of families over a period of years, attitudes supportive to financial progress did not make a decisive difference in the actual position of families eleven years later. Intervening influences were overriding.

The purchasing power of families has not increased in recent years, as had been the pattern. The share of total income of lower-income families has declined while that of higher-income families has increased. Also, in contrast to low-income families, affluent families have large assets and are composed of well-educated individuals, and the accompanying opportunity for the higher income of an upper-level occupation.

Economic risks are of two types: those related to general economic conditions and those that strike more personally. While individuals cannot control the general impact of economic factors, they can prepare themselves to be in a strong employment situation either in their occupation, by improving their skills, or among occupations, by developing multiple skills.

Personal economic risks of ill health, property losses, premature retirement, or death may be shared through private and through social means. Both social and private insurance programs seek to reduce the critical resource impacts. An apparent effect of prepaid social-security programs has been the encouragement of individuals to save from assets to supplement social-security income at retirement. At the same time, earnings from employment have declined.

Assets contribute to overall financial security by allowing consumption over the life cycle or by increasing the family's financial resources through investment. They minimize the impacts of emergencies. Low-income families are less likely to have this source of security.

Budgeting has an allocating role in planning, and record keeping provides information for controlling current plans and developing later ones. Differences in situations affect the need for detail in both budgeting and record keeping. Greater opportunity for control accompanies greater detail.

Families may introduce their children to financial planning and implementing in a number of ways. Any one way of providing money to children—through allowances, doling, or encouraging opportunities for earning—may or may not promote the child's learning about the value of money. A combination of approaches will provide the clearest insight.

Factors affecting planning and implementation include the nature of income flow, organization patterns, and changing price levels. The stability, frequency, and amount of income characterize the nature of its flow. In general, steady and frequent income payments facilitate sequencing and controlling, especially checking.

Organization patterns for financial management vary greatly; young families or newly formed groups have to evolve satisfactory plans for roles or procedures. Income flow and organization patterns do not determine the amount of resource allocation to any item or determine which item will be purchased. Instead, they influence decision-making processes and help designate responsibilities.

Changing price levels further affect financial planning and implementing. Hedging price changes by spreading holdings over both fixed and variable assets provides some protection against major price effects. Emphasizing variable-dollar assets during inflationary and fixed-dollar assets during deflationary periods involves careful management.

Satisfactions of husbands and wives with their financial management accompany the more tangible effects of levels of living and net worth. The components of net worth reflect decisions affected by other systems, especially the economic system. Human capital increases often follow from financial outlays for education and training, although the cost may not be borne directly by the individual or family.

Notes

1. Marilyn M. Dunsing, ed., *Proceedings of the Symposium on Perceived Economic Well-Being* (Champaign-Urbana: University of Illinois, 1983).
2. Kristan Rinker Crosby, "Perceived Levels of Living and Family Welfare," M.S. thesis (Columbus: The Ohio State University, 1970), pp. 58–59.
3. Virginia T. Rowland, Richard A. Dodden, and Sharon Y. Nickols, "Perceived Adequacy of Resources: Development of a Scale," *Home Economics Research Journal* 14 (December 1985): 224.
4. Greg J. Duncan, with Richard D. Coe, Mary E. Corcoran, Martha S. Hill, Saul D. Hoffman, and James N. Morgan, *Years of Poverty, Years of Plenty: The Changing Economic Fortunes of American Workers and Families* (Ann Arbor: University of Michigan, Institute for Social Research, Survey Research Center, 1984), p. 5.

5. Ibid., p. 25.

6. Hazel Kyrk, *The Family in the American Economy* (Chicago: University of Chicago Press, 1953), pp. 166–167.

7. Duncan, *Years of Poverty, Years of Plenty,* pp. 26–27.

8. Ibid., p. 27.

9. Marilyn Marshall, "The Gaither Quints: The Miracle of Multiple Births," *Ebony* 40 (December 1985): 36, 40.

10. U.S. Department of Commerce, Bureau of the Census, *Money Income of Households, Families, and Persons in the United States: 1984,* Consumer Income Series P-60, No. 151 (Washington, D.C.: U.S. Government Printing Office, 1986), p. 76.

11. Duncan, *Years of Poverty, Years of Plenty,* p. 23.

12. Gordon E. Bivens and Carol B. Volker, "A Value-Added Approach to Household Production: The Special Case of Meal Preparation," *Journal of Consumer Research* 13 (September 1986): 277.

13. U.S. Department of Commerce, Bureau of the Census, *Money Income of Households, Families, and Persons in the United States: 1984,* Series P-60, No. 151, pp. 41–42.

14. Robert B. Avery and Gregory E. Elliehausen, "Financial Characteristics of High-Income Families," *Federal Reserve Bulletin* 72 (March 1986): 165.

15. Robert B. Avery, Gregory E. Elliehausen, and Glenn B. Canner, "Survey of Consumer Finances, 1983: A Second Report," *Federal Reserve Bulletin* 70 (December 1984): 863.

16. Avery and Elliehausen, "Financial Characteristics of High-Income Families," p. 167.

17. Ibid., p. 168.

18. U.S. Department of Agriculture, Agricultural Research Service, "Cost of Food at Home Estimated for Food Plans at 4 Cost Levels, January 1986, U.S. Average," *Family Economics Review* (April 1986): 36.

19. Francille Maloch and C. R. Weaver, "Orientation of Expenditures to Day of Pay," *Journal of Consumer Affairs* 5 (Summer 1971): 140.

20. Ibid., pp. 142–143; see also Ruby Turner Norris, *The Theory of Consumer's Demand* (New Haven: Yale University Press, 1952), p. 100.

21. Reuben Hill, *Family Development in Three Generations* (Cambridge, Mass.: Schenkman, 1970), p. 24.

22. Ibid., p. 206.

23. Tahira K. Hira, "Socio-Economic Characteristics of Families in Bankruptcy," *Canadian Home Economics Journal* 32 (Winter 1982): 28.

24. Ibid., p. 31.

25. Karen Schnittgrund, Marilyn Dunsing, and Jeanne Hafstrom, "Children and Money . . . Attitudes and Behavior of 52 Grandparent and Parent Families," *Illinois Research* 15 (Spring 1973): 13.

26. Hill, *Family Development in Three Generations,* pp. 216–219.

12

Work and family

This chapter discusses the family and work, which can be broadly defined as "physical or mental effort or activity directed toward the production or accomplishment of something. At its best, when it is generative, work is creating, producing, organizing, taking care. Work is doing."[1] Men, women, and children engage in work for pay and work in the home, which we will refer to as household labor or family work. Interest in the balance between family work and paid work is heightened by the increasing numbers and percentage of families with two earners.

Selected current trends and facts about work and family include:

- The majority of married couples are dual earners.
- Women are increasingly employed in clerical, professional, or technical and managerial jobs, rather than as operatives in factories.
- Single-earner families are somewhat larger than dual-earner families and more often include grown children or elderly relatives.
- Dual-earner families generally have more education than single-earner families.
- Dual-earner families comprise a higher percentage of black than white or Hispanic families.
- Dual-earner average family income is higher than for traditional families, but average earnings of husbands in traditional families are greater than those in dual-earner families.[2]
- Nearly half of all wives with children one year old or under are in the labor force,[3] with almost 30 percent working full time all year long.

This chapter emphasizes role interrelationships of family members in both paid work and family systems. While work for wages or profit may impact heavily on the family system, the impact of families on work conditions and benefits is increasingly recognized.

Family system and paid work interactions

The relationship between the family system and the work of husbands and wives is, in some cases, compartmentalized with rather impermeable boundaries around the "work" system; other family and work systems have permeable boundaries. Especially for men, employment demands are met with the family adjusting to those demands. Over time, wide variations in the interpretation of work demands probably occur. Women, particularly, experience "nagging worries which follow them to work, whether it be the house which needs cleaning or the child who looked unhappy when leaving for school."[4]

The interrelation of household work performance and employment demands may be classed as:[5]

- Traditional: Husband is employed; his employment has priority over family responsibilities; wife's role is performing household and family work.
- Additive: Each spouse maintains traditional activities and one or both add another dimension, e.g., where the wife adds outside employment but keeps her role inside the home.
- Transitional: The division of household labor is based on skills, ability, and interests, rather than on gender-based expectations; employment demands on the wife may sometimes take precedence over family duties; the husband may allow family responsibilities to overlap employment role.
- Reversed traditional: The husband fulfills the household responsibilities while the wife works away from home; the wife may separate employment and family responsibilities or permit employment responsibilities to affect the family setting.

With increased employment of women outside the home, the traditional category no longer predominates; evidence suggests that the additive group is relatively common.[6] Families in which members work together for wages or profit (such as farm families) and families in which members work in the home setting both exemplify systems with close interrelationships between systems. A young newspaper carrier may relinquish family activities for business responsibilities, and often other family members become quite involved with the carrier's duties when he or she has school activities or other commitments.

The timing of employment and motherhood may be sequential, with several variations of the employment-motherhood-employment pattern; or women may simultaneously engage in employment and motherhood. Various timing patterns are graphically presented in Figure 12.1.

Since family and work systems interact, many couples experience intersystem conflicts with the arrival of their first child. During the transition to parenthood, the emotional climates of the workplace and the family—with their tensions and responsibilities—affect one another.[7]

Paid work is closely integrated in the family system when it is done at home. The increase in cottage industries brings attention to its obstacles and advantages, but relatively limited empirical research is available about paid work in the home.

The organizational skill requirements may be greater for persons doing paid work at home when they must structure both paid work and family work. Isolation from social interactions is cited as a frequent problem.[8] Developing paid work space out of previously open family space can create problems for some families. Accompanying the savings on clothes, gasoline, parking, lunches, and other expenses is a change in or lessening of child care problems.

A British homeworker reports this schedule:

> I get the kids off to school, then do the washing and clean round for ten o'clock when the work is delivered. I work through until lunchtime, stop for a sandwich, and continue until four in the afternoon. About six, after tea and clearing it up, I work another hour, get the youngest off to bed, start again about eight and work until eleven at night. Sometimes I stop work at nine and get up early the following morning so it will be ready at ten in the morning, when the delivery comes.[9]

Telecommuting is projected to increase in the coming years. In the United States, the computer, or "electronic cottage," makes telecommuting possible. Both men and women whose work is linked by telephone and com-

FIGURE 12.1 *Employment timing patterns among white wives by family life-cycle stage*

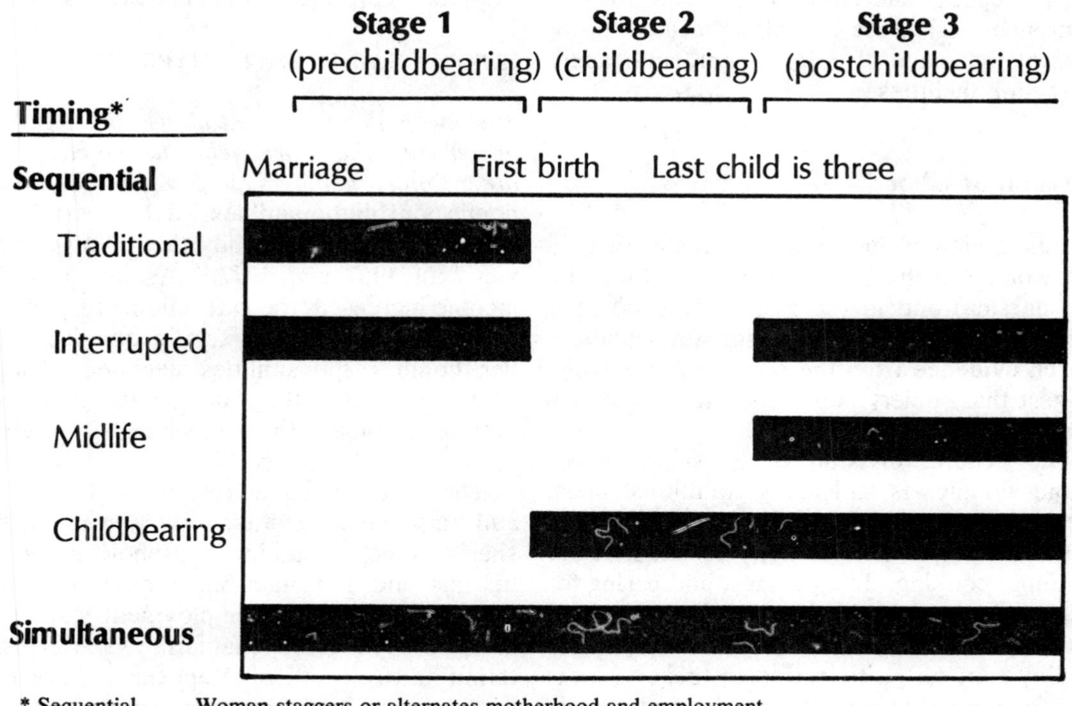

* Sequential	Woman staggers or alternates motherhood and employment.
Traditional	Motherhood follows employment subsequent to the first child, with no intention of return to work.
Interrupted	Employment-motherhood-employment sequence, interrupting education or employment to exclusively devote time to motherhood, subsequent to reentry into the labor force.
Midlife	Employment follows motherhood sequence, with full-time parenting, then employment.
Childbearing	Employment follows motherhood without having established an employment pattern prior to childbearing.
Simultaneous	Overlapping parenthood and paid work throughout the life cycle.

Source: Adapted from Ellen Van Velsor and Angela M. O'Rand, "Family Life Cycle, Work Career Patterns, and Women's Wages at Midlife," *Journal of Marriage and the Family* 46 (May 1984): 365–373. See also Pamela Daniels and Kathy Weingarten, *Sooner or Later: The Timing of Parenthood in Adult Lives* (New York: W. W. Norton & Co., 1982), pp. 98–99. Copyrighted 1984 by the National Council on Family Relations, 1910 W. County Rd. B, Suite 147, St. Paul, Minn. 55113. Reprinted by permission.

puter to an office or industrial site are more often conducting business at home, either part-time or full-time.

Organizations that make extensive demands on the family system have often provided benefits and services to families to increase their understanding of and commitment to the organization. One study of military families proposes that the organizational support of the employer increases the family's overall commitment to the employer and the commitments of employed family members to their jobs. Improved family support policies are likely to yield benefits for employers in such areas as employee retention, performance, and morale.[10]

Employee benefits particularly helpful to families are good-quality, convenient child-care facilities, a food service available for long periods throughout the day, medical and hospital insurance, assistance for minor medical problems at the place of employment, and family recreation facilities.

Division of labor

A radical view proposes that activities of men and women in the home (except child bearing and nursing) and in the marketplace be fully interchangeable.[11] Casual observation and research evidence from the contemporary scene suggest that society is a considerable distance from such a view.

The general division of household labor among couples is still along traditional lines, with women doing the larger share of household tasks. Wives remain primarily responsible for cleaning, cooking, doing dishes, and caring for children in most families, even when they hold outside jobs. The chief effect of wives' outside employment on participation in these tasks is that they are substantially less likely to retain sole responsibility for them. Women often directly supervise the household work of others, maintain quality control over the products, and assume a general managerial role.[12]

Husbands primarily do the stereotypically masculine tasks of maintaining the house and yard, and they increase their participation only a little if their wives work. Bill-paying responsibilities are almost equal between husband and wife, and her work status has little effect on who has primary responsibility.[13]

Children are the most likely to help by cleaning house, though they may be simply cleaning up after themselves. First-born girls contribute more time to household work than boys, but the traditional pattern does not extend to second-born children.[14]

Various hypotheses about the household division of labor have been examined, and each hypothesis has some research support, suggesting that multiple factors affect the division of labor and consequent time allocations to tasks.

RESOURCE AND POWER HYPOTHESIS

The more the wife's earnings, the more her power and the more help she receives from other family members. The wife's relative economic contribution influenced the division of labor in the home in a study that involved interviews in 1967 and 1977.[15] As the husband's income increased, the wife's home responsibilities increased; as the wife's income increased, her home responsibilities declined. Another study found that the "smaller the differential between spouses, the greater male housework participation becomes."[16]

The wife's tangible resources, her income and employment status, were associated with sharing time-consuming household tasks with her husband. For husbands, a mixture of tangible resources (wife's employment status) and intangible resources (egalitarian sex-role orientation and role salience) appear to have influenced sharing of time-consuming household tasks.[17] Role salience is the importance placed on the values of family, employment, and community roles.

TIME AVAILABILITY HYPOTHESIS

The wife's employment reduces time available for household tasks, and she will have fewer household responsibilities than if she is not employed. A study with a nationwide sample of 1,364 couples showed the wife's employment status more than the husband's affecting the division of labor.[18]

The wife's time in family work is affected by her outside employment hours and the age of the younger child, but the husband's and children's household work time was not found to be significantly related to time spent in outside employment by their wife and mother in a study of

210 families with two children in the south-central United States.[19] In another study, working wives received more help than nonworking wives.[20]

When child care and housework are included, "in families with employed mothers, the number of hours the wife worked per week was the strongest single predictor of fathers' participation, affecting all forms but solo interaction and child-care tasks."[21] Solo interaction is between the father and child alone. "Neither fathers' nor mothers' occupational prestige, flexibility of hours worked, nor satisfaction with that flexibility affected fathers' participation" in housework.[22]

In still another study, husbands whose wives worked full-time, who had more feminine sex-role orientations, and were in households with more children helped their wives more with child care.[23]

The evidence is mixed, but the fact remains that husbands, on the average, spend more time in paid work than wives, wives spend more time in household or family work, and the work days of the husband and wife are becoming similar in length (Figure 12.2). Thus, time availability for both husbands and wives is similar.

SEX-ROLE HYPOTHESIS

The sex-role attitudes of husbands (in particular) and wives affect the division of labor. The husband's attitude more strongly affected the division of labor according to the nationwide study previously cited.[24] A greater traditional attitude on the part of mothers toward the male role has been associated with less participation by fathers in family work, while the less traditional her views, the greater the father's participation in family work. The converse regarding the father's values was not found to similarly affect the father's participation in housework.[25]

Husbands who tend to agree that interchangeable rather than specialized roles are the preferred norm for spousal behavior accept more responsibility for tasks associated with child care, meal preparation, and cleaning.[26] ". . . it is not employed wives with liberal sex role attitudes who reduce their family time most in relation to their job hours, but employed wives with conservative attitudes."[27] Sex-role ideology did not have consistent effects on the division of labor in several nationwide studies, but perhaps it is a matter of the measurement of sex-role attitudes.[28]

PREFERENCE-FOR-HOUSEWORK HYPOTHESIS

The division of family labor relates to the wife's (particularly) or husband's preference for housework. The division of labor was found to be congruent with the wife's preference for housework in the study of the 1,364 couples previously cited.[29] A high percentage of wives (43 percent) indicated a preference for household work over paid work, compared with 8 percent of the husbands indicating that preference.[30]

Wives' perception of household tasks as being important or pleasant affects their time and work-quality contributions to the tasks. For a wife's increased ranking of importance of one point on a scale of ten, she did thirty more tasks above the average number of tasks, with a maximum of 300 additional tasks each month.[31] A ranking increase of one, in terms of pleasantness of the task, meant an increase of nineteen additional tasks per month.

Family system accommodations

To allow for similar career and family commitments of both spouses, the family system and its members often accommodate the work system. Changes made by family members do not necessarily alter gender-role expectations and, consequently, household work patterns. Proba-

FIGURE 12.2 *Length of work day for husband and wife*

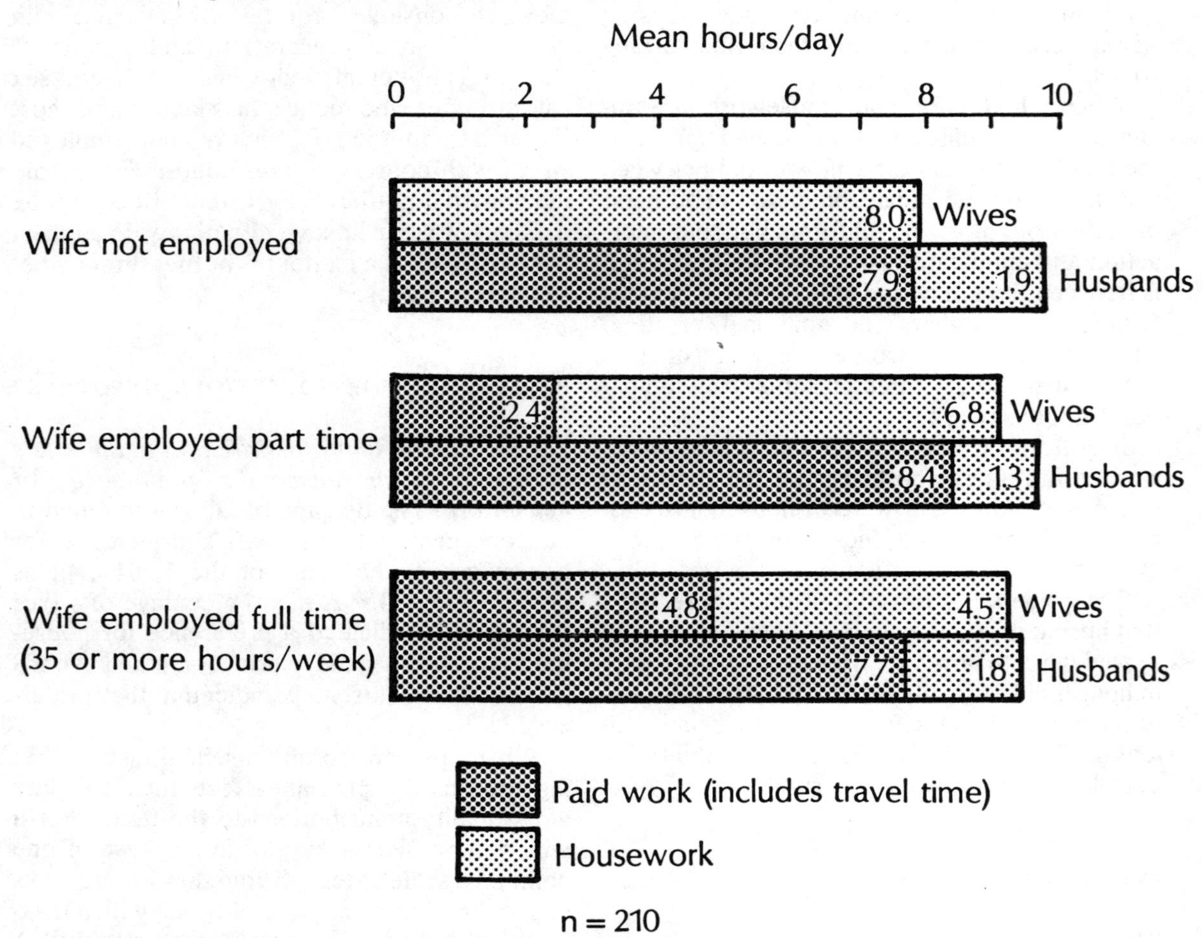

Source: Karen D. Fox and Sharon Y. Nickols, "The Time Crunch: Wife's Employment and Family Work," *Journal of Family Issues* 4 (March 1983): 75. Copyright © 1983 by Sage Publications, Inc. Reprinted by permission of Sage Publications, Inc.

bly the greatest change in families in recent years is a reduction in the amount of household work brought about by the reduction in the number of children and the increasing social acceptance of childlessness. Some families are also spacing children in relation to career demands. The teacher who has her children during the summer is an example.

Another accommodation within the family system is the marriage of people with different degrees of family and work orientation. Generally, women have been less committed to careers and more oriented to the family. A reversal of roles, where men who get major satisfaction from family endeavors marry women oriented to careers, is the case among some couples today and may be a situation that will increase.[32]

When two careers are considered, relocation for career and family development can be a complex situation. Career choices that seem best for the family may mean that the individual man or woman must alter or postpone reaching a career goal. A corporate employee who is requested to move may decide that an additional move is not good for the family, even though it would be good for reaching a career goal.

Of employees asked to relocate, an estimated one-third to one-half will object, and many will refuse to relocate.[33] Recognition of the importance of the careers of both men and women continues to grow, while challenges remain in making the decisions and living with the consequences. Commuter marriages, where spouses live apart due to job locations and meet periodically during nonwork periods, require sufficient financial and emotional resources for successful functioning.

Less stress may be felt in commuter marriages among (1) couples who are older, (2) who have been married longer, (3) with at least one established career and (4) those without childrearing responsibilities.[34] Younger, less established couples grappled with less firmly established professional identities and with fewer shared experiences and thus felt the separation more keenly, as reported in the same study.

Input

DEMANDS

Many individuals and families in recent years have been challenged to balance the increasing involvement in work for pay and its related role requirements against family demands. The following case notes both demands and needed resources for the complexities of conflict in maternal and professional roles.

> Of course there are conflicts as you attempt to finish law school with two children and a third on the way. You're tired as you attempt to nurse your new baby, prepare dinner for a tired commuter husband, put cranky little ones to bed and study for an all-important exam. Again, the only way to survive is to be as flexible as possible about goals, maintain a sense of humor, and have strong faith in the grace of God. I sometimes shock my students by saying that my children were and are terribly valuable to me. Having children forces one to grow up oneself and makes one a better person, lawyer, teacher, etc.[35]

Values for women, in particular, shifted between 1970 and 1980. An important change was the increase in women's desire "for high-status professional careers and commitment to the career-based values necessary to success."[36] Table 12.1 presents the life-style commitment, vocational aspiration, and career values for 1970 and 1980 college graduates.

The authors of the study are rather pessimistic about the potential of undergraduates' meeting their current expectations. They conclude: "Today's aspiring professionals will face difficult choices: lowering career aspirations or consciously rejecting parenthood."[37] Another writer suggests the stability in adulthood of women's achievement orientation.[38] The major time of concern in implementing that value orientation is during early motherhood, when circumstances strongly inhibit women's pursuit of career values through full-time employment.[39]

RESOURCES

The average earnings of husbands in traditional families are greater than those in dual-earner families, but, as noted earlier, dual-earner family average income is higher than that of traditional families. The wages for the wife vary by the timing of her employment, in relation to the family life cycle. The following are typical impacts of the employment patterns on wages of employed wives (see Figure 12.1):

- Simultaneous
  Working throughout the life cycle yields significantly greater wages per hour, on the average, than for any other group.[40]

TABLE 12.1 *Life-style commitment, vocational aspiration, and career values by sex and decade of graduation*

	Men		Women	
	1970	*1980*	*1970*	*1980*
Number sampled	833	527	866	560
	Percent			
Life-style commitment[1]				
Family-directed	15	15	34	19
Family-accommodated	28	27	38	34
Career-accommodated	15	10	7	16
Career-directed	13	10	5	8
Other-directed	28	38	17	23
Vocational aspiration				
Professional	59	48	16	44
Other	41	52	84	56
Career Values[2]				
None	17	10	35	12
One	18	19	27	21
Two	20	19	20	21
Three	18	19	11	23
Four	14	16	4	13
Five	12	17	3	9

Source: Adapted from Mary C. Regan and Helen E. Roland, "Rearranging Family and Career Priorities: Professional Women and Men of the Eighties," *Journal of Marriage and the Family* 47 (November 1985): 986–987. Copyrighted 1985 by the National Council on Family Relations, 1910 W. County Rd. B, Suite 147, St. Paul, Minn. 55113. Reprinted by permission.

[1] Life-style commitment
Family-directed = family is the most important goal and any other goal except career is secondary
Family-accommodated = family most important goal, career secondary
Career-directed = career is most important, and any other goal except family is secondary
Career-accommodated = career most important, family secondary
Other-directed = neither family nor career is most important

[2] Career values: a five-item scale reflecting commitment to the career values of leadership, prestige, recognition, power, and monetary reward.

- Interrupted
  Yields higher average wages than childbearing pattern; early labor force participation may substitute for education advantage in wage determination.[41]
- Childbearing
  Less advantage in labor market; educational background has little effect on wages, probably reflecting the conflict between employment and child-rearing demands.[42]
- Midlife
  Yields same average wage rates as childbearing pattern and results in relatively higher returns to education and experience.[43] The timing pattern may be advantageous due to less conflict with family roles.

With higher incomes, families are able to secure more paid assistance for household and family work. In examination of time spent on household work, those families with higher family income (with other factors controlled statistically) were found to spend somewhat (but not dramatically) less time in household work. Families with higher incomes also eat out more often; and in one study, the wives averaged one half-hour less in meal preparation and clean-up each time the family ate out.[44]

Human resources are important in coping with role conflicts between work and family. In a study of dual-earner families with preschool children, feelings of self-esteem and high levels of career commitment were associated with less role conflict and greater coping effectiveness, while spouse support was associated with social support (help received from persons other than spouse), greater coping effectiveness, and reduced role conflict.[45]

The interrelationship of resource demands at work and in the family is felt when both spouses are under time pressures.

> I was slow to realize that Joe and I can go along pretty well as long as we both don't hit a crunch at the same time. But then we really get into trouble at home because there isn't anybody who has the extra time to fill in. It's awful. It gets very tense. It's hard on the kids. All the things that are stable in our lives, like an evening meal, go out the door because nobody's home to fix it and it's havoc. Now that it has happened a few times, we know what was wrong. But I don't know how to guard

> against it. . . . But when we both need that time and it is not there—it just isn't good. Then you live through it and you put the pieces together afterwards, but it takes a toll. Because our work lives are really not all that flexible, there are times when it really has to be heavy for both of us. Thank God it is not all that often.[46]

The health of family members can be viewed as a resource; in one study, the poorer the wife's health, the longer the time spent in household work.[47]

Throughput

Planning and implementing household or family work, and its relation to paid work, is the focus of this section. Planning and organizing time in dual-earner families is reportedly practiced more frequently by wives than husbands, though both spouses rate relatively high in their use of organization. A vice president of a metropolitan museum and mother of two (the younger, aged two and a half) suggests that "her secret for running her house is the same as that for running her office: organization. 'I think in two-week segments and try to project everything in advance.' "[48] "Perhaps wives in dual-career families . . . feel more personal and societal pressure than their husbands to achieve success in multiple roles and thus are more conscious of planning their time and organizing their schedules."[49]

In dealing with the demands of employment and paid work, husbands and wives use various coping strategies differentially. Wives more than husbands compartmentalize family and paid employment responsibilities. In the same study, both husbands and wives extensively used the organization strategy, but the husbands' use significantly exceeded that of the wives. Two actions characterized this strategy: "When I am pressured to do many things at once, I organize and plan my time." "When increased demands are made of me, I set priorities and do the most important things first."[50]

PLANNING

Standard setting. When people live together and share household work, they often have different standards for the work. Among couples who shared household work, over half reported that earlier in their marriage the wives had generally advocated much higher standards of household orderliness and cleanliness than did their husbands. When the wife was in charge of doing the household chores, no conflict resulted; but when the couples decided to share chore responsibility, wives pushed for doing chores at the frequency they specified and in the manner that they preferred. They often fretted about the house's condition and experienced embarrassment from unexpected visitors. Husbands also wanted to do the chores according to their own ideas of frequency and in the manner (often unconventional) that appealed most to them. "Husbands consistently felt wives were too finicky and wives regarded husbands as too sloppy."[51]

Most couples coped with this disparity in standards by lowering the wives' expectations and raising the husbands' expectations. The wives being busy with jobs or school work usually precipitated the change, accompanied by heated discussions and practical experiments. "Both spouses generally professed to be happier with the new standard."[52] For example, one person may sort and separately launder clothes by color and degree of soil, pretreat the stains or spots, and vary the water temperature and cleaning agents. Another person may toss all the clothes in the wash with no variation in pretreatment, water temperature, or detergent use. One solution is for the person with higher standards always to do the laundry; another is to agree on a standard somewhere between the two; and another is for the person doing the laundry to use his or her standard.

Wives utilized the strategy "reducing responsibilities" less than their husbands in a study of university administrators. The strategy that can be viewed as changes in standards was measured by responses to the following statements: "If my job demands become too great, I change my standards of job performance." "I can easily say 'No' when asked to assume an overload of responsibilities at my job." "My home responsibilities justify my not accepting more responsibilities on the job."[53] Among wives of university administrators, those holding professional or administrative positions reported "reducing responsibilities" as a way of coping with demands less than those holding jobs with fewer demands in time, effort, and educational requirements. Perhaps this is some evidence of the "superwoman" with a high commitment to both family and career. Thus "career-oriented" wives would be less likely than "career-earner" wives to change performance standards at work or to use home responsibilities as a reason for reducing employment responsibilities.[54]

Another example of a change in standards as a way of coping with demands is simplification of meal preparation. A couple reported that one spouse cooks while the other babysits with the children before dinner. "Whoever wants to have a hassle-free time does the cooking. . . . And if it's been a terrible day for both of us, we order pizza."[55]

Action sequencing. Women continue to have the main responsibility for reconciling paid work with family life. The family work day's length affects many aspects of how wives (but not husbands) allocate time within the home. "Males are primarily responsible for the length of the work day, but wives seem to be more responsive to their husband's work schedules than vice versa."[56]

External forces, such as when the children come home from school or when the mother and father go to work may place constraints on the sequences of household activities. Flexibility in job requirements helps individuals meet both job and family demands. Flexible work schedules, leaves of absence, parental leaves for childbirth, and part-time work status provide alternatives for meeting family needs. Flexible schedules (traditionally available to many professionals and more recently to other workers) may facilitate the fulfilling of family goals, such as having a parent instead of another care-giver take a sick child to the doctor.

Among families with a member employed by the federal civil service, flextime was found most beneficial for families without children. Mothers from both single-parent and dual-earner families felt stressed whether or not on flextime. The study found that men on flextime with employed wives spent about the same time on family work as men whose wives were not employed; however, they spent more time on family work than their standard-time counterparts—and they report less stress.[57]

Relief from work–family stress requires more than limited shifts in work hours. Such shifts may change the times when tasks are done (which can be helpful), but they do not necessarily increase opportunities or inclinations to share family activities. Among full-time pharmaceutical workers, women with four-day work weeks used the fifth day for housework and spent more total time on housework than standard-time workers.[58] In the study of civil service workers, single-parent mothers on flextime spent eight hours more per week on household work than did single-parent mothers on standard work-week schedules.[59]

Other changes in the occupational or paid work system can broadly impact the family system; for example, greater flexibility in place of work; parental leave programs; shorter, reduced-pay work days for parents; increased child-care programs; and more after-school programs.[60]

Technological changes, such as "telecommuting," can impact action sequencing within the home rather dramatically. The clustering of household activities to provide for blocks of time for paid work may be similar to working outside the home, but increased flexibility in the day as well as convenience in location encourage working for pay in the home.[61]

Scheduled paid work and household work shape some of the specific action sequences. Paid work at night and on weekends may constrain the action sequencing or scheduling of volunteer and family or household work. "Dual-earner husbands are more likely than dual-earner wives to report such stressful work schedule characteristics as weekend work, an early starting time, a late finishing time, a large number of hours per week, and a second job."[62] When wives work nondaytime shifts, husbands experience conflicts in their own schedules, but wives are not equally affected by their husband's shift work. The husband's weekend work, however, brought increased schedule conflicts for wives.[63]

Although scheduling is complicated by both spouses working frequently at different hours, the schedule of paid work for the single parent greatly affects the sequencing of family activities. Women aged eighteen to forty-four with a preschool child are often employed at other than regular daytime hours—one in six of all full-time employed women and one in five of part-time women are in some form of shift work.[64] "Non-day employment is almost twice as likely among unmarried mothers than among the married," suggesting that economic necessity is highly relevant to working times.[65]

Having some control over the pattern of hours to work helps buffer nonstandard work schedules for men and women. Because of the family demand usually experienced by women, some flexibility of schedule is often more important to them than to men.[66]

Parental work and volunteer schedules complicate sequencing of household activities, and the complexity of scheduling is compounded by the children's many activities, such as special tutoring, ballet classes, sports events, club meetings, and paid work (Figure 12.3). The goals and priorities of family members affect action sequencing. For example, preparing special food for an elderly parent or a child may be considerably more important to a family than vacuuming the living room, and thus the one activity is sequenced before the other. Forces within the home, some of which are inherent in the tasks themselves, combine to limit the discretion available for sequencing some tasks. Tasks in which completion of one task depends on the completion of another are considered interdependent. Before washing the breakfast dishes, the breakfast must be prepared and consumed or abandoned.

In a study of both husbands and wives and the content of organization within the household, the natural flow or prerequisite quality of tasks was found especially applicable to the sequencing of early-morning activities. "[O]ver the course of a household day, perhaps as much as a third of the activities are constrained by some sort of necessary order. . . . [M]eal preparation activities are apparently the critical contributor."[67]

Clustering compatible activities can be an efficient sequencing technique. Shopping for various items all available at a single shopping center is an example of clustering the sequence of activities by location. Many tasks related to family and household care may be incompatible due to location and individual family member demands. Going to the post office for a registered letter and mopping the kitchen floor are incompatible because of location.

IMPLEMENTING

Technology, paid work patterns, and the characteristics of household work interact and influence the implementation of plans to meet the demands of families and individuals. Here we will review the impact of technology and the characteristics of household work.

Technology. Availability of household equipment tends to reinforce stereotyped task assignments and reduce the amount of help from others.[68] Work may be accomplished with increased ease (facilitated) and at higher standards because equipment enables an individual

FIGURE 12.3 *Sequencing*

by Lynn Johnston

Source: For Better or for Worse. Copyright 1986 Universal Press Syndicate. Reprinted with permission.

to do a job more easily and thoroughly. Equipment enables some individuals or families to undertake tasks that were not formerly done in the home.

Contrary to the opinion of many, average time used by wives for household work has not been drastically reduced because of technological developments in automatic equipment, such as dishwashers, clothes dryers, and garbage disposals. Much of a family's work cannot readily be automated. Some activities are easier to do because of new equipment, and sometimes more can be accomplished because changes in technology have made the work easier.[69]

Another writer describes the impact of technology on household work:

> The level of technology applied to housework is a long way behind that in industry. Domestic technology affects particular tasks but not the job of housework as a whole. . . . Differential ownership of mechanical aids, and the differences in the possession of amenities, may affect the way housework is done, and they may have some influence on attitudes to work tasks, but they do not appear to affect satisfaction with work.[70]

And another writer states:

> There is little doubt that an individual housewife can save time using a dishwasher or clothes dryer instead of doing these chores by hand. In the long run, amid the press of all other household tasks that have to be performed, however, the mere presence of the machines makes little difference in housework time.[71]

Little evidence was found in another study that appliance ownership is related to less time being spent on household tasks. There was a positive relationship between the number of appliances owned that require continuous attention and the time spent in related tasks.[72]

> Modern household technology facilitated married women's workforce participation not by freeing women from household labor but by making it possible for women to maintain decent standards in their homes without assistants and without a full-time commitment to housework. The technological and social systems for doing housework had been constructed with the expectation that the people engaged in them would be full-time housewives. When the full-time housewives be-

gan to disappear, those systems could not adjust quickly.[73]

Household work characteristics. Household work can be described as follows:

Varied: involves different tasks on a typical day.[74]

Repetitive: includes tasks that are performed again the next day or sooner.[75]

Brief: most household tasks in the United States are 15 minutes in length, with the average task lasting 25 minutes.[76] This contrasts to countries where long periods of time may be spent, for example, cooking bread products, such as chapaties in India.

Time-consuming: total household work time averages almost 7 hours a day;[77] less time is spent when both spouses work outside the home.

Amenable to dovetailing: on the average, three tasks are done at once, e.g., cooking breakfast, feeding the baby, and washing a load of clothes.[78]

Complex: includes working mainly with things, with considerable involvement with family members.[79]

Internal standards: set by individuals or families, unlike paid work.

A number of characteristics of individuals and families have been found to be associated with effective time use (Table 12.2).

Controlling household activities (checking and adjusting the standards or sequences of planned actions) is accomplished in a variety of ways. Checking against standards is often subjective, as with the readiness of food or the sheen on a car when waxing it.

Some homemakers may check the sequence of household activities according to a written plan for a day or a longer period of time, while others may use a mental activity sequence. Highly specific plans may require careful checking to meet their exacting standards and sequences. An activity such as redecorating a room can involve specific plans and frequent checking to insure completion as planned. For such projects, adjustments are often necessary to accommodate subtle variations from expected effects, such as when using a more intense paint color.

As indicated in Chapter 8, the environmental situation can facilitate or deter the progress of actions. The household space use and equipment available affect how household work takes place. In one study, two-story houses were associated with more time spent on household work or other activities.[80]

These features are called facilitators (positive or negative); in day-to-day activity, they are not ordinarily involved directly in planning and implementing household activities. If environmental conditions are altered, they temporarily become a part of conscious planning until their impacts on the daily routines are stabilized.

Facilitating conditions may only slightly influence the actual time use in household work, but they may markedly increase the sense of order, enjoyment, and satisfaction. An example one faces each day is the order of one's clothes closet. The needed shoes and clothes are eventually found in a poorly organized closet, and the total time spent seeking the articles is probably not great, but the easy flow of readily finding clothes and shoes in well-organized space can facilitate the beginning of the day.

Individuals and families are capable of adapting to work areas as well as to other parts of their environment. A family may identify poorly designed spaces while inspecting a house, but these spaces—if not changed before or soon after the family moves in—are often readily adapted to. Adaptability reduces the necessity but not the benefits of well-designed work areas.

Storage and work-area arrangements deserve close attention when they are frequently used or when improvements would sufficiently

TABLE 12.2 *Characteristics of effective time users*

Characteristic	*More efficient time use*	*Less efficient time use*
Personal		
Age	Middle age	66 years or older
Retirement	Not retired	Retired
Education	Graduate or professional school	Other
Local group participation	Moderate to high	Lower
Family		
Cohesiveness (group work, play and other experiences)	More frequent	Less frequent
Task variety	High	Low
Income	Higher	Lower

Source: Florence S. Walker and Anne M. Parkhurst, "Identification of Differences in Time Management," *Home Economics Research Journal* 11 (September 1982): 58.

increase the use and enjoyment to justify the improvement costs. Arrangement of storage areas may be based on several criteria, such as increasing the facilitation of the work, increasing the satisfaction with the work process, protecting children and others incapable of judgment about proper use and care of supplies and equipment, or protecting a product from heat or sunlight. Choices in storage design may also be influenced by the visual and esthetic impact.

Storage can be either independent of or interdependent with work areas. Storing items within the worker's limits of reach is appropriate for storage independent of work areas, but it is probably more important in storage that is part of a work area. In either case, placing frequently used and/or heavy items within easy reach lessens the likelihood of lifting strain.[81] For increased exercise, frequently used light articles stored on a lower level can be reached by a deep knee bend.

The best storage height for minimum heart rate and energy consumption is between 28 and 52 inches above floor level. Using storage space 4 inches above the floor requires about 16 more heart beats per minute than using storage 52 inches above the floor.[82] The physiological importance of tasks varies for workers, depending on their general state of health, including pregnancy, age, and vision. Work heights are especially important when an activity is done frequently, when it involves heavy lifting, when performed for long periods, or when the person has physical problems.

For both sitting and standing activities, elbow height is related to good working positions. If the work surface is too high for the person and the job, the worker's elbow and arm will be in a strained position; if it is too low, the person may adjust his or her whole body downward, resulting in poor posture. Recommendations based on elbow height provide for arm positions with freedom of movement.

The median height of American women is 5 feet 4 inches, with a median elbow height of 40.3 inches;[83] the median height of American men is 5 feet 9 inches, with a median elbow height of 43.5 inches.[84] The preferred distance below the elbow for standing work is 3–5 inches, depending on the activity. A 36-inch counter height is therefore close to the preferred working-surface height for the average woman, although it is low for the average man.

The seated working position has additional work-area requirements compared with the standing position. The preferred work-surface height is from one-half inch below to 1 inch above elbow height, and there should be enough room under the work surface for freedom of leg movement. The thickness of the work surface is limited if both optimum work height and adequate leg clearance are provided.[85]

The desirability of different work heights for different tasks and for different people must be balanced with other realities, such as the difficulty in modifying some work areas, the impracticality of changing work areas in rented apartments and houses, and the effort needed to modify work areas when the family or individual expects to move frequently.

Output

Output from family or household work includes the accomplishment of tasks and the satisfaction and stresses associated with that accomplishment. Output from paid work is income and the satisfaction associated with the income. The output from the interaction between family and paid work may be satisfaction, or the role conflict may bring stress, strain, or depression.

FAMILY WORK

Household members determine "what has to be done and who will do it" by tasks.[86] Tasks are the "conceptual unit through which the work is originally defined and allocated. . . . [T]ime is merely an input. . . . Tasks, however, reflect a combination of input and output."[87] Tasks reflect the resulting commodity itself.

The allocation of tasks, or the division of labor, has been considered earlier, but here the focus is on the consequences of that division of labor, especially in relation to paid work. The wife's satisfaction with her husband's contribution to housework and child care is more important than the actual levels of family work by the husband.[88]

> An employed wife's wanting her husband to do more housework and childcare is an extremely powerful predictor of poor family adjustment as well as overall well-being. . . . The more childcare she does, the better her adjustment if she is satisfied with her husband's childcare participation, but the worse her adjustment if she is not satisfied.[89]

Fathers are concerned about their participation in family work and its interference with their careers; they also may be critical of their wives for expecting or needing their participation. "If participant fathers are critical of their wives, their wives feel guilty, blaming themselves and their work for tension and conflict. . . . [A]s fathers increasingly juggle family work with paid work, they are coming to resemble mothers with respect to the conflicts and tensions they face."[90]

Satisfaction with family or household work varies among women and men. "Class factors such as family income and husband's status do not account for significant differences in housewives' reported satisfaction. Working-class women are not 'more satisfied' with full-time housework, whether this is interpreted to mean a comparison to working-class employed women or to middle-class housewives. Insofar as housework varies in meaning or rewards, it seems to be along a dimension largely independent of class."[91]

RELATIONSHIP OF PAID AND FAMILY WORK

Satisfaction with paid work and the relationship between work and family demands, as indicated by life satisfaction and separately by marital and job satisfaction, presents a mixed picture. When many studies based on over 2,500 couples were examined, the wife's employment status had little or no effect on the husband's or wife's marital satisfaction.[92] Yet in an analysis of a large nationwide sample in 1977, husbands with higher occupational status and higher educational levels had a lower sense of well-being and satisfaction when their wives were employed outside the home.[93]

The effects of family income and wife's employment interact; that is, for husbands with higher incomes, the wife's employment has a greater negative impact on the husband's distress. Husbands with employed wives also feel more distress when their spouse's salary is competitive.[94]

For two-earner couples who were professionally employed, high- and low-quality marriages were identified.[95] The characteristics of marriage making up the high- and low-quality marriages related to work and family are given in Table 12.3. Of particular interest here are the following findings:

1. "The greater the socioeconomic adequacy of the family, the greater the marital quality."
2. "The greater the role-fit, the greater the marital quality." Role-fit means a lack of role conflict and the presence of role-sharing.
3. "The more effective the communication between spouses, the more the marital quality."[96]

Congruence between the woman's desire to be employed outside the home and actual employment is important in her satisfaction. Also important is the husband's attitude toward her participation in the labor force after the birth of the first child. A young mother would feel "forced" to work outside the home after children are born if her husband insisted that she work, even though she did not want to work. The lower the family's resources, the more any insistence of the work role outside the home is thought of as "forced."[97]

ROLE CONFLICTS AND STRAINS

Role strain among working parents may be expressed in a number of ways, including time shortages, income inadequacy, and job tension. Table 12.4 presents barriers or demands and resource-related factors associated with these three types of role strain.

The multiplicity of roles handled by single-parent families increases the complexity of the situation and, for many, the stress. Being a single parent was the only determinant of role strain resulting in time shortages, income inadequacy, and job tension in a study of 468 working parents in a Southeastern metropolitan area.[98]

Divorced mothers in metropolitan areas in Ohio did not see their jobs as creating difficulties in managing family responsibilities and did not select their jobs on the basis of their home responsibilities. The women, who worked primarily in clerical, sales, and kindred occupations, generally did not think their jobs created stress or excessive demands. However, "dissatisfaction with management of employment and family responsibilities increased when job stress and job demands increased."[99]

In the case of divorced mothers, nonroutine home demands most often revolve around children. For example, illness of children requiring several days of special care or the inability of the regular caretaker to care for them most often led the divorced mother to handle the situation herself.[100] The divorced mother relied on herself to deal with employment and child-care conflicts under the following conditions:

1. The employment was less stressful and time-demanding from their viewpoint.
2. The children were young.
3. Help from friends and relatives was not readily available.
4. They were experienced as a parent.[101]

The importance of housework to the mother was found to reduce the leisure time with chil-

TABLE 12.3 *Characteristics of marriages of high and low quality in two-earner families*

High-quality marriages	*Wives*
	They report little or no difficulty discussing work-related activities, problems, and achievements with their husbands.
	They perceive husbands as supportive with childrearing and household tasks.
	They are satisfied with their work situations.
	Husbands
	Their support for wives' careers has increased since marriage.
	Their perceptions of wives' role overload, and stress levels are similar to what wives report.
	Marital dyad
	They agree husband's career is preeminent.
	They are more likely to be involved in similar career pursuits.
	They have older children and more jointly share child-care responsibilities.
	They are working with levels of emotional, sexual, intellectual, recreational, and social intimacy within the relationship.
Low-quality marriages	*Wives*
	They report much difficulty discussing work-related activities, problems, and achievements with their husbands.
	They perceive husbands as less supportive with child-rearing and household tasks.
	They are more likely to have made a career change during marriage.
	They are acutely dissatisfied with the level of emotional intimacy in the relationship.
	Husbands
	Their support for wives' careers has decreased since marriage.
	Their perceptions of wives' role overload and stress levels are lower than wives report.
	Marital dyad
	There is less agreement regarding whose career is preeminent.
	They are less likely to be involved in similar career pursuits.
	They have younger children and report much stress due to conflict with children's schedules and/or child-care arrangements.
	They are dissatisfied with levels of emotional, sexual, intellectual, recreational, and social intimacy within the relationship.

Source: Sandra Thomas, Kay Albrecht, and Priscilla White, "Determinants of Marital Quality in Dual-Career Couples," *Family Relations* 33 (October 1984): 513–521. Copyrighted 1984 by the National Council on Family Relations, 1910 W. County Rd. B, Suite 147, St. Paul, Minn. 55113. Reprinted by permission.

dren in one study, with the mother's orientation to housework affecting that leisure time more than the total time available.[102] Further, the more important the housework to the mother, the more likely she was to restrict the child's behavior in exploring the environment.[103]

Career-oriented women do not necessarily find motherhood more stressful than women who are not career-oriented,[104] but stress does often occur. Figure 12.4 illustrates the stress Andrea feels about returning to work after the birth of her first child.

TABLE 12.4 *Factors associated with role strain of working parents*

Types of role strain		
Time shortage	*Income inadequacy*	*Job tension*
Factors: demands		
Being a single parent	Being a single parent	Being a single parent
Having preschool and school-age children	Having first child relatively soon after marriage	Having youngest child under six years old
Experiencing family changes (birth, death, someone leaving home) within last year	Experiencing family changes within last year	Serious illness of a family member within last year
Wife's occupational status higher than husband's	Husband's occupational status relatively low	Equal occupational status of husband and wife
		Inadequate time for family activities
Long work hours, overtime, and moonlighting		Overtime and dissatisfaction with work hours and scheduling
Factors: resource-related		
	Having an unemployed spouse	
	Being in service sector	Being in public relations
Low income	Low income	Low job satisfaction
	Long job tenure	Long job tenure
	Low education	Less than college education
	Black	Low self-satisfaction

Sources: Patricia Voydanoff and Robert F. Kelly, "Determinants of Work-Related Family Problems among Employed Parents," *Journal of Marriage and the Family* 46 (November 1984): 881–892. Copyrighted 1984 by the National Council on Family Relations, 1910 West County Road B, Suite 147, St. Paul, Minnesota 55113. Reprinted by permission.

Robert F. Kelly and Patricia Voydanoff, "Work/Family Role Strain Among Employed Parents," *Family Relations* 34 (July 1985): 367–374. Copyrighted 1985 by the National Council on Family Relations, St. Paul, Minnesota. Reprinted by permission.

Most of us are depressed at some time. Spouses may become depressed to varying degrees under different circumstances. Spouses may, in particular, experience depression when employment preferences are unmet. Husbands with employed wives who prefer that they not be employed experience depression more often than others; unemployed wives wishing to work experienced depression more often. "Also, wives are less depressed if their husbands help with the housework, and the husbands are not more depressed as a result of helping."[105] The

FIGURE 12.4 *Role tension*

Source: Cathy. Copyright 1986 Universal Press Syndicate. Printed with permission. All rights reserved.

lowest depression among spouses occurs when husband and wife agree on their employment and when they share household work, according to a study of 680 couples in a nationwide sample.

Among a smaller sample of women in a Northeast urban community, women with the most complex roles—mothers, wives, and employees—reported the lowest levels of depressive symptoms. Perhaps women with high initial levels of psychological well-being undertake more complex roles, or they may be less sensitive to stress that is role-specific.[106] Interpersonal interactions, particularly within the family, were cited as the greatest source of dissatisfaction and stress.

In a number of studies cited in this chapter, the spouses' sharing of household task responsibilities and the wife's perception of the husband's contribution to housework and child care have been noted as important in satisfaction and well-being. Among wives of dairy farmers, the husband's involvement in the home was associated with supportiveness; the husband's support or perceived lack of it determined stress levels of the wives more than the actual role conflict or actual duties.[107] Role conflict was found to be unrelated to the work loads of the farm and the household.

ECONOMIC VALUE OF HOUSEWORK

The economic value of unpaid productive work has not, until recently, been recognized because the product is not sold. Such productive activity, however, is accepted as economic activity even though it remains difficult to evaluate. The fact that services are performed that would incur direct costs if a paid worker performed them is now recognized, as is the point that the value added to products at home before consumption increases their total worth. Table 12.5 presents a typology of economic evaluation methods related to unpaid household work.

Included in Table 12.5 is value of input or wages foregone, that is, opportunity cost as a method for valuing unpaid household work. In comparison to the most commonly used method of valuation, market wages, the opportunity cost method estimates higher average values of an hour of wife's home work time.[108] The opportunity cost measure is also called the shadow, or reservation, wage. "It takes on this name because at such a wage the individual is indifferent to selecting between time spent at home and time spent in market work."[109]

Traditionally, the economic value of unpaid productive work has been excluded from the gross national product (GNP). The service con-

TABLE 12.5 *Typology of economic evaluation methods related to unpaid household work*

Inputs, volume
- Volume of labor inputs, in time
- Volume of labor inputs, in workers

Inputs, value
- Wage, substitute household worker
- Wage, equivalent market function
- Wage, equivalent market qualifications
- Wage, foregone or opportunity cost of time
- Wage, average for all workers
- Wage, average for female workers
- Wage, minimum
- Returns in other activities
- Value of noncash benefits
- Bride price (applicable in Africa, in particular)
- Labor costs in market enterprises

Output, volume
- Volume of output by activity

Output, value
- Gross output, value derived from consumer expenditures on material inputs
- Value added, derived from consumer expenditures on material inputs
- Gross output value, at price of equivalent market product
- Value added, at price of equivalent market product

Source: Luisella Goldschmidt-Clermont, *Economic Evaluations of Unpaid Household Work: Africa, Asia, Latin America and Oceania,* Women, Work and Development Series, No. 14 (Geneva: ILO, 1987), p. 12. Copyright © 1987 International Labour Organisation, Geneva.

tributions of volunteers in many agencies and groups have not been valued and included in the GNP, nor have household members' contributions, such as household repair and maintenance, meal preparation, cleaning, chauffeuring, or other services. When the value of goods and services produced outside the market system is excluded, the value of the total economic production is underestimated. The value of unpaid productive work has been estimated to be 35 percent of GNP.[110]

Table 12.6 presents the market valuation of household work calculated on an estimate of costs for the services. The real cost of hiring someone to get the house cleaned, the laundry done, the dishes washed, and so on, is used in the estimated economic value. Average wage time used by wife and husband with the corresponding family size was used as the basis for the calculations.

Unpaid productive activities, if evaluated, could provide a basis for calculating benefits ordinarily available only to people gainfully employed outside the home. Legislation has been proposed that would allow homemakers' work to be valued as self-employment income for Social Security coverage and make benefits available similar to those for workers now under the Social Security system. People outside the paid work force have been covered by Social Security only through their spouses, parents, or guardians. With changing life-styles and an increasing divorce rate, such proposals recognize needs for alternative methods of protection for economically vulnerable persons.

Money estimates may be made to establish the reasonable value of productive contributions that are no longer available to the household because of the death or disability of a family member. Litigation involving premature death or disability is increasing in frequency, as is the size of settlements. The wife and/or mother's contribution is of especially high value since she typically spends more time in household work than the father or other family members. The average values for household work shown in Table 12.6 can provide a start for projecting potential losses. Projections into the future need to reflect likely changes in family composition as children reach independence, potential changes in outside employment, and anticipated price effects. In particular cases, adjustments may rightfully be made above or below the average as evidence of skills in the household contribution or in outside earnings. Such projections were made in the case of a mother killed in a car–train collision. The ages of the three children were under-one, three, and five years old. The value of the mother's contribution to the household until the youngest child becomes eighteen years of age has been com-

TABLE 12.6 *Average weekly dollar value of time contributed by various members in all household work (all values to nearest dollar)*

Number of children	*Age*	*Employed-wife households*			*Nonemployed-wife households*		
	Wife	*Wife*	*Husband*		*Wife*	*Husband*	
0	under 25	$ 90	$35		$135	$22	
	25–39	95	35		154	31	
	40–54	113	20		161	40	
	55 and over	113	29		141	53	
	Youngest child	*Wife*	*Husband*	*Teens*	*Wife*	*Husband*	*Teens*
1	12–17	$128	$46	$23	$184	$52	$27
	6–11	154	30	—	180	39	—
	2–5	119	39	—	174	45	—
	1	159	11	—	191	44	—
	under 1	*	*	—	209	40	—
2	12–17	$120	$41	$20	$192	$42	$20
	6–11	138	39	22	190	40	20
	2–5	159	46	28	211	42	18
	1	162	97	*	225	42	*
	under 1	196	41	*	241	39	*
3	12–17	$ 96	$40	$21	$173	$27	$20
	6–11	165	39	32	191	42	30
	2–5	196	54	*	205	36	19
	1	221	62	*	222	42	28
	under 1	166	54	*	256	39	*
4	12–17	$167	$36	$32	$161	$26	$20
	6–11	139	26	21	205	37	21
	2–5	*	*	*	231	38	22
	1	*	*	*	226	50	16
	under 1	*	*	*	263	50	*
5–6	12–17	*	*	*	—	—	—
	6–11	*	*	*	$220	$54	$32
	2–5	*	*	*	229	39	18
	1	*	*	*	189	14	*
	under 1	*	*	*	261	49	19
7–9	6–11	—	—	—	*	*	*
	2–5	*	*	*	$227	$55	$27
	1	—	—	—	*	*	*
	under 1	—	—	—	292	50	*

* Averages not calculated because there were fewer than 4 cases
— No cases
Source: William H. Gauger and Kathryn E. Walker, "The Dollar Value of Household Work," *Information Bulletin* 60, rev. (Ithaca: New York State College of Human Ecology, 1980), p. 11.

puted. The mother worked as a secretary before marriage, and it was assumed that she would have returned to work part time when the youngest child became six years old, full time when the youngest child became twelve years old. Her net economic contribution to the family until the youngest child became eighteen was estimated to be $168,500.

A case of both parents dying from a chlorine gas leak resulted in a $235,000 judgment for the loss of the mother's contribution and $185,000 for the loss of the father's.[111] The Ohio Supreme Court affirmed the loss of the mother's contribution.

Summary

The interrelationship of paid and household work is one of the most explicit examples of the interface of the family and employment systems. The interface is increasingly significant for the large numbers of men and women employed outside the home. Women are increasingly employed outside the home when the children are young. Social support is important for families coping with the demands of work and family, especially those families with young children.

Family members accommodate outside employment and its demands by having small families, spacing children by career demands, evolving differing spousal commitment to careers, and living between work sites or commuting when spousal employment locations differ.

Employment has long impacted on family systems, but today employers are providing more benefits to accommodate family members, especially women. These benefits often fall short of requirements, especially in day care, but flexible work times and limited parental leaves are helping fulfill some of the needs.

Flexible work times affect the scheduling of household work. Work-for-pay schedules today show a remarkable amount of non-day work, especially for unmarried mothers.

As women's career aspirations increase, the value shifts—especially of women—bring increased conflict between work and family. The financial resources to meet family needs are generally greater when both spouses work outside the home. The timing of employment for wives affects their earnings; employment continuity is the most financially rewarding pattern (on hourly rate comparisons).

The division of labor within the household is hypothesized to vary with: (1) resources and power of the husband and wife, (2) time availability of spouses and, to some extent, children, (3) sex-role attitudes of both husbands and wives, and (4) preference for housework.

Organization of both family and paid work is necessary in managing demands faced by both spouses. Wives with professional employment do not reduce their responsibilities as much as wives with less demanding jobs, indicating a tendency toward being "superwomen."

When both spouses work outside the home and share household responsibilities, agreement on standards for tasks is quite different from when only one person completes the tasks. Many couples arrive at a compromise that represents a new standard when differences are great.

The characteristics of tasks and the myriad demands of family members' schedules affect the sequencing of tasks by all family members. Clustering compatible activities can increase efficiency in sequencing tasks.

Increased technology impacts the implementation of household tasks, but modern household equipment does not significantly reduce the time spent on household work. Characteristics of household tasks include variety, repetitiveness, brevity of single tasks, time-consuming nature of total household tasks, amenability to dovetailing, complexity, and adjustable quality through individual standards. These characteristics affect the flow of work and attitudes toward it.

Characteristics affecting time-use efficiency include age, retirement status, level of education, participation in community and group activities, family cohesion, variety of family activities, and income. The environmental situation can facilitate the progress of household activities, but it may have little effect on the time spent on household activities. Good storage and well-chosen work heights can promote efficiency and forestall fatigue in household work.

The degree of the wife's satisfaction with the husband's contribution to housework is more important than the actual division of labor. Husbands tend to be concerned about their participation in housework in relation to their career demands. When both spouses work outside the home, conflicts and tensions of husbands and wives become more similar.

Time shortages, income inadequacy, and job tensions are three major role strains felt by spouses when both work, and they are especially felt by working single parents. Divorced mothers rely heavily on their own strengths to deal with employment and child care conflicts. Children present a particular challenge for single parents when they are ill or when the regular caregiver is unavailable.

Marital and job satisfaction of husbands and wives seems not directly related according to most recent studies, although some indicate that husbands at higher occupational and educational levels have a lower sense of well-being and satisfaction when their wives are employed. Differences have been identified in families with both spouses employed outside the home regarding the quality of the marriage relationship, work-related concerns, role overload, and emotional intimacy.

A wife's fulfillment of her desire to work outside the home is important to her satisfaction and well-being. Women, more often than men, experience depression. The woman's homemaker role and expectations are associated with a number of depressive symptoms. Generally, full-time homemakers and employed women are found to differ little in the prevalence of depression, although employed women are found to be depressed more by feelings of financial deprivation.

The economic value of household work is currently the subject of considerable study. Such valuations could be used as bases for participation in the Social Security system, and they are now used in litigation involving the premature death or disability of a wife or mother.

Notes

1. Pamela Daniels and Kathy Weingarten, *Sooner or Later: The Timing of Parenthood in Adult Lives* (New York: W. W. Norton, 1982), p. 96.
2. Howard Hayghe, "Dual-Earner Families, Their Economic and Demographic Characteristics," in *Two Paychecks: Life in Dual-Earner Families,* ed. by Joan Aldous (Beverly Hills: Sage Publications, 1982), p. 27–40.
3. Howard Hayghe, "Rise in Mothers' Labor Force Activity Includes Those with Infants," *Monthly Labor Review* 109 (February 1986): 43.
4. Frank A. Johnson and Colleen L. Johnson, "Role Strain in High-Commitment Career Women," *Journal of American Academy of Psychoanalysis* 4 (January 1976): 31.
5. Phyllis J. Johnson and Francille M. Firebaugh, "A Typology of Household Work Performance by Employment Demands," *Journal of Family Issues,* 6 (March 1985): 85–87. Copyright © 1985 by Sage Publications, Inc. Reprinted by permission of Sage Publications, Inc.
6. Ibid.
7. Jay Belsky, Maureen Perry-Jenkins, and Ann C. Crouter, "The Work–Family Interface and Marital Change Across the Transition to Parenthood," *Journal of Family Issues* 6 (June 1985): 218.
8. Tammara H. Wolfgram, "Working at Home," *The Futurist* 18 (June 1984): 31–34; and Margot Slade, "Working at Home: The Pitfalls," *The New York Times* (October 21, 1985) p. 15.
9. Sheila Allen and Carol Wolkowitz, "The Control of Women's Labour: The Case of Home Working," *Feminist Review* 22 (February 1986): 39.
10. Dennis K. Orthner and Joe F. Pittman, "Family Contributions to Work Commitment," *Journal of Marriage and the Family* 48 (August 1986): 580.
11. Halcyone H. Bohen and Anamaria Viveros-Long, *Balancing Jobs and Family Life: Do Flexible Work Schedules Help?* (Philadelphia: Temple University Press, 1981), p. 194.
12. Catherine White Berheide, Sarah Fenstermaker Berk, and Richard A. Berk, "Household Work in the Suburbs," *Pacific Sociological Review* 19 (October 1976): 504.
13. Michael Geerken and Walter R. Gove, *At Home and at Work* (Beverly Hills: Sage Publications, 1983), p. 92.

14. Margaret Mietus Sanik and Kathryn Stafford, "Boy/Girl Differences in Household Work," *Journal of Consumer Studies and Home Economics* 10 (September 1986): 217.

15. Elizabeth Maret and Barbara Finlay, "The Distribution of Household Labor among Women and Dual-Earner Families," *Journal of Marriage and the Family* 46 (May 1984): 357–364.

16. Suzanne Model, "Housework by Husbands: Determinants and Implications," *Journal of Family Issues* 2 (June 1981): 225–237.

17. Gloria W. Bird, Gerald A. Bird, and Marguerite Scruggs, "Determinants of Family Task Sharing: A Study of Husbands and Wives," *Journal of Marriage and the Family* 46 (May 1984): 354.

18. Joan Huber and Glenna Spitze, *Sex Stratification* (New York: Academic Press, 1983), p. 90.

19. Karen D. Fox and Sharon Y. Nickols, "The Time Crunch: Wife's Employment and Family Work," *Journal of Family Issues* 4 (March 1983): 61–82.

20. John G. Condran and Jerry G. Bode, "Rashomon, Working Wives, and Family Division of Labor: Middletown, 1980," *Journal of Marriage and the Family* 44 (May 1982): 421–426.

21. Rosalind C. Barnett and Grace K. Baruch, "Determinants of Fathers' Participation in Family Work," Working Paper 136, rev. (Wellesley: Wellesley College, Center for Research on Women, 1986), p. 20.

22. Ibid.

23. Jane Clarkson Perlmutter and Karen Smith Wampler, "Sex Role Orientation, Wife's Employment, and the Division of Household Labor," *Home Economics Research Journal* 13 (March 1985): 243.

24. Huber and Spitze, *Sex Stratification,* p. 91.

25. Barnett and Baruch, "Determinants of Fathers' Participation in Family Work," p. 21.

26. Bird et al., "Determinants of Family Task Sharing," p. 353.

27. Joseph H. Pleck, *Working Wives/Working Husbands* (Beverly Hills: Sage Publications, 1985), p. 72.

28. Ibid., p. 76

29. Huber and Spitze, *Sex Stratification,* p. 91.

30. Ibid., p. 87.

31. Sarah Fenstermaker Berk, *The Gender Factory* (New York: Plenum Press, 1985), p. 146.

32. Constantina Safilios-Rothschild, "Dual Linkages Between the Occupational and Family Systems: A Macrosociological Analysis," *Signs* 1 (Spring 1976): 59.

33. Allie C. Kilpatrick, "Job Change in Dual-Career Families: Danger or Opportunity?" *Family Relations* 31 (July 1982): 363–368.

34. Harriet Engel Gross, "Dual-Career Couples Who Live Apart: Two Types," *Journal of Marriage and the Family* 42 (August 1980); 574.

35. Lucia A. Gilbert, Carole Kovalic Holahan, and Linda Manning, "Coping with Conflict Between Professional and Maternal Roles," *Family Relations* 30 (July 1981): 424.

36. Mary C. Regan and Helen E. Roland, "Rearranging Family and Career Priorities: Professional Women and Men of the Eighties," *Journal of Marriage and the Family* 47 (November 1985): 989.

37. Ibid., p. 991.

38. Catherine A. Faver, "Women, Careers, and Family," *Journal of Family Issues* 2 (March 1981): 106.

39. Ibid., p. 108.

40. Ellen Van Velsor and Angela M. O'Rand, "Family Life Cycle, Work Career Patterns, and Women's Wages at Midlife," *Journal of Marriage and the Family* 46 (May 1984): 365–373.

41. Ibid., p. 370.

42. Ibid., p. 372.

43. Ibid., p. 370.

44. Jeanne L. Hafstrom and Vicki R. Schram, "Housework Time of Wives: Pressure, Facilitators, Constraints," *Home Economics Research Journal* 11 (March 1983): 245–256.

45. Margaret R. Elman and Lucia A. Gilbert, "Coping Strategies for Role Conflict in Married Professional Women with Children," *Family Relations* 33 (April 1984): 317–328.

46. Bohen and Viveros-Long, *Balancing Jobs and Family Life,* p. 181.

47. Hafstrom and Schram, "Housework Time of Wives," p. 252.

48. Beverly Stephen, "Moment of Truth: Having a Second Child," *Working Woman* (April 1986): 176.

49. Bird et al., "Role-Management Strategies," p. 69.

50. Ibid., p. 68.

51. Linda Haas, "Role-Sharing Couples: A Study of Egalitarian Marriages," *Family Relations* 29 (July 1980): 294.

52. Ibid.

53. Bird et al., "Role-Management Strategies," p. 68.

54. Ibid.

55. Stephen, "Moment of Truth," p. 133.

56. Paul William Kingston and Steven L. Nock, "Consequences of the Family Work Day," *Journal of Marriage and the Family* 47 (August 1985): 619–629.

57. Bohen and Viveros-Long, *Balancing Jobs and Family Life,* p. 132.

58. Walter R. Nord and Robert Costigan,

"Worker Adjustment to the Four-Day Week: A Longitudinal Study," *Journal of Applied Psychology* 58 (February 1973): 60–66.

59. Bohen and Viveros-Long, *Balancing Jobs and Family Life,* p. 132.

60. Ibid.

61. Erik Larson, "Working at Home: Is It Freedom or a Life of Flabby Loneliness?" *The Wall Street Journal* (February 13, 1985), p. 34.

62. Joseph H. Pleck and Graham L. Staines, "Work Schedules and Family Life in Two-Earner Couples," *Journal of Family Issues* 6 (March 1985): 61–82.

63. Ibid.

64. Harriet B. Presser, "Shift Work among American Women and Child Care," *Journal of Marriage and the Family* 48 (August 1986): 551.

65. Ibid., p. 561.

66. Graham L. Staines and Joseph H. Pleck, "Work Schedule Flexibility and Family Life," *Journal of Occupational Behaviour* 4 (April 1986): 152.

67. Richard A. Berk and Sarah Fenstermaker Berk, *Labor and Leisure at Home* (Beverly Hills: Sage Publications, 1979), pp. 233–234.

68. Christine E. Bose and Philip L. Bereano, "Household Technologies: Burden or Blessing?" In *The Technological Woman Interfacing with Tomorrow,* ed. Jan Zimmerman (New York: Praeger Publishers, 1983), p. 88.

69. Charles Alexander Thrall, "Household Technology and the Division of Labor in Families," Ph.D. diss., Harvard University, 1970.

70. Ann Oakley, *The Sociology of Housework* (New York: Pantheon, 1974), pp. 96–98.

71. John P. Robinson, "Housework Technology and Household Work," in *Women and Household Labor,* ed. Sarah Fenstermarker Berk (Beverly Hills: Sage Publications, 1980), pp. 53–67.

72. Rebecca P. Lovingood and Jane L. McCullough, "Appliance Ownership and Household Work Time," *Home Economics Research Journal* 14 (March 1986): 326.

73. Ruth Schwartz Cowan, *More Work for Mothers* (New York: Basic Books, 1983), pp. 209, 213.

74. Catherine White Berheide, "Women's Work in the Home: Seems Like Old Times," *Marriage and Family Review* 7 (Fall–Winter 1984): 37–55.

75. Ibid., p. 41.

76. Ibid., p. 43.

77. Ibid.

78. Ibid.

79. Carmi Schooler, Joanne Miller, Karen A. Miller, and Carol N. Richtand, "Work for the Household: Its Nature and Consequences for Husbands and Wives," *American Journal of Sociology* 90 (July 1984): 97–124.

80. Hafstrom and Schram, "Housework Time of Wives," p. 252.

81. Rose E. Steidl and Esther Crew Bratton, *Work in the Home* (New York: Wiley, 1968); 279.

82. Tessie Agan, Stephan Konz, and Lucy Tormey, "Extra Heart Beats As a Measurement of Work Cost," *Home Economics Research Journal* 1 (September 1972): 32.

83. Edmund Churchill, Thomas Churchill, John T. McConville, and Robert M. White, "Anthropometry of Women in the U.S. Army—1977," *Report No. 2—The Basic Univariate Statistics, Technical Report NATICK/TR-77/024* (June 1977): 46, 85.

84. Albert Damon, Howard W. Stoudt, and Ross A. McFarland, *The Human Body in Equipment Design* (Cambridge: Harvard University Press, 1971), pp. 64, 70.

85. Joan S. Ward and N. S. Kirk, "The Relation Between Some Anthropometric Dimensions and Preferred Working Surface Heights in the Kitchen," *Ergonomics* 13 (November 1970): 786.

86. Berk, *The Gender Factory,* p. 40.

87. Ibid.

88. Joseph H. Pleck, "Husbands' and Wives' Family Work, Paid Work, and Adjustment," Working Paper 95 (Wellesley: Wellesley College, Center for Research on Women, 1982), pp. 7–8.

89. Ibid., pp. 7–9.

90. Grace K. Baruch and Rosalind C. Barnett, "Consequences of Fathers' Participation in Family Work: Parents' Role-Strain and Well-Being," Working Paper 159 (Wellesley: Wellesley College, Center for Research on Women, 1986), p. 20.

91. Myra Marx Ferree, "Class, Housework, and Happiness: Women's Work and Life Satisfaction," *Sex Roles* 11 (December 1984): 1073.

92. Drake S. Smith, "Wife Employment and Marital Adjustment: A Cumulation of Results," *Family Relations* 34 (October 1985): 485.

93. Sandra C. Stanley, Janet G. Hunt, Larry L. Hunt, "The Relative Deprivation of Husbands in Dual-Earner Households," *Journal of Family Issues* 7 (March 1986): 3–20.

94. Michael Fendrich, "Wives' Employment and Husbands' Distress: A Meta-analysis and a Replication," *Journal of Marriage and the Family* 46 (November 1984): 878.

95. Sandra Thomas, Kay Albrecht, and Priscilla White, "Determinants of Marital Quality in Dual-Career Couples," *Family Relations* 33 (October 1984): 513–521.

96. Ibid., p. 518.

97. Geerken and Gove, *At Home and at Work,* pp. 80–81.

98. Patricia Voydanoff and Robert F. Kelly, "Determinants of Work-Related Family Problems Among Employed Parents," *Journal of Marriage and the Family* 46 (November 1984): 881–892.

99. Phyllis J. Johnson, "Non-Routine Management of Employment and Family Responsibilities by Divorced Mothers," Ph.D. diss., The Ohio State University, 1978, p. 81.

100. Ibid.

101. Phyllis J. Johnson, "Divorced Mothers' Management of Responsibilities: Conflicts Between Employment and Child Care," *Journal of Family Issues* 4 (March 1983): 100.

102. Joan Toms Olson, "The Impact of Housework on Child Care in the Home," *Family Relations* 31 (January 1981): 79.

103. Ibid., p. 77.

104. Nancy Pistrang, "Women's Work Involvement and Experience of New Motherhood," *Journal of Marriage and Family Living* 46 (May 1984): 445.

105. Catherine E. Ross, John Mirowsky, and Joan Huber, "Dividing Work, Sharing Work, and In-Between: Marriage Patterns and Depression," *American Sociological Review* 48 (December 1983): 809.

106. Denise B. Kandel, Mark Davies, and Victoria H. Raveis, "The Stressfulness of Daily Social Roles for Women: Marital, Occupational and Household Roles," *Journal of Health and Social Behavior* 26 (March 1985): 73.

107. Alan Berkowitz and H. Wesley Perkins, "Stress Among Farm Women: Work and Family As Interacting Systems," *Journal of Marriage and the Family 46* (February 1984): 164.

108. Cathleen D. Zick and W. Keith Bryant, "Alternative Strategies for Pricing Home Work Time," *Home Economics Research Journal* 12 (December 1983): 143.

109. Ibid., p. 137.

110. Martin Murphy, "The Value of Nonmarket Household Production: Opportunity Cost Versus Market Cost Estimates," *The Review of Income and Wealth* 24 (March 1978): 249.

111. John Nussbaum, "3 Orphans Win $1.3 Million in Fatal Chlorine Gas Leak," *The Plain Dealer,* Cleveland (October 24, 1970), pp. 1A, 6A.

Part Three

Applications to situations

13

Family life cycle and young families

Family life cycle describes the movement of family members through stages from formation to dissolution. The family life cycle serves as an indicator of demands placed on the personal and managerial systems at particular phases in the family life span. Individuals and families want to provide adequate resources over the life span and meet needs at all stages. An overview of transitions in goals, decisions, income, and use of resources by families over the life span is discussed in terms of the family life-cycle concept. The special circumstances of young families are considered more fully in this chapter. Middle and older stages are discussed in Chapter 14.

Concept of family life cycle

DEFINITION

Families' progress through life will vary in social-emotional and economic demands—children are born, attend school, leave home, one or both spouses retire.

Probably the most frequently used definition of family life cycle is in relation to ages of children and their presence in the home (Table 13.1). While many families remain intact and follow the usual family life stages, the more common pattern of life stages does not describe others: premarital births; early death of spouses; marriages ending in dissolution or divorce; remarriages; or children from other families joining new households.

The changes that occur in a family over the years, such as adding or losing family members, result in changes in family boundaries.[1] Uncertainties exist regarding boundaries when a divorced man has a female companion who stays with him during the week but is not there on the weekends when the children come. It has been proposed that "the greater the boundary ambiguity at various developmental and normative junctures throughout the family life-cycle, the higher the family and individual dysfunction."[2]

The family or household life cycle can be viewed as a flow rather than a precise linear set of stages. Because of this, it may be easier to conceptualize a "family life spiral." The spiral reflects the general relationships between generations; the developmental tasks of one generation lead to or are associated with changes in other generations. Parents have children who are grandchildren to the senior generation. The middle years of childhood occur while the parents are settling down and grandparents are making plans for retirement (Figure 13.1). The persons who make up each of the generations,

TABLE 13.1 *Families across the life cycle*

	Stages of the family life cycle
Stage 1	Young couples without children "Formulating and negotiating individual and couple goals and mutually acceptable lifestyles"
Stage 2	Families with preschoolers (birth to 5 years) "Oriented toward growth and nurturance" of children
Stage 3	Families with school-age children (ages 6 to 12) "Focused on the education and socialization of children"
Stage 4	Families with adolescents (ages 13 to 18) "Preparing their teenager to be launched from the home"
Stage 5	Launching families (adolescent, age 19 or older) "Parental roles and rules are changing, and the family is occupied with successfully launching its children"
Stage 6	Empty-nest families (all children gone) "Oriented toward couple needs and establishing more differentiated relationships with children and grandchildren"
Stage 7	Families in retirement (male over 65) "Occupied with couple maintenance as well as relationships with extended family and friends"

Source: Adapted from David H. Olson, Hamilton I. McCubbin, Howard L. Barnes, Andrea S. Larsen, Marla J. Muxen, Marc A. Wilson, *Families: What Makes Them Work,* pp. 22–23. Copyright © 1983 by Sage Publications, Inc. Reprinted by permission of Sage Publications, Inc.

i.e., the parent or grandparent generation, may be married couples or single parents—the concept is similar.[3]

The family life cycle for single parents is complex; when compared to two-parent families, differences exist in the "*number, timing, and length of the critical transitions experienced.*

First, all types of single-parent families experience more and longer critical transitions between equilibrium stages than two-parent families.

Second, single parents who marry and add a child experience even more transitions and more structural disorder than single parents who do not remarry.

Third, among single parents who remarry, widowed remarrieds are least vulnerable to divorce (less even than couples in first marriages)."[4]

RESOURCES AND DEMANDS

In looking at a single generation, for the one-half of families whose lives flow along the lines of the stages presented in Table 14.1, resources and demands do not follow the linear relationship from earlier stages of the family life cycle to the latter stages. Generally, resources (such as income) increase for the first fifteen years or so of marriage, then remain relatively stable, and finally decline in the latter stages of the cycle, i.e., after thirty-five years of marriage.

Figure 13.2 presents the median income for households by age of household head. Median household income increases to the age range 45–54 and then decreases. Resources are often scarce when consumption needs (demands) are greatest. The economic pressures on young families rise sharply in the early years of marriage. Some years ago, it was proposed that a way be sought to distribute resources more evenly over the life cycle. A larger portion of total lifetime income would thus be available in the early marriage years when demands are greater.[5]

Expenditure patterns across the life cycle vary as follows: Compared to other age groups, families headed by persons aged thirty-four spend more money on "clothing, shelter, household operations, house furnishings and equipment, automobile purchase and operation, recreation, alcoholic beverages and tobacco, and other transportation."[6] The young family is

FIGURE 13.1 *Family life spiral*

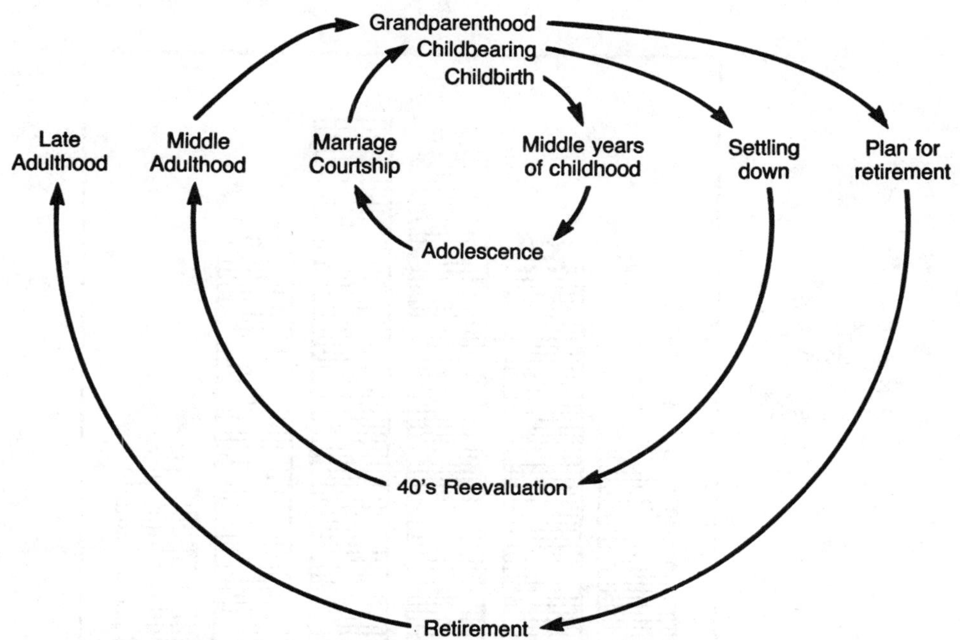

Source: Lee Combrinck-Graham, "A Developmental Model for Family Systems," *Family Process* 24 (June 1985): 142.

more mobile, invests more in human capital, and has less stock in consumer durables than older age groups.

Compared to non-aged groups, aged families "spend relatively more on household utilities, medical care, personal care, gifts and contributions; they allocate relatively less to clothing, house furnishings and equipment, automobile purchase and operation, education, and recreation. For shelter, household operations, and transportation, the aged group spends relatively more than middle-aged groups but less than the young." Reasons suggested for these patterns include the relative immobility of the aged consumer; reduced involvement in outdoor activities; possession of consumer durables accumulated over a lifetime; retirement; and less urgency in investing in human capital.[7] Table 13.2 presents expenditures by age of household head, excluding taxes and other savings and investments.

An analysis of expenditures for clothing by family life cycle, including categories that accounted for nontraditional families, found that the effects of "socioeconomic and demographic variables, particularly income, are much larger than the effect of family life cycle on expenditures."[8]

Time as a resource remains the same over the family life cycle, but available time is at a minimum when demands from young children and employment are at a peak. Changes in time use in household activities hypothesized by Walker and Woods are presented in Figure 13.3. They write:

> Household production time of all workers in the family rises as the number of children increases

FIGURE 13.2 *Median money income of households, by age of householder* in 1984*

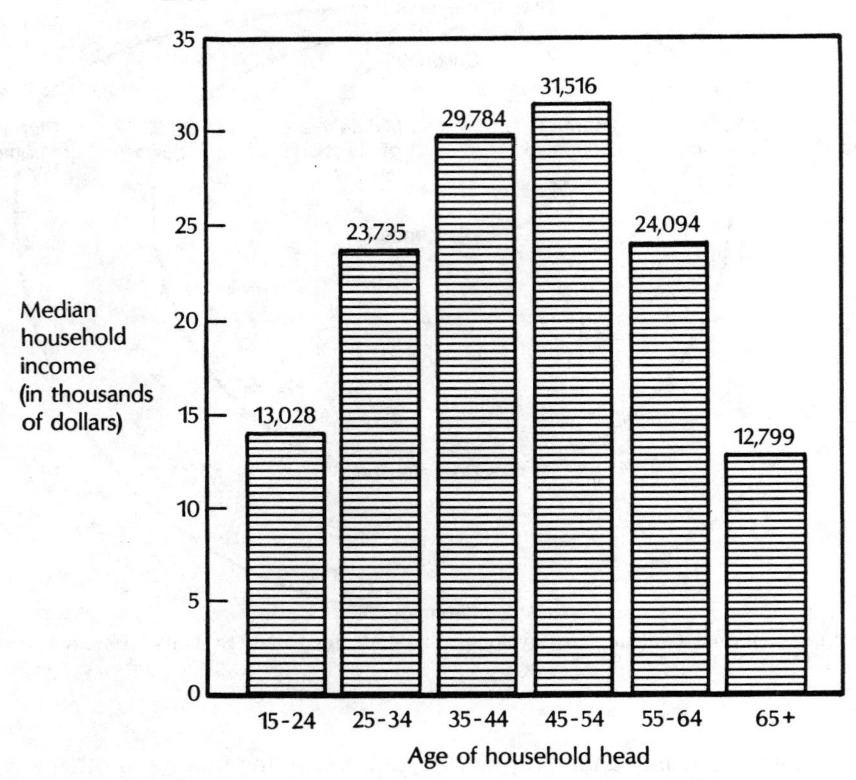

* Householder: Person in whose name the home is owned or rented; if jointly held, may be either husband or wife.
Source: U.S. Department of Commerce, Bureau of the Census, Current Population Reports, "Money Income of Households, Families and Persons in the United States, 1984," Series P-60, No. 151 (Washington, D.C.: U.S. Government Printing Office, 1986), p. 24.

and as the children reach school age, then drops abruptly as children enter the teen years. Time continues to decline as the children leave home, but more slowly. The time level for older couples whose children have all left home remains higher than that of the young married couple, since the older couple frequently continues to live in the more complex physical and social environment, which usually evolves during the child-rearing years.[9]

ENVIRONMENT

A major component of the physical and social environment is the residence of families. The view of moving as involving much risk increases with the stages in the family life cycle.[10]

Families in varying stages of the life cycle were asked about their residential preference in terms of the specific characteristics that were

TABLE 13.2 *Expenditures of households, by age of household head, 1984*

	Age of household head						
Expenditure	*Under 25*	*25–34*	*35–44*	*45–54*	*55–64*	*65–74*	*75 and over*
Food	2,030	3,063	4,342	4,337	3,747	2,831	1,912
Alcoholic beverages	364	353	344	339	272	179	90
Housing	3,740	7,107	8,698	7,878	6,451	4,848	3,972
Apparel and services	787	1,186	1,646	1,620	1,224	715	346
Transportation	3,303	4,641	5,142	6,112	4,477	3,041	1,450
Health care	305	626	795	1,061	1,060	1,340	1,487
Entertainment	678	1,107	1,505	1,274	1,027	604	291
Personal care	105	160	238	265	258	211	148
Reading	66	136	173	173	149	130	93
Education	601	209	367	517	275	88	101
Tobacco	151	220	266	313	260	173	65
Miscellaneous	129	321	404	441	355	172	135
Cash contributions	106	368	1,056	1,131	828	762	878
Personal insurance and pensions	814	2,009	2,725	3,162	2,619	778	229
Total	13,178	21,506	27,702	28,623	23,000	15,873	11,196

Source: U.S. Department of Labor, Bureau of Labor Statistics, "Consumer Expenditure Survey Results from 1984," *News,* USDL 86-258 (June 22, 1986), (Washington, D.C.: U.S. Dept. of Labor, 1986), Table 3.

most important, second most important, and third most important in a new place to live. Table 13.3 includes the most important and second most important variables.

Housing costs are important at each stage of the family life cycle, and no other variable appears as either the first or second most important variable at all stages. The variables reflect both resources and demands.

The quality of life varies across the life cycle and varies in the different perspectives of the husband and the wife. (See Figure 13.4)

The measure of quality of life included satisfaction with marriage and family life; friends; health; home; education; time; religion; employment; mass media; financial well-being; neighborhood and community.[11] The quality of life for wives is lowest at the launching period, when adolescents begin to leave home. The highest quality of life was reported at the empty-nest and retirement stages (Stages 6 and 7).[12]

Young families

Young families are faced with the challenges of family formation and parenthood. The concept of the family as a system takes on new meaning as the parents interact with the child and as the child impacts on the parents. The myriad relationships outside the family system that evolve as the child matures also create many new systemic relationships.

Making arrangements so that the grandparents and children will have time together, taking care to meet and choose a babysitter who will best fit one's needs and values, finding out about chil-

FIGURE 13.3 *Hypothesized relationship between time use and family composition*

Source: Adapted from K. E. Walker and M. E. Woods, *Time Use: A Measure of Household Production of Family Goods and Services.* By permission, The American Home Economics Association, Washington, D.C., 1976: p. 29.

dren's activities offered in a community, meeting with teachers and other professionals who work with family members, attending PTA meetings, serving as scout leaders and sports coaches, and so on, may all be part of the fabric of everyday family life . . .[13]

The interactions between persons related to the child or the child's activities illustrate the many relationships that are absent in childless family systems.

Increased responsibilities accompany the flow of changes from dependence on one's parents to independence from them, to marriage and having children. Managerial skills and resources grow along with the changes.

Some writers refer to the birth of the first child as a crisis, but reference is more appropriately made to a transition to parenthood, since crises are most often unexpected and unplanned. The transition to parenthood is a difficult time for some parents, particularly teenagers.

Teenage marriages that include responsibilities of children due to premarital pregnancies result in early marital dissolutions more frequently than among childless couples. Teenage marriages in general have a higher likelihood of divorce, dissolution, or separation than do marriages of older people. "Furthermore, young teenage brides or grooms (ages 14 to 17) are more likely to have a marriage dissolved than older teenagers (ages 18 to 19)."[14] In spite of the difficulties that many teenagers experience, it is important to differentiate between successful and unsuccessful teenage parenting.

The timing of parenthood and its accompa-

TABLE 13.3 *Level of importance of variables in a new place to live, by family life cycle*

Life-cycle stage	*Most important*	*Second most important*
Young (less than 45), single	Housing costs Peace and quiet Opportunities for advancement	Healthiness of environment Housing costs Convenience to medical facilities
Young, married, no children	Housing costs Convenience to work Job security	Housing costs Quality of local services Friendliness of neighbors
Young, married, young children (0–5 years)	Housing costs Quality of schools Job security	Quality of schools Healthiness of environment Job security
Married (any age), at least one child (6–17 years)	Housing costs Quality of schools Job security	Quality of schools Housing costs Job security
Old (more than 45), married, no children in home	Housing costs Convenience to medical facilities Peace and quiet	Convenience to medical facilities Housing costs Quality of local services
Old, widowed	Housing costs Convenience to medical facilities Public transportation	Property taxes Peace and quiet Convenience to church

Note: The items were most often mentioned as first or second, irrespective of prior or subsequent choices.
Source: Adapted from William J. McAuley and Cheri L. Nutty, "Residential Preference and Moving Behavior: A Family Life-Cycle Analysis," *Journal of Marriage and the Family* 44 (May 1982): 301–309. Copyrighted 1982 by the National Council on Family Relations, 1910 W. County Rd. B, Suite 147, St. Paul, Minn. 55113. Reprinted by permission.

nying demands receive emphasis throughout this section.

INPUT: DEMANDS

Values and goals. The most important decision, personally and managerially, made by young couples is whether or not to be parents.

Some subcultures, such as the Swiss in Wisconsin or the Amish, provide a supportive environment for early marriage and adolescent parenting. The community and the parents support and even encourage the marriage.[15] The newlyweds are immediately involved in the family's economic activities, where goals are deeply ingrained.

In many other settings, the value and cost of having and rearing children may have little relation to the pressure of family and society to have children. One study included young parents and grandparents and sought their ideas about the value and cost of children; the ranking and mean scores on a "value of children" scale revealed some global similarities between gender and generation (Table 13.4). However, the correlation between husbands and wives was significant only for costs of children; there were no significant correlations for mothers and daughters; and for father-and-son pairs, only continuity, tradition, and security were significantly related.[16]

Childhood is an important time for the clarification of goals for the coming years. Young mothers often rethink their career goals and make adjustments in the timing of their goals; families who have been ready to move when it is advantageous for the husband's or wife's career now weigh the effects on their children and may reorient their goals related to career advancement. Certainly parenthood is not all negative in relation to careers. In some families, the responsibility of children may revitalize or redirect career goals upward. The birth of a child is also a time when the housing environment is examined, which may result in changes being made in goals or in the family moving.

In a statewide study in Pennsylvania, home ownership increased from 12 percent for never-married individuals to 42 percent for families

TABLE 13.4 *Mean scores for "value of children" scales, by descending order, for mothers (M), fathers (F), grandmothers (GM), and grandfathers (GF)*

Item	*M*	*F*	*GM*	*GF*
Decision-mindedness: "Having children is seen as a decision which is preceded by weighing the financial, career, and time constraints that children impose."	1	2	4	5
Goals and incentives: "Children are seen as providing a sense of purpose in life and a stronger marital bond."	2	1	1	1
Cost of children: "Children are perceived as limiting parents in their range of activities and as exacting an economic cost."	3	3	2	3
Parenthood satisfaction: "Children are viewed as providing parents with a sense of purpose and achievement."	4	4	3	2
Continuity, tradition, and security: "Children are seen as providing support for aged parents and as helping to continue the family name and traditions."	5	5	6	6
Role motivations: "Parenthood is seen as a reflection of sex- and age-role socialization."	6	6	5	4
Social status: "Having children is viewed as associated with community acceptance and importance."	7	7	7	8
Happiness and affection: "Childbearing is perceived as a means of expressing and receiving love and happiness."	8	8	8	7
External control: "Having children is seen as an inevitable outgrowth of pressure by family and society to have children."	9	9	9	9

Source: Adapted from Richard L. Leavy and Olga B. Hough, "The Value and Cost of Children: Cross-Generational and Sex Differences in Perceptions Among Parents," *Home Economics Research Journal* 12 (September 1983): 57–62.

who were young with no children, to 62 percent for families with at least one child, but none older than five years old.[17]

Events. Events often increase in importance for couples when a child is born. Unexpected illnesses and accidents may make it necessary to alter plans. With a second child, occurrences that were events with the first child may be anticipated. In the case of single-parent families in which one parent has visitation privileges, an example of an event is the last-minute request for a shift in the time of visitation and an extended delay in arrival of the person transporting the child for the visitation.

INPUT: RESOURCES

Help from relatives. Help from parents and other relatives is a resource extension for many young families. Help is given in many forms: outright gifts, advice, or assistance in obtaining money, goods, or services.

In a study of seventy-five Mexican families who had been married one to five years, every family had received some goods and services from their families (Table 13.5). The monetary value of the contributed goods was greater than that for services or the money received. Interfamily transfers have been and continue to be a part of our culture.

Proximity to family of origin affects the amount of contact with families in the transition to parenthood, but "it does not determine the function of such contact (emotional and material support) or the value and meaning of the relationship that motivate such contact . . ."[18]

Income. Young families often begin with relatively low incomes. Resource increases may coincide with increasing financial needs if there is time to make personal and financial adjustments before the first pregnancy and if there is time before the next pregnancy to move ahead. Young low-income people with limited skills or with other resource limitations are particularly vulnerable to expanding family demands.

TABLE 13.5 *Help received by families married one to five years*

Type of help	*Percent receiving help*	*Average annual dollar value*
Goods		
Clothing	96	253
Meals	96	88
Household equipment	83	334
Food	83	71
Household furnishings	81	167
Restaurant guest	79	115
Tools	59	125
Baby furniture	59*	183
Other goods	20	895
Car or car related	10	381
Housing	8	1,713
Services		
Use of		
Tools	63	120
Household equipment	55	113
Car	44	110
Storage	32	205
Other	25	107
Provided		
Babysitting	89*	234
Lodging	65	185
Other services	63	65
Household repairs	51	108
Transportation	47	127
Homemaking	43	175
Personal services	35	47
Car repairs	31	50
Nursing care	23	249
Money		
Unspecified purpose	63	422
Savings	40	128
Money substitutes	33	28
Interest-free loans	17	142
Insurance	15	171
Education	7	674

* Based on number of families with a child.
Source: Adapted from Mary M. Smith and Pamela N. Olson, "Interfamily Transfers to Beginning and Elderly Families," *Home Economics Research Journal* 13 (December 1984): 188–189.

In 1981, in families in which the wife and

husband were employed full time year-round, husbands fifteen to twenty-four years old made an average of $14,610, while wives made $10,510; for husbands aged twenty-five to thirty-four, the average income was $19,580, for wives $13,640.[19] These couples made up about 23 percent of all the married couples with earnings income in 1981. For wives working full time, the earnings picture follows:[20]

	Average earnings in 1981
All children under six years old	$ 9,699
Some children under six years old, and some six to seventeen years old	9,165
All children six to seventeen years old	10,852
No children under eighteen years old	11,634

These data are for married women, but the picture for single-parent mothers is just as dismal, if not more so (see Chapter 16).

Credit use. If income decreases, as when the wife does not return to work after having a child, young families can have problems paying debts. When incomes decline, families frequently find it difficult to adjust expenditures, partly because it is difficult to reduce their level of living, but often because their needs continue to increase. Optimism about increases in earnings and high demands for consumer goods encourage young families to use consumer credit. Young families are more likely to use credit cards than older families, and the probability of their paying finance charges is high.[21]

THROUGHPUT

Planning and implementing. Planning the number and spacing of children is important in the lives of young families. As the trend for women to be employed in higher-paying jobs continues, there will be greater economic incentives for couples to postpone childbirth. Extensions of educational and training periods also contribute to postponement of childbirth. Plans may be altered and children born sooner if the quality and quantity of day-care facilities increase.[22]

Planned pregnancies resulted in mothers who are more likely "to have prepared themselves for parenthood and to be less bothered by parental responsibilities and restrictions; but they also experience fewer gratifications from the parental role. It is suggested that planning increases perceived competency, financial security, and so on, but also reflects introspectiveness and concern (or even hesitancy) about the effect of children on the individual and on a marriage."[23]

The transition to parenthood requires some adjustments and, thus, coping strategies for dealing with change. Young parents reported they had their routines and plans interrupted by their child.[24] Flexibility and adaptability are called for from both parents.

A family coping inventory for parents with new babies has been developed that is effective for use with mothers; the authors recognize the need for modification for use by fathers.[25] The coping behavior grouped around the patterns of (1) seeking social support and self-development, and (2) maintaining family integrity. Included in seeking social support and self-development were such items as "engaging in relationships and friendships," "keeping in shape," and "becoming independent"; maintaining family integrity included "trying to be a parent to the baby and other child(ren)" and "doing things with child(ren)."[26] Another coping pattern—being religious, thankful, content—was not consistent with all groups, but it was a factor with one group of parents. Items included in that pattern were "believing in God," "telling myself I have things to be thankful for," and "belief that life would not be any better without baby."[27]

Several coping strategies are effective, including a positive view of the situation, deciding the dominant role (motherhood or career) so that some decisions can be made more easily at points of conflict in roles, "compartmentalizing roles," and "compromising standards."[28] These coping strategies would seem to be useful in both the personal and managerial systems. The setting of standards for particular circumstances as presented in this book, rather than comprising standards, reflects the coping strategy.

Family size and spacing affect the way resources are allocated to meet goals and events. A number of rather complex factors affect the size and spacing of families, including: unwanted pregnancies or difficulty in conceiving; marital disruptions; infant deaths; incongruence of sex of child with desired sex; changes in living arrangements; wives' plan for work outside the home; and social mobility.[29] Much of the research has been cross-sectional—that is, at a point in time—rather than longitudinal. Longitudinal studies would give some much-needed answers to the sequential questions of differences in reasons for having the first child or the second or third child.

During the first pregnancy, slight changes in gender-typed household roles occur during early pregnancy, during late pregnancy, and postpartum (Table 13.6). Changes undoubtedly occur with the second pregnancy, with a number of factors affecting the change, such as age of the first child, ease of the pregnancy, and whether the mother is employed outside the home.

The roles of husbands and wives for performing household tasks ordinarily include some balance of sharing and specialization.

> [T]he transition to parenthood traditionalizes sex role patterns not so much by reducing the tendency of men and women to take on tasks typically done by members of the other sex but rather by an increase in the extent to which women carry out kinds of tasks that traditionally have been done by women.[30]

In a study of families with children between six and seventeen, children were found to increase their participation in household tasks as they grew older. Further, task stereotyping was obvious in the task participation; particularly, girls washed dishes and cared for clothing, while many more boys than girls helped with maintenance of the home, yard, car, and pets.[31]

As the years of marriage increase, the roles become more patterned. Also, the husband's household responsibilities tend to decrease with age. Role patterns are influenced by such factors as education, occupation, skill, age, and interest.

The very complexity of these interrelationships makes it difficult to identify the factors that have a major influence. In the individual situation, the roles are determined by what will work to the best advantage of the individuals involved—that is, if the decisions are made with managerial insight.

The resources used over the early stages of the family life cycle vary considerably by the number of children in the family. When examining the cost of raising children to adulthood, there are variations by geographic regions.

Costs of raising urban children from birth to age eighteen, estimated in 1987, ranged from $95,867 in the Midwest to $106,687 in the West. Costs of raising rural nonfarm children were lowest in the Midwest at $89,278 and highest in the West at $111,439. These estimates do not include the costs associated with the birth of children (Table 13.7).

Whether individual families consider the initiation of parenthood as a crisis or a transition, many changes occur in plans. Implementation of plans may be considerably altered by the circumstances that did not prevail when there was a couple only.

OUTPUT

Demand responses. Parents are changed themselves by parenthood; the output from the per-

TABLE 13.6 *Household task participation by husbands and wives during early pregnancy, during late pregnancy, and postpartum*

	Wives			*Husbands*		
Household task domain	*Early pregnancy*	*Late pregnancy*	*Post partum*	*Early pregnancy*	*Late pregnancy*	*Post partum*
	Percent usually doing the task					
Neatness chores Setting the table Picking up clothes Making bed Ironing	70	65	72	29	36	36
Essential frequent tasks Food shopping Laundry Cooking Washing dishes Cleaning house	66	61	72	32	41	36
Infrequent tasks Car repairs Appliance repairs Carpentry Taking out trash	19	42	24	83	63	74

Source: Adapted from Wendy A. Goldberg, Gerald Y. Michaels, and Michael E. Lamb, "Husbands' and Wives' Adjustment to Pregnancy and First Parenthood," *Journal of Family Issues* 6 (December 1985): 491.

sonal system that impacts on the managerial system is described by a father on his daughter's first birthday:

> All I know is that here is my home, I have a completely different feeling than I ever expected I'd have. Everything has changed. I guess I knew that was bound to happen, but I couldn't have predicted in precisely what ways. Quite simply, I am a different person than I was a year ago.
>
> I just went into Amanda's room and looked down at her. She never knew me as the man I was before. She may never be aware that, just by living, she has changed another life so much.[32]

Couples expecting a first child and couples who had not yet decided to have children were interviewed over a period of two years to learn more about changes occurring with the birth of the first child. The couples expressed ambivalent feelings, with less satisfaction in their overall relationship.[33]

Partners already vulnerable from lack of sleep and major shifts in their own self-image, their roles in the world of family and work, and their intimate relationships, find themselves startled by unexpected differences and increased conflict. The slightest hint of disapproval or impatience in one's spouse can feel more distressing than before. New fathers and mothers feel both excited and interested in the baby, but they are also weighed down by a new sense of responsibility; it is not unusual for one or both to feel trapped in the "foreverness" of the parent role. In this context, the normal changes and differences that occur as men and women become parents may have negative consequences for the quality and stability of the marriage.[34]

Changes in the mother's labor-force partici-

TABLE 13.7 *Estimates of the cost of raising a child, moderate-cost level, 1987*

Area	*Total*	*Food at home*	*Food away from home*	*Clothing*	*Housing*	*Medical care*	*Education*	*Trans-portation*	*All other*
					Dollars				
Midwest									
Urban	95,867	19,633	2,390	6,460	31,790	6,174	1,932	14,448	13,040
Rural, nonfarm	89,278	18,202	2,200	6,018	29,838	5,642	1,932	13,874	11,572
Northeast									
Urban	101,222	22,436	2,644	6,756	33,992	6,174	2,424	13,426	13,370
Rural, nonfarm	104,600	19,462	2,896	7,084	33,874	6,858	2,424	17,434	14,568
South									
Urban	104,431	19,969	2,768	6,830	34,540	6,858	2,904	15,460	15,102
Rural, nonfarm	108,615	20,641	3,082	6,866	36,254	6,174	2,904	16,928	15,766
West									
Urban	106,687	21,005	3,082	6,572	34,728	7,542	2,424	15,966	15,368
Rural, nonfarm	111,439	20,445	2,896	6,940	34,972	7,390	2,904	18,392	17,500

Source: U.S. Department of Agriculture, Agricultural Research Service, Family Economics Research Group, "Updated Estimates of the Cost of Raising a Child," *Family Economics Review* (October 1987): 36–37.

pation due to the birth of the first child will depend on her education, economic situation, and prebirth work experience. The extent of the first child's demands on the mother that may cause her to leave the labor force appears to differ considerably with each of these variables.[35] For example, one new mother in a comfortable economic position may choose to withdraw from paid employment and invest her time in human capital development at home, while another in less comfortable circumstances may arrange outside child care and keep her job to maintain an acceptable level of living.

While each of us knows cases of fathers' unusual time and effort in the care of a child, the mother primarily furnishes or arranges for child care. In many cases, the birth of a first child increases the new mother's total responsibilities because of the child-care responsibility.[36] When mothers are employed outside the home, child care during working hours often takes place somewhere outside the home. Securing acceptable child care is a continuing challenge for most young families. Often the family may try several kinds of child care before the "right" one is found.

Resource changes. Concerning human resources, both young mothers and fathers report that fatigue is a problem in parenthood. In such cases, the system should be examined for factors that contribute to the tired feelings. The physical effort in caring for a child and stress associated with child care contribute to feelings of fatigue. Not knowing whether children are really ill or whether their behavior is like that of other babies are typically stressful. Management, particularly planning, is more difficult under stress and uncertainty. Young families are often dissatisfied with their material resources, especially their savings and reserve funds.

Summary

Stages of the family life cycle are based on one or more of several factors: years of marriage; timing of family landmarks, such as birth of first child; ages of children and their presence in the home; age of responsible adult(s); and marital status.

Conceptualizing the flow of families is perhaps easier through the family spiral rather than the more linear life cycle. The concept of family life cycle is used in analyzing management as an indicator of the varying demands on families. Income patterns, as well as expenditures, differ relative to the years of marriage and the ages of the couple. The bases for residential preference change over the life cycle, with housing costs appearing as an important variable. Use of time in household production activities peaks with increases in the number of children and the attainment of school age. The quality of life differs from the viewpoints of husbands and wives, but the highest level of satisfaction is in the later years of marriage.

The most critical decision made by young couples is whether to have children. The value of children, cost of children, and parenthood satisfaction are viewed similarly by generation and gender. The period of transition to parenthood is a time of goal clarification; it is also frequently a time for changes in the environment, with the move to a larger apartment or to a house.

Resources in the form of help from relatives—gifts, advice, loans, or other assistance—continue to be a part of the American scene. Income generally increases in the early years of marriage. Many mothers of young children work to add to family income. Young families use credit; and in the case of consumer credit, they are more likely than older families to pay finance charges.

Family planning decisions and the resultant family size and spacing are among the most important of all decisions managerially and personally. Parents are faced with many changes in their lives and in the management of their family resources. The increased time and effort in caring for a child are most often made by the mother, in combination with child-care services. Children assist to some extent with household tasks, and sex stereotyping of the task participation continues.

Planning is more complex in the transition to parenthood than it was before children were born and the resource base changed. Physical energy of both parents may be sapped and financial resources strained during the early years of parenthood. Direct costs of raising a child from birth to age eighteen vary by region, ranging from $89,000 to $111,000.

Notes

1. Pauline G. Boss, "Normative Family Stress: Family Boundary Changes Across the Life-Span," *Family Relations* 29 (October 1980): 447.
2. Ibid.
3. Lee Combrinck-Graham, "A Developmental Model for Family Systems," *Family Process* 24 (June 1985): 142.
4. Reuben Hill, "Life Cycle Stages for Types of Single Parent Families: Of Family Development Theory," *Family Relations* 35 (January 1986): 28.
5. Lester C. Thurow, "The Optimum Lifetime Distribution of Consumption Expenditures," *The American Economic Review* 59 (June 1969): 329.
6. Yung-Ping Chen and Kwang-Wen Chu, "Household Expenditure Patterns: The Effect of Age of Family Head," *Journal of Family Issues* 3 (June 1982): 246.
7. Ibid., pp. 245–256.
8. Janet Wagner and Sherman Hanna, "The Effectiveness of Family Life Cycle Variables in Consumer Expenditure Research," *Journal of Consumer Research* 10 (December 1983): 290.
9. Kathryn E. Walker and Margaret E. Woods, *Time Use: A Measure of Household Production of Family Goods and Services* (Washington, D.C.: American Home Economics Association, Center for the Family, 1976), p. 28.
10. William J. McAuley and Cheri L. Nutty, "Residential Satisfaction, Community Integration, and Risk Across the Family Life Cycle," *Journal of Marriage and the Family* 47 (February 1985): 128.
11. David H. Olson and Hamilton I. McCubbin

with Howard L. Barnes, Andrea S. Larsen, Marla J. Muxen, and Marc A. Wilson, *Families: What Makes Them Work.* (Beverly Hills: Sage Publications, 1983), pp. 181–182.

12. Ibid.

13. Lydia O'Donnell, "The Social Worlds of Parents," *Marriage and Family Review* 5 (Winter 1982): 31.

14. John R. Weeks, *Teenage Marriages* (Westport, Conn.: Greenwood Press, 1976), p. 90.

15. Pauline G. Boss, "Premature Parenting: Making Responsible Decisions to Slow It Down," speech, August 10, 1977, Annual Meeting, State of Ohio Department of Education, Home Economics, Columbus, Ohio.

16. Richard L. Leavy and Olga B. Hough, "The Value and Cost of Children: Cross Generational and Sex Differences in Perceptions among Parents," *Home Economics Research Journal* 12 (September 1983): 61.

17. McAuley and Nutty, "Residential Satisfaction," pp. 127–128.

18. Jay Belsky and Michael Rovine, "Social-network Contact, Family Support, and the Transition to Parenthood," *Journal of Marriage and the Family* 46 (May 1984): 461.

19. U.S. Department of Commerce, "Earnings in 1981 of Married-Couple Families by Selected Characteristics of Husbands and Wives," Current Population Reports, Series P-23, No. 133 (Washington, D.C.: U.S. Government Printing Office, 1984), p. 30.

20. Ibid., p. 26.

21. Lewis Mandell, *Credit Card Use in the United States* (Ann Arbor: The University of Michigan, 1972), p. 17.

22. S. K. Happel, J. K. Hill, and S. A. Low, "An Economic Analysis of the Timing of Childbirth," *Population Studies* 38 (July 1984): 310.

23. Renee Hoffman Steffensmeier, "A Role Model of the Transition to Parenthood," *Journal of Marriage and the Family* 44 (May 1982): 330–331.

24. Lynda Cooper Harriman, "Personal and Marital Changes Accompanying Parenthood," *Family Relations* 32 (July 1983): 392.

25. Jacqueline N. Ventura and Pauline G. Boss, "The Family Coping Inventory Applied to Parents with New Babies," *Journal of Marriage and the Family* 45 (November 1983): 874.

26. Ibid., p. 873.

27. Ibid.

28. Judith A. Myers-Walls, "Balancing Multiple Role Responsibilities During the Transition to Parenthood," *Family Relations* 33 (April 1984): 270; and M. M. Paloma, "Role Conflict and the Married Professional Woman," in *Toward a Sociology for Women,* ed. by C. Safilios-Rothschild (Lexington, Mass.: Xerox College Publishing, 1972).

29. N. Krishnan Namboodiri, "Sequential Fertility Decision Making and the Life Course," in *Determinants of Fertility in Developing Countries, Vol. 2: Fertility Regulation and Institutional Influences,* ed. by Rodolfo A. Bulatao and Ronald D. Lee (New York: Academic Press, 1983) pp. 444–472.

30. Susan M. McHale and Ted L. Huston, "The Effect of the Transition to Parenthood on the Marriage Relationship," *Journal of Family Issues* 6 (December 1985): 422.

31. Frances L. Cogle and Grace L. Tasker, "Children and Housework," *Family Relations* 31 (July 1982): 395.

32. Bob Greene, *Good Morning, Merry Sunshine* (New York: Atheneum, 1984), p. 306.

33. Carolyn Pape Cowan, Philip A. Cowan, Gertrude Heming, Ellen Garrett, William S. Coysh, Harriet Curtis-Bloes, and Abner J. Boles III, "Transitions to Parenthood: His, Hers, and Theirs," *Journal of Family Issues* 6 (December 1985): 475.

34. Ibid., p. 476.

35. Steven D. McLaughlin, "Differential Patterns of Female Labor-Force Participation Surrounding the First Birth," *Journal of Marriage and the Family* 44 (May 1982): 417–418.

36. Jay Belsky, Graham B. Spanier, and Michael Rovine, "Stability and Change in Marriage Across the Transition to Parenthood," *Journal of Marriage and the Family* 45 (August 1983): 575; and Susan M. McHale and Ted L. Huston, "The Effect of the Transition to Parenthood on the Marriage Relationship," *Journal of Family Issues* 6 (December 1985): 422.

14

Family life cycle: middle years and the elderly

Middle years in the family life cycle

Middle years in the family life span range from the time the youngest child starts to school until retirement of one or both spouses. Early middle years in the family life span involve the period from the time the youngest child starts to school until that child leaves home. Late middle years are from the time the youngest child leaves home until retirement of one or both spouses.

Early middle years are described by Sheehy:

> Life becomes less provisional, more rational and orderly in the early thirties. We begin to settle down in the full sense. Most of us begin putting down roots and sending out new shoots. People buy houses and become very earnest about climbing career ladders. . . . This coincides with the couple's reduced social life outside the family and the in-turned focus on raising their children.[1]

Turning forty may be accompanied by a midlife crisis. Some of the stress of midlife includes "coming to terms with the limits of success, giving up dependency relationships at home and at work, signs of physical aging, and contemplation of time running out."[2] The time when midlife crisis occurs will differ. This is the case when some part of one's life has not followed the usual pattern, e.g., late marriage, late child bearing, never marrying, or changing careers at a time that may postpone crisis.

INPUT

Demands. Goals of families in the middle years are focussed on the education and socialization of children, preparing teenagers to be launched from home, careers of both spouses, financial security, and housing. Among women forty to fifty-five years of age, retirement, savings, and investment goals were reported as important.[3]

Value orientations may shift during the middle years and, consequently, goals may change. Although physical and intellectual changes are slow, emotional growth and development may move markedly.[4] Response to changes in individual family members during this period differ for families operating in a relatively open or closed system. Family members have varied and changing goals that may or may not match the families' material resources. In the case of relatively open and expansive families, new resources may be sought to help reach the new goals, or drastic alterations may be made in other resource uses.

An event occurring during the middle family years that may be particularly disruptive is the abrupt departure of a spouse. Departure of a spouse necessitates a major reorientation in a family, whether it is the wife or husband. After departure of a spouse through separation, divorce, or death, the capacity for earning may need to be increased.

Another event in this period of the family life span that can be difficult to deal with is unemployment. Among middle-aged married women in a nationwide study, high unemployment rates affected those who were not previously well established in the labor force. "Among women who had worked most of the time in the recent past, a small minority, generally the less educated, also experienced job loss due to business conditions and considerable unemployment."[5] Family responsibilities and health are also important reasons for irregular work patterns.

Resources. The result of unemployment or departure of a spouse is frequently reduced material resources with increased personal demands. If the event leads to a long-term situation, resource use must be altered or new resources found. In dealing with either the departure of a spouse or unemployment, family members previously not employed may have to seek work; those already employed may have to take an additional part-time job if one is available.

Family income peaks in the age group forty-five to fifty-four; this holds true whether or not the wife is in the labor force (Table 14.1). Women who begin paid employment after childbearing, that is, at midlife, achieve "the same average wage level as wives who enter during childbearing, but with payoffs to their educational level."[6] Job continuity and sequence are also important factors affecting the wages attained by women who enter the labor force during midlife. The sequence of childbearing and employment is somewhat more advantageous in terms of wage attainment than the pattern of entry during childbearing.[7] Generally, it appears that "delayed marriage, higher family incomes during middle work years (about age forty), and liberal sex-role attitudes during middle work years enhance chances for labor-market success."[8]

Work expectations for persons aged thirty-five will both influence labor-force behavior and significantly increase employment during childbearing years. In one study, for those women who planned to be employed, marital history and educational attainment had little to do with their employment. More highly educated women stayed home with their children when they were young.[9]

> The midlife woman who has been employed throughout adulthood is least likely to experience poverty at midlife or later. . . . The midlife women employed intermittently throughout adulthood and who is no longer a wife or mother fares worst under the current set of public programs. There exists no federal cash transfer entitled programs that provide for women before retirement age unless they have dependent children, with the exception of disability insurance. However, disability insurance is not paid to career homemakers who become disabled or chronically ill.[10]

Many Chicago-area women aged twenty-five to fifty-four expect to retire early, seeing their husband's pension as the major income source during retirement. The women report plans for later retirement when they need to be financially independent, when the income need is greater, or when they have a high commitment to their work, even though they have relatively low economic needs.[11]

Occupational changes with consequent income advances are often made during the early middle years; for people with limited schooling and during the older middle years, the move is downward in the occupational ladder.[12]

TABLE 14.1 *Median family income, by age of male head, with and without wife in paid labor force for all races, 1983*

Age of male head	Median family income: All families	Wife in labor force: Wife employed full time	Wife in labor force: Wife employed part time	Wife not in labor force
	Dollars			
18–24 years	16,679	20,867	16,627	12,788
25–34 years	25,970	30,826	25,581	21,637
35–44 years	32,591	37,415	32,085	27,855
45–54 years	35,872	40,596	36,906	30,005
55–64 years	29,171	35,122	32,931	24,943
65+ years	17,263	26,728	21,410	16,268

Source: U.S. Department of Commerce, Bureau of the Census, Current Population Reports, "Money Income of Households, Families and Persons in the United States: 1983," Series P-60, No. 146 (Washington, D.C.: U.S. Government Printing Office, 1985), pp. 71–74.

THROUGHPUT

The middle years for families are marked for many by working toward goals set in earlier years. For some, this means that repeat-use plans are used again and again. A "static life plan" is based on a maturity myth that all will be well in the forties if you keep working toward it.

> [A static life plan] insists that we follow rules set down by others in accordance with external demands of society. . . . A static life plan creates a situation in which stagnation and loss of self becomes inevitable. . . . A static life plan means that change, whether in the external world or inside ourselves, will be a cause for anxiety.[13]

The effect of this static life plan, or morphostatic system, on planning and implementing is a reduction in the alternatives considered and dissatisfaction when plans are not precisely met.

A life strategy of operating as a morphogenic system incorporates anticipation of change, contributing to a general or directional view that can accept a variety of goals and various plans for meeting them.[14] "Shifting gears is the process by which we choose change; our life strategy is the open-minded attitudes that allow us to make that choice."[15] With the more open, adaptive, and expansive view, new plans will be needed to meet varying goals.

Having a life dominated by continuity does not mean that a family or individuals in the family cannot change directions. The sameness of life for some people in midlife may make them take stock and seek change and plan for it within the same environment.

One writer identified the ages between thirty-nine and forty-two as ones where people "know how to use their time, how to delegate authority, how to make decisions, how to make policy, and how to administer systems."[16] Many women manage multiple roles well, with high coping abilities.

In the mid-forties, dealing with teenagers and elderly parents—both of whom may require material resources but who want to make their own decisions—is a special challenge. Making and implementing plans that involve either teenagers or elderly parents can be difficult.

Relatively little is known about the planning of expenditures by teenagers, although one writer has commented on the extent of choices that teenagers have: "Kids are given more latitude. We are a more prosperous society and we let them buy their own clothes. We think if we allow them to make more choices they will develop more responsibilities."[17] The weekly incomes of teenage boys and girls are similar, but the expenditures differ (Table 14.2).

Clothing and cosmetics and fragrances account for 43 percent of the expenditures by teenage girls, while movies, dating, entertainment, gasoline and auto, and clothing account for 48 percent of the expenditures by teenage boys. Expenditure patterns do not reveal the responsibility assumed in relation to the choices, but choice-making is good experience before children leave home for college or work.

TABLE 14.2 *Teenage income and expenditures*

	Boys aged 16–19	*Girls aged 16–19*
	Dollars	
Income		
Allowance	21.80	22.05
Earnings	31.65	32.55
Total	53.45	54.60
Expenditures		
Food and snacks	6.60	3.90
Clothing	8.15	15.40
Personal grooming	3.45	2.40
Cosmetics and fragrances	—	10.25
Movies, dating, and entertainment	8.90	4.30
Gasoline and auto	8.50	4.40
Records	.90	1.45
Books, paperbacks	.95	1.10
Coin-operated video	1.90	.30
Magazines	.95	.70
School supplies	.80	.85
Cigarettes	.20	.25
Hobbies	2.00	—
Total	43.30	45.30
Savings	10.15	9.30

Source: Rand Youth Poll, Teenage Economic Power, 1983, cited in Doris L. Walsh, "Targeting Teens," *American Demographics* 7 (February 1985), p. 25.

Careful planning of expenditures of families in support of the costs of vocational training or a college education is necessary for some families. The expenses for education are met by support from parents, by the student's savings and earnings, and, for many, by receiving some type of financial aid. Nevertheless, as most users of this book are aware, the period is often marked by a drain on family resources.

Private university costs averaged $10,199 in 1986–87, with tuition amounting to $2,899 of that cost. Public university costs averaged $5,604, when living on campus; the lower tuition made most of the difference from private institutions. Tuition is expected to rise 6–7 percent annually, and charges for room and board about 5 percent per year throughout 1988–89.[18]

Participation of family members in household work changes for a time, but as the years of marriage increase, the roles become more patterned. The husband's responsibilities tend to decrease with years of marriage. Children increase their participation in household tasks as they grow older, according to a study of families with children between ages six and seventeen. Task stereotyping was obvious in the task participation; girls washed dishes and cared for clothing, while many more boys than girls helped with maintenance of the home, yard, car, and pets.[19]

OUTPUT

Families in the middle years may have one or both spouses experiencing a midlife crisis. The midlife crisis may be expansive and growth-producing, while for others there is an effort to cling to the status quo (morphostatic response). Some turn to sports and exercise in competition for time with the family. A regressive shift in priorities may occur, regressive in that one moves away from complicated tasks to simpler ones, such as running. Some women return to work at midlife. For working-class women who have limited options, employment may not open new vistas or be expansive. For them, midlife is probably the most difficult time.[20]

"If we have confronted ourselves in the middle passage [around age fifty] and found renewal of purpose around which we are eager to build a more authentic life structure, these may well be the best years."[21] Families begin to gain a new stability as children are launched into their adulthood. The middle years bring different satisfactions for men and women, though they will be more similar as career expectations become more alike.

White women in midlife, ages thirty-five to fifty-five, were interviewed to determine their psychological well-being. Being a paid worker was associated with higher self-esteem; being a wife or mother was not predictive of well-being; and being a mother did not predict pleasure/happiness. Family income predicted all three measures of well-being, self-esteem, depression (or lack of it), and pleasure, which contained indicators of happiness, satisfaction, and optimism. The authors suggest that multiple roles may be a prerequisite for well-being.[22]

In the middle years, the satisfaction of meeting many long-term goals is realized: home ownership, children raised to maturity, and progress in occupations.

The elderly

The aging population can be divided into the following categories:[23]

Older	age fifty-five and over
Elderly	age sixty-five and over
Aged	age seventy-five and over
Very old	age eighty-five and over

Some general facts about the aging population follow:

- Growth in the elderly population over the past two decades has been twice that of the other population groups.
- The very old population showed a 165 percent increase between 1960 and 1982.
- The ratio of elderly to other population groups will be one to five in 1990; in 2025, it will be one to three.
- The median income of the elderly has increased more over the last two decades than that of younger population groups.
- Approximately one in seven elderly Americans live in poverty.[24]

Elderly Americans are predominantly women: They outnumber men by a ratio of three to two. Approximately half of all elderly women are widows compared to only one in eight elderly men. This is probably a result of the fact that men have a shorter life expectancy, that they usually marry women younger than themselves, and that widowers have a higher remarriage rate than widows.[25]

THROUGHPUT

Demands. Today there are many elderly people who live full lives, with continued personal growth and development. Retirement is a new phase in their lives, a time to enjoy travel and pursue projects of long-standing interest.

Goals and event demands change in the lives of the elderly as their situations change. Maintaining their level of living, and attention to health, housing, environment, family relations, and financial management, are goals frequently requiring attention from the elderly.

Retirement brings a reduction in time at work and a consequent increase in time available for leisure. Developing leisure competence should be a major goal for late adulthood. It can be viewed as having three dimensions: physical care, intellectual growth, and social expansion.[26] Physical care of oneself means giving attention to exercise, nutrition, rest, and relaxation—an orientation to preventive measures as opposed to remedial measures.

Dr. Seuss suggests:

In those green-pastured mountains
of Fatta-fa-Zee
everybody feels fine
at a hundred and three
'cause the air that they breathe
is potassium-free
and because they chew nuts
from the Tutt-a-Tutt tree
This gives strength to their teeth,
it gives length to their hair,
and they live without doctors,
with nary a care.[27]

from *You're Only Old Once!*

Intellectual growth through university course work, use of libraries, or the pursuit of former or new hobbies is limited primarily by motivation and resourcefulness.[28] Social expansion is the third vital dimension, with making new friends and interacting with individuals other than family members as important components. Realizing that specific needs can be met through volunteer work can be helpful in identifying meaningful community activities.[29]

Relatively little information is available on events, which are another form of demands. Events originating from changes in health and/or accidents seem to occur with increasing frequency as people grow older. These events often affect the lives of the children and friends of the elderly. Consider the following example.

Mrs. Mawson fell in the backyard late one evening as she was going to her car. She broke her leg but managed to crawl back into the house and contact her daughter, Barbara, by telephone. Barbara and the family physician managed to get Mrs. Mawson to the hospital. Barbara was planning to go to Europe in four days. The management of her responsibilities was stretched to the limit by visiting her mother in the hospital (18 miles away) and visiting her father in a nursing home (35 miles away). The accident was an unplanned occurrence in the life of Mrs. Mawson and Barbara that required carefully managed resources to meet the demands.

The elderly are probably less able to respond quickly and effectively to events. When time is not essential, responses to events based on experience can be wise ones. Physical limitations often slow the response. A study of injury severity in fire incidents involving apparel found that people over sixty-five had a significantly lower percentage of relatively minor burns and a higher percentage of burns covering 50 percent or more of the body. The author of the study suggests that defensive capabilities become limited with age.[30]

Events in the lives of individuals that can be traumatic are notification of early retirement or the death of a spouse. In many cases, early retirement can be foreseen due to ill health or to economic circumstances in a community or a company. When early retirement or personal losses are not anticipated, receipt of such notices can be events of major importance.

Resources. Resources that contribute heavily to a person's flexibility in activities and capacity for meeting goals are good health, economic solvency, religiosity, and social support of someone—such as a spouse, close friend, or relative—to serve as a confidant. These human and material resources held by older families are interrelated in their impact on family management.

Having good health is probably one of the most important human resources of the elderly. Poor health, compounded by limited financial resources, contributes to the concerns of many older people. Chronic health problems affect 86 percent of the elderly to some degree. While health problems are significant, they are largely ones that can be treated and that do not impair the capacity to work. Long-term and/or serious illness can drain resources severely and even bring instant poverty.[31]

For many over age sixty-five, barriers exist for participation in health maintenance organizations (HMOs) as an alternative to traditional Medicare Supplementary Insurance. Lack of knowledge of alternatives (such as HMOs), reluctance to change from supplementary insurance, financial constraints, and negative attitudes toward the concept can each serve as barriers to participation and possibly to less-effective health care.[32]

One person made the following comments in relation to HMOs: "Wouldn't want to pay a set amount to a doctor as an insurance benefit; would totally change the relationship with the doctor. The only way I'd pay in advance is if it were conceptualized as a retainer that I would draw against as I received care."[33] Another noted: "Have no money to pay for it and wouldn't drop my insurance. If I dropped it, I might be able to get insurance or I might have to wait six months to cover a preexisting condition. I wouldn't take that risk."[34]

Wide variation exists in the financial resources of the elderly, just as with any other age group. Resources in the form of eligibility for a pension before age sixty-two are the best predictor of early retirement for women, although asset income and health did not affect early retirement plans.[35] At age sixty-five, eligibility for a pension continues to be the significant reason for women's retirement.[36]

Income is the coping resource that seems to make the difference among the elderly. Income allows purchase of needed services when one's spouse, relatives, or friends are unable to render the services. For example, when poor health prohibits driving to the grocery store or doctor's office, sufficient income allows the elderly person to take a taxi or hire someone to drive his/her car.[37]

Upon retirement, the average couple "initially loses about one-third of its previous income, while non-married women, with less to begin with, lose somewhat less."[38] Sources of income for those with low income prior to retirement include an important component of earnings: Many often earn as much as they did before retirement and still collect their Social Security check.[39] These low-income earners also had fewer pensions other than Social Security, and their asset income amounted to only about one-tenth of total income, compared to as much as one-fourth of aggregate income for the high-income group (Figure 14.1).

Resources are particularly limited for most single elderly persons who occupy a single room. For one such group at the Guinevere Hotel, a number of the tenants had to move out when the rent was raised a small amount, "a reminder of the unalterable reality of drastically circumscribed funds."[40]

When the elderly have assets, such as a home or certificates of deposit, they also feel a sense of financial security. But often there is reluctance to use assets that have been designated for precautionary purposes or anticipated major expenses; or they may not be available for meeting current day-to-day needs.[41] As an eighty-eight-year-old woman living with her ninety-five-year-old husband put it:

> We have a bond up in the bank, we put it there a long time ago. And Fred, he says, we're not going to cash that, but unless we just have to, until we have to have it for burial expenses; $1,000, and we would have to cut it down to $900 before we could get the food stamps. And Fred says he won't do it. I never insist because after all . . . he worked hard to get the money to buy that bond and I think he should have the say-so.[42]

Relatives and children are an important source of services for some elderly persons. In a large study conducted in the New York metropolitan and Miami–Fort Lauderdale areas, older persons reported turning to relatives and children for daily care and attention, for providing home nursing care, and emotional succor when upset.[43] Far more than for any other group (friends, neighbors, formal organizations), the elderly reported calling on relatives

FIGURE 14.1 *Income shares at time of Social Security benefit receipt, by level of previous income*

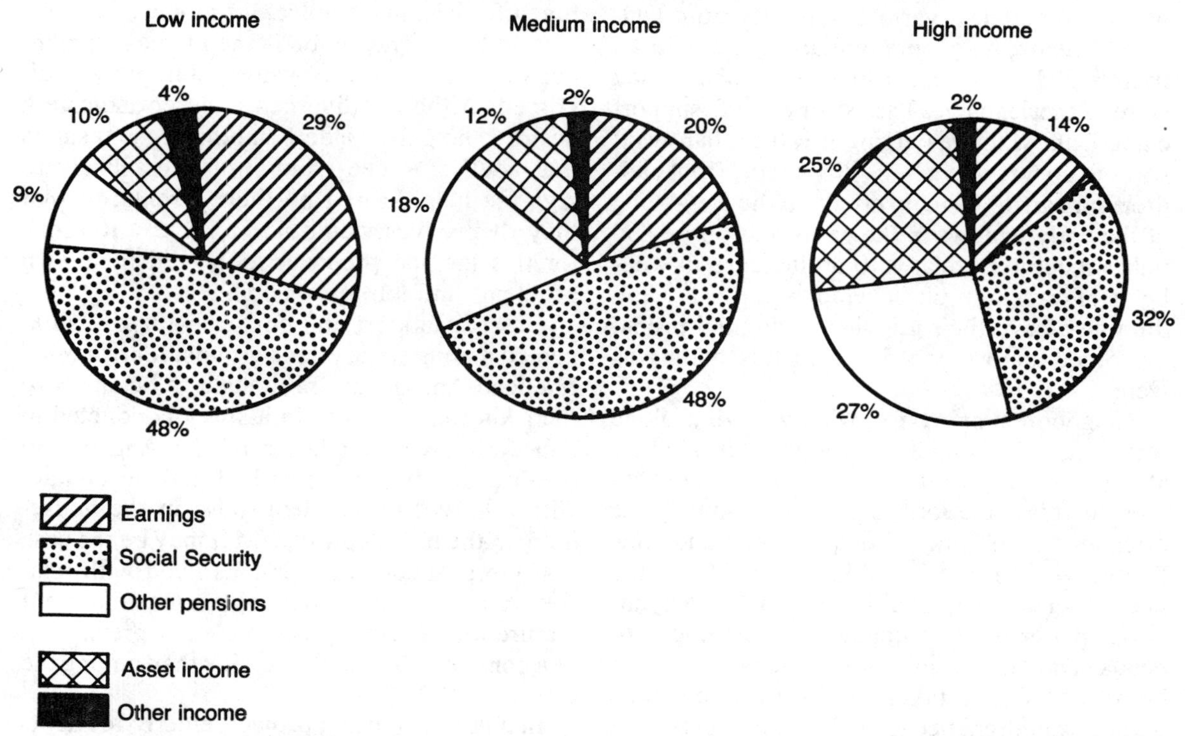

Source: Alan Fox, "Income Changes at and after Social Security Benefit Receipt: Evidence from the Retirement History Study," *Social Security Bulletin* 47 (September 1984): 10.

and children for storing clothes and doing laundry, and managing money, bills, bank account, and Social Security. Family and friends are reported giving assistance in transportation and housekeeping.[44]

Racial differences in intergenerational support exist, with elderly black parents giving and receiving more support than elderly white parents; "however, the greater amount of help that is received by older blacks is, to a large extent, the result of socio-economic factors. The increased amount of help that they give to the middle and younger generations appears to be a combination of cultural and socio-economic factors. Among black families, attitudes of respect for generation play a part in determining family support behavior."[45]

Ties with children and siblings became more intimate after widowhood, as reported in a study of elderly women in Omaha, Nebraska; "primary and confidant ties with other kin are allowed to disintegrate."[46] Both married and widowed elderly women relied on children when they had health or financial problems.

A study of widowhood in Chicago divided the widows into two phases: the *crisis-loss-phase* group, made up of women continuing to grieve acutely and widowed 18 months or less, and the *transition-phase* group, composed of women widowed between 19 and 35 months and who were experiencing limited grieving.[47] The widows reacted to various supports from widowed friends, neighbors, children, and married friends differently according to the phase they were experiencing. The strength of support came from who was giving it rather than what sort of support was given. "[S]upport from children appears to have no effect on the well-being of the early widows in the crisis-loss phase and only moderately relates to an increase in well-being of transition-phase widows. . . ."[48] Children also have their grieving to do, and probably other factors contribute to this finding as well.

Neighbor support for widows living alone was least for childless widows in another study.[49] A number of factors possibly contributes to this situation: Childless widows have often had a lifetime of employment and thus limited time for getting to know neighbors; the marital relationship of childless couples may involve patterns of intimacy and fulfillment of needs; and the neighbors themselves may not be comfortable in taking on care for neighbors without children because they anticipate that the person will not be a neighbor for long, or they may fear that involvement could lead to a greater commitment than they want to make.

Two recent studies of the childless elderly revealed that their personal and social resources did not differ significantly from elderly persons with children.[50] It may be that childless couples develop a self-reliance through the years that prepares them for later times in their lives.

Indeed, there is no assurance that children will care for their elderly parents or that the exchange of personal and social resources will be what is desired by one or the other. Reciprocity is the general pattern among most elderly who receive help from members of their informal network of friends, relatives, and children.[51] The elderly provide such help as babysitting, running errands, home repairs, transportation, house and yard work, food, advice on family and financial management, help in time of crisis, and the loan of money.[52]

Another phenomenon is the increasing number of elderly parents whose children are divorced. Although divorced children indicate a desire to help their elderly mothers, the result is that adult divorced children are less likely to give the help desired by their parents, or that they themselves would like to give.[53] Reasons for this include preoccupation with their own problems and job responsibilities.

Greater support and contact with kin is expected among some ethnic groups; for example, Mexican-Americans are thought to be closer to their kin than Anglos. In a study conducted in San Antonio, one-quarter of the Anglos and one-fifth of the Chicanos had had no contact with relatives (other than those in the household) in the past two weeks.[54] It may be the case that more Mexican-Americans lived with relatives and had more relatives. One important feature for the elderly is the greater prevalence of a confidant among the Anglos than among the Chicanos.[55]

In a public housing project, elderly residents often help each other, and this may well be critical assistance. In the following example, assistance in dealing with an event was particularly important.

> Herbert Watson, a man in his late sixties with a past history of heart disease, describes how he obtained skilled assistance when he unexpectedly fainted in his room: 'When I came to, I dragged myself to the phone. I was frightened to stand up because I didn't know if I would fall over again and maybe break a leg or a hip. No one was in the office, so I called this lady upstairs who is a practical nurse. She came right down and helped me over to the bed. She took my blood pressure and said it was way down. After a while I was O.K., but she stayed with me until she was sure I could manage.'[56]

Resources that are available only through public ownership may be very important to the aged. These services are often essential if the elderly, without spouses or relatives, are to remain independent in their living arrangements.

At a minimum, public transportation is needed by many for grocery shopping and visits to the doctor. In a city with public transportation, older nondrivers reported that riding as a passenger was their most common means of transportation to visit children and other relatives and friends, to see the doctor, to shop, and to attend religious services and other community events. While public transport was often not dependable, being a passenger had the advantages of getting to otherwise inaccessible places, was enjoyable, and easier where there were physical limitations.[57] These factors have particular relations to sequencing problems in planning.

"Dissatisfaction pertaining to convenience for traveling to a public library, shopping place, bank, doctor or clinic, public park, restaurant, post office, and church or synagogue" was associated with "general feelings of unhappiness, little anticipation of the future, and self-assessed poor health" for elderly respondents in North Carolina.[58]

More sophisticated widows were found to use community resources, while those in special need often did not. "The existing helping persons and groups are failing these women, at the time during the husband's fatal illness, immediately after his death, when the widow is trying to build a new life, and when she stabilizes herself in a life style and support system, extensive or restricted as those may be."[59]

Community services are limited in a number of ways for the elderly. Three reasons are proposed:

1. Too large a social emphasis has been placed both on the roles of the elderly individual to care for himself (herself) and on the family to provide services for its members.
2. The economic status of the aged makes them captive consumers of whatever services are available.
3. Our own cultural aversion to old age and to death.[60]

Because community services often lack coordination, individual needs may not be met. The social and economic position of the individuals, their awareness of available services, and determination to receive those services affect whose needs are met.

THROUGHPUT

Planning. Planning for retirement is difficult because uncertainties are prominent during the time when planning must be done. The uncertainties include time of death of self and spouse, income, retirement needs, especially health care, and date of retirement.[61]

Retirement among two-earner couples should be viewed as a family process or within the household framework. An analysis of hypothesized retirement patterns "suggests a certain amount of equality in decisions to retire since the pattern chosen depends on the characteristics of both spouses, not just the husband's."[62]

Three retirement patterns named for the relationship to the wife are:

Joint: both spouses work and withdraw from the labor force simultaneously;
Substitute: wife works beyond the husband's retirement, "substituting" for her husband;
Secondary: husband works "longer or more steadily than the wife," whose work is "secondary" to her role in the family.[63]

The analysis of almost 2,000 couples married during the initial stage of the study found that the joint pattern of retirement was more prevalent when one spouse was older and when the wife was an unpaid worker in a family business.

The substitute or secondary retirement patterns were found when one spouse made lower wages or when one spouse lacked pension coverage.[64] Support was clearly found for an interdependent view of husband and wife in the retirement decision.

Chapter 11 includes a discussion of saving to meet retirement goals. The interaction of the family system with the economic system is dramatically evident with the elderly individual or family, and the results must be taken into account in planning. The effects of unchecked inflation on the material resources of the family are particularly serious for individuals who have fixed incomes and assets.

Social Security was designed as a supplemental retirement system, yet many individuals receive only Social Security benefits, some at the very lowest levels. For those receiving minimal Social Security benefits as their major source of income, the incomes are woefully inadequate.

Planning for needs in old age is also made difficult by the rising level of living of other families and individuals. Anticipation of the effects of this comparison on an individual is not easy.

The importance of standard setting is likely to increase for the elderly. Retired people must often plan expenditures more closely than at any time in their lives, except in the beginning years of marriage.

Compared to nonretired households, "retired households allocated a larger part of an increase in total budget to shelter, medical care, and gifts and contributions, other things being equal. They allocated less of an increase in budget to food, food away from home, and household operations and expenses and much less to household furnishings, clothing, recreation, vacations, and vehicle purchases."[65] Table 14.3 gives annual budgets for retired couples at three levels of living, updated to 1985 dollars.

In long-term planning, the elderly often must consider the need for institutional care. About 5 percent of the elderly population in the United States live in institutions.[66] Choices are sharply curtailed in many institutional arrangements, and planning is limited.

TABLE 14.3 *Annual budgets for retired couples at three levels of living, urban United States, autumn 1981, adjusted to 1985 price levels.*

Budget item	Level of living		
	Lower	*Intermediate*	*Higher*
		Dollars	
Total budget	8,404	11,893	17,537
Total family consumption	8,041	11,178	16,236
Food	2,452	3,256	4,092
Housing	2,771	3,956	6,187
Transportation	613	1,189	2,172
Clothing	268	450	691
Personal care	230	243	493
Medical care	1,450	1,458	1,455
Other family consumption	375	623	1,228
Other items	424	838	1,524

Sources: U.S. Department of Labor, Bureau of Labor Statistics, "Three Budgets for a Retired Couple," Autumn, 1981. *News,* USDL 82-266; and "CPI Detailed Reports," December 1981, p. 10, and December 1985, p. 8.

The number of options available generally decline in old age. The effect of limited social choices is a narrowing of managerial activity. In recent years, elderly people have resisted the downturn in social choices, with some choosing to remarry in later years and others, though limited in number, choosing an alternative lifestyle, such as communal living.

Flexibility is an attribute of planning that needs to be high when the elderly person lives in an age-heterogeneous situation. The need for flexibility is less in an age-homogeneous setting, where the variety of situations is reduced and expectations are standardized.[67]

Planning for retirement seems to be an important prelude to satisfaction in outcomes. For men who had retired before their company's mandatory retirement age, ill-adjusted retirees were twice as likely to have done little planning as were well-adjusted retirees. Making plans before rather than after retirement is important. For both blue- and white-collar workers with high adjustment to retirement, over 70 percent had made retirement plans before actual retirement.[68]

In a study of union workers aged sixty and older who had planned retirement, changes in the husband's decision-making patterns occurred during the first two years of retirement. Decisions about the husband's working and about the care of and repairs to the house that had been made frequently by the husband became almost completely husband-dominated. The decisions that were almost equal before retirement—that is, where the husband and wife contributed equally to the decision—became more nearly equal after retirement. The decisions were: what trips to take, when to go to the doctor, what evening activity to engage in, and what to do for relatives—involving both standard setting and sequencing aspects. The questions of food expenditures and visits of relatives moved toward being more equal in husband and wife involvement after retirement. What to have for meals became more wife-dominated in the two years after the husband's retirement.[69]

Implementing. Implementation of plans may be considerably altered by the changes in the physical capacity of the aged. The pace of activities is generally slowed, and help is increasingly needed as years progress and chronic health conditions develop.

Table 14.4 shows the percentage of those sixty-five years of age and older who have chronic conditions and who need help in activities.

TABLE 14.4 *Percentage of persons 65 years and over with chronic conditions needing help in activities*

	Age		
Activity	*65–74*	*75–84*	*85 and over*
Any activity	6	14	40
Shopping*	4	12	36
Chores	4	10	29
Handling money	2	5	18
Meals	2	6	22

* Excludes persons who only need help in getting to the store.
Source: Adapted from Barbara A. Feller, "Americans Needing Help to Function at Home," *Vital and Health Statistics,* No. 92, (Washington, D.C.: U.S. Department of Health and Human Services, National Center for Health Statistics, 1983); and Marilyn Doss Ruffin, "Contribution of the Family to the Economic Support of the Elderly," *Family Economics Review* (October 1984): 8.

For the actual performance of tasks, some changes were noted following retirement. "Husbands tended during the first year of retirement to turn over more of the household tasks to their wives than had been the case before retirement."[70]

Couples who had been married for fifty years or longer and with one member seventy-five years old or older were asked about the division of responsibilities for household tasks. Table 14.5 reveals that the "masculine" tasks of yard work, car maintenance, and making household repairs were responsibilities of husbands, and one task often considered feminine, cleaning house, was a male responsibility. Planning family social events and shopping were shared by husbands and wives.[71]

Farmers, blue-collar workers, small businessmen, and salaried and self-employed professionals were studied, at a ten-year interval, in regard to their participation in household activities. "Blue-collar workers experienced greater life satisfaction if they were involved in masculine tasks. The retired, and to a lesser extent the partially retired, had more positive evaluations of life if they participated more in masculine household tasks."[72] Masculine tasks included lawn care, gardening, and repairing broken things.

Output. Retirement may bring a time when people take stock of met demands and used resources and the information is fed back to alter goals. Some goals may be recognized as being

TABLE 14.5 *Actual division of responsibility for household tasks for elderly husbands and wives*

Task	Report by husbands			Report by wives		
	Husband	Wife	Shared	Husband	Wife	Shared
	Percent					
Cooking meals	9	87	3	3	91	6
Washing dishes	16	50	34	12	69	19
Washing clothes	16	68	16	13	78	9
Writing letters	6	53	41	9	63	28
Shopping	9	38	53	12	47	41
Cleaning house	59	38	3	50	44	6
Earning money	50	—	50	44	—	56
Yard work	60	12	28	66	9	19
Car maintenance	87	3	10	97	—	3
House repairs	88	9	3	82	9	9
Family social events	—	22	89	6	63	28
Family decisions	3	3	94	3	3	94

Source: Timothy H. Brubaker, "Responsibility for Household Tasks: A Look at Golden Anniversary Couples Aged 75 Years and Older," in *Social Bonds in Later Life,* ed. Warren A. Peterson and Jill Quadagno (Beverly Hills: Sage Publications 1985), p. 33. Copyright © 1985 by Sage Publications, Inc. Reprinted by permission of Sage Publications, Inc.

highly unlikely of ever being met and may be discarded, while others are shifted in priority.

There is evidence to support the model in Figure 14.2 that suggests that postretirement well-being for men depends on many factors: personal attributes, preretirement well-being, the nature of the retirement decision (whether voluntary or mandatory), and postretirement resources (health and finances).[73] Although the model does not specify social supports, other writers suggest that informal support networks, coping efforts, socialization for old age, access to and coordination of formal services all contribute to the well-being of the elderly.[74]

Fewer widows and widowers aged sixty to seventy-nine report having a less happy and exciting life than married people of the same age. Sixty-eight percent of widows reported a great deal of satisfaction with family life, compared with only 39 percent of the widowers.[75] Divorced or separated men share the negative outlook of widowers, just as divorced or separated women do. The negative effects are greater among men, however, with 71 percent of the divorced or separated women reporting a great deal of satisfaction with friendships, compared to only 38 percent of the men.[76]

Analysis of differences between childless and parent elderly revealed that although the parent elderly had a larger network of friends, including family, the satisfaction with friendships and presence of a confidant suggest little or no difference between the childless and elderly parents.[77] The childless were more satisfied with their housing, while more elderly parents owned their own homes. The childless elderly reported better health and satisfaction with their health than the elderly parents; and finally, the childless elderly were somewhat more satisfied with their income, standard of living, and ability to afford major items than the elderly parents.[78]

FIGURE 14.2 *Model of determinants of postretirement well-being for men*

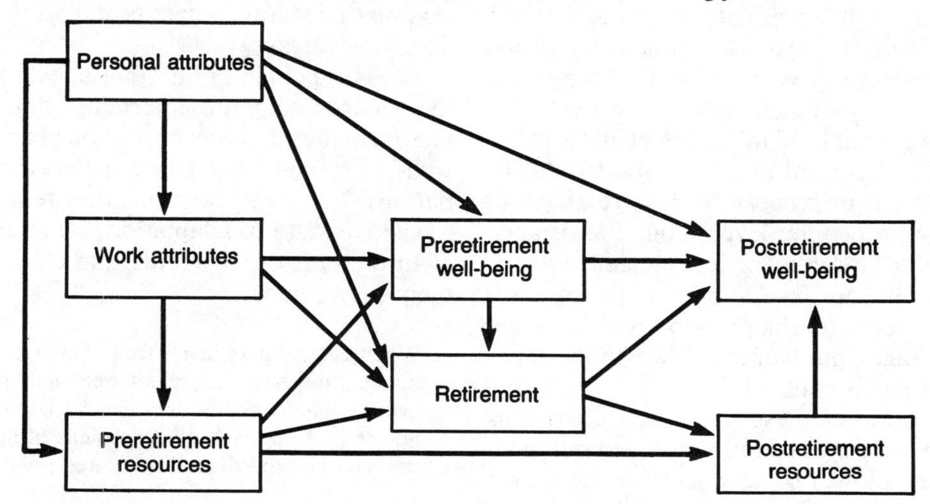

Source: Joan E. Crowley, "Longitudinal Effects of Retirement on Men's Psychological and Physical Well-Being." Reprinted by permission of the publisher, from *Retirement Among American Men* by Herbert S. Parnes, Joan E. Crowley, R. Jean Haurin, Lawrence J. Less, William R. Morgan, Frank L. Mott, and Gilbert Nestel (Lexington, Mass.: Lexington Books, 1985), p. 150. Copyright 1985 by D. C. Heath and Company.

Environment. Housing alternatives open to the elderly include: remaining in their own home; living in an age-mixed or age-segregated area; or living in a retirement community, in a nursing home, or in an extended-care facility.[79]

Many elderly people choose the first alternative. Such a choice can mean that an individual or a couple remains in a large house that is appropriate for a big family but not for one or two people. Staying in the same neighborhood in urban areas that have changed drastically may mean that the risk of crime is great. Older people often have the disadvantage of having inadequate material and human resources to maintain their homes.

In a study of impaired clients of social agencies in Philadelphia, it was found that the clients who remained in their homes had some sort of "control center." "The control center arranged the home environment so as to maximize the person's amount of knowledge and control over his or her total environment."[80]

The control center was located in the living room, and generally a favorite chair was the focus of the center. The telephone and television set were placed in reach of the person. The front door and window were in view, and often the chair was close enough to the window to allow looking at the entrance and sidewalk. "Side tables, often of substantial size, were placed on one or both sides of the chair. In addition to holding the telephone and sometimes the remote control for the television, these surfaces were covered with objects and information of highest salience to the person: telephone numbers, medicine, water, snacks, mail, checkbook, magazines, pencil, and sometimes photographs."[81]

In day-to-day living, it is often the "little" things that can make the difference in the ability of the elderly to cope and exercise their preference to remain independent. Shopping for food can be difficult to cope with. In a study of the elderly in small towns, proximity to the store, the long aisles of larger stores, the cost of a phone, the cost of food (although eligible, many elderly people do not apply for food stamps), and the weight of grocery bags were all problems for some people. Even limited assistance of the right type can make independence possible: "I pay her for it. She goes to get my groceries, you see . . . she goes to town, buys my groceries, takes the laundry down to the laundromat, brings it back."[82]

Identification of these needs and provisions of appropriate service could often extend independence at a lower social cost than alternative programs. Where food cannot be prepared, group meal programs are a success story in providing a strategic service. Home care and daily living assistance programs provided as a community service allow many of the elderly to remain in their homes.

Openness of families and communities to the possibilities for continuing involvement of the elderly is also an advantage—as where retirement and day-care facilities offer opportunity for creative interchanges between young and old.[83]

Values related to housing—for example, privacy—are often very important at all stages of the life cycle, but they are particularly so to the elderly. A Jewish man relates his concerns:

> Now, what the hell are you afraid about at your age? I'm over seventy years old and I'm afraid. Of what? Of *what?* Of having no place to live. Maybe I won't find a place. Or maybe they will put us together with other people. I couldn't stand that. I'd die before that time. I need my privacy too. I don't want other people *that* close. Like Harry Tobasch upstairs. I want him close, but not *that* close.[84]

In another study, retired residents who lived in an age-integrated community had higher morale than those in an age-segregated community. The respondents were matched for age, sex, marital status, religious affiliation, and participation rates.[85]

As with people of all other ages, changes in the environment are intermingled with other factors in their relative impact on perceptions of well-being, making positive and negative contributions. Environmental qualities tend to affirm a positive state of adaptation, for example.

In the best of all worlds, the elderly choose their environment.

> When elderly people are free to choose their residence, they tend to select one that meets their needs. Their needs include both the cultural norms that apply to all regardless of age and the special age- and disability-related needs.[86]

Summary

Middle years in the family life span are characterized by stability combined with the realization that youth and vigor are fading. Value orientations may shift during middle years; consequently, emphasis on particular goals may change. Traumatic events that occur in some families during the middle years are the abrupt departure of a spouse and loss of employment. The husband's departure may result in the displacement of homemakers who have dedicated their lives to caring for family members and maintaining the home. Material resources often peak during the middle years, although demands also may continue to be high for major expenditures, such as education or vocational training for children.

Management by middle-year families may be morphostatic or morphogenic in nature; for families who have a "static life plan," limited alternatives are considered, and dissatisfaction occurs when plans are not met. Midlife families may respond to midlife crises in an expansive mode and actually seek change, being morphogenic in outlook.

Output, in terms of satisfaction and happiness, seems to be viewed differently for men and women in their middle years. Launching children into adulthood is often a satisfying part of the middle years.

The elderly population of the United States is increasing, especially the number of people eighty-five years old and over. Women dominate the elderly. Goals of maintaining their level of living—with attention to health, housing, environment, family relations, financial management, and leisure competence—are important to many of the elderly. Events are probably greater among the elderly than during the years of late adulthood, most often surrounding accidents and health-related matters.

Resources among the elderly are often limited—both human and material—especially among individuals and couples in their seventies and eighties.

The resource most critical in old age is health. Income makes a critical difference in the ability of the elderly to cope with the pressures of aging. Help and support from relatives, children, friends, neighbors, and the general community are important to aging individuals and couples to maintain their own housing arrangements. Childless widows and elderly parents whose children are divorced both present special cases in terms of help from others.

Widowed and divorced women receive more services than any other group of elderly people, although that is limited. Community resources—public transportation, recreation facilities, and health-care facilities—can be very important to the elderly.

Decisions and task allocations seem to be clearly gender-based. Planning by the elderly often is marked by limited options; planning for retirement affects satisfaction with retirement. Postretirement well-being is affected by personal attributes, preretirement well-being, whether retirement decision was voluntary or mandatory, and postretirement resources.

The living environment may affect the elderly more than other groups; changes in the environment are potentially traumatic.

Notes

1. Gail Sheehy, *Passages* (New York: Bantam, 1976), p. 43.
2. Michael P. Nichols *Turning Forty in the 80's* (New York: W. W. Norton, 1986), p. 153.
3. Judy McKenna and Sharon Y. Nickols, "Planning a Retirement Security: A Study of Women in the Middle Years" (Stillwater: Oklahoma State University, Family Study Center [n.d.]), p. 4.
4. Joanne Sabol Stevenson, *Issues and Crises During Middlescence* (New York: Appleton-Century-Crofts, 1977), p. 24.
5. Lois Banfill Shaw, *Unplanned Careers: The Working Lives of Middle-Aged Women* (Lexington, Mass.: Lexington Books, 1983), p. 57.
6. Ellen Van Velsor and Angela M. O'Rand, "Family Life Cycle, Work Career Patterns, and Women's Wages at Midlife," *Journal of Marriage and the Family* 46 (May 1984): 372.
7. Ibid., p. 370.
8. Sandra Hanson, "A Family Life-Cycle Approach to the Socio-economic Attainment of Working Women," *Journal of Marriage and the Family* 45 (May 1983): 335.
9. Cynthia Rextroat, "Women's Work Expectations and Labor-Market Experience in Early and Middle Family Life-Cycle Stages," *Journal of Marriage and the Family* 47 (February 1985): 131–142.
10. Judy Long and Karen L. Porter, "Multiple Roles of Midlife Women," in *Women in Midlife,* ed. Grace K. Baruch and Jeanne Brooks-Gunn (New York: Plenum Press, 1984), pp. 109–159.
11. Helena Znaniecka Lopata and Kathleen Fordham Norr, "Changing Commitments of American Women to Work and Family Roles," *Social Security Bulletin* 43 (June 1980): 6.
12. A. J. Jaffe, "The Middle Years: Neither Too Young nor Too Old," *Industrial Gerontology,* Special Issue (September 1971): 43.
13. Nena O'Neill and George O'Neill, *Shifting Gears* (New York: Avon Books, 1975), pp. 86–87.
14. Ibid., p. 86.
15. Ibid., p. 90.
16. Stevenson, *Issues and Crises During Middlescence,* p. 158.
17. Doris L. Walsh, "Targeting Teens," *American Demographics* 7 (February 1985), p. 41.
18. Jean Evangelauf, "Colleges' Charges to Students Rising 6 pct This Fall," *The Chronicle of Higher Education* 32 (August 6, 1986): 24.
19. Frances L. Cogle and Grace L. Tasker, "Children and Housework," *Family Relations* 31 (July 1982): 395–399.
20. Ibid., pp. 62, 113.

21. Sheehy, *Passages* p. 46.

22. Grace K. Baruch and Rosalind C. Barnett, "Role Quality, Multiple Role Involvement and Psychological Well-Being in Midlife Women," Working Paper 149 (Wellesley, Mass.: Wellesley College, Center for Research on Women, 1986), pp. 10–15.

23. Cynthia M. Taeuber, "America in Transition: An Aging Society," U.S. Department of Commerce, Bureau of the Census, Special Studies Series P-23, No. 128 (Washington, D.C.: U.S. Government Printing Office, 1983), p. 1.

24. Ibid.

25. Jacob S. Siegel, "Demographic Aspects of Aging and the Older Population in the United States," U.S. Department of Commerce, Bureau of the Census, Special Studies Series P-23, No. 59 (Washington, D.C.: U.S. Government Printing Office, 1982), p. 17.

26. Winnifred E. Peacock and William M. Talley, "Developing Leisure Competence: A Goal for Late Adulthood," *Educational Gerontology* 11 (Nos. 4–6, 1985): 267.

27. Theodor Seuss Geisel, *You're Only Old Once!* (New York: Random House, 1986).

28. Peacock and Talley, "Developing Leisure Competence," p. 268.

29. Ibid., p. 271.

30. Laura Baker Buchbinder, "Human Activity Patterns and Injury Severity in Fire Accidents Involving Apparel," *Journal of Fire and Flammability/Consumer Products* 1 (March 1974): 4–18.

31. Robert N. Butler, *Why Survive? Being Old in America* (New York: Harper and Row, 1975), p. 4.

32. Sandra L. Titus, "Barriers to the Health Maintenance Organization for the Over 65's," *Social Science & Medicine* 16 (1982): 1767, 1774.

33. Ibid., p. 1773.

34. Ibid.

35. Lois Banfill Shaw, *Midlife Women at Work* (Lexington, Mass.: Lexington Books, 1986), p. 125.

36. Ibid., p. 127.

37. Ronald L. Simons and Gale E. West, "Life Changes, Coping Resources, and Health among the Elderly," *International Journal of Aging and Human Development* 20 (1984–1985): 184.

38. Alan Fox, "Income Changes at and after Social Security Benefit Receipt: Evidence from the Retirement History Study," *Social Security Bulletin* 47 (September 1984): 3.

39. Ibid., p. 8.

40. Joyce Stephens, *Loners, Losers, and Lovers* (Seattle: University of Washington Press, 1976), p. 40.

41. James H. Schulz, *The Economics of Aging* (Belmont, Calif.: Wadsworth, 1976), p. 23.

42. Mary E. Heltsley, "Coping—The Aged in Small Town, U.S.A.," *Journal of Home Economics* 68 (September 1976): 49.

43. Eugene Litwak, *Helping the Elderly* (New York: Guilford Press, 1985), p. 44.

44. J. R. Weeks and J. B. Cuellar, "The Role of Family Members in the Helping Networks of Older People," *The Gerontologist* 21 (June 1981): 388–394.

45. Elizabeth Mutran, "Intergenerational Family Support among Blacks and Whites: Response to Culture or to Socioeconomic Differences," *Journal of Gerontology* 40 (May 1985): 382.

46. Trudy B. Anderson, "Widowhood As a Life Transition: Its Impact on Kinship Ties," *Journal of Marriage and the Family* 46 (February 1984): 112.

47. Elizabeth A. Bankoff, "Social Support and Adaptation to Widowhood," *Journal of Marriage and the Family* 45 (November 1983): 829.

48. Ibid., p. 836.

49. Shirley L. O'Bryant, "Neighbors' Support of Older Widows Who Live Alone in Their Own Homes," *The Gerontologist* 25 (Spring 1985): 309.

50. Pat M. Keith, "A Comparison of the Resources of Parents and the Childless Men and Women in Very Old Age," *Family Relations* 32 (July 1983): 403–409; see also Judith Rempel, "Childless Elderly: What Are They Missing?" *Journal of Marriage and the Family* 47 (May 1985): 343–359.

51. Eleanor Palo Stoller, "Exchange Patterns in the Informal Support Networks of the Elderly: The Impact of Reciprocity on Morale," *Journal of Marriage and the Family* 47 (May 1985): 335–342.

52. Ibid., p. 339.

53. Victor G. Circirelli, "Adult Children's Helping Behavior to Elderly Parents: The Influence of Divorce," *Journal of Family Issues* 5 (September 1984): 419–440.

54. Kyriakos S. Markides and Harry W. Martin, *Older Mexican Americans* (Austin: The University of Texas, Center for Mexican American Studies, 1983), p. 30.

55. Ibid., pp. 31, 33.

56. Janice A. Smithers, *Determined Survivors* (New Brunswick, N.J.: Rutgers University Press, 1985), p. 125.

57. Frances M. Carp, "Retired People As Automobile Passengers," *The Gerontologist* 12 (Spring 1972): 67.

58. Mohamed Abdel-Ghany, "Quality of Life from the Perspective of the Elderly," *Home Economics Research Journal* 6 (September 1977): 43.

59. Helena Znaniecka Lopata, "Widowhood: Social Norms and Social Integration," in *Family Factbook* (Chicago: Marquis Academic Media, 1978), pp. 217–225.

60. Elizabeth W. Markson, Gary S. Levitz, and Maryvonne Gognalons-Caillard, "The Elderly and the Community: Reidentifying Unmet Needs," *Journal of Gerontology* 28 (October 1973): 508.

61. James H. Schulz and Guy Carrin, "The Role of Savings and Pension Systems in Maintaining Living Standards in Retirement," *Journal of Human Resources* 7 (Summer 1972): 348.

62. John C. Henretta and Angela M. O'Rand, "Joint Retirement in the Dual Worker Family," *Social Forces* 62 (December 1983): 516.

63. Ibid., p. 507.

64. Ibid., p. 515.

65. Charles E. McConnel and Firooz Deljavan, "Consumption Patterns of the Retired Household," *Journal of Gerontology* 38 (July 1983): 480–490.

66. U.S. Department of Commerce, Bureau of the Census, "Demographic and Socio-economic Aspects of Aging in the United States," Current Population Reports, Series P-23, No. 138 (Washington, D.C.: U.S. Government Printing Office, 1984), p. 73.

67. Jaber F. Gubruim, "Toward a Socio-Environmental Theory of Aging," *The Gerontologist* 12 (Autumn 1972, Part 1): 282.

68. Elizabeth M. Heidbreder, "Factors in Retirement Adjustment: White-Collar/Blue-Collar Experience," *Industrial Gerontology* 12–13 (Winter 1972): 77.

69. Woodrow W. Hunter, "A Longitudinal Study of Preretirement Education," U.S. Department of Health, Education, and Welfare, Welfare Administration, Research Grants Branch Project 151 (Ann Arbor, The University of Michigan, 1968), pp. 81–82.

70. Ibid., p. 84.

71. Timothy H. Brubaker, "Responsibility for Household Tasks: A Look at Golden Anniversary Couples Aged 75 Years and Older," in *Social Bonds in Later Life,* ed. Warren A. Peterson and Jil Quadagno (Beverly Hills: Sage Publications, 1985), p. 33.

72. Pat M. Keith, Cynthia D. Dobson, Willis J. Goudy, and Edward A. Powers, "Older Men: Occupation, Employment Status, Household Involvement, and Well-Being" *Journal of Family Issues* 2 (September 1981): 345.

73. Joan E. Crowley, "Longitudinal Effects of Retirement on Men's Psychological and Physical Well-Being," in *Retirement among American Men,* ed. Herbert S. Parnes, Joan E. Crowley, R. Jean Haurin, Lawrence J. Less, William R. Morgan, Frank L. Mott, and Gilbert Nestel (Lexington, Mass.: Lexington Books, 1985), p. 151.

74. Russel Ward, "Informal Networks and Well-Being in Later Life: A Research Agenda," *The Gerontologist* 25 (February 1985): 56.

75. Herbert H. Hyman, *Of Time and Widowhood* (Durham, N.C.: Duke University Press, 1983), p. 89.

76. Ibid.

77. Judith Rempel, "Childless Elderly: What Are They Missing?" *Journal of Marriage and the Family* 47 (May 1985): 343–348.

78. Ibid., p. 346.

79. James E. Montgomery, "The Housing Patterns of Older Families," *The Family Coordinator* 21 (January 1972): 40–45.

80. M. Powell Lawton, "The Elderly in Context," *Environment and Behavior* 17 (July 1985): 501–519.

81. Ibid., p. 515.

82. Heltsley, *Coping,* p. 48.

83. Debra Kneeland, "Meeting Across the Generations," *The Des Moines Register* (November 30, 1977), p. 1B.

84. Thomas J. Cottle, *Hidden Survivors, Portraits of Poor Jews in America,* (Englewood Cliffs, N.J.: Prentice-Hall, 1980). p. 17.

85. Houshang Poorkaj, "Social-Psychological Factors and 'Successful Aging,' " *Sociology and Social Research* 56 (April 1972): 299.

86. Earl W. Morris and Mary Winter, *Housing, Family and Society* (New York: Wiley, 1978), p. 220.

15

Families with handicapped members

In the United States, almost 25 million people have handicapping conditions that place limitations on their work, housekeeping, or school activities.[1] In addition, chronic health conditions limit major activities for 40 percent of the population over age sixty-five.

In almost all cases, handicaps and chronic or extended illness can make formidable differences in managerial demands and responses at any point in the life cycle.

Families respond to chronic illness, acute illness, accidents, and handicapping conditions of family members in very different ways. Conceptually, however, the family's response may be characterized by two phases. The first phase is called "precrisis," or adjustment phase.[2] This assumes that families are stable and functioning in rather predictable ways; "demands (from stressors, hardships, and prior strains . . .) interact with existing resources . . . , with the family's definition of demands . . . , and with the family's resistance coping behaviors to result in a level of adjustment which varies depending on how well needs or demands are being met."[3] The family tries not to move into a crisis.

Following this adjustment phase, when family crisis results and changes are clearly called for, families may enter the adaption phase. The imbalance in demands and resources is so great that disequilibrium occurs and new resources must be found or other changes made in order to cope with the situation. "Family adaption, then, describes the outcome of family efforts to achieve a new level of homeostasis, which was upset by the crisis."[4]

A handicapped member's situation both affects and is affected by the family's management. The degree and nature of the effects relate to a number of factors:

1. the time in the family life cycle at which the handicap occurs
2. the role of the handicapped person: parent or child-provider or dependent
3. the severity, duration, and likely outcome of the handicapping condition
4. the managerial skills acquired before the occurrence of the handicapping condition

All of these factors impinge on management within the family system. Each factor has special implications for the demands and resources of the family and how the system can respond. Society's increasing awareness and efforts in support of the interests of handicapped people to maintain normal lives, where the surrounding conditions are permissive, have been positive factors in overcoming stigmas based on misunderstanding and limited involvement. Even so, each situation places its own demands and constraints on family systems.

Input

DEMANDS

Whether the handicapping condition existed before the family was formed or after makes considerable difference in the nature of its impact on demands. When people with a handicapping condition marry, they realize that limitations exist, and expectations are adjusted accordingly. Goals are established within those realities.

Handicapping conditions that occur after formation of the family—whether to a parent or a child—introduce requirements, often of a crisis nature, that need to be met. They also introduce the need for changes in previously formed expectations and goals. Depending on the circumstances, the impacts on the goals may be toward higher qualitative experiences in meeting goals, such as greater family cohesion, or they may be conflict-producing rather than expansive. Values of families where there is a disability are similar to those of other families.

When the handicapping condition shifts a member's role from that of helping to formulate family goals to one around whom the goals revolve, which places limits on other family goals, the member's role image shifts. If the condition is severe and has long-term goal effects, the shift may be traumatic. If the condition occurs early in the life cycle and is permanent, goals may need to be drastically adjusted to meet reduced potential and continuing demands. The possibility of rehabilitation is an important factor in the eventual impact on goals.

If the disability or illness is temporary, the adjustments to its special demands only delay the reconcentration on longer-term goals. If, however, the condition will be terminal, many life goals may be telescoped or permanently set aside. Consideration of possible eventualities can facilitate adaptation. An orientation to contingency goal setting can be a factor in positive adjustment or adaptation.

In families in which there is a child with a chronic disease or disability, the husband and wife may disagree on goals. One study found that parents of a diabetic child have lower goal agreement and greater parental role tension than parents of nondiabetic children.[5] Less agreement on goals, as with other factors affecting demands, can increase the difficulty of management.

An important part of effective management is identification of realistic purposes to which responses can be directed. Such goal adjustments are closely associated with interactions between the personal and managerial subsystems.

People can learn from another person's traumatic experience. Susan Sontag has explained the fears that gripped her during the diagnosis and the early stages of treatment for cancer and then the positive perspective that followed in the urgency of "having priorities and trying to follow them."[6]

RESOURCES

When a family member acquires a handicapping condition, questions arise about the sufficiency of resources and the effects on both the personal and managerial concerns of the family.

Are potential income losses manageable through insurance or employment of another family member if the major earner is disabled? To what extent would extra expenses be covered through insurance and/or savings? Are there alternatives for covering the management of the household? How can the stress on interpersonal relations be minimized if adults or dependent children become disabled? What differences will the severity or duration of the disability make? Matching the demands of family member(s) with handicapping conditions with human and material resources to meet their special needs is a major family challenge.

Major problems of rearing developmentally disabled children are resource-related: time demanded and money problems (Table 15.1). Physical demands of caring for a child were also reported by almost one-fourth of the parents as a major problem. Table 15.1 includes problems that are centered in the personal subsystem as well.

Material. The material resources of families are inadequate for long-term demands following from conditions arising early in the life cycle. Human resources of adults are either reduced or need to be rechanneled. Reduced earnings or other capacities for contributing to family functioning are likely, either short- or long-term.

Disability income available to workers through Social Security is a source of basic support. When the disability strikes those not covered, alternative sources are needed, but they are available only to a limited degree. The resourcefulness of individuals within the family group can make a difference in the response.

TABLE 15.1 *Parents' perception of major problems of rearing developmentally disabled children*

Problem	*Number*	*Percent*
Personal subsystem		
Social stigma	15	7
Adjustment of brothers and sisters	6	3
Adjustment of parents	9	4
Discipline problems	30	14
Managerial subsystem		
Physical demands of caring for child	50	23
Time demanded	100	45
Money problems	60	27
Knowledge of social services	14	6
Lack of services	17	8
Other	58	26

Source: Adapted from William R. Dunlap and J. Selwyn Hollinsworth, "How Does a Handicapped Child Affect the Family? Implications for Practitioners," *The Family Coordinator* 26 (July 1977): 289. Copyrighted 1977 by the National Council on Family Relations. Reprinted by permission.

Incomes for disabled people are lower than for nondisabled people. And disabled people often are employed in occupations that are generally lower paid—for men, as farmers, household service workers, farm and nonfarm laborers; in the case of women, as household service workers or laborers. Besides providing lower pay, the jobs commonly held by the disabled are those that have relatively low education requirements and where employment and scheduling are flexible. Handicapped people are too often categorized as being incapable of employment, even though their particular incapacity has little effect on their ability to do many jobs. This situation is now being scrutinized more closely than in the past. Both acute illnesses and chronic conditions often cause heavy strains on families' financial resources. Costs of illness or other care on top of ongoing needs are likely to drain savings unless there is insurance to meet at least major medical costs.

Human. In the case of families with members having handicapping conditions, the care giver's health and internal strengths, support from other family members and friends, and community support all make important contributions to the welfare of the family.

Resources internal to care givers dominated their responses to Alzheimer's patients concerning their burden in care giving. Confidence in problem solving and in reframing problems, spiritual support, and extended family help were all associated with feeling less burden in care giving. Passivity of the care giver was associated with feeling a greater burden in care giving. The extent of the burden was associated with the health status of the care giver.[7] Confidence in problem solving and in reframing problems can come with education and experience. And social programs can extend assistance beyond the immediate care giver to the extended family to help them understand the importance of their support.

Help from relatives and friends can be very important in meeting the demands of care for handicapped family members.

Among severely handicapped people in families, help for household responsibilities was received from relatives in about 17 percent of the cases. For those who have never been disabled, help for household responsibilities from relatives was around 11 percent. Financial assistance from relatives was limited.[8] While relatives contribute household help more often than financial aid, the incidence is not high enough to suggest that relatives can provide more than occasional relief. Such help can make the difference at critical times, but distance and other demands on relatives make long-term support difficult.

The family's capacity for care of a handicapped person is greater than that of the population at large because, among other reasons, care of a disabled person can be shifted to family members who have more time.[9]

Help from the community is another important resource for families with handicapped members. More community resources were needed by families with severely disabled persons than by families with mildly or moderately disabled members.[10]

A case study of a family with three boys with Duchenne muscular dystrophy (who will probably die before age twenty-five) reveals community support as well as interested professional help. A sorority and a service fraternity have committed themselves to working with the family on a long-term basis. The help on a day-to-day basis is provided by a student who is living with the family for a semester. The group raised funds for a van fitted for a wheelchair and raised money for the parents to take a trip to their homeland, Germany. "From the time the first to the time the last boy dies, the continuity and support of these young people may make the crucial difference in the endurance as well as the lifelong perspective of the family."[11]

A number of social agencies, publicly supported as well as private, provide specialized services to handicapped people. Since the needs of the handicapped are rarely isolated, this specialization of social services often makes it difficult for handicapped people to tap the range of resources available to them. Community resources, family capabilities, and the handicapped or dependent person's condition interact to affect the quality of care received.

Throughput

PLANNING

Effective planning is called for in families with handicapped members in order to compensate for the condition. "Some examples may include planning facilitating conditions to improve the work environment, searching for needed resources to accomplish tasks, or planning more specific time schedules because of dependence upon others (as in the case of transportation)."[12]

Acute conditions most often follow from events that are not foreseeable. Chronic conditions, on the other hand, may provide opportunities for developing contingency plans. A person losing sight or hearing can anticipate alternatives such as learning Braille or lip reading. Finding the optimum balance between preparation for a likely contingency and not becoming too dependent is not an easy task. But at least the chronic condition provides an opportunity for preparation.

If the handicapping condition is present as the family is formed, realistic standards can be established in relation to the givens of the material and human resources that are present. Individuals can provide reinforcement to each other and complement each other's capacities when one or even two adults have handicapping conditions. These effects can relate to standards and sequences. As an example, Figure 15.1 shows a couple in a kitchen having little space

FIGURE 15.1 *Kitchen area with inadequate space for assisting wife with limited vision*

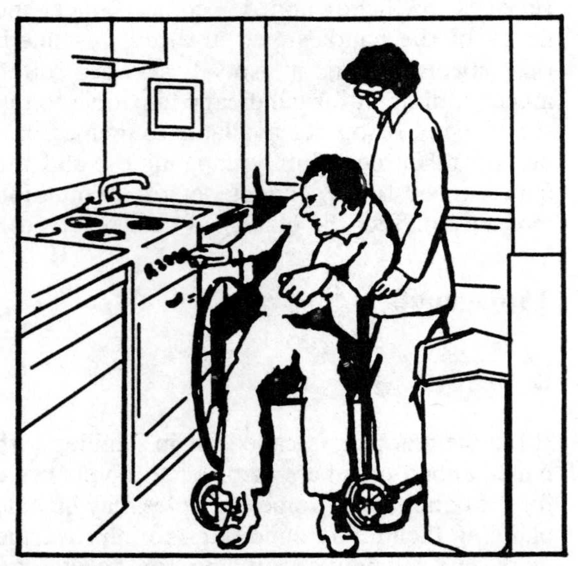

Source: Marianne Parker and Francille M. Firebaugh, "An Experience in Home Management," *Illinois Teacher* 15 (May–June 1972): 235. Reprinted with permission.

for a wheelchair. The wife has impaired vision and cannot see the degree markings on the oven thermostat or read fine-print labels and instructions. The husband's clearer vision, but limited mobility, complement her greater mobility and limited vision. Standard setting and sequencing are interrelated aspects of planning to which the strengths of each contribute.

Financial protection in cases of extreme demands is likely to be adequate where attention has been given to planning and resources are adequate to follow the plans. However, freedom from financial worries does not simplify the problem of giving needed attention to people—both ill and well—in periods of crisis. Some compromise from preferred standards is likely to be required in striving for an optimum balance in meeting the care needs of various family members. Whether care of the disabled person is in the home or outside, the sequencing of related attention and tasks calls for careful planning. In more severe and permanent handicapping situations, plans may need to involve critical changes in the patterning of the family system. For other conditions, situations may settle back into more familiar patterns with the handicapped person bearing the major adjustment.

IMPLEMENTING

Participation in household activities is important in examining differences in families who have a disabled member, particularly an adult. Of those severely disabled, women participate in far more of the household activities than men, with the least difference in heavy chores (Table 15.2). The differences are reflected in the patterns of participation for people never disabled. Small things can make a difference in one's ability to be independent or mobile, but they often need to be adapted to the special situation.

For people with handicapping conditions that do not involve a wheelchair, crutches, or braces, many special facilitating conditions to improve the environment can be identified. Individuals with limited vision may need special space arrangements; elderly people may need arrangements for easy access to the bathroom and the kitchen; obese people must make some changes in the environment to satisfy their daily needs.

The increasing awareness and attention to the needs of physically handicapped people—the provision of ramps, elevators, and accessible restrooms, for instance—have added considerably to their mobility. These changes serve to increase choices and the freedom to participate.

Dealing with handicapping conditions or with family members having them is affected by the flexibility and creativity of those involved.[13]

TABLE 15.2 *Participation in household activities by currently disabled and nondisabled men and women*

Participation	Currently disabled			Nondisabled	
	Severe	Occupational	Secondary work limitation	Recovered	Never disabled
	Percent by type of disability				
Men					
Shopping for family meals	41	46	52	53	54
Heavy chores	20	41	54	67	75
Light chores	50	59	61	64	69
Money handling	49	55	62	55	62
Women					
Shopping for family meals	70	83	80	91	96
Heavy chores	23	40	37	67	73
Light chores	86	91	84	91	97
Money handling	60	67	62	67	71

Source: Paula A. Franklin, "Impact of Disability on the Family Structure," *Social Security Bulletin* 40 (May 1977): 14–15.

Output

DEMAND RESPONSES

The degree to which a sense of meeting demands in a handicapping situation is effective depends on both the extent to which goals have been adjusted realistically and the adequacy of the management response. Where handicapping conditions existed before family formation, the goals that evolve in that context are more likely to lead to satisfaction than when handicapping conditions occur later. The challenges are compounded for adults who have both the demands of the handicapping event and the long-range goal adjustment to face.

The degree to which demands are considered to be met satisfactorily relates to the factors alluded to in the introduction to the chapter. The person's role as one responsible to others or as a dependent can influence the level of expectation or readiness to make adjustments in goals. Dependent people may feel freer to adapt to their individual needs relating to the handicap than the person whose goals have involved the welfare of others. In the latter case, satisfactions in adjusting to the handicap may be complicated by concerns for the needs of others not being served as intended. The likely outcome of the handicapping condition affects whether goal adjustments can be viewed as temporary or final. Adjustment and accompanying satisfaction may be more likely with either extreme, compared to situations where uncertainty prevails for an extended period.

The wife of a disabled husband may change her role and life-style significantly as she responds to his disability. She may return to a career, or she may be confined to caring for him. The circumstances surrounding the changes and the spousal relationship will affect the acceptance of the disability and the subsequent changes in life-style.

Wives who have husbands with chronic conditions were less satisfied with most family roles and relationships than wives with well husbands. Included in the satisfaction variables were the personal attention received from the husband, the time husbands and wives spent together, the husband's personality, and his role as companion. Also significantly different was the decreased satisfaction with the husband's help around the house and the husband's roles as father and husband.[14]

Families with wives who become disabled may not change as dramatically as those in which the husbands develop handicapping conditions.[15] This is the case where the wives have not worked outside the home or where they have had lesser involvement in a career. In the coming years, this difference will surely subside. Men must often take on more responsibilities in household activities when their spouse is disabled; this will change as the division of labor within the household alters. This particular study did not examine the satisfaction of husbands with chronically ill wives.

Stress is an outcome of dealing with members of the household who have handicapping conditions. In a study of the family stress of hemodialysis, several findings have relevance to this discussion:

1. The greater the amount of crisis, the greater the family vulnerability, and the greater the vulnerability, the more that dialysis is perceived as a crisis;
2. Families were more disorganized and less capable of handling additional stress if they felt dialysis was a stressor and they had experienced a number of stress-related disruptions in the previous year;
3. Income level, patient employment, and spousal employment were all positively related to the dialysis patient's family's ability to organize and handle additional stress.[16]

The stage in the life cycle has implications for responsibilities that exist and the degree to which adjustment to goal expectations is needed. Achieving satisfaction can be difficult for young people who have set specific life goals at high levels of achievement. Managerial skills in adapting goals realistically, in planning effectively in relation to the human and material resources available, and in exercising control in implementing actions can be important to maintaining balance in the system or helping it to respond positively.

To maintain balance in the system, the negative-feedback mechanism is particularly important. The process of learning to cope is often one of learning to live within defined achievable levels. Recognizing deviations that would throw the system out of balance and taking steps to move back on target is a response to negative feedback. An example would be a minor accident due to physical overexertion in the process of rehabilitation. A negative-feedback response would be to return to the planned schedule to avoid a serious impact on the rehabilitation process. Once a level to permit expanded activity is safely achieved, a positive-feedback response would be to take advantage of the increased skill and energy level to assume more responsibility. This might be in relation to meeting one's own needs in some other way that strengthens the family system.

Two contrasting situations illustrate the range of responses that may follow from handicapping situations:

> Andy, aged 20½, was injured in a motorcycle accident two years ago. He is a paraplegic who is currently enrolled as a full-time student in architecture. . . . He married a shy college student named Marie B. during her freshman year and they have a 3-month-old baby. . . . He wishes he could have more quiet time to work on his studies and that Marie would spend less time complaining about her minor aches and pains. After all, there is no comparison between her symptoms and what he has overcome with his disability. . . . She indicates that Andy does not help her with the baby or the apartment. He is totally absorbed with his studies, his group of paraplegic buddies, and his physical hygiene regimen, which takes considerable time in the morning and evening. . . . The infant is normally developed for 3 months. Marie considers him a good baby and expresses some guilt at taking out her frustrations toward Andy and anger with herself on the baby by ignoring his cries for prolonged periods of time.[17]
>
> A 23-year-old woman named Elaine was in the terminal stages of metastatic carcinoma. . . .

> She and her husband had been married for four years, and most of that time she had been in and out of hospitals. . . . Jack, the 25-year-old husband, was angry and frustrated. . . . [H]e felt guilty because of his anger and frustration, . . . yet she was the embodiment of their ruined hopes and dreams. . . . In a few weeks, Elaine was admitted to the hospital and died. Jack still had much grief work left to do, but he had surprised himself with how well he had held up during the last few days, and he said that he realized that most of his worries and concerns had been for himself and his own foggy future rather than for Elaine. He said that this had been "a beastly way to grow up," but he had grown up a lot in the past year.[18]

In these illustrations of negative and positive growth experience lie many varied possibilities for greater and lesser cohesion in anticipations and satisfactions. The challenges are especially great because both demand and resource inputs to management present adjustment problems.

RESOURCE CHANGES

In a study of time use across a number of states, women with handicapping conditions spent less total time in housework but more time in social/recreational and personal care activities than women without handicapping conditions. Exceptions to the pattern of fewer hours spent in housework were more time spent in maintenance of home, yard, car, and pet (related to older age of women) and more time spent in management (related to the handicap of the woman).[19]

Husbands of the handicapped women spent less time per week (9.5 hours) in total household work activities than did husbands of nonhandicapped women. The families with handicapped women also had no more outside help than those families with nonhandicapped women. The children of handicapped women spent about the same amount of time on household work activities as did children in families with nonhandicapped women.[20] It appears that handicapped women themselves make adjustments in household work activities. It is also likely that standards change to accommodate the lessened human energy base.

"Handicapped men spent more hours per week in housekeeping and physical care of family members than nonhandicapped men": They spent a total of 17.83 hours per week, while nonhandicapped men spent 13.72 hours per week. The handicapped men also spent less time in paid and unpaid work and more time in social/recreational activities and personal care than nonhandicapped men.[21]

The amount of "time demanded" was the problem mentioned most frequently by parents of developmentally disabled children (Table 15.1). A disability does affect how time is spent by people assuming household responsibilities.

Shifts in a family's allocation of material resources accompany handicapping conditions. Families are pressed to meet medical costs and to control the condition, as well as to find ways to facilitate living within the constraints placed on them. There are, in addition, lost opportunities for achieving a desired family life-style or limited energies for adapting. At the same time, the development of the human capacity for coping and the ability to direct resources purposefully to meet the existing realities often expand individual and family potential in unparalleled ways—evidencing positive feedback effects.

Summary

The demands of handicapping conditions on families and the availability of resources to meet them vary according to the role of the handicapped person, the nature and timing of the handicapping condition, and the managerial skills acquired to respond. Although any handicapping condition has traumatic effects, the continuity of the system is less affected when the handicapped member is a dependent. The resources of the system can be rallied around the dependent member, whereas the lost inputs of responsible members—in addition to the demands of the handicapping condition—place major strains on the capacity to cope. Regardless of the role of the handicapped member, the ability to cope is, in turn, influenced by whether the handicapping condition is severe and/or of long duration. If there has been time to build up material resources or to acquire the needed skills to simplify the making of an adequate response to the situation, the overall problem is alleviated managerially.

Planning ahead to meet handicapping situations, particularly acute ones, is difficult—except as material resource needs can be anticipated, as through insurance or savings. In such a situation, the ability to make realistic adjustments in terms of standards and sequences takes on special significance. Limited mobility or dexterity has direct relations to an ability to implement both the desired standards and sequences anticipated in the planning process. Planning within the limits of the handicapping condition becomes a major asset in personal management.

Changing the living environment can facilitate the actions of handicapped people and enable them to maintain life as normally as possible.

Awareness of the need to make adjustments in the public arena to extend the mobility of handicapped individuals has increased recently. As a result, extended involvement in economic, political, and social affairs has been increasingly possible for the handicapped, though much remains to be done.

The ability of families with handicapped members to manage effectively is often influenced by the availability of extended family, social, or public services at critical times. Internally, the capacity to adjust to the limits of the handicapped person's condition and to build positively as the situation permits is important to the optimum satisfaction of all family members.

Notes

1. U.S. Department of Health and Human Services, Public Health Service, "Current Estimates from National Health Interview Survey: United States, 1981," Series 10, No. 141 (Washington, D.C.: U.S. Government Printing Office, 1982), p. 24.
2. Joan M. Patterson, "Critical Factors Affecting Family Compliance with Home Treatment for Children with Cystic Fibrosis," *Family Relations* 34 (January 1985): 81.
3. Ibid.
4. Ibid.
5. Alan J. Crain, Marvin Sussman, and William B. Weil, "Effects of a Diabetic Child on Marital Integration and Related Measures of Family Functioning," *Journal of Health and Human Behavior* 7 (Summer 1966): 122–127.
6. © 1978 New York Times News Service, "Intellectual Sontag Comes to Grips with Cancer," *Ames Daily Tribune* (February 20, 1978), p. 13.
7. Clara C. Pratt, Vicki L. Schmall, Scott Wright, and Marilyn Cleland, "Burden and Coping Strategies of Caregivers to Alzheimer's Patients," *Family Relations* 34 (January 1985): 27–33.
8. Paula A. Franklin, "Impact of Disability on the Family Structure," *Social Security Bulletin* 40 (May 1977): 7.
9. Janet Zollinger Giele, "A Delicate Balance: The Family's Role in Care of the Handicapped," *Family Relations* 33 (January 1984): 91.
10. Ibid., p. 88.
11. Deborah Kaplan and Judith S. Mearig, "A Community Support System for a Family Coping with Chronic Illness," *Rehabilitation Literature* 38 (March 1977): 79–82.
12. Arlene Holyoak and Jane Meiners, "Time Allocation of the Handicapped and Their Spouses: Comparison with Families Including No Handicapped Members," in *The Balancing Act: Thinking Globally, Acting Locally,* ed. Sharon Y. Nickols, Proceedings of a workshop sponsored by The Family Economics/Home Management Section of the American Home Economics Association (Washington, D.C.: American Home Economics Association, 1985), pp. 181–195.
13. Lynne C. Rustad, "Family Adjustment to Chronic Illness and Disability in Mid-Life," in *Chronic Illness and Disability Through the Life Span,* ed. Myron G. Eisenberg, LaFaye C. Sutkin, and Mary A. Jansen (New York: Springer Publishing, 1984), p. 231.
14. Jeanne L. Hafstrom and Vicki J. R. Schram, "Chronic Illness in Couples: Selected Characteris-

tics, Including Wife's Satisfaction with and Perception of Marital Relationships,'' *Family Relations* 33 (January 1984): 195–203.

15. Rustad, ''Family Adjustment to Chronic Illness,'' pp. 222–242.

16. Susan D. Molumphy and Michael J. Sporakowski, ''The Family Stress of Hemodialysis,'' *Family Relations* 33 (January 1984): 33–39.

17. Joanne Sabol Stevenson, *Issues and Crises During Middlescence* (New York: Appleton-Century-Crofts, 1977), pp. 147–148.

18. Ibid., pp. 149–150.

19. Holyoak and Meiners, ''Time Allocation of the Handicapped,'' p. 187.

20. Ibid., pp. 190–193.

21. Ibid., p. 191.

16

Single-parent families

The prevalence of single-parent families represents one of the most significant social changes in this decade. Projections indicate that 40 percent of children will be in a single-parent family due to divorce, 12 percent due to premarital birth, 5 percent due to long-term separation of their parents, and 2 percent due to the death of a parent. These projections are based on an assumed continuation of the current divorce and premarital birth rate.[1]

The implications for the personal and managerial subsystem relations are extensive. The changing significance of single parenthood is the culmination of a variety of factors of social change not fully understood.

Varied circumstances accompanying single-parent status are shown on Table 16.1.

Premarital pregnancy, separation or divorce, the death of a spouse, and adoption are all directly related to the single-parent status. Each of these factors has special conditions surrounding the single and parenting roles that make them unique with respect to the responsibilities, problems, and benefits that pertain. Although children are still more likely to live with their mother than their father following divorce, living with the father is occurring more frequently, and more singles of both sexes are adopting children.

In 1983, 75 percent of all children under age eighteen lived with both parents (Table 16.1). Of those family units with children, one in five was headed by a single parent. For children living with their mother only, divorce was the most common cause among white single-parent families; in black families, the most prevalent cause was the fact that the mother had never married.

Between 1960 and 1983, there was a fivefold increase in the number of families headed by never-married females.[2] The illegitimacy rate for both whites and blacks had also increased during this period. Other factors included "rising ages at first marriage and thus increases in the numbers of never-married women relative to ever-married women, increase in the number of never-married women who are mothers, and especially among whites, a declining tendency to put illegitimate children up for adoption."[3]

Female-headed single-parent families have tended to be tagged as "broken," "disorganized," and "disintegrated" rather than recognized as an alternative choice in life-style.[4]

The prevalence of social attitudes that char-

TABLE 16.1 *Families with children under 18 by parental status: 1985*

Parental status	*Total*	*Families*		
		White	*Black*	*Spanish*
		Number in thousands		
	62,475	50,836	9,479	6,057
		Percent*		
Both parents	73.9	80.0	39.5	67.8
Mother only	20.9	15.6	51.0	26.6
Divorced	8.5	8.1	11.3	7.3
Married, spouse absent	5.4	4.1	12.4	11.1
Single, never married	5.6	2.1	24.8	6.5
Widowed	1.5	1.3	2.5	1.7
Father only	2.5	2.4	2.9	2.2
Neither parent	2.7	2.0	6.6	3.3

* Due to rounding, a 1-percentage-point difference may occur.
Source: U.S. Department of Commerce, Bureau of the Census, *Statistical Abstract of the U.S. for 1987,* 107th ed. (Washington, D.C.: U.S. Government Printing Office, 1986), p. 48.

acterize female-headed families as outside the scope of "normal" family situations has placed single mothers in a defensive position. Society has been especially concerned that the children headed by women would not be properly disciplined, would "get into trouble," or would become confused in their sex-role identity. As a result, single mothers often tried to assume a "super-woman" role or seek the security of remarriage.[5]

Differences in the management of single-parent family systems, as with other families, follow from variations in the demands and resources. The level and the balance between these systems inputs provide the bases of differences in management by single-parent households.

Input

TEENAGE

Teenage mothers may be very successful in parenting, but on the whole, they are probably the most vulnerable single parents. Teenage pregnancies result in abortions (38 percent), out-of-wedlock births (22 percent), births after marriage (17 percent), miscarriages (13 percent), and births that are legitimized after premarital conception (10 percent).[6] Teenage parenthood has been found to be associated with suboptimal health and development of both mother and infant[7] and extended periods of economic dependence that have long-term negative economic consequences for the family. Understanding some of the characteristics of teenage mothers further emphasizes their vulnerability.

In a study of young women thirteen to eighteen years old seeking birth control information or pregnancy tests, pregnant adolescents were found to be more likely than those seeking birth control information "to have had a traditional sex role orientation, to perceive themselves to be competent in more highly sex-typed activities, to have lower aspirations and school grades, and to have less of a sense of personal control over events in their lives."[8] Of the variables found to be associated with these two situations, lower socioeconomic status of pregnant adolescents was the most explanatory. Pregnant teenagers were also younger and more likely to believe in God determining their lives.

Adequate investment in human resources is particularly important to teenage mothers, as completion of their education and attainment of employment skills will contribute to an increased long-term earning capacity and a decrease in welfare dependence.[9] A major source of assistance for many teenage mothers is their family of origin. Pregnant adolescents may be faced with the situation of staying with their parents and receiving more help than if they left home for an uncertain marriage. Assistance with child care is also more likely when adolescent mothers remain with their parents. The pregnant adolescent receives more help in couple-headed families than single-parent families, probably because of greater economic resources and physical space in their homes.[10]

In an experimental test where free educational day care was provided for children of teenage mothers, it was found that mothers having access to these facilities were more likely to complete high school, obtain postsecondary education, and become self-supporting compared with a control group of teenage mothers who did not have access to the facilities.[11] Having free educational day care afforded teenage mothers the opportunity to direct resources to their own human-capital development. The situation arising when the developmental task of the parent conflicts with the developmental tasks of children or elderly parents is a challenging one, but it is one that is not infrequently faced.

Results from this experimental study emphasize the importance of resource availability, since a higher proportion of teenage mothers who received the free educational day care were able to stop receiving public child support, compared to those who did not receive free day care.[12]

Assistance and encouragement can intensify the goal to remain in school. This can be given by parents, counselors, or—possibly most important—support groups of peers in the same circumstances.[13]

The realization of an unplanned pregnancy can be described as an event demand. Young pregnant teenagers face high-risk biological and psychological demands associated with the pregnancy that more-mature teenagers and young women can often deal with without complications.

The interruption of addressing personal goals in order to deal with the demands of a baby can be frustrating to the teenage mother.

> It is early afternoon, and the smells of dirty diapers and grease mingle in the bleak Minneapolis apartment. The TV is tuned to "All My Children," and Stephanie Charette, 17, has collapsed on the sofa. Her rest is brief. Above the babble of the actors' voices comes a piercing wail. Larissa, her three-week-old daughter, is hungry. In an adjacent bedroom, Joey, one and a half years old and recovering from the flu, starts to stir. Stephanie, who is an American Indian, and one of ten children herself, first became pregnant at 15. It was "an accident," she explains. So, too, was her second baby. "I'm always tired," she laments, "and I can't eat." Before Joey's birth, before she dropped out of school, Stephanie dreamed of being a stewardess. Now her aspirations are more down to earth. "I want to pay my bills, buy groceries and have a house and furniture. I want to feel good about myself so my kids can be proud of me. It has been a long, long while," she confides, "since I had a good time."[14]

DIVORCED OR SEPARATED

The cost of divorce in terms of human capital depreciation generally rests with the wife, who has stayed at home rearing children. Absence from the labor force for periods of child rearing hampers her professional progress. The opportunity cost for wives of high-status husbands is generally higher than for wives of lower-class men. Human capital depreciation, however, is still important to lower-class women because they have lost their place in the seniority system.[15] It is important to keep the cost of depreciation of human capital prominent in legal and legislative matters related to divorce.

Women who remain consistently attached to the labor force should not suffer any more than men in regard to their human capital resources, unless they choose specifically not to advance in their work due to home and employment pressures.

While other goals with implications for interchanges with the personal subsystem are involved, of course, the interrelated ones of parenting and providing the means for maintaining the family are central for most divorced mothers.

A specific goal of divorced mothers, reflected in the perceived need for life insurance, was examined in an Ohio study. Three major reasons for life insurance were stated by the mothers: to meet a family income need, for savings and disability protection, and for death and burial expenses. Divorced mothers with young children and with limited education felt a need for life insurance based on family income requirements; older divorced mothers with limited education and few assets felt a need for life insurance for savings and disability protection; and young divorced mothers with low incomes felt a need for life insurance to cover funeral expenses. For each of the bases for the perceived need for life insurance, social-psychological factors were important—for example, family orientation, financial security, and perception of risk.[16]

Divorced women with young children, generally having fewer resources than their male counterparts, need to be goal oriented. After divorce, a person frustrated by either no direction or too specific direction from someone else is free to set a new course.

A recently divorced mother—with a boy age seven and girl age four—whose income is $25,000 to $30,000 notes: "I have found the financial re-adjustment to be difficult, and at times very stressful. Since the divorce has been final, I feel more in control of my financial situation. I am learning to budget my money more effectively and am setting goals for future financial planning."[17]

Single-parent fathers who have custody of their children often experience a change in their resource base. In a study of 1,136 single-parent fathers, 66 men reported having to relinquish their job and 43 men reported having been fired.[18] It was found that difficulties associated with a reduced income were greater than those associated with actual income level; that is, "a father whose income falls from $25,000 a year to $20,000 a year will find things more difficult than will a father earning $16,000 a year who experiences no drop in income after the breakup."[19]

The family resource base, particularly household income, drops drastically for separated and divorced women, and that reduction seems to be permanent.[20] Table 16.2 indicates that the median income for female-headed households is considerably lower than that of male-headed households.

Source of income for separated and divorced women will differ by level of income. Lower-income households depend primarily on public assistance, and women with higher income depend on their earnings and, in the early years

TABLE 16.2 *Money income for single-parent households*

Marital status	*Total households*	*Median income*
	Thousands	*Dollars*
Male-headed households		
Wife absent	1,282	15,775
Widowed	1,664	11,727
Divorced	3,345	20,631
Female-headed households		
Husband absent	2,564	8,851
Widowed	9,484	8,806
Divorced	6,037	13,486

Source: U.S. Department of Commerce, Bureau of the Census, *Statistical Abstract of the U.S. for 1985*, 105th ed. (Washington, D.C.: U.S. Government Printing Office, 1986), p. 443.

after divorce, child-support payments and alimony.[21] Women who are employed prior to marriage have a far better chance of shielding their household from a large drop in level of living after divorce than those who are minimally employed at the time of divorce.[22] In addition, reduction in income is usually associated with a substantial change in standard of living, with expenditures on food, housing, and other related items all being reduced. The reduction in living standards will likely continue as long as women remain head of the household, since real-income levels do not rise, on average, over time.[23]

When income levels of male and female divorced custodial parents are matched, no differences in their resource management behaviors are evident, except that females tend to have less life insurance than their male counterparts.[24] The substantial difference in the resources of male and female divorced custodial parents that is often noted in the literature is likely due to the differences in income levels.

For many women, the period after divorce (or the death of the husband) can bring on a regressive (entropic) period from which welfare, job training, an employment struggle, or remarriage provides the basis on which eventual stability depends.[25]

WIDOWED

Compared to divorce and separation, the shift to single parenthood due to death of one of the partners is less common, although it is no less, and often more, traumatic. Wives are more likely than husbands to be left with children under eighteen years of age. The children of widowed parents are more likely to be older than in other single-parent situations.[26] While the parenting and economic responsibilities may not be as critical, the patterns of dependency and other circumstances accompanying widowhood can be as traumatic and demanding as other causes leading to single parenthood.

According to a study of widows, 40 percent of those fifty to sixty years old considered seeking work after the death of their spouse.[27] In future years, many more widows will have work experience, as more women are now in the labor force.

Previous work experience, available money resources, and supportive family members are important contributors to the long-term adjustment of widows.

ADOPTIVE

Single parents who have chosen to adopt children, by comparison, must demonstrate their strong interest in becoming adoptive parents and their economic capacity to meet the related commitments. This preparation contrasts with teenage parenthood. Assuming the parenting role, especially of children who are older and more difficult to place, presents special problems to those who assume single-parent responsibility. Single applicants who want to adopt young infants are well educated, have employment stability, make plans, and are competent.[28] Many single applicants are also willing to adopt older or handicapped children.

In the early stage of the parenting cycle, the interrelations of the demands and resources seem to be particularly problematic. Different routes to single-parent roles also place demand-resource relations at different levels. In the following discussion, implications of these differences for management are considered.

Throughput

TEENAGE

The harsh realities of the need for planning are noted by Michelle, a fourteen-year-old in San Francisco who is concerned about her future: "I have to get my money together," she frets.

"I have to think ahead." She is going to have her baby in three weeks, and her pregnancy has caused a new way of thinking: "I used to think, ten years from now I'll be 24. Now I think, I'll be 24, and my child will be ten." Planning takes on a new meaning in these circumstances.[29]

Finding ways to make the most of challenges through planning and implementing can be an awesome task. Teenage single parents encounter especially difficult situations. Strong demands and limited resources both tend to make the managerial response short-term and highly reactive and responsive. There is little opportunity for evolving alternative solutions. For many teenagers, the physical demands of work, child care, and maintaining a household become so overriding that quality aspects of standards often have to be subordinated.

The problem of managing limited resources to meet nutritional needs, for example, can be difficult, particularly if there was no previous opportunity to learn how to allocate and control expenditures over a given time period. If income varies, experience in controlling may need to emphasize adjusting. At a time when nutritional needs are highly important, the pregnant teenager is often ill equipped to meet them. The kinds of food selected are often not the ones most adequate for maintaining health of both the unborn child and the pregnant mother. The quality and quantity of the nutrition obtained in the food purchased is a standard-setting consideration, while spreading the purchases over the needed time period is a sequencing matter.

Employment can be continued up to the time of birth, but loss of income following childbirth and preceding a return to the labor force can be a major adjustment problem. Even for two-parent families, the period immediately following childbirth is a critical one. Where the prior adjustment period is short, marital instability is more likely to develop. For the single teenager, the prospects are equally or more complex because the demands need to be faced alone, unless there are supportive people to compensate.

After the birth of the child, physical demands are heavy and sequencing of the related activities becomes difficult. The additional responsibilities for child care—many of which are "on demand," such as feeding and diapering—make control of the time resource difficult. Under such circumstances, maintaining the quality of desired activity or learning skills for reaching them is almost impossible. These circumstances combine to tax even the most resourceful young people and often bring a sense of discouragement and futility, unless there are support services within either the family or community. The source of income for families headed by women is important for their sense of control over their fate because of the stigma attached to welfare and the unreliability of child-support payments.

Indeed, given the present alternatives for financial support, the mother who fully assumed both roles (mother and provider) and earned her family's support was more likely to be better off than the mother who stayed home and depended upon unreliable, unstable, controlling, or stigmatizing sources of income.[30]

The teenage single parent with major resource constraints in terms of time and money (although balanced with the optimism and resilience of youth) probably follows a more directional than specific goal-oriented planning procedure. Persons in unpredictable situations with less experience on which to build are likely to identify success as "keeping one's head above water."

Standard-setting and sequencing decisions are often made on the basis of the cheapest alternative, accepting whatever sacrifice in quality occurs.

Within the resource constraints, decisions are also likely to be oriented to alternatives that focus on satisfactions in returns, although growing awareness of risks may lead to an increasing interest in ways to reduce uncertainties. The ambivalence that accompanies a teenage mother's maturing processes, in combination with an infant's demands, can mitigate against the mother's ability to reach her potential in making choices that bring high benefits in relation to the resources used. Achieving optimum results may be frustrated by the pressures of the moment, by limited reserves, or by inadequate consideration of existing possibilities. Yet, some positive net balance must be found, whether through individual effort or with strategic outside support, for success to be achieved.

At critical times, a morphostatic approach may be needed to break even each day—gaining control through negative feedback, until the demands themselves lessen. Unless further demands occur—a second pregnancy, illness, or another costly event—the early, heavy demands of a child are reduced eventually and goals can be established. With gradual progress, the cycle can be turned into a morphogenic one, building on positive feedback.

DIVORCED OR SEPARATED

Divorced or separated people with older children have more flexibility, as a rule, in balancing responsibilities and outside employment than do teenage parents. Following divorce, single parents can also be under heavy pressure and feel a lack of direction during the initial period of accepting the change and learning new roles in situations of resource constraints. In other instances, single parenthood may be less pressured and more goal-oriented after the anxieties of a traumatic relationship are limited.

The planning style of single-parent mothers and fathers was investigated in a study using the morphostatic and morphogenic planning framework described in Chapter 7.

In this Minneapolis sample, most of the single parents engaged in a planning process. One group used strategies that involved "*creating* new resources or *substituting* one resource for another, e.g., time for money. A new goal or want was added to their demand structure with the understanding that the necessary resources would be found if they were not already available."[31] Another style of planning was viewing "available resources as givens that could not be modified. Rather, when it was necessary to juggle demands and resources, they chose to modify their demands."[32] For mothers, the educational level was associated with the more expansive style of planning: creating new resources, etc. The relationship did not exist with the fathers. Differences in household income did not explain the planning styles; the family life-cycle stage was rather grossly measured and did not correlate with the planning styles.

For single-parent fathers, either divorced or widowed, the economic problem is not as great as is coordination or sequencing of household responsibilities. Fathers report that it is not the unfamiliarity with household tasks and child care that is demanding, but rather the totality of their roles that is overburdening.[33] Fathers, prior to their single-parent role, have apparently had more experience with child care than with the integrating of household demands. Planning for structuring activities in order to provide adequate supervision is also of concern. The regularity of the housework is "what gets you down"—the management logistics.

Single-parent fathers assume a large proportion of household responsibilities. If they do receive help, it is daughters who are more active contributors than sons.[34] Table 16.3 provides information on the allocation of household work responsibilities in a study of 1,136 families.

Divorced mothers in clerical and sales occupations were more likely to assume child-care responsibilities that conflicted with employment "when they had employment that was less stressful and time demanding, when help from friends and relatives was not readily available, when the children were younger and when they had experience managing dual responsibilities.[35] In these circumstances, the boundaries between employment and the family seem to be

TABLE 16.3 *Person(s) who usually take care of household work in families with single fathers*

Task	*Father*	*Children*	*We all do*	*Other*
		*Percent**		
Cooking	65	2	28	6
Cleaning	36	5	55	5
Laundry	53	5	36	6
Shopping	71	1	25	3

* The figures for each task may total more than 100 percent, due to rounding.
Source: Geoffrey L. Greif, "Children and Housework in the Single Father Family," *Family Relations,* 34 (July 1985): 355. Copyrighted 1985 by the National Council on Family Relations, 1910 W. County Rd. B, Suite 147, St. Paul, Minn. 55113. Reprinted by permission.

permeable. Pleck[36] describes this type of boundary as asymmetrically permeable, i.e., allowing family responsibilities to overlap employment.

By examining time-use patterns, insights can be gained concerning the use of resources to meet demands in both the personal and managerial systems. Employed single mothers spend less time on household tasks (food preparation, dishwashing, and cleaning activities) than employed mothers in two-parent households[37] (Table 16.4). When the age of the younger child is statistically controlled, time spent in physical child care is lower for employed married mothers than for single mothers. Analysis revealed no difference between the two groups in time spent in nonphysical care of children. The single employed mother sacrifices on the time spent in personal care, including sleep.

Another important part of throughput is decision-making at various points, in both the personal and managerial systems. Adolescents in mother-only households make more decisions than those in two-parent families. "The mother, faced with the problem of controlling an adolescent without a father, is less likely to make decisions without input from the youth and is more likely to allow the youth to make his or her own decision."[38] Decisions included in the study were those involving the choice of clothing and

TABLE 16.4 *Time use by employed and unemployed mothers in single- and two-parent families in hours per day*

	Employed mothers		*Nonemployed mothers*	
Activity	*One-parent families*	*Two-parent families*	*One-parent families*	*Two-parent families*
		Time in hours per day		
Household tasks	1.8	3.3	4.0	6.0
Child care	1.0	0.8	1.5	1.4
Personal care	9.2	9.7	10.9	10.2
Recreation	2.4	2.6	5.5	4.9
Volunteer work	0.6	0.1	1.2	1.0
Paid work	8.7	7.6	—	—
Other	0.2	—	0.8	0.3

Source: Margaret Mietus Sanik and Teresa Mauldin, "Single Versus Two Parent Families: A Comparison of Mother's Time," *Family Relations* 35 (January 1986): 55. Copyrighted 1986 by the National Council on Family Relations, 1910 W. County Rd. B, Suite 147, St. Paul, Minn. 55113. Reprinted by permission.

friends, the spending of money, the use of time, and constraints on social activities. Both parents and adolescents were asked the questions.

WIDOWED

Widowhood for both men and women is more likely to be faced after the children are grown than before. But where there are young children, adjustments are particularly great. A parent's lingering illness introduces difficult problems that may seem impossible to sequence because of uncertainties in scheduling. Illness also can make unforeseen claims. Financial resources may be drained. Under these circumstances, the spouse may have trouble assuming the responsibilities for resource use ordinarily performed by his or her partner.

Once the transition to widowhood occurs, responses to particular circumstances can be similar to those of the divorced parent. Friends or community groups are more likely to offer support to widows than divorced individuals during the transitional period, however.

ADOPTIVE

Adoptive parents are presumed to be especially oriented to planning in relation to their single-parent roles. The way in which their single-parent status affects their general sense of satisfaction in meeting their goals and in using their resources to that end is too new a phenomenon to interpret, generally. The individual circumstances are unique and provide the setting within which the particular managerial processes make coping and enhancing possible.

While limited information is available about the management by adoptive parents, what is available suggests a heavy leaning on the parents or relatives for child-care support.[39] The planning and checking of arrangements by an agency on the means by which the additional responsibility will be met probably strengthens the likelihood of success. In addition, while the single adoptive parent does not have the previous experience of growing into the responsibility in a shared way (as is the case with other single-parent roles, except for the premarital ones), the role is planned for and is not precipitated by relationship or other problems. The trade-offs could well yield a balance to support success.

Output

For young teenage parents, met demands may be the satisfaction of meeting another day with enough resources for basic necessities. During periods of negative demand and resource balances, the output effects can be discouraging until either additional outside support or positive feedback effects can bring shifts in the balance. The abilities to set and meet goal and event demands satisfactorily and to be effective in resource acquisition and use are both important for effective management in the long run. Community or social agencies provide important support services to single female parents, particularly.

Being happy and not feeling isolated are important to the general well-being of the single parent. The roles of the community, organizations, neighbors, steady romantic involvements, as well as relatives and friends should not be overlooked. Female single parents have a wider social support system than male single parents. In a sample of low-income single parents in a rural area dominated by divorced mothers, informal support through groups, friendships, and relatives had a positive effect on their general well-being.[40] Social support was also found to be important in predicting physical and mental health of single parents.[41]

Single parents recently divorced or widowed, whether men or women, face major adjustments in their lives. Goal demands during the adjustment period are likely to shift to a short-term basis, a likely change in perspective, regardless of available resources. Resource aspects may be supportive if adequate or complicating if limited. Even though the adjustment is successful, the need for a shorter orientation may minimize an underlying unsatisfactory response until security in new roles is achieved and new directions identified. Successful management of adversity can lead to a greater overall sense of satisfaction and security than might have otherwise been possible. These adjustments involve continuing interchanges with the personal subsystem.

Probably the most goal-oriented single parents are fathers who have sought the role at the time of divorce or persons who have sought it through adoption. Their resource positions are also relatively strong, monetarily. Although other skills may well be limited, they are ones that appear to be acquired acceptably within the context of the situation.

The several single-parent situations involve varying throughput processes. While differences within each of the circumstances leading to single parenthood are almost as great as among them, each has been shown to have special managerial implications for the ways demands are met and resources are used effectively.

Summary

Single parenthood is an increasingly significant family form, commonly entered through a change in marriage status, but increasingly through premarital parenthood. Increases in teenage pregnancy are the recent phenomenon given major attention in the chapter, not only because of current general interest but also because of its special and long-run effects. Teenage mothers often bear major responsibilities because marriages are highly unstable. Though men are obtaining custody of children more often than in the past, those who seek to do so are likely to be more established and able to bear the economic responsibilities. The inexperience and limited schooling of both male and female teenage parents mitigate against them without sources of support, either through family, community, or government agencies.

Single parents—never married, divorced, separated, widowed, adoptive—are child-oriented families. Demands and resources, as inputs to the family system, place the question of managing in relation to the interests of the child or children high on the list. Compared to couples with no previous parenting experience, the individual responsibility is compounded. Those with previous experience need to reorder their roles and their priorities. The extent to which adequate resources are available—money, helping services, time, skills—increases the flexibility within which planning can be done and the likelihood of success. Teenagers lack both experience and resources. Older divorced, separated, and widowed men may have more money resources than skills and time; the reverse is more likely the case with women.

Single adults are being successful in their efforts to adopt children. Reliance on extended-family support is common, although community services may be utilized. Interest, responsibility, and adequate resources are all factors to be demonstrated before adoption, factors that may be missing to some degree in the other avenues open to the single-parent role.

Notes

1. Arthur J. Norton and Paul C. Glick, "One Parent Families: A Social and Economic Profile," *Family Relations* 35 (January 1986): 16.
2. Herbert L. Smith and Phillips Cutright, "Components of Change in the Number of Female Family Heads Age 15 to 44, an Update and Reanalysis: United States, 1940–1983," *Social Science Research Journal* 14 (September 1985): 241.
3. Ibid.
4. Ruth A. Brandwein, Carol A. Brown, and Elizabeth Maury Fox, "Women and Children Last:

The Social Situation of Divorced Mothers and Their Families," *Journal of Marriage and the Family* 36 (August 1974): 498.

5. Ibid., p. 499.

6. Kimball Miller and Charles S. Field, "Adolescent Pregnancy: A Combined Obstetric and Pediatric Management Approach," *Mayo Clinic Proceedings* 59 (May 1984): 312.

7. Barry S. Zuckerman, Deborah K. Walker, Deborah A. Frank, Cynthia Chase, and Beatrix Hamburg, "Adolescent Pregnancy—Biobehavioral Determinants of Outcome," *The Journal of Pediatrics* 105 (December 1984): 857.

8. Carol J. Ireson, "Adolescent Pregnancy and Sex Roles," *Sex Roles* 11 (August 1984): 189.

9. Dianne S. Burden and Lorraine V. Klerman, "Teenage Parenthood: Factors That Lessen Economic Dependence," *Social Work* 29 (January–February 1984): 14.

10. Frank F. Furstenberg, Jr., "Implicating the Family: Teenage Parenthood and Kinship Involvement," in *Teenage Pregnancy in a Family Context: Implications for Policy,* ed. Theodora Ooms (Philadelphia: Temple University Press, 1981), pp. 138–143.

11. Frances A. Campbell, Bonnie Breitmayer, and Craig T. Ramey, "Disadvantaged Single Mothers and Their Children—Consequences of Free Educational Day Care," *Family Relations* 35 (January 1986): 67.

12. Ibid.

13. Miller and Field, "Adolescent Pregnancy," pp. 311–317.

14. Claudia Wallis, "Children Having Children," *Time* 126 (December 9, 1985): 79.

15. Jeanne Wielage Smith and Elizabeth Smith Beninger, "Women's Nonmarket Labor: Dissolution of Marriage and Opportunity Cost," *Journal of Family Issues* 3 (June 1982): 261.

16. Mary Ann Noecker Guadagno, "Selected Factors Affecting Perceived Need for Life Insurance by Divorced Mothers," Ph.D. diss. (Columbus: The Ohio State University, 1978) pp. 68–75, 78–79.

17. Mary Lou Branson, "Resource Management: Divorced Custodial Fathers Compared to Divorced Custodial Mothers," *Family Perspectives* 17 (Spring 1983): 106.

18. Geoffrey L. Greif, *Single Fathers* (Lexington, Mass.: Lexington Books, 1985), p. 63.

19. Ibid.

20. Robert S. Weiss, "The Impact of Marital Dissolution on Income and Consumption in Single-Parent Households," *Journal of Marriage and the Family* 46 (February 1984): 126.

21. Ibid.

22. Joyce M. Larson and Norleen M. Ackerman, "Human Capital As Related to the Income of Households Recently Headed by Women: Descriptive Findings," in *Thinking Globally, Acting Locally,* Proceedings of a Workshop Sponsored by the Family Economics/Home Management Section of the American Home Economics Association (Washington, D.C.: American Home Economics Association, 1985), p. 305.

23. Weiss, "The Impact of Marital Dissolution," p. 126.

24. Mary Lou Branson and Glen Jennings, "A Comparison of Resource Management Behaviors of Male and Female Divorced Custodial Parents," in *Social and Economic Resources: Managing in a Complex Society,* Proceedings of the Conference for the Southeastern Regional Association Family Economics–Home Management (Baton Rouge: Louisiana State University, 1985) p. 2.

25. Susan Maizel Chambre, "Welfare, Work, and Family Structure," *Social Work* 22 (March 1977): 105.

26. Heather L. Ross and Isabel V. Sawhill, *Time of Transition* (Washington, D.C.: The Urban Institute, 1975), p. 28.

27. Leslie A. Morgan, "Continuity and Change in the Labor Force Activity of Recently Widowed Women," *The Gerontologist* 24 (October 1984): 530.

28. Joan F. Shireman and Penny R. Johnson, "Single Persons As Adoptive Parents," *Social Service Review* 50 (March 1976): 108.

29. Wallis, "Children Having Children," pp. 78–79.

30. Sally Bould, "Female-Headed Families: Personal Fate Control and the Provider Role," *Journal of Marriage and the Family* 39 (May 1977): 347–348.

31. Cheryl Buehler and M. Janice Hogan, "Planning Styles in Single-Parent Families," *Home Economics Research Journal* 14 (June 1986): 359.

32. Ibid.

33. Rita D. Gasser and Claribel M. Taylor, "Role Adjustment of Single Parent Fathers with Dependent Children," *The Family Coordinator* 25 (October 1976): 400.

34. Geoffrey L. Greif, "Children and Housework in the Single Father Family," *Family Relations* 34 (July 1985): 357.

35. Phyllis J. Johnson, "Divorced Mothers' Management of Responsibilities: Conflicts Between Employment and Child Care, *Journal of Family Issues* 4 (March 1983): 100.

36. Joseph H. Pleck, "The Work–Family Role System," *Social Problems* 24 (April 1977): 417–427.

37. Margaret Mietus Sanik and Teresa Mauldin,

"Single Versus Two Parent Families: A Comparison of Mother's Time," *Family Relations* 35 (January 1986): 55.

38. Sanford M. Dornbusch, Merrill J. Carlsmith, Steven J. Bushwall, Philip L. Ritter, Herbert Leiderman, Albert H. Hastorf, and Ruth T. Gross, "Single Parents, Extended Households, and the Control of Adolescents," *Child Development* 56 (October 1985): 334.

39. Shireman and Johnson, "Single Persons As Adoptive Parents," p. 108.

40. Nancy Wells Gladow and Margaret P. Ray, "The Impact of Informal Support Systems on the Well-Being of Low-Income Single Parents," *Family Relations* 35 (January 1986): 113–123.

41. Shirley M. H. Hanson, "Healthy Single Parent Families," *Family Relations* 35 (January 1986): 131.

17

Blended families

Reconstituted, blended, or remarried-couple households—whatever the title given this type of family—comprise some of the most complex family systems in the United States today. Some facts illustrate their prevalence and make-up:

- In one of five couple households, one or both spouses have been divorced
- In most remarried-couple households, one spouse has children at the time of remarriage
- Three sets of children under eighteen—his, hers, and theirs—occur in only a small portion of remarriages
- Most divorced women retain custody of the children; thus stepfathering is far more prevalent than stepmothering[1]
- One in six children lives in a blended family[2]
- Divorce is higher among remarried couples than in first marriages[3]

Blended families without children from each spouse's former marriage plus children from the new marriage do not experience the full complexity of the recombinant family system. In viewing the family as a system, the boundaries of the system can be most evident in the case of the blended family. Spouses may draw sharp boundaries between a blended family system maintained by ex-spouses. Children may physically move in and out of two systems and learn to compartmentalize their lives. Boundary problems often occur around holidays. Stepfamilies eventually develop their own traditions and as members of the family contribute to the new traditions.[4]

A family life cycle for blended families helps conceptualize the many changes and adjustments that take place in the process of establishing new relationships and roles. The three major stages are the early stage (getting started), middle stage (restructuring), and later stage (solidifying the stepfamily).[5]

In blending two families throughout the life cycle, it is possible to adapt to and to accommodate the new stepparent and the energy that person brings from another family system. In other cases, the family system may expect the new member (a stepparent) to meet their expectations without changing—to assimilate a new stepparent.[6]

A woman in her twenties whose parents divorced when she was in high school wrote about her experience, conveying a greater sense of assimilation than accommodation:

> Remarriage introduces complications. The new family requires patience and effort to make it work. It is a challenge. The stepmother is confronted with the onerous burden of making peace

> with her husband's children. She must establish her identity and, should she be so ambitious, establish a rapport with the children. The process involves an attempt to understand the background of the child and become familiar with the former childhood relationships between children and parents. . . . All the influences and circumstances are never recovered. The pieces rarely fit. The result is too often a distorted, inaccurate portrayal of the nuclear family.[7]

Complications associated with remarriage and blended families arise when couples and their children are at different stages of the life cycle. When a father of teenage children marries a younger woman with young children, the blending process is often not easy, but the process is probably no more complex than in the case where both families have teenagers, particularly of different sexes.

Some families maintain boundaries around the parent and children in an effort to compartmentalize potential problems or concerns. Privacy for individuals within the household may be of considerable importance, and the concept of boundaries may be defined to include physical boundaries.

Input

VALUES AND GOALS

Value differences in blended and other family types merit close consideration in understanding the functioning of a blended-family system. A seventeen-year-old reflecting on her stepparents illustrates the differing values of her biological and blended family and the accommodation she made:

> I've had to adapt to my stepparents. They're different. My stepfather is sterner and quiet. My stepmother is emotional, while my real mother is more self-contained. My stepmother uses frozen foods and doesn't buy expensive cereals I like. My real mother is a gourmet cook. There is more discipline at my stepmother's. I like the discipline, but there are problems. For example, my stepmother wouldn't let me wash my clothes unless I filled the washer. But at my mother's I find them too family-oriented. We all had to eat together. I am not interested in family to that extent. In that sense I feel freer at my stepmother's. She accepts me as an adult.[8]

Couples who join two families together need to recognize and give advance consideration to "their functions as stepparents, their attitudes to child-rearing, and their plans for home and money management."[9] If new spouses and their children have not worked through some prominent value and standard differences before, or at least in the early months of marriage, everyday living can be difficult. The following case is an example of "reverse" assimilation, asking the new system to incorporate the stepmother and her expectations:

> Connie thought she could win them all over by mapping out a homemaker's role for herself. She began reorganizing the home, shifting the kitchen utensils to make everything more functional for her management. She went shopping for her favorite recipes, all gourmet dishes. In short, she displaced Paul and his sons from their household routines. No negotiations were held about the division of family and household responsibilities. . . . Things were no longer in their accustomed places; meals defied his nutritional bias.[10]

Working through values and standard differences might have helped avoid some of the friction that developed. In the therapy that the family received, some deep-seated factors contributing to the tensions were identified and openly discussed.

Couples may hold intimacy as a goal for themselves, while they consider maintenance of equilibrium and closeness as a goal in their parent-child relationships.[11] Recognizing and dealing with such basic differences in goals makes possible reduced competition between systems. "In general, members of one subsystem can more easily tolerate requests for time, space, or money which come from a member of that subsystem than requests which come from another subsystem."[12] For example, a child will accept his mother's request that she spend time with his stepfather more readily than the stepfather's statement that he deserves time with the child's mother.[13]

RESOURCES

Management in blended families presents the special challenge of conflicting demands and often limited resources. For a parent with children from a former marriage living in another household, the goal of stability and financial security for the current family must be balanced against the goal and commitment to provide support for children living in another household—and perhaps to furnish alimony for a former spouse. The result of dealing with those conflicting goals is often a family with a tenuous resource base.

Child support payments in 1978 were received by 41.4 percent of women reporting children under 21 from previous marriages living at home (Table 17.1).

Parallel data are not available from men, but in another survey, in 77.1 percent of the cases, men reported providing financial support to children under eighteen living elsewhere. No easy explanation can be found to deal with the apparent wide difference in providing and receiving child support payments—the difference in ages, under eighteen and under twenty-one, seems insufficient to make such a difference.

The strong interrelationship between the personal and managerial subsystems of a family are particularly evident in blended families. Complex personal subsystem functions may present managerial subsystem challenges in managing limited resources. Child support and/or alimony obligations often come when newly blended families are experiencing high resource demands. Savings will be used, outside employment of both spouses becomes a near certainty, and a second job may be needed for one spouse. Men more than women report a negative relationship with their ex-spouses.[14] The most likely explanation is the man's child support or alimony requirements, which may be seen as costly to the current marriage.[15]

TABLE 17.1 *Men and women reporting children from a previous marriage and providing or receiving child-support payments*

Men reported to have children under 18 from a previous marriage living elsewhere.	3,382,000
Men reported providing financial support to children living elsewhere, "regularly," "occasionally," or "seldom."	2,605,000 (71.1%)
Women reported children under 21 from previous marriage living in the household.	5,720,000
Women reporting receipt of child-support payments in 1978, "regularly," "occasionally," or "seldom."	2,368,000 (41.4%)

Source: Men: June 1980 Current Population Survey Public Use Tape; Women: U.S. Bureau of the Census (1981, Table 1). In Andrew Cherlin, Jeanne Griffith, and James McCarthy, "A Note on Maritally Disrupted Men's Reports of Child Support in the June 1980 Current Population Survey," *Demography* 20 (August 1983): 386.

The blended family's resource base may erode, and the level of living be reduced, when support of two families or child-support payments are involved. A remarried woman gave a report:

> "My new husband and I have some arguments over money. I worry that we won't have enough at the end of the month for his child and our taxes. We never save." She said that money is the thing she worries about more than anything else, and life for her now is very different: "We don't entertain. We invite people for a pot of soup and French bread. We don't buy clothes. We don't travel much. It's a source of tension . . ."[16]

Support from kin, specifically grandparents,

a common resource for traditional nuclear families, may or may not continue when the family changes through divorce. Most children, regardless of which spouse has the custody,

> . . . continue to see their grandparents at least during the year. Somewhere between two-thirds and three-fourths of the children see their noncustodial grandparents a few times a year or more, and about a third see them at least once or twice a month. Thus divorce rarely breaks the ritual ties between the first and third generations although it usually removes grandparents from day-to-day or even week-to-week contact with grandchildren.[17]

Roughly one in ten grandparents in the study contributed to the financial support of a child.[18] Various writers suggest that blended families have more family and thus will receive more support and have more exchange within the family network. That likely occurs in some families.

When the middle-age child changes roles and becomes the "patron" for his or her parents, the situation of job responsibilities, relationships with children and stepchildren, and demands of the current spouse may make assistance of aging parents difficult to give. The effect of multiple marriages on parental support and the subsequent assistance for parents by children is not clearly established.

Throughput

Divorce and remarriage can be viewed in a morphostatic or morphogenic fashion. The new relationships that are formed can be expansive and growth-producing (morphogenic) for the adults and children involved. With permeable boundaries from the system and probably less well defined roles than in an initial nuclear family, opportunities for new ways of coping and managing are found.[19]

For example, children in remarried families see additional role models and have a wider variety of experiences, and this diversity can result in morphogenic behavior. This diversity can also be frustrating to those children who respond to constant change quite differently: Their response is morphostatic—a struggle to restore equilibrium to their lives.[20]

Planning in blended families is complicated by the number of other family systems that interface with the blended family. Conflict often arises over visitation of children. Agreements can help blended families and other involved families to have more control over their lives and thus more opportunity for planning. Suggestions for blended-family parents in maintaining relationships with former family members follow:

1. "Don't take the other parent for granted."
2. "Be orderly." This may mean clear scheduling of visits and writing memos after visits.
3. "Use businesslike communications and recordkeeping" to convey the information and plans you have developed.
4. "Make no assumptions. Have everything explicit." Patterns of being with children will change, and parents will need to check the expectations of the other parent, such as whether the father will continue with scouting.
5. "Give the other parent the benefit of the doubt." When the other parent is late in bringing the child or has to cancel a child's weekend stay, before attributing negative reasons for such behavior, realize that there may be another explanation.
6. "Keep your feelings in check."[21]

In managing financial resources, spouses may pool money, regardless of biological parentage of children, or maintain separate accounts for their biological children.[22]

Planning-conscious couples may make prenuptial agreements about their net worth and the disposition of their estates while agreeing to pool their current incomes for household expenses or deciding to maintain money from different sources in separate accounts. Two examples illustrate pooled and separate resource arrangements:

> Mike Robinson and Fran Becker Robinson have been together in a stepfamily household for the past five years, with his two boys and her three children—two adolescent daughters and nine-year-old Sammy. . . . Resources of time, services, goods and cash are distributed according to an individual family member's needs.[23]

Fran's hospital dietician salary and Mike's shoe store profits go into their joint checking account. Both draw on the account for household expenses (Figure 17.1).

Separate resource management can be seen in the Marshall/Linton stepfamily made up of Harry Marshall, Sheila Linton Marshall, and her three sons, ages eight to thirteen:

> The boys live in the household full time, but visit their father (who lives in another state) for summer and extended school vacations. Harry's oldest daughter, Greta, is away at college, and Ginny, 16 years old, lives with her mother and new stepfather in another stepfamily. Neither of

FIGURE 17.1 *Pooled resource management*

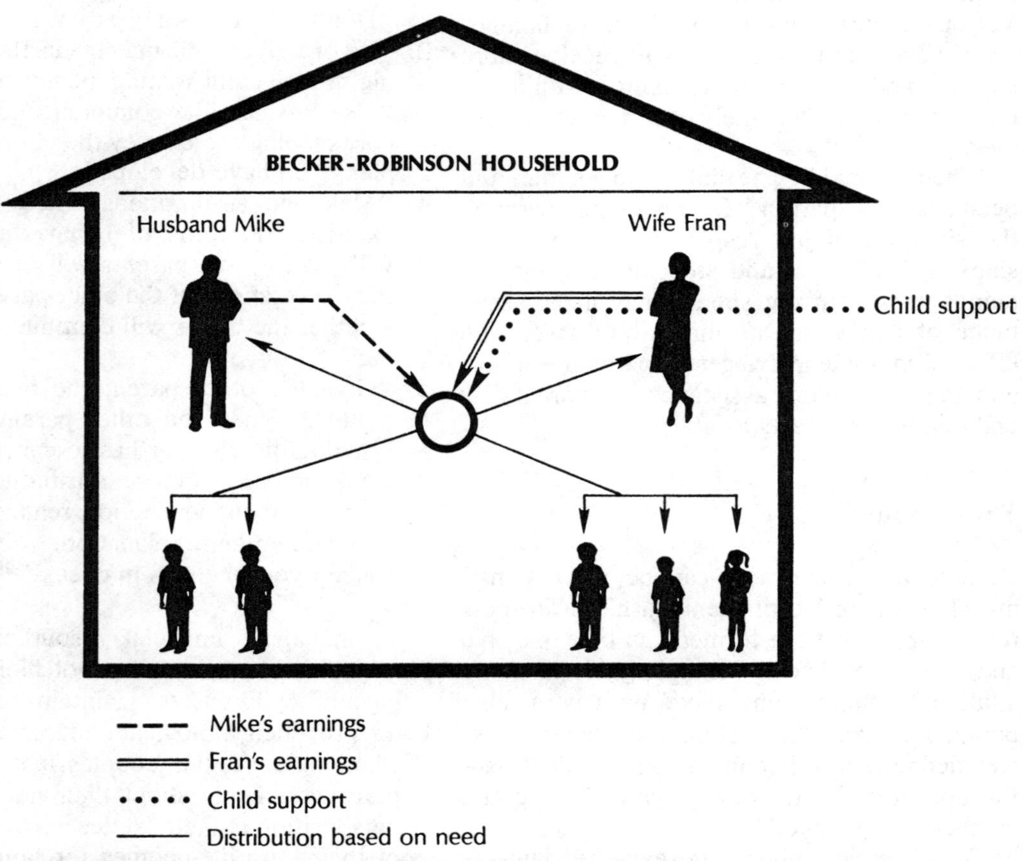

Source: Adapted from Barbara Fishman, "The Economic Behavior of Stepfamilies," *Family Relations* 32 (July 1983), 363. Copyrighted 1983 by the National Council on Family Relations, 1910 W. County Rd. B, Suite 147, St. Paul, Minn. 55113. Reprinted by permission.

FIGURE 17.2 *Separate resource management*

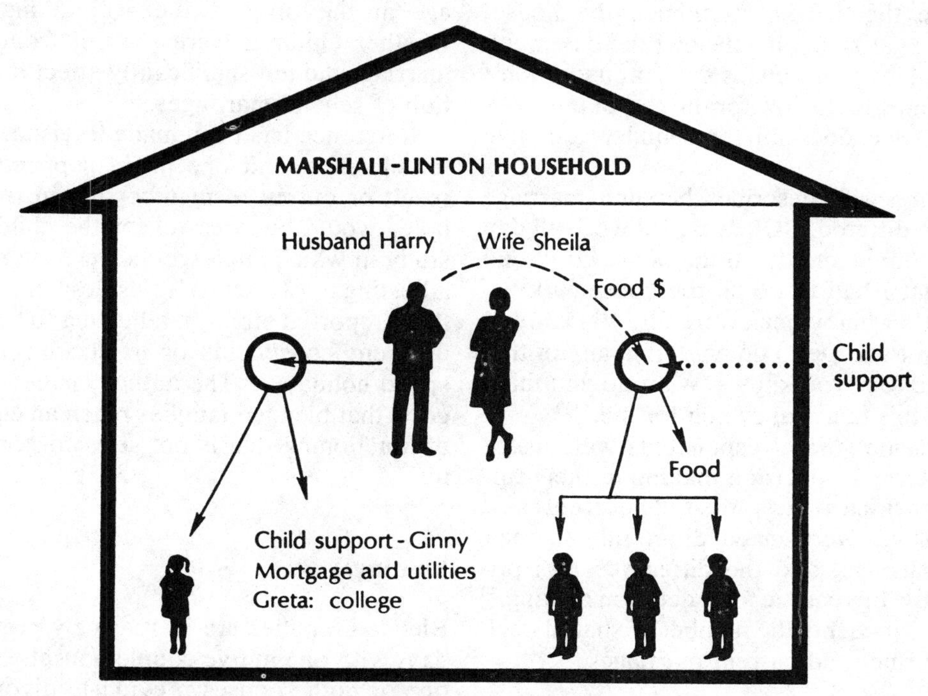

Source: Adapted from Barbara Fishman, "The Economic Behavior of Stepfamilies," *Family Relations* 32 (July 1983), 363. Copyrighted 1983 by the National Council on Family Relations, 1910 W. County Rd. B, Suite 147, St. Paul, Minn. 55113. Reprinted by permission.

> Harry's children lives under the Marshall/Linton roof, although Ginny visits every other weekend and vacations. Greta's visits are sporadic. Harry has an executive position with a large oil company. Sheila is an unemployed teacher who has chosen to be at home, at least for this time in her family life.[24]

Sheila reports that her husband gives her a fixed amount each week for his portion of the food and other expenses. She adds that to her checking account along with the child-support payments (Figure 17.2).

Although each family must work out financial management to serve both familial and individual needs, it appears that pooling money is a unifying process, while maintaining separate accounts "encourages biological loyalties and personal autonomy."[25]

Task performance and decision-making patterns were compared between former marriages and current marriages in a study that interviewed individuals after separation and then reinterviewed them three years later.[26]

> [Both men and women viewed] their second marriages as more egalitarian than their first marriages. Females are less likely than males to see their partners as sharing decisions and tasks and share tasks more or less equally in their second marriages. However, the females even more than the males experienced a sharp movement away from a marriage based on strictly defined roles.[27]

A wife describes her current marriage and their division of labor, "I went out shopping with a friend on Monday and I got home and he'd done the dishes, vacuumed the house, burned the garbage, and cleaned the basement. He does all my work on his days off and I don't have anything to do now for the rest of the week (laughing). He does all the laundry too, five loads."[28]

The same wife describes her first marriage and how it differed, "Oh Jeez, I'd work all day and come home and do all the housework, and be told that I had to do all the housework because that's what women were for, you know. I mean 'don't ask me to do anything, any of that stuff,' he'd say, you know. 'What do you think I am.' So this is a real switch for me."[29]

In the same study, respondents were asked about patterns of decision making in their current and past marriages. Most (80 percent) said that decisions were made differently in their second marriage, and the difference was primarily in the increase in joint decision making.[30] Figure 17.3 presents the number of shared decisions in former and current marriages.

Output

Satisfaction from marriage does not seem to differ between first-married and remarried couples.[31] Remarried couples reported they felt inadequate in their marital role performance more often than first-married couples in the same study. Reasons for these feelings of inadequacy may cluster around the complexity of the role.[32] Yet, differences in first-married and remarried individuals exist: The remarried individuals report poorer physical health, more frequent use of alcohol and drugs (31 percent compared to 19 percent in first marriages), and more frequent experiences of difficult times than for first-married individuals.[33] In spite of these differences, the outcome of remarriage in terms of morale and outlook is similar to first-marrieds. From an analysis of 10,000 couples, black couples who remarried were less likely to get a divorce or dissolution than first-married couples; remarried white couples were more likely to dissolve their marriage than first-married couples. The age at the time of the second marriage or whether children were present from the first marriage did not significantly affect the dissolution of second marriages.[34]

Reference has been made to visitation rights for children, and one might suppose that the result or output of membership in two households would be stressful for the children. In a study in which adolescents were queried about adjusting to two sets of rules, less than a third of them reported stress in adjusting to rules in the different households or in deciding where to spend holidays.[35] The author of the study suggests that blended families reach an equilibrium of functioning that is not stressful for the family.

Summary

Blended families are increasingly prevalent today, with one in five couple households having one or both spouses previously divorced. The major stages in the life cycle of blended families include getting started, restructuring, and solidifying the stepfamily. When the ages of the children of the spouses are widely different, the complexity of the newly formed system is complex; so, too, are the blended families with all teenage children. Boundaries of the several systems may be drawn differently: Where relations between former spouses are very good, the boundaries for the children may be quite permeable.

Blended families deal with a melding of established values and goals. Requests for time, space, or money that often reflect value and goal differences are more acceptable from a member of the original system than from a member of the newer system.

Use of resources and the resource base for blended families are complicated by child-support and alimony payments and the arrangements for the children to spend time with their other parent. Support from kin, especially

FIGURE 17.3 *Shared decisions in current and former marriages*

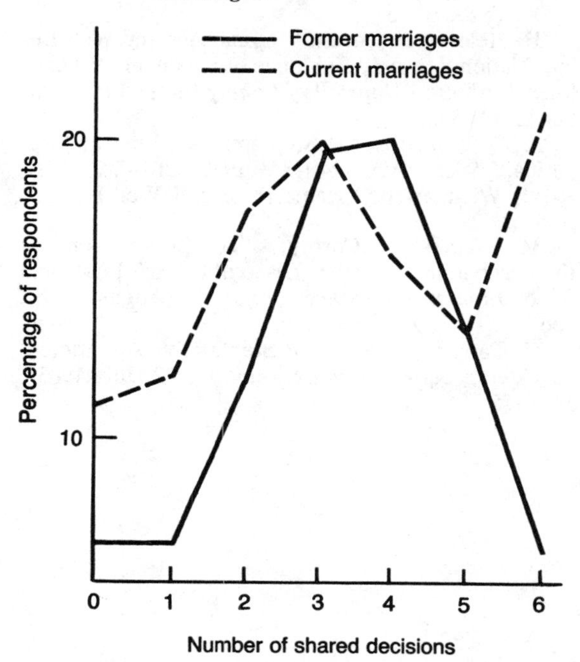

Source: Frank F. Furstenberg, Jr. and Graham B. Spanier, "Conjugal Succession," *Recycling the Family: Remarriage After Divorce,* p. 73. Copyright © 1984 by Sage Publications, Inc. Reprinted by permission of Sage Publications, Inc.

grandparents, may or may not continue with blended families. Contact with grandparents continues for at least a few times a year. Some writers suggest that blended families have more family members and thus more exchange.

Children in blended families may find the experience expansive, or morphogenic, in nature, as they are surrounded by different role models and have different experiences. Other children, and probably other spouses, struggle to maintain as near status quo as possible.

Resources of blended families may be pooled or kept quite separate. Prenuptial agreements are advisable for arriving at accord on net worth and the disposition of estates, as well as for deciding how to deal with current income.

Blended marriages are reported as being more egalitarian than first marriages and as having more joint decision making.

The outlook is similar for remarried couples compared to first-married couples, although remarried individuals report poorer physical health, more use of alcohol and drugs, and more frequent experiences of difficult times.

Reaching successful levels of functioning that are not stressful for them is a challenge that blended families continue to face.

Notes

1. Andrew Cherlin and James McCarthy, "Remarried Couple Households: Data from the June 1980 Current Population Survey," *Journal of Marriage and the Family* 47 (February 1985): 23–30.
2. Ibid., p. 23.
3. Michael A. Smyer and Brian F. Hofland, "Divorce and Family Support in Later Life," *Journal of Family Issues* 3 (March 1982): 61–77.
4. Emily B. Visher and John S. Visher, *Stepfamilies: A Guide to Working with Stepparents and Stepchildren* (New York: Brunner/Mazel, 1979), p. 214.
5. Patricia L. Papernow, "The Stepfamily Cycle: An Experiential Model of Stepfamily Development," *Family Relations* 33 (July 1984): 355–363.
6. Marilyn O. Kent, "Remarriage: A Family Systems Perspective," *Social Casework: The Journal of Contemporary Social Work* 61 (March 1980): 149.
7. Leslie Aldridge Westoff, *The Second Time Around* (New York: Viking Press, 1977), p. 114. Copyright © 1975, 1977 by Leslie Aldridge Westoff. Reprinted by permission of Viking Penguin, Inc.
8. Ibid., p. 110. Reprinted by permission.
9. Lilian Messinger, *Remarriage: A Family Affair* (New York: Plenum Press, 1984), p. 174.
10. Ibid., p. 171.
11. Jamie Kelem Keshet, "From Separation to Stepfamily," *Journal of Family Issues* 1 (December 1980): 528.
12. Ibid., p. 529.
13. Ibid.
14. Lucile Duberman, *The Reconstruction of the Family: A Study of Remarried Couples and Their Children* (Chicago: Nelson-Hall, 1975), p. 77.
15. Ibid., p. 78.
16. Westoff, *The Second Time Around,* p. 57. Reprinted by permission.

17. Frank F. Furstenberg, Jr., and Graham B. Spanier, *Recycling the Family: Remarriage after Divorce* (Beverly Hills: Sage Publications, 1984), p. 149.
18. Ibid., p. 150.
19. Visher and Visher, *Stepfamilies,* pp. 207–222.
20. Ibid., p. 172.
21. Isolina Ricci, *Mom's House/Dad's House* (New York: Macmillan, 1980), pp. 105–107.
22. Barbara Fishman, "The Economic Behavior of Stepfamilies," *Family Relations* 32 (July 1983): 359.
23. Ibid., pp. 362–363.
24. Ibid., p. 364.
25. Ibid., p. 359.
26. Furstenberg and Spanier, *Recycling the Family,* pp. 77–78.
27. Ibid., p. 77.
28. Ibid., p. 79.
29. Ibid.
30. Ibid., p. 73.
31. Helen Weingarten, "Remarriage and Well-Being: National Survey Evidence of Social and Psychological Effects," *Journal of Family Issues* 1 (December 1980): 546.
32. D. S. Jacobson, "Stepfamilies: Myths and Realities," *Social Work* 24 (May 1979): 202–207.
33. Weingarten, "Remarriage and Well-Being," p. 555.
34. James McCarthy, "A Comparison of the Probability of the Dissolution of First and Second Marriages," *Demography* 15 (August 1978): 356.
35. Patricia Lutz, "The Stepfamily: An Adolescent Perspective," *Family Relations* 32 (July 1983): 367–375.

18

Low-income families

Interest and concern for the poor and homeless increased during the mid-eighties with famine in Africa and increasing homelessness in the United States. Poverty exists around the world, not just in developing or disaster-stricken areas such as Africa. A startling demographic characteristic of the U.S. homeless is that 20 percent are young, with two or three children.[1]

In a longitudinal study, persistently poor families were defined as those who were poor in eight or more of the ten years of the study. Only one-sixth of those classified as persistently poor lived in families headed by an able-bodied man of working age; almost half of these men had actually worked in at least five of the ten years of the study.[2]

Nearly half of all poor families in the United States are female-headed households, which constitutes an increasing trend and results in the feminization of poverty. Over thirty-five million people live in poverty when poverty levels are defined to exclude noncash benefits. The poverty rate in 1985 for the total population was 14.0 percent; for blacks, 31.3 percent; and for those of Spanish origin, 29.0 percent. Approximately half of the adults in poverty work in salaried jobs; of this group, 17 percent (one million people) work full-time year-round and still remain in poverty.[3]

A continuing question is whether a cycle of poverty exists, that is, are children who grow up in families who live in poverty likely to continue in poverty and to be on welfare? The Michigan Study of Income Dynamics found that children who live in female-headed households are less likely than those who live in two-parent households to graduate from high school.[4] The study findings suggest "that policies aimed at equalizing the incomes of different family forms and minimizing the stress that accompanies marital disruption may be quite successfully eliminating some of the intergenerational disadvantages attributed to family structure and single mothers."[5]

Whether or not welfare dependency causes black women to head their households has been explored. The question is complex, and we have seen a continued increase in female-headed households, especially among blacks. It appears that the availability of black men is a key contributor to female-headed households. Black men in the marriageable years disappear "via mortality, incarceration, and institutionalization."[6]

Low-income status can be short- or long-term in nature. Young couples and independent individuals may have low incomes while attending school, or a family may experience a low-income period when a member loses a job. Many low-income statistics do not distinguish temporary from long-term income status, but in this chapter, we focus on the implications for management of families who experience low incomes over time.

Input

DEMANDS

Values and goals. Persons in poverty hold values and goals that differ from those not in poverty. The differences are not so much in terms of the nature of the interests or needs but in how they are expressed qualitatively or the degree to which they are fulfilled. Poor parents want their children to be educated, but the goals for their education may be considerably lower than the goals of middle-class or high-income families. The low-income family's value of a nice place to live may translate into a place to exist, depending on the level of poverty.

A short report of a low-income mother of three young children illustrates the goals of a family in poverty. Joyce Reeves, thirty-four, "a stout, haggard divorcee," lives in a small trailer near Morehead, Kentucky.

> [The $457 monthly welfare check] is barely enough to pay for rent and the family's daily bread. Chicken is fancy meat; soup beans and potatoes, standard fare. Only the two youngest children ever get breakfast; an egg is a Saturday morning treat. Mrs. Reeves wears men's shoes she retrieved from a garbage dump. But, she has her dream: a secure job, a home, Christmas presents that the children want instead of presents that they need and, she says, "one night when I could lay down and not have to worry."[7]

Despite valuing education, persons in dire poverty are often forced to make decisions in conflict with education. María, a Peruvian street peddler of Lima who faces life's harsh realities, makes such a decision:

> She touches Teresita gently to wake her. María has decided that today the child will have to miss school; she needs Teresita to help with the accounting while she sells. Her daughter knows how to figure the cost of purchases and is quick at giving change from bills, whereas María is slow and clumsy, often making mistakes; she is illiterate. Chabelita is changed, wrapped in a shawl asleep. Teresita is awake and coughing badly. María coaxes her into swallowing half of a teaspoon of kerosine—the cheapest medicine available. There is no money for a doctor.[8]

Events. The conditions of families in poverty produce frequent events. Involuntary events that occur among the low-income population may be more difficult to cope with than is the case for the same events in high-income groups. One study revealed that education was the key factor in the frequency of these involuntary events, with those persons having a college education experiencing fewer of these events. The specific events were becoming widowed, becoming divorced, major unemployment, involuntary job changes, work loss due to illness, becoming disabled, involuntary residential moves, and major decreases in family income.[9] These involuntary events may have unexpected or low probability, but the response to them is related to education.

The need to respond to events often shatters hopes of attaining minimal goals. A report of a Boston-area woman reveals some of the stresses resulting from events:

> Her husband supported the family, which included eight children, through a home-based business for which the family truck was essential. The truck broke down at Christmas time, when the children were expecting new boots, and one daughter needed expensive dental treatment. The respondent, who was a diabetic, learned that she had also developed rheumatoid arthritis. The family was not supported by welfare and not eligible for Medicaid benefits, and their medical bills precluded fixing the truck. The family business came to an effective halt and financial crisis ensued.[10]

RESOURCES

Material. The poverty income guideline in 1986 was $11,000 for a family of four.[11] The poverty definition is based on the cost of an economy food plan, multiplied by three (based on the assumption of food costs as a third of expenditures by low-income families). This figure is then adjusted for family size and updated according to the Consumer Price Index (CPI). Many suggestions for improving the poverty definition have been made; for example, the inclusion of noncash income, using a different multiplier (the cost of food is nearer one-fifth, rather than one-third, of all consumption) and a more realistic food plan for calculating the base. The lack of inclusion of geographic variation is a problem, and the current CPI indexing of the level also contributes to an accounting of the poor that is continually in question. The Bureau of the Census has developed nine alternative measures of poverty that value noncash benefits. The number of people in poverty is greater when seven of the nine alternative measures are used because of reductions in noncash benefit programs.[12]

Low-income individuals and families may experience wide swings in income. Farm families and self-employed individuals and families often have highly volatile incomes. Management of resources becomes more complex with such instability.

Coping with income instability is a necessity for survival. Poor families, particularly black families,

> . . . have learned to survive external conditions which they view as highly unpredictable and arbitrary. These external forces are totally unresponsive to their daily needs and fluctuate so greatly as to require continual rearrangements in household composition. Irregular employment unpredictably alters an individual's ability to contribute to the household income. . . . In order to cope with all these disruptive external influences, the poor have developed extended networks of economically cooperating kin and friends. . . . These networks extend well beyond household boundaries and represent relatively stable social relationships which are maintained throughout periods of uncertainty and economic fluctuation, providing a reasonable degree of stability and economic security.[13]

Migrant families probably experience the most severe fluctuations in income. Harvest-time wages may be cut by bad weather, poor crops, or other conditions. One migrant worker said, "I just want a job all year 'round so money will keep coming in for living expenses."[14]

The degree to which instability and insecurity can be tolerated differs among individuals and families. Even so, a high tolerance does not imply that dealing with continuous income instability is comfortable. One family's financial situation has been described as follows:

> During the winter and spring of this year, financial crises tended to occur on a regular basis several times each month. When bills were due on the first of the month, the Schakelfords were usually completely broke. They would borrow from Al, Mack and Kate, Barry's (husband in the Schakelford family) mother and stepfather (whom they rarely saw), or me, to get them through until the fourth when Bobbi's (wife) emergency welfare was supposed to be issued. . . . [O]n the fourth the crisis usually subsided temporarily. . . .[15]

When the welfare check for the uncle (Walt) did not come on time, another crisis ensued. Hocking guns and equipment was considered, but the major items had already been hocked. Discussing the late arrival of his check, Walt said, "Well, I don't know where it is. They probably sent it to the wrong address, 'cause they do almost every time. But it was supposed to be here on Friday, and today's Wednesday and there ain't no check. I don't know what we're going to do. We ain't hardly got no money left."[16]

Welfare programs include Aid to Families with Dependent Children (AFDC); Supplementary Security Income (SSI), which is a consolidated program for the aged, blind, and disabled; state-administered General Assistance payments; and food stamps, although not cash welfare. "Most welfare recipients remain on the welfare rolls for relatively short periods of time, . . . most are not totally dependent on welfare income in a given year; and . . . even for those who are, this dependency is short-lived."[17] In a longitudinal study, only 25 percent of respondents were found to receive welfare in a ten-year period, with 4.4 percent receiving welfare in eight or more of the ten years, and only 2 percent receiving welfare that amounted to over half of their family income.[18] A return to self-sufficiency is the current pattern.

Government benefits (or welfare) are important for some low-income families and individuals for minimal support for living costs and medical care. In no state does any AFDC family receive cash or noncash transfers "that bring their total income up to poverty level. These families are poor regardless of alimony, child support, welfare benefits, or their own earnings, and they remain poor after receiving welfare benefits because of the level at which these are provided."[19]

To receive noncash benefits, the household income or assets (resources) must fall below a specified level; that is, they are means tested.[20] Over 60 percent "of the households below the poverty level received some form of means-tested non-cash benefits in 1984."[21]

> The Federal government pays slightly more than half the total cost of AFDC; the states pay the remainder. Within broad federal guidelines, the state sets eligibility standards and benefit levels. Both vary widely from state to state. For example, two-parent families in which the father is unemployed or incapacitated are eligible for AFDC in only about half the states. In 1983 a single mother with two children received $96 per month in Mississippi and $530 per month in Vermont.[22]

Those families living below the poverty line who did not receive means-tested, noncash benefits failed to receive them "either because of reluctance to apply, lack of knowledge about available programs or the application process, or failure to qualify because of ownership of assets such as a house."[23] Major noncash benefits are Medicaid and food stamps (Figure 18.1).

Medicaid furnishes medical assistance for low-income, aged, blind, or handicapped individuals and households with dependent children.

Federal policy in the 1980s has raised the AFDC qualification thresholds. In a Michigan study of 279 families for which the AFDC benefits had been terminated, the most serious problems they faced were:

> . . . lack of money (28%); lack of food (10%); having something bad happen to their children (14%); having someone close die (9%); and own illness (7%). Women with lower income experienced somewhat more crises, particularly those involving crime and lack of money, but the relationship was not strong—probably because the income range was limited relative to overall need and because nearly all experienced several serious crises during the year.[24]

For the aged and disabled, Social Security and Medicare programs are important government benefit programs. Individuals contribute to both Social Security and Medicare, and neither program is means-tested, that is, the benefits are not based on income or assets. Social Security, received by over fourteen percent of the population, provides direct cash payments to families or individuals. The Social Security payments are often very important to the low-income aged. Medicare payments for hospital and physician services are made to the purveyors of the aged and disabled. Medicare covers only about one-half of the medical costs, and it does not cover long-term care nor, in some cases, acute-care needs. "By and large, the households facing the greatest insecurity are those (numbering nearly half of all aged house-

FIGURE 18.1 *Percent of the total U.S. population receiving federal means-tested benefits*

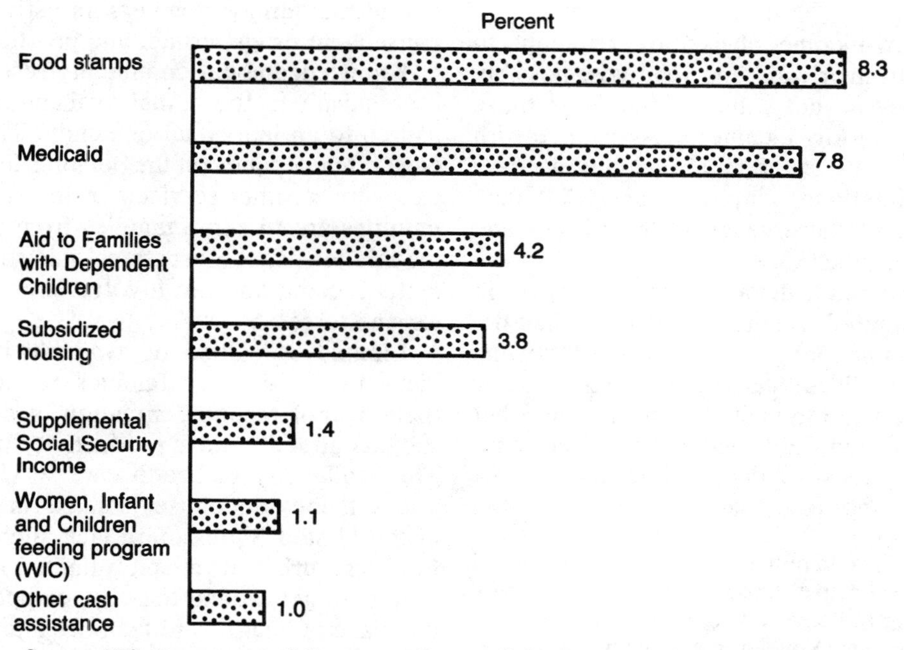

Source: U.S. Department of Commerce, Bureau of the Census, "Population Profile of the United States 1983/84," Current Population Reports, Series P-23, No. 145 (Washington, D.C.: Government Printing Office, 1985), p. 32.

holds) that have incomes between the poverty level and the average."[25]

In general, low-income individuals and families have very few assets. Having limited amounts of capital increases the vulnerability to event situations. Younger low-income families tend not to own their houses, while low-income elderly families are likely to own theirs.

Low-income consumers are generally regarded as poor credit risks. Efforts are being made to develop techniques for appraising credit worthiness suited to the needs of low-income consumers.

Low-income families who have the potential for meeting payments may be denied access to such credit as bank cards, while more generous policies are applied to more-affluent families. The poor may be paying high costs for credit or may be limited in the alternatives credit can provide. Education or counseling can help low-income families avoid overextension or delinquency in making payments.[26]

Whether obtaining credit at the discount store or the used-car lot or by less formal borrowing from family members, some low-income consumers are regularly in debt.

> You know, I'll always be in debt. I know that. I'll never be out of debt. So I might as well get a little further in debt. That's the only way a person can afford to buy anything, if you don't have but so much money, and getting a little further in debt won't hurt you none. That is, if you can meet the payments.[27]

Human. Help from relatives or organizations and arrangements with neighbors and informal groups can bridge gaps that occur when earnings or other assistance are insufficient or unstable.

Some low-income blacks are reluctant to seek help from friends and relatives, possibly because they do not want to impose on those who also have low incomes.[28] Assistance with child care is one of the most common needs.[29] In other situations, families share what they have based on the urgency of their needs and the needs of others.

The poor can demonstrate creativity in stretching limited resources in meeting their demands in caring for their families. The following report exemplifies sharing resources. Ruby Banks took a cab to visit Virginia Thomas, her baby's aunt, and they swapped some hot corn bread and greens for diapers and milk. In the cab going home, Ruby said:

> I don't believe in putting myself on nobody, but I know I need help everyday. You can't get help by just sitting at home, laying around, house-nasty and everything. You got to get up and go out and meet people, because the very day you go out, that first person you meet may be the person that can help you get the things you want. I don't believe in begging, but I believe that people should help one another. I used to wish for lots of things, like a living room suite, clothes, nice clothes, stylish clothes—I'm sick of wearing the same pieces. But I can't, I can't help myself because I have my children and I love them and I have my mother and all our kin. Sometimes I don't have a damn dime in my pocket, not a crying penny to get a box of paper diapers, milk, a loaf of bread. But you have to have help from everybody, so don't turn no one down when they come round for help.[30]

Social networks consisting of family members or friends are known as natural helping networks as opposed to formal helping networks. Natural helping networks often have stress associated with them because of the emotional ties that are involved. Sometimes paid services or formal helping networks can moderate or relieve some stresses in the lives of low-income women.[31] Negative networks are those that attract family members into street life and consequent drugs, crime, and prostitution.[32]

Knowledge about community resources is a prerequisite to the actual availability of a resource to an individual or family. This knowledge often depends on the person's literacy and exposure to other services or officials. If communities are to serve families from a range of income levels, the programs must be conveniently located and not involve large additional expenditures.

Limited utilization of available health services by low-income families can compound their overall resource situation in other ways such as affecting their productivity on the job. The availability of health care services determines their extent of use; isolated rural counties in the United States often lack such services. For some urban dwellers, a limited knowledge of how to get around the city, compounded by the maze of health-care facilities and accompanying complicated procedures, makes health care services also "unavailable." Most health care comes from private physicians, but the poor use emergency rooms and hospital clinics more often than do other groups.

Health Maintenance Organizations (HMOs) can provide an effective medical service delivery, but there are problems with integrating the poor and uninsured population into the HMOs. Some have urged HMOs to have 10 percent of their total enrollment composed of the poor[33]:

> An employed population is usually a more healthy population than the unemployed or never-employed poor. . . . The HMO is an attractive and economically viable program for many informed subscribers, but it is not a panacea for the poor's health care problems. An HMO without an adequate mix of self-sufficient, health-responsible subscribers might be weakened by having too many people without the health skills required for HMO membership.[34]

Throughput

PLANNING

Families without experience or ability to process alternative solutions are especially vulnerable to the uncertainties of irregular and fluctuating income or to an inadequate income to meet their goal and event demands. Young families with too many pressures may be unable to find adequate solutions soon enough to avoid lost time in establishing basic financial security, formidable debts, or dissolution of the family.

Many low-income people have a sense of readiness to meet demands rather than a specific plan to meet demands. Some people or families are morphogenic in nature with a desire, but not necessarily the skill, to take advantage of opportunities that rarely seem to come.

Some low-income people and families exist in a rather closed system, convinced that "what will be, will be." This sense of fatalism can permeate the system and affect planning considerably. A fatalistic view can mean greater frequency of events because fewer such occurrences are anticipated.

The O family has a fatalistic view. Mr. O had a back injury and now receives welfare—a regular, if limited, income. They are resigned to the managerial role of responding to circumstances. They are happy with their seven children, ages one to eleven, having planned originally to have only two or three. They have their ups and downs, but things are usually the same. . . . Neither Mr. nor Mrs. O believes that they have much control over what happens to them. "This control is in God's hands and all we can do is to make the best of it. It does not do much good to have ambitions which are not part of His plan."[35] Mrs. O is thus content with her attention to whatever she is doing at the moment.

Researchers in Iowa studied the internal–external orientation of lower-income families—a measure that reflects the degree of fatalism. They found that greater internal control (less fatalistic in outlook) was associated with higher incomes and greater agreement between spouses on family matters.[36] The study examined realistic standards, defined in terms of the frequency with which expectations are met. Husband–wife agreement on family matters was associated with increase in the likelihood that realistic standards were set during planning and that family demands and goals were met.[37] A model from the study appears in Figure 18.2.

Internal–external orientation indirectly rather than directly influenced planning through the extent of husband–wife agreement.[38] Higher levels of education were associated with more realistic standard setting for husbands, but the relationship was not significant for the wives.[39]

Planning is affected by the resource flow and constraints attached to the resources coming into the family system. The impact of government benefits on families and individuals brings about continued discussion on the most appropriate form of the benefits-in-kind versus cash benefits and the basis for the benefits, whether flexible or standardized.

In-kind versus cash benefits. To what extent should benefits be directed toward meeting identifiable special needs with appropriate support goods and services? Or does cash assistance make it more possible for recipients to exercise the needed flexibility in their particular circumstances? Some who advocate in-kind transfers feel that because low-income families have many different needs, people should keep attuned to the variety of benefits required and respond accordingly. Proponents of cash transfers counter that cash is not only more helpful to low-income families but is also less expensive to the taxpayer.[40] A related proposal is a guaranteed income program that could be administered through a negative tax process.

Receiving assistance in-kind—that is, for a

FIGURE 18.2 *A path model for wives and husbands for factors affecting planning*

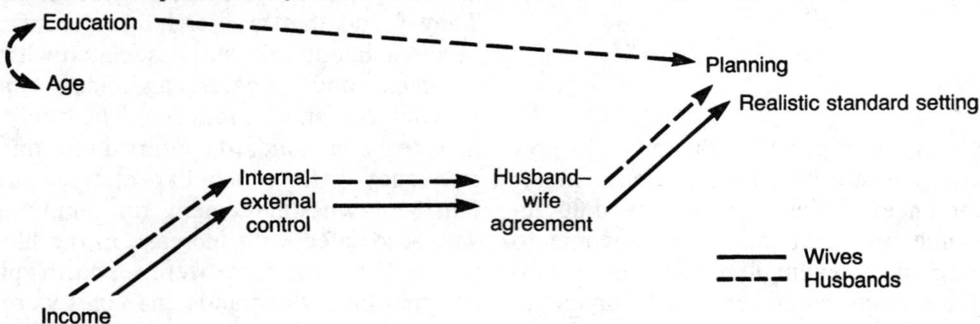

Source: Adapted from Jodie Johnson Brown, Mary E. Heltsey, Richard D. Warren, "Planning in Low Income Families: Influence of Locus of Control and Dyadic Consensus on Realistic Standard Setting," *Home Economics Research Journal* 11 (September 1982): 74.

specific commodity, such as food, housing, or medical care—limits choice making to that commodity and does not allow for choice across varied needs. Cash assistance would allow more choice, and better choices are likely to be made. Cash assistance permits meeting of individual needs in the most flexible manner, and it promotes individual responsibility in determining what is effective use of available resources.[41]

Flexible versus standardized guidelines. Flexibility in assistance programs is urged by some, so that caseworkers can exercise discretion. On the other hand, standardization is seen by advocates as avoiding the inequities of well-intended welfare caseworkers whose discretion inevitably results in arbitrary treatment of recipients.[42] Managerially, the assistance that most nearly fits the family needs is most desirable. Whether or not this is more possible with discretion or standardization is debatable, since outside interpretation is assumed in one case and defined in the other. Guidelines that provide ranges within which discretion could be exercised would seem to be a desirable middle ground.[43]

IMPLEMENTING

Implementing plans can be challenging under conditions of severely limited time or money resources. For example, effective choices in food shopping call for: (1) considering the economy of buying in larger-size containers, recognizing that resources are tied up longer, that the possibility of loss or damage during storage exists, and that there's a tendency on the part of some to use up the contents at a faster rate than for smaller containers, (2) avoiding impulse buying, and (3) careful planning through reading store specials. It may be difficult for low-income consumers to be effective in using these methods. Low-income consumers are often forced to shop at stores with higher prices and fewer choices due to lack of transportation. Transportation costs may be considerably offset by a decision to shop at a store with good prices and selections.

Hispanic consumers may be disadvantaged in the market place for several reasons: "(a) their socio-economic characteristics; (b) their appearance, language and migration patterns; (c) their values, goals and attitudes; and (d) their residence in poverty areas."[44] Definitive research is lacking about the Hispanic group that appears to face barriers to effective consumption.

Time constraints for the working poor are exemplified by María, the Lima street peddler:

> When my boy gets sick, I first try to cure him with a laxative; this way I clean his stomach. But, if he develops a fever I take him to a private doctor rather than to the emergency services in the hospital which is always crowded with patients. One usually wastes the whole day waiting for one of the doctors instead of selling at the marketplace.[45]

Low-income individuals and families are often represented as being oriented to the present in terms of their time perspective: How can they project into the future while trying to get together enough to live on today? One way to examine a family's present or future time orientation is to study the way it handles unexpected income. In an Oregon study in which the observer-participant saw two cases of windfall close at hand, she found a reality orientation, rather than a present or future one.[46]

The first case of windfall was from transfer income. Carol and Leonard received retroactive unemployment compensation. They claimed their repossessed car with the unexpected funds, applied part of the money to unpaid bills, bought a used car, and spent the remainder to repair a clothes dryer that had quit. Carol and Leonard have five children, including a handicapped child. The observer-participant noted that the expenditures seemed rational and, rather than lacking foresight or having a present orientation, represented decisions "conditioned by real material circumstances."[47]

The second case reported by the observer-participant relates to Ed and Sadie, who unexpectedly sold a small piece of property they owned and once lived on. With nine children at home, including a daughter with her two children, the windfall was a cause for celebration.

The first week, they bought food in bulk quantities. The next week, a dilapidated, old pickup truck appeared in the yard, followed by an old, pink Rambler station wagon and a white Ford sedan (the latter two inoperative). Within three months, Ed had repaired the cars and sold them for double his purchase price.

To an unknowing person, the food- and car-buying sprees might appear to be examples of a poor person's orientation to the present; but information about the food in relation to the family's needs and about the investment of money to make productive use of his skills suggests that they looked ahead and took advantage of opportunities.[48]

Output

DEMAND RESPONSES

The sense of well-being of low-income people is fairly low, but the sense of well-being increases as income increases, when people have less than a college education. The relatively high levels of satisfaction for lower-income college-educated people can be attributed to their service occupations, such as the ministry, where other satisfactions create a sense of well-being.[49] At higher levels of income, it would seem that expectations in relation to income are either difficult to satisfy or are out of phase for many.

In a study of sixty-three low-income single parents in a rural area in Washington, their happiness "was most affected by the psychological intimacy available to the single parent."[50]

Unemployed men and their spouses were compared to employed men and their spouses in a study in a Midwestern city:

> Unemployment of the husband was found to have no effect on worker self-esteem, but a negative effect on marriage and family relations. . . . Among the unemployed, traditional compared to

egalitarian marital role expectations were found to be related to lower marital adjustment and communication and less harmony in family relations.[51]

RESOURCE CHANGES

Because of the dynamic nature of individuals and families, generalizations about management in various family situations are difficult. Many who are low-income today were not low-income yesterday. "Only a little over one-half of the individuals living in poverty in one year are found to be poor in the next, and considerably less than one-half of those who experience poverty remain persistently poor over many years."[52]

Balancing resources with demands means considering the total situation as rationally as possible. When money is very limited, the least-cost choice in consumer purchases is often the only option open. Further, the strategy for decisions for low-income families or individuals is the need to minimize uncertainties or risks. Yet, persistently poor are described as buying "something which brings temporary color and show into a drab life, but the object purchased quickly falls apart or into disuse."[53]

One writer suggests that shopping for some low-income consumers may be a social event that helps their well-being and self-definition, especially in comparison to middle-class white consumers.[54]

Data on time use by low-income families are insufficient to make generalizations. The limited information that is available indicates that socioeconomic level has little influence on the use of time for major household work.[55] Case study data suggest wide variation in the use and organization of time among low-income individuals and families.

Environment

The immediate neighborhood can provide a familiar setting for families and individuals with shared values, a place of personal safety, and a sense of community. For low-income urban mothers, such characteristics were rated on average between "not so good" and "good."[56] Poor neighborhoods are often areas with a high crime rate. In some cities, residents are collectively protecting their environment and managing public housing complexes.

> Compared to more affluent city dwellers, poor men and women exercise little choice about where and among whom to live. Buying power and renting are limited by poverty, of course. Those who must depend on public housing or on publicly subsidized housing are further limited in their choice of a residential location. Discrimination against racial and ethnic minorities, single-parent families and families with many children often sets up additional barriers, so that the decision about where to locate is hardly a choice at all.[57]

Satisfaction with specific aspects of housing varies by income level (Figure 18.3). The rating of safety at night, convenience, heating, being well built, and being a good place to live all fell below the mean satisfaction rating for those with relatively low incomes.

The following description of the housing satisfaction of one person illustrates the relative nature of the satisfaction with specific aspects of housing:

> What I dislike is when people mess up the hallways, when they don't cooperate, and when the elevator is broken. I have to carry the baby upstairs. What I do like is that I have the type of kitchen and bath that I can keep clean. It's easier to keep these apartments clean except the dust that comes in from having so many windows. They also just put these new locks on which are sturdier than the old ones, and you can't lock yourself out as easy as you could with the others. You know when I lived over on Waterman Street, the apartments used to get so cold in the winter time that you had to put the baby's blankets into the oven to warm them up so he wouldn't be too cold. You could talk to the landlady all of the time

FIGURE 18.3 *Satisfication ratings of housing qualities by income*

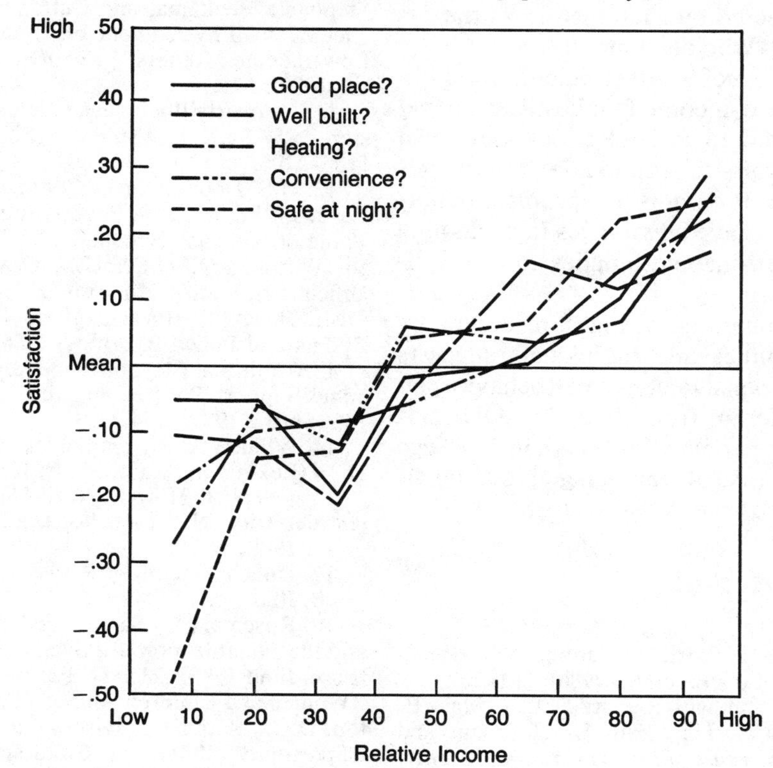

Source: Adapted from Angus Campbell, Philip E. Converse, and Willard L. Rodgers, *The Quality of American Life,* p. 126. © 1976 by Russell Sage Foundation, New York. Reprinted by permission of Basic Books, Inc.

and complain about there not being enough heat, but she never turned it up. That is one thing you don't have to worry about here in the project, because in winter time it's always warm in these apartments.[58]

Summary

The goals of low-income families are similar to those of other income groups, but they differ in extent and are altered by the reality of situations. The conditions of poverty combine to introduce event situations for many families that reduce the possibility of achieving their goals.

Low-income families and individuals who are chronically limited in resources have income problems in both amount and stability. Besides economic conditions and unemployment, the level and stability of incomes relate to health, education, occupation, and age. Transfer payments through public and social programs such as AFDC and Social Security provide major support. Some low-income families also have a network of assistance among relatives and neighbors, which includes exchange of goods and services. Other supports that are available to more-affluent families to meet stress conditions are often not as readily available to low-income families—credit and health services, for example.

Planning and implementing the use of resources are affected by such factors as the extent of husband–wife agreement.

Government benefits affect planning and implementing by low-income families. Cash benefits, as compared to in-kind allocations, also provide opportunity to respond flexibly to their special situation. Programs that promote opportunity for choice have advantages in promoting the ability of low-income families toward self-reliance.

Evidence concerning changed resources by low-income families and individuals suggests rational and responsive consumer behavior, although it is different from that of middle-class consumers. For people with less than a college education, the sense of well-being of individuals increases as income increases.

Notes

1. Constance Holden, "Counting the Homeless," *Science* 234 (October 17, 1986): 281–282.
2. Greg J. Duncan with Richard D. Coe, Mary E. Cocoran, Martha S. Hill, Saul D. Hoffman, and James N. Morgan, *Years of Poverty, Years of Plenty: The Changing Economic Fortunes of American Workers and Families* (Ann Arbor: Institute for Social Research, Survey Research Center, University of Michigan, 1984), p. 53.
3. U.S. Department of Commerce, "Money Income and Poverty Status of Families and Persons in the United States, 1985," Current Population Reports, Series P-60, No. 154 (Washington, D.C.: U.S. Government Printing Office, 1986), pp. 34–35.
4. Sara McLanahan, "Family Structure and the Reproduction of Poverty," *American Journal of Sociology* 90 (January 1985): 898.
5. Ibid.
6. William A. Darity, Jr., and Samuel L. Myers, Jr., "Does Welfare Dependency Cause Female Headship? The Case of the Black Family," *Journal of Marriage and the Family* 46 (November 1984): 776.
7. "Life below the Poverty Line," *Newsweek* 99 (April 5, 1982): 20.
8. Ximena Bunster and Elsa M. Chaney, *Sellers and Servants* (Westport, Conn.: Praeger Publishers, 1985), p. 82.
9. Duncan, *Years of Poverty,* pp. 26–27.
10. Diana Dill, Ellen Field, Jacqueline Martin, Stephanie Beukema, and Deborah Belle, "The Impact of the Environment on the Coping Efforts of Low-Income Mothers," *Family Relations* 29 (October 1980): 505.
11. "Poverty Income Guidelines: Annual Revision," *Federal Register* 51 (February 11, 1986): 5105–5106.
12. U.S. Department of Commerce, Bureau of the Census, "Estimates of Poverty Income Including the Value of Noncash Benefits: 1985," Technical Paper 56 (Washington, D.C.: U.S. Government Printing Office, 1986); and "Analysis of Poverty Using Non-Cash Benefits" (Washington, D.C.: Center on Budget and Policy Priorities, 1986).
13. Colin C. Blaydon and Carol B. Stack, "Income Support Policies and the Family," *Daedalus* 106 (Spring 1977): 154.
14. William A. Rushing, *Class Culture and Alienation* (Lexington, Mass.: D. C. Heath, 1971), p. 113.
15. Joseph T. Howell, *Hard Living on Clay Street* (Garden City, N.Y.: Anchor Books, 1973), p. 78.
16. Ibid., p. 79.
17. Duncan, *Years of Poverty,* p. 91.
18. Ibid., p. 77.
19. Rosemary C. Sarri, "Federal Policy Changes and the Feminization of Poverty," *Child Welfare* 64 (May–June 1985): 235; D. Pearce and H. McAdoo, "Women and Children Alone in Poverty" (Washington, D.C.: National Advisory Council on Economic Opportunity, 1981); and Children's Defense Fund, "A Children's Defense Budget: An Analysis of the 1984 Budget" (Washington, D.C.: Children's Defense Fund, 1984).
20. U.S. Department of Commerce, Bureau of the Census, "Characteristics of Households and Persons Receiving Selected Noncash Benefits: 1984," *Current Population Reports,* Series P-23, No. 145 (Washington, D.C.: U.S. Government Printing Office, 1985), p. 1.
21. Ibid.
22. "Women, Children, and Poverty in America," Working Paper, (New York: Ford Foundation, 1985), p. 9.
23. U.S. Department of Commerce, Bureau of the Census, "Characteristics of Households and Persons Receiving Selected Noncash Benefits: 1984," p. 34.
24. Sarri, "Federal Policy Changes" p. 244.
25. John L. Palmer and Stephanie G. Gould, "The Economic Consequences of an Aging Society." *Daedalus* 115 (Winter 1986): 316.
26. Joan S. Tabor and Jean S. Bowers, "Factors Determining Credit Worthiness of Low Income Consumers," *Journal of Consumer Affairs* 11 (Winter 1977): 51.

27. Howell, *Hard Living on Clay Street* p. 183.
28. Richard E. Ball, "Family and Friends: A Supportive Network for Low-Income American Families," *Journal of Comparative Family Studies* 14 (Spring 1983): 62.
29. Michelene Malson, "The Social Support System of Black Families," *Marriage and Family Review* 5 (Winter 1982): 44–45.
30. Carol B. Stack, *All Our Kin Strategies for Survival in a Black Community* (New York: Harper and Row, 1974), p. 32.
31. Deborah E. Belle, "Impact of Poverty on Social Networks and Supports," *Marriage and Family Review* 5 (Winter 1982): 101.
32. Ibid., p. 96.
33. Mary Jane Fisher, "HMOs Urged to Provide Health Care for Poor, Uninsured, Unemployed," *National Underwriter* 90 (January 18, 1986): 2.
34. Ralph Segalman and Asoke Basu, *Poverty in America* (Westport, Conn.: Greenwood Press, 1981), pp. 259–260.
35. Janet M. Fitchen, "The People of Road Junction: The Participant Observer's Study of a Rural Poverty Area in Northern Appalachia, with Particular Reference to the Problems of Employment of Low Income Women," in *A Study of the Effects on the Family Due to Employment of the Welfare Mother,* Vol. III, Report to Manpower Administration, U.S. Department of Labor [n.d.], p. 348.
36. Jodie Johnson Brown, Mary E. Heltsey, and Richard D. Warren, "Planning in Low Income Families: Influence of Locus of Control and Dyadic Consensus on Realistic Standard Setting," *Home Economics Research Journal* 11 (September 1982): 74.
37. Ibid., p. 73.
38. Ibid., p. 70.
39. Ibid.
40. Laurence J. Lynn, Jr., and Mark D. Worthington, "Incremental Welfare Reform: A Strategy Whose Time Has Passed," *Public Policy* 25 (Winter 1977): 71.
41. Ibid.
42. Ibid., pp. 72–73.
43. Ivan F. Beutler, "Comprehensive Development of a Standard of Need for Iowa Aid-to-Dependent-Children Recipients," Home Economics Research Institute Bulletin 101 (Ames: Iowa State University, 1978), pp. 64–66.
44. Alan R. Andreasen, "Disadvantaged Hispanic Consumers: Research Perspective and Agenda," *The Journal of Consumer Affairs* 16 (Summer 1982): 56, 58.
45. Ximena Bunster and Elsa M. Chaney, *Sellers and Servants* (Westport, Conn.: Praeger Publishers, 1985), p. 96.
46. Jan M. Newton, "Economic Rationality of the Poor," *Human Organization* 36 (Spring 1977): 55.
47. Ibid., pp. 52–55.
48. Ibid., pp. 53–55.
49. Angus Campbell, Philip E. Converse, and Willard L. Rodgers, *The Quality of American Life* (New York: Russell Sage Foundation, 1976), p. 57.
50. Nancy Wells Gladow and Margaret P. Ray, "The Impact of Information Support Systems on the Well-Being of Low-Income Single Parents," *Family Relations* 35 (January 1986): 122.
51. Jeffry H. Larson, "The Effect of Husband's Unemployment on Marital and Family Relations in Blue-Collar Families," *Family Relations* 33 (October 1984): 510.
52. Duncan, *Years of Poverty,* p. 3.
53. Segalman and Basu, *Poverty in America,* p. 29.
54. Alan R. Andreasen. "The Differing Nature of Consumerism in the Ghetto," *The Journal of Consumer Affairs* 10 (Winter 1976): 187.
55. Kathryn E. Walker and Margaret E. Woods, *Time Use: A Measure of Household Production of Family Goods and Services* (Washington, D.C.: American Home Economics Association, Center for the Family, 1976), p. 253.
56. Belle, "Impact of Poverty" p. 101.
57. Ibid., p. 94.
58. Lee Rainwater, *Behind Ghetto Walls* (Chicago: Aldine, 1970), p. 18.

Glossary of terms

Absolute values are meanings independent of surrounding conditions.

Action sequencing is the ordering of parts of an activity or specifying succession among activities.

Actuating is putting plans into effect.

Adaptability is the ability of a marital or family structure to change its power structure, role relationships, and relationship rules.[1]

Adjusting is changing a planned standard, sequence, or underlying process to increase the chances of the desired output.

Affective domain is the positive or negative feeling derived from experience leading to the internalized adoption of a value system.

Boundaries separate a system's area of influence from that of other systems.

Budget is a plan for the allocation of available resources among various needs and wants.

Certainty is complete knowledge of consequences of a decision.

Checking is the examination of actions and outcomes in relation to planned standards and sequences.

Clarity in plans is the specification of standards and sequences.

Closed systems make no significant exchanges with their environments.

Cognitive domain is the perception of values, goals, and related criteria and the potential of the situation for their fulfillment.

Cohesion is the emotional bonding that family members have toward one another.[2]

Communication is the process of using messages to engender meaning in the minds of others.[3]

Complexity in plans is the degree of interrelationships between people and tasks.

Conceptual foresight is the ability to relate anticipated future situations to the present.

Consuming is the reduction of available resources through "using up" their utility value.

Contingency planning specifies alternative standards and sequences of action for indefinite conditions.

Controlling is the checking of actions and outcomes for conformity to plans and, if necessary, adjusting standards or sequences.

Cybernetic strategy proceeds through trial and error, using feedback as the mechanism for correction.

Decision making is the process of evaluation in choosing or resolving alternatives. When decision making involves more than one person:

- **Consensual decision making** concludes with equal assent and commitment to a decision.
- **Accommodation decision making** concludes with the acceptance of the desire of a dominant person without reconciliation of all views.
- **De facto decision making** results from a lack of dissent; any course of action committed to is undeliberated and happenstance.

Decision strategies are a set of procedures for relating anticipated benefits to objectives.

Demand clarification is the refinement of objectives consistent with values; both goals and events may be clarified.

Demand responses are the output from managerial actions relating to values and satisfactions.

Demands are goals and/or events requiring action.

Directional planning identifies areas of activities and preferences for action.

Dissaving is credit use against anticipated future income.

Dovetailed tasks are those activities receiving intermittent attention until they are completed.

Ecological systems represent the totality of organisms and environments that interact interdependently.

Ecosystem identifies a functional unit for the study of its interrelationships to the total environment.

Entropy is the tendency of all forms of organization to move to disorganization or death.

Environment is the external setting within which a system functions.

Equifinality is similar results coming from different initial circumstances or conditions.[4]

Events are unexpected or low-probability occurrences (contingencies) that require action.

Exchanging involves interchanges of equal values and therefore affects the makeup, but not necessarily the value, of the household resource inventory.

External systems are the functioning units outside the system of focus that interact with it directly or indirectly.

Extrinsic value is the meaning or worth derived from the relation of one thing to another.

Facilitating conditions are situation characteristics that assist the progress or flow of actions, but are not directly accounted for as resources.

Family life cycle describes the movement of family members through stages from formation to dissolution.

Family system is composed of personal and managerial subsystems that interact through communication processes to develop intrasystem dynamics of cohesion, adaptability, and functionality.

Feedback is information about output that reenters the system as input to affect succeeding output.[5]

Flexibility in plans is the range of acceptable standards and sequences of action.

Foresight is awareness of the relation of possible future events and present situations.

Functionality is the ability of family members to use their human and material resources to anticipate and meet demands.

General values prevail over time and are met through a variety of actions.

Goals are value-based objectives or anticipated outcomes.

Heuristics are procedures that provide relatively simple guidelines for decision making, such as representativeness, availability, or anchoring and adjusting.

Human capital of an individual or family at a point in time is the total stock of human capacities for affecting future resources and their use.

Human resources are all the means vested in people that can be used for meeting goals and events: cognitive insights, psychomotor skills, affective attributes, health, energy, and time.

Implementing is actuating standards and sequences and controlling the action.

Implementing in morphostatic systems is change resistant and deviation correcting.

Implementing in morphogenic systems is open to adapting plans and to accepting altered outcomes; it is deviation amplifying or change producing.

Implementing in random systems is unstructured.

Incremental strategy progresses toward a final solution through a series of additive stages.

Input is matter, energy, and information entering a system in various forms to affect the throughput (transformation) processes in the achievement of outcomes or outputs.

Interdependent activities are tasks in which completion of one is dependent on the completion of another.

Interface is the common or shared boundary of systems.

Interference "distorts the information transmitted to the receiver or distracts him or her from receiving it."[6]

Intrinsic value is the inherent and self-sufficient meaning or quality of an experience.

Intuition yields an immediate decision, bypassing well-defined, conscious steps.

Intuitive decision making conceptualizes or comprehends all steps of the process without explicit interpretation of the parts.

Investment is an asset varying both in value and earnings with economic conditions.

Level of living is the quantity and quality of goods and services currently consumed or available.

Leveling describes congruence in all parts of a message.

Linkage is a fixed interaction pattern forming bonds among the systems.

Macroenvironment is composed of the surroundings of societal, natural, and structured systems beyond the microenvironment.

Management is planning and implementing the use of resources to meet demands.

Material assets are the stock of goods that have value: available durable and nondurable goods, savings, and investments.

Material resources are nonhuman means for meeting goals and events: natural and processed consumption goods, housing, household capital, physical energy, money, and investments.

Messages are stimuli flowing from a sender to a receiver.

Microenvironment of a family is composed of its immediate social aspects and physical habitats.

Morphogenic systems are adaptive and growth supporting in response to change.

Morphostatic systems are stable and deviation correcting in response to change.

Multifinality is different results following from similar initial conditions.

Natural and structured systems are the physical and biological settings within which related societal systems function.

Negative entropy is the tendency, particularly of open systems, to maximize the ratio of resources that enter the system to those expended.

Negative feedback is output formation returning as input to promote corrective measures to maintain the system in a desired state.

Net worth is the market value of the stock of available resources minus obligations.

Nonmanaged actions use resources to meet demands, bypassing planning and implementing plans.

Objective probability is the ratio of the number of actual occurrences to the total number of possible occurrences in a particular situation.[7]

Objective value components are the attributes or properties of resources capable of meeting the evaluative criteria.

Open systems interrelate continually with their environments.

Optimizing strategy is the use of objective and/or subjective probabilities to determine the most satisfying solutions.

Output is matter, energy, or information produced by a system in response to input and throughput (transformation) processes.

Overlapped tasks are two or more activities receiving intermittent and/or concurrent attention until they are completed.

Particularistic resource exchanges depend for their value on the significance of given relationships.

Perceptual foresight is the ability to project to the future from the present.

Personal system is composed of two major subsystems: developmental and values.

Developmental subsystem fosters growth of four interrelated capacities: cognitive, emotional, social, and physical.

Values subsystem translates experiences and understandings into intrinsic and extrinsic meanings.

Planning is a series of decisions concerning future standards and/or sequences of action.

Planning in morphogenic systems is flexible, generally for nonroutine, nonprogrammed activities, and results in adaptive, expansive behavior.

Planning in morphostatic systems is relatively rigid, generally for routine, short-term activities, and results in maintaining the current status.

Planning in random systems is spontaneous, fluid in nature, and results in unstructured behaviors.

Positive feedback accepts deviations from expected outcomes and promotes rather than inhibits change.[8]

Probability is the relative possibility that a particular situation will occur.

Producing is creating additional resources or utilities from available resources.

Protecting is minimizing potential economic losses at the cost of risk sharing.

Quality is the property or image of what is desired.

Quantity is a definitive or estimated amount of what is desired.

Random strategy is taking a course of action that lacks insight into outcomes but that has intrinsic, spontaneous, or emergency interest in a response.

Reality in plans is the feasibility of achieving the chosen standards and sequences.

Relative values are meanings that depend on their context for interpretation.

Repeat-use plans employ previously developed standards and/or sequences.

Resource assessment is analyzing means to meet particular demands.

Resource changes are the output from managerial actions affecting the flow and composition of human and/or material means.

Resource flow follows from system actions in response to demands.

Resource stock is the sum of available means for meeting demands at a point in time.

Resources are means capable of meeting demands.

Risk is the hazard or chance of loss.

Satisficing strategy seeks alternatives only until an acceptable aspiration level can be met.[9]

Sequence of action is the order of parts of an activity or specific succession among activities.

Single-use plans are those plans used only once or as part of the development of a repeat-use plan.

Societal systems are sociocultural, political, economic, and technological mechanisms and processes through which society's roles in relation to its members are met.

Specific values are satisfied in a single action or by achieving given goals.

Standard of living is the quantity and quality of goods and services that an individual or group desires.

Standard setting is the reconciliation of resources with demands.

Standards are operational criteria that reflect qualities and/or quantities that reconcile resources with demands.

Subjective probability is a measure of the decision maker's belief in the outcome.

Subjective value components provide the criteria to be met to achieve goals.

Subsystem is a set of components functioning together for a purpose fulfilling the same conditions as a system and playing a functional role in a larger system.

System is an integrated set of parts and functions to accomplish goals.

Throughput is the transformation of matter, energy, or information by a system from input to output.

Transferring is the reduction of available resources through voluntary or mandatory transfers to users outside the household.

Uncertainty is the lack of knowledge of consequences of a decision.

Universalistic resource exchanges depend for their value on the generality of interrelationships.

Utility is the satisfaction of the intrinsic or extrinsic values derived from the usefulness of resources.

Marginal utility is the added satisfaction from the last unit used.

Value content is the subjective-objective meaning that accompanies value judgments.

Values are meanings relating to what is desirable or has worth.

Notes

1. David H. Olson, Hamilton I. McCubbin, Howard Barnes, Andrea Larsen, Marla Muxen and Marc Wilson, *Families: What Makes Them Work* (Beverly Hills: Sage Publications, 1983), p. 47.
2. Ibid.
3. James C. McCroskey, Carol E. Larson, and Mark L. Knapp, *An Introduction to Interpersonal Communication* (Englewood Cliffs, N.J.: Prentice-Hall, 1971), pp. 3–4.
4. Walter Buckley, *Sociology and Modern Systems Theory* (Englewood Cliffs, N.J.: Prentice-Hall, 1967), p. 79.
5. A. D. Hall and R. E. Fagen, "Definition of Systems," *General Systems* 1 (1956): 23.
6. Stewart L. Tubbs and Sylvia Moss, *Human Communication* (New York: Random House, 1983), p. 36.
7. Jess Stein, ed., *The Random House Dictionary of the English Language* (New York: Random House, 1967), p. 1146.
8. Buckley, *Sociology and Modern Systems Theory*, p. 58.
9. Herbert A. Simon, "Theories of Decision-Making in Economics and Behavioral Science," *The American Economic Review* 49 (June 1959): 277.

Bibliography

ABDEL-GHANY, MOHAMED. "Quality of Life from the Perspective of the Elderly." *Home Economics Research Journal* 6 (September 1977): 38–48.

ACKOFF, RUSSELL L. *Redesigning the Future*. New York: Wiley, 1974.

ACKOFF, RUSSELL L., and EMERY, FRED E. *On Purposeful Systems*. Chicago: Aldine-Atherton, 1972.

ADLER, MORTIMER J. *A Guidebook to Learning for the Lifelong Pursuit of Wisdom*. New York: Macmillan, 1986.

AGAN, TESSIE; KONZ, STEPHAN; and TORMEY, LUCY. "Extra Heart Beats As a Measurement of Work Cost." *Home Economics Research Journal* 1 (September 1972): 28–33.

AGOR, WESTON H. "How Top Executives Use Their Intuition to Make Important Decisions." *Business Horizons* 29 (Jan.-Feb. 1986): 49–53.

ALDOUS, JOAN. "A Framework for the Analysis of Family Problem Solving." In *Family Problem Solving,* ed. by Joan Aldous, Thomas Condon, Reuben Hill, Murray Straus, and Irving Tallman. Hinsdale, Ill.: Dryden Press, 1971.

ALEXIS, MARCUS, and WILSON, CHARLES Z. *Organizational Decision Making*. Englewood Cliffs, N.J.: Prentice-Hall, 1967.

ALLEN, AGAITHA, and THOMPSON, TERESA. "Agreement, Understanding, Realization, and Feeling Understood as Predictors of Communicative Satisfaction in Marital Dyads." *Journal of Marriage and the Family* 46 (November 1984): 915–921.

ALLEN, SHEILA, and WOLKOWITZ, CAROL. "The Control of Women's Labour: The Case of Homeworking." *Feminist Review* 22 (February 1986): 25–51.

ALWIN, DUANE F.; CONVERSE, PHILIP E.; and MARTIN, STEVEN S. "Living Arrangements and Social Integration." *Journal of Marriage and the Family* 47 (May 1985): 319–334.

"Analysis of Poverty Using Non-Cash Benefits." Washington, D.C.: Center on Budget and Policy Priorities, 1986.

ANDERSON, TRUDY B. "Widowhood As a Life Transition: Its Impact on Kinship Ties." *Journal of Marriage and the Family* 46 (February 1984): 105–114.

ANDREASEN, ALAN R. "The Differing Nature of Consumerism in the Ghetto." *The Journal of Consumer Affairs* 10 (Winter 1976): 179–190.

ANDREASEN, ALAN R. "Disadvantaged Hispanic Consumers: Research Perspective and Agenda." *Journal of Consumer Affairs* 16 (Summer 1982): 46–61.

ANNETT, JOHN. *Feedback and Human Behavior*. Baltimore: Penguin Books, 1969.

ARONS, STEPHAN. "Compulsory Education." *Saturday Review* 55 (January 15, 1972): 52–57.

ATER, E. CAROLYN, and DEACON, RUTH E. "Interaction of Family Relationship Qualities and Managerial Components." *Journal of Marriage and the Family* 34 (May 1972): 257–263.

AVERY, ROBERT B., and ELLIEHAUSEN, GREGORY E. "Financial Characteristics of High-Income

Families." *Federal Reserve Bulletin* 72 (March 1986): 163–177.

AVERY, ROBERT B.; ELLIEHAUSEN, GREGORY E.; and CANNER, GLENN B. "Survey of Consumer Finances, 1983: A Second Report." *Federal Reserve Bulletin* 70 (December 1984): 857–868.

AVERY, ROBERT B.; ELLIEHAUSEN, GREGORY E.; KENNICKELL, ARTHUR B.; and SPINDT, PAUL A. "The Use of Cash and Transaction Accounts by American Families." *Federal Reserve Bulletin* 72 (February 1986): 87–108.

BALL, RICHARD E. "Family and Friends: A Supportive Network for Low-Income American Families." *Journal of Comparative Family Studies* 14 (Spring 1983): 51–65.

BANDLER, RICHARD; GRINDER, JOHN; and SATIR, VIRGINIA. *Changing with Families,* Vol. 1. Palo Alto: Science and Behavior Books, 1976.

BANKOFF, ELIZABETH A. "Social Support and Adaptation to Widowhood." *Journal of Marriage and the Family* 45 (November 1983): 827–839.

BARCLAY, NANCY ANN. "Organization of Household Activities by Home Managers," Ph.D. dissertation. Columbus: The Ohio State University, 1970.

BARNETT, ROSALIND C., and BARUCH, GRACE K. "Determinants of Fathers' Participation in Family Work." Working Paper 136. (rev.). Wellesley, Mass.: Wellesley College, Center for Research on Women, 1986.

BARUCH, GRACE K., and BARNETT, ROSALIND C. "Consequences of Fathers' Participation in Family Work: Parents' Role-Strain and Well-Being." Working Paper 159. Wellesley, Mass.: Wellesley College, Center for Research on Women, 1986.

———. "Role Quality, Multiple Role Involvement and Psychological Well-Being in Midlife Women." Working Paper 149. Wellesley, Mass.: Wellesley College, Center for Research on Women, 1986.

BAVELAS, JANET BEAVIN, and SEGAL, LYNN. "Family Systems Theory: Background and Implications." *Journal of Communications* 32 (Summer 1982): 99–107.

BEARD, DORIS MARIE. "Morphostatic and Morphogenic Planning Behavior in Families: Development of a Measurement Instrument." Ph.D. dissertation. Columbus: The Ohio State University, 1975.

BEARD, DORIS MARIE, and FIREBAUGH, FRANCILLE M. "Morphostatic and Morphogenic Planning Behavior in Families: Development of a Measurement Instrument." *Home Economics Research Journal* 6 (March 1978): 192–205.

BEAVERS, W. R., and OLSON, D. H. "Epilogue." *Family Process* 22 (1983): 97–98.

BELL, DAVID G.; CHAFETZ, JANET SALTZMAN; and HORN, LORI HEGGEM. "Marital Conflict Resolution." *Journal of Family Issues* 3 (March 1982): 111–132.

BELLE, DEBORAH E. "Impact of Poverty on Social Networks and Supports." *Marriage and Family Review* 5 (Winter 1982): 89–103.

BELSKY, JAY, and ROVINE, MICHAEL. "Social-Network Contact, Family Support, and the Transition to Parenthood." *Journal of Marriage and the Family* 46 (May 1984): 455–462.

BELSKY, JAY; PERRY-JENKINS, MAUREEN; and CROUTER, ANN C. "The Work–Family Interface and Marital Change Across the Transition to Parenthood." *Journal of Family Issues* 6 (June 1985): 205–220.

BELSKY, JAY; SPANIER, GRAHAM B.; and ROVINE, MICHAEL. "Stability and Change in Marriage Across the Transition to Parenthood." *Journal of Marriage and the Family* 45 (August 1983): 567–577.

BERGER, R. M.; GUILFORD, J. P.; and CHRISTENSEN, P. R. "A Factor-Analytic Study of Planning Abilities." *Psychological Monographs* 71, Whole No. 435 (1957): 15–28.

BERHEIDE, CATHERINE WHITE. "Women's Work in the Home: Seems Like Old Times." *Marriage and Family Review* 7 (Fall–Winter 1984): 37–55.

BERHEIDE, CATHERINE WHITE; BERK, SARAH FENSTERMAKER; and BERK, RICHARD A. "Household Work in the Suburbs." *Pacific Sociological Review* 19 (October 1976): 491–518.

BERK, RICHARD A., and BERK, SARAH FENSTERMAKER. *Labor and Leisure at Home*. Beverly Hills: Sage Publications, 1979.

BERK, SARAH FENSTERMAKER. *The Gender Factory*. New York: Plenum Press, 1985.

BERKOWITZ, ALAN, and PERKINS, H. WESLEY. "Stress among Farm Women: Work and Family as Interacting Systems." *Journal of Marriage and the Family* 46 (February 1984): 161–166.

BEUTLER, IVAN F. "Comprehensive Development of a Standard of Need for Iowa Aid-to-Dependent-Children Recipients." Home Economics Research Institute Bulletin 101. Ames: Iowa State University, 1978.

BIRD, GERALD A.; BIRD, GLORIA W.; and SCRUGGS, MARGUERITE. "Role-Management Strategies Used by Husbands and Wives in Two-Earner Families." *Home Economics Research Journal* 12 (September 1983): 63–70.

BIRD, GLORIA W.; BIRD, GERALD A.; and SCRUGGS, MARGUERITE. "Determinants of Family Task Sharing: A Study of Husbands and Wives." *Journal of Marriage and the Family* 46 (May 1984): 345–355.

BIVENS, GORDON E. "The Grants Economy and Study of the American Family: A Possible Framework for Trans-Disciplinary Approaches." *Home Economics Research Journal* 5 (December 1976): 70–78.

BIVENS, GORDON E., and VOLKER, CAROL B. "A Value-Added Approach to Household Production: The Special Case of Meal Preparation." *Journal of Consumer Research* 13 (September 1986): 272–279.

BLAYDON, COLIN C., and STACK, CAROL B. "Income Support Policies and the Family." *Daedalus* 106 (Spring 1977): 147–161.

BOHEN, HALCYONE H., and VIVEROS-LONG, ANAMARIA. *Balancing Jobs and Family Life: Do Flexible Work Schedules Help?* Philadelphia: Temple University Press, 1981.

BOSE, CHRISTINE E., and BEREANO, PHILIP L. "Household Technologies: Burden or Blessing?" In *The Technological Woman Interfacing with Tomorrow,* ed. by Jan Zimmerman. New York: Praeger Publishers, 1983.

BOSS, PAULINE G. "Normative Family Stress: Family Boundary Changes Across the Life-span." *Family Relations* 29 (October 1980): 445–450.

———. "Premature Parenting: Making Responsible Decisions to Slow It Down." Speech, August 10, 1977, Annual Meeting, State of Ohio Department of Education, Home Economics. Columbus, Ohio.

BOULD, SALLY. "Female-Headed Families: Personal Fate Control and the Provider Role." *Journal of Marriage and the Family* 39 (May 1977): 339–349.

BOULDING, ELISE. "Familial Constraints on Women's Work Roles." *Signs* 1 (Spring 1976): 95–117.

BOULDING, KENNETH E. *Economics as a Science.* New York: McGraw-Hill, 1970.

BRANDEWEIN, RUTH A.; BROWN, CAROL A.; and FOX, ELIZABETH MAURY. "Women and Children Last: The Social Situation of Divorced Mothers and Their Families." *Journal of Marriage and the Family* 36 (August 1974): 498–514.

BRANSON, MARY LOU. "Resource Management: Divorced Custodial Fathers Compared to Divorced Custodial Mothers." *Family Perspectives* 17 (Spring 1983): 101–107.

BRANSON, MARY LOU, and JENNINGS, GLENN. "A Comparison of Resource Management Behaviors of Male and Female Divorced Custodial Parents." In *Social and Economic Resources: Managing in a Complex Society,* Proceedings of the Conference for the Southeastern Regional Association Family Economics–Home Management. Baton Rouge, Louisiana: Louisiana State University, 1985.

BROWN, JODIE JOHNSON; HELTSEY, MARY E.; and WARREN, RICHARD D. "Planning in Low-Income Families: Influence of Locus of Control and Dyadic Consensus on Realistic Standard Setting." *Home Economics Research Journal* 11 (September 1982): 67–75.

BRUBAKER, TIMOTHY H. "Responsibility for Household Tasks: A Look at Golden Anniversary Couples Aged 75 Years and Older." In *Social Bonds in Later Life,* ed. by Warren A. Peterson and Jil Quadagno. Beverly Hills: Sage Publications, 1985.

BUCHBINDER, LAURA BAKER. "Human Activity Patterns and Injury Severity in Fire Accidents Involving Apparel." *Journal of Fire and Flammability/Consumer Products* 1 (March 1974): 4–18.

BUCKLEY, WALTER. *Sociology and Modern Systems Theory.* Englewood Cliffs, N.J.: Prentice-Hall, 1967.

BUEHLER, CHERYL, and HOGAN, M. JANICE. "Planning Styles in Single-Parent Families." *Home Economics Research Journal* 14 (June 1986): 351–362.

BUNSTER, XIMENA, and CHANEY, ELSA M. *Sellers and Servants.* Westport, Conn.: Praeger Publishers, 1985.

BURDEN, DIANNE S., and KLERMAN, LORRAINE V. "Teenage Parenthood: Factors That Lessen Economic Dependence." *Social Work* 29 (January–February 1984): 11–16.

BUTLER, ROBERT N. *Why Survive? Being Old in America.* New York: Harper and Row, 1975.

CALLAHAN, SIDNEY CORNELIA. *The Working Mother.* New York: Macmillan, 1971.

CAMPBELL, ANGUS; CONVERSE, PHILIP E.; and

RODGERS, WILLARD L. *The Quality of American Life*. New York: Russell Sage Foundation, 1976.

CAMPBELL, FRANCES A.; BREITMAYER, BONNIE; and RAMEY, CRAIG T. "Disadvantaged Single Mothers and Their Children—Consequences of Free Educational Day Care." *Family Relations* 35 (January 1986): 63–68.

CAPON, NOEL, and KUHN, DEANNA. "Can Consumers Calculate Best Buys?" *Journal of Consumer Research* 8 (March 1982): 449–453.

CARP, FRANCES M. "Retired People As Automobile Passengers." *The Gerontologist* 12 (Spring 1972): 66–72.

CHAMBRE, SUSAN MAIZEL. "Welfare, Work, and Family Structure." *Social Work* 22 (March 1977): 103–108.

CHEN, YUNG-PING, and CHU, KWANG-WEN. "Household Expenditure Patterns: The Effect of Age of Family Head." *Journal of Family Issues* 3 (June 1982): 233–250.

CHERLIN, ANDREW; GRIFFITH, JEANE; and MCCARTHY, JAMES. "A Note on Maritally Disrupted Men's Reports of Child Support in the June 1980 Current Population Survey." *Demography* 20 (August 1983): 385–389.

CHERLIN, ANDREW, and MCCARTHY, JAMES. "Remarried Couple Households: Data from the June 1980 Current Population Survey." *Journal of Marriage and the Family* 47 (February 1985): 23–30.

Children's Defense Fund. "A Children's Defense Budget: An Analysis of the 1984 Budget." Washington, D.C.: Children's Defense Fund, 1984.

CHURCHILL, EDMUND; CHURCHILL, THOMAS; MCCONVILLE, JOHN T.; and WHITE, ROBERT M. "Anthropometry of Women in the U.S. Army—1977," Report No. 2: "The Basic Univariate Statistics," Technical Report NATICK/TR-77/024 (June 1977).

CHURCHMAN, C. WEST. *The Systems Approach*. New York: Delacorte, 1968.

CIRCIRELLI, VICTOR G. "Adult Children's Helping Behavior to Elderly Parents: The Influence of Divorce." *Journal of Family Issues* 5 (September 1984): 419–440.

CLELAND, DAVID I., and KING, WILLIAM R. *Management: A Systems Approach*. New York: McGraw-Hill, 1972.

COGLE, FRANCES L., and TASKER, GRACE L. "Children and Housework." *Family Relations* 31 (July 1982): 395–399.

COMBRINCK-GRAHAM, LEE. "A Developmental Model for Family Systems." *Family Process* 24 (June 1985): 139–150.

CONDRAN, JOHN G., and BODE, JERRY G. "Rashomon, Working Wives, and Family Division of Labor: Middletown, 1980." *Journal of Marriage and the Family* 44 (May 1982): 421–426.

COTTLE, THOMAS J. *Hidden Survivors, Portraits of Poor Jews in America*. Englewood Cliffs, N.J.: Prentice-Hall, 1980.

———. *Perceiving Time: A Psychological Investigation with Men and Women*. New York: Wiley, 1976.

COWAN, CAROLYN PAPE; COWAN, PHILIP A.; HEMING, GERTRUDE; GARRETT, ELLEN; COYSH, WILLIAM S.; CURTIS-BLOES, HARRIET; and BOLLES, ABNER J., III. "Transitions to Parenthood: His, Hers, and Theirs." *Journal of Family Issues* 6 (December 1985): 451–481.

COWAN, RUTH SCHWARTZ. *More Work for Mothers*. New York: Basic Books, 1983.

CRAIN, ALAN J.; SUSSMAN, MARVIN; and WEIL, WILLIAM B. "Effects of a Diabetic Child on Marital Integration and Related Measures of Family Functioning." *Journal of Health and Human Behavior* 7 (Summer 1966): 122–127.

CROOG, SYDNEY H.; LIPSON, ALBERTA; and LEVINE, SOL. "Help Patterns in Severe Illness: The Roles of Kin Network, Non-Family Resources, and Institutions." *Journal of Marriage and the Family* 34 (February 1972): 32–41.

CROSBY, KRISTAN RINKER. "Perceived Levels of Living and Family Welfare." Master's thesis. Columbus: The Ohio State University, 1970.

CROWLEY, JOAN E. "Longitudinal Effects of Retirement on Men's Psychological and Physical Well-Being." In *Retirement among American Men*, ed. by Herbert S. Parnes, Joan E. Crowley, R. Jean Haurin, Lawrence J. Less, William R. Morgan, Frank L. Mott, and Gilbert Nestel. Lexington, Mass.: Lexington Books, 1985.

"Cutting the Waist, Trimming the Fat." *Ebony* 40 (October 1985): 52–56.

DAMON, ALBERT; STOUDT, HOWARD W.; and MCFARLAND, ROSS A. *The Human Body in Equipment Design*. Cambridge: Harvard University Press, 1971.

DANIELS, PAMELA, and WEINGARTEN, KATHY. *Sooner or Later: The Timing of Parenthood in Adult Lives*. New York: W. W. Norton, 1982.

DARITY, WILLIAM A., JR., and MYERS, SAMUEL L.,

JR. "Does Welfare Dependency Cause Female Headship? The Case of the Black Family." *Journal of Marriage and the Family* 46 (November 1984): 765–779.

DAVEY, ALICE J., and PAOLUCCI, BEATRICE. "Family Interaction: A Study of Shared Time and Activities." *Family Relations* 29 (January 1980): 43–49.

DAVIS, HARRY L. "Decision Making Within the Household." *Journal of Consumer Research* 2 (March 1976): 241–260.

DEJESUS, CAROLINA MARIA. *Child of the Dark.* Transl. by David St. Clair. New York: New American Library, 1962.

DILL, DIANA; FIELD, ELLEN; MARTIN, JACQUELINE; BEUKEMA, STEPHANIE; and BELLE, DEBORAH. "The Impact of the Environment on the Coping Efforts of Low-Income Mothers." *Family Relations* 29 (October 1980): 503–509.

"Domestic Financial and Nonfinancial Statistics." *Federal Reserve Bulletin* 72 (June 1986): A40, A52.

DORNBUSCH, SANFORD M.; CARLSMITH, MERRILL J.; BUSHWALL, STEPHEN J.; RITTER, PHILIP L.; LEIDERMAN, HERBERT; HASTORF, ALBERT H.; and GROSS, RUTH T. "Single Parents, Extended Households, and the Control of Adolescents." *Child Development* 56 (October 1985): 326–341.

DOUGLAS, SUSAN P. "Examining Family Decision-Making Processes." *Advances in Consumer Research* 10 (1983): 451–453.

DRABEK, THOMAS E.; KEY, WILLIAM H.; ERICKSON, PATRICIA E.; and CROWE, JUANITA L. "The Impact of Disaster on Kin Relationships." *Journal of Marriage and the Family* 37 (August 1975): 481–494.

DUBERMAN, LUCILE. *The Reconstruction of the Family: A Study of Remarried Couples and Their Children.* Chicago: Nelson-Hall, 1975.

DUNCAN, GREG J., and MORGAN, JAMES N. "An Overview of Family Economic Mobility." In *Years of Poverty, Years of Plenty: The Changing Economic Fortunes of American Workers and Families.* Greg J. Duncan et al. Ann Arbor: University of Michigan, Institute for Social Research, Survey Research Center, 1984.

DUNCAN, GREG J.; with COE, RICHARD D.; CORCORAN, MARY E.; HILL, MARTHA S.; HOFFMAN, SAUL D.; and MORGAN, JAMES N. *Years of Poverty, Years of Plenty: The Changing Economic Fortunes of American Workers and Families.* Ann Arbor: University of Michigan, Institute for Social Research, Survey Research Center, 1984.

DUNLAP, WILLIAM R., and HOLLINSWORTH, J. SELWYN. "How Does a Handicapped Child Affect the Family? Implications for Practitioners." *The Family Coordinator* 26 (July 1977): 286–293.

DUNSING, MARILYN M., ed. *Proceedings of the Symposium on Perceived Economic Well-Being.* Champaign-Urbana: University of Illinois, 1983.

EILON, SAMUEL. "What Is a Decision?" *Management Science* 16 (December 1969): B-172–B-189.

EISENHARDT, KATHLEEN M. "Control: Organizational and Economics Approaches." *Management Science* 31 (February 1985): 134–149.

ELLIS, CAROLYN. "Community Organization and Family Structure in Two Fishing Communities." *Journal of Marriage and the Family* 46 (August 1984): 515–526.

ELMAN, MARGARET R., and GILBERT, LUCIA A. "Coping Strategies for Role Conflict in Married Professional Women with Children." *Family Relations* 33 (April 1984): 317–328.

ERDOES, RICHARD. "My Travels with Medicine Man John Lame Deer." *Smithsonian* 4 (May 1973): 30–38.

EVANGELAUF, JEAN. "Colleges' Charges to Students Rising 6 Percent This Fall." *The Chronicle of Higher Education* 32 (August 6, 1986): 1, 24–30.

FAVER, CATHERINE A. "Women, Careers, and Family." *Journal of Family Issues* 2 (March 1981): 91–112.

FAWCETT, JACQUELINE. "The Family as a Living Open System: An Emerging Conceptual Framework." *International Nursing Review* 22 (July–August 1975): 113–116.

FELLER, BARBARA A. "Americans Needing Help to Function at Home." *Vital and Health Statistics,* No. 92. Washington, D.C.: U.S. Department of Health and Human Services, National Center for Health Statistics, 1983.

FENDRICH, MICHAEL. "Wives' Employment and Husbands' Distress: A Meta-analysis and a Replication." *Journal of Marriage and the Family* 46 (November 1984): 871–879.

FERREE, MYRA MARX. "Class, Housework, and Happiness: Women's Work and Life Satisfaction." *Sex Roles* 11 (December 1984): 1057–1074.

FILIATRAULT, PIERRE, and RITCHIE, J. R. BRENT. "Joint Purchasing Decisions: A Comparison of

Influence Structure in Family and Couple Decision-Making Units." *Journal of Consumer Research* 7 (September 1980): 131–140.

FISHER, MARY JANE. HMOs Urged to Provide Health Care for Poor, Uninsured, Unemployed." *National Underwriter* 90 (January 18, 1986): 2, 23.

FISHMAN, BARBARA. "The Economic Behavior of Stepfamilies." *Family Relations* 32 (July 1983): 359–366.

FITCHEN, JANET M. "The People of Road Junction: The Participant Observer's Study of a Rural Poverty Area in Northern Appalachia, with Particular Reference to the Problems of Employment of Low Income Women." In *A Study of the Effects on the Family Due to Employment of the Welfare Mother,* Vol. 3. Report to the Manpower Administration, U.S. Department of Labor [n.d.].

FOA, URIEL G. "Interpersonal and Economic Resources." *Science* 171 (January 1971): 345–351.

FOA, URIEL G., and FOA, EDNA B. *Societal Structures of the Mind.* Springfield, Ill.: Charles C Thomas, Publisher, 1974.

FOLGER, JOSEPH P., and POOL, MARSHALL SCOTT. *Communication.* Glenview, Ill.: Scott, Foresman, 1984.

FOX, ALAN. "Income Changes at and after Social Security Benefit Receipt: Evidence from the Retirement History Study." *Social Security Bulletin* 47 (September 1984): 3–23.

FOX, KAREN D., and NICKOLS, SHARON Y. "The Time Crunch: Wife's Employment and Family Work." *Journal of Family Issues* 4 (March 1983): 61–82.

FRANKLIN, PAULA A. "Impact of Disability on the Family Structure." *Social Security Bulletin* 40 (May 1977): 3–18.

FRIEDMAN, KATHIE, "Households and Income Pooling Units." *In Households and the World Economy,* ed. by Joan Smith, Immanuel Wallerstein and Hans-Dieter Evers. Beverly Hills: Sage Publications, 1984.

FURSTENBURG, FRANK F., JR. "Implicating the Family: Teenage Parenthood and Kinship Involvement." In *Teenage Pregnancy in a Family Context: Implications for Policy,* ed. by Theodora Ooms. Philadelphia: Temple University Press, 1981.

FURSTENBURG, FRANK F., JR., and SPANIER, GRAHAM B. *Recycling the Family: Remarriage after Divorce.* Beverly Hills: Sage Publications, 1984.

GALVIN, KATHLEEN M., and BROMMEL, BERNARD J. *Family Communication Cohesion and Change.* Glenview, Ill.: Scott, Foresman, 1982.

GARRISON, M. E., and WINTER, MARY. "The Managerial Behaviour of Families with Preschool Children." *Journal of Consumer Studies and Home Economics* 10 (September 1986): 247–260.

GASSER, RITA D., and TAYLOR, CLARIBEL M. "Role Adjustment of Single Parent Fathers with Dependent Children." *The Family Coordinator* 25 (October 1976): 397–401.

GAUGER, WILLIAM H. and WALKER, KATHRYN E. "The Dollar Value of Household Work," *Information Bulletin* 60, rev. Ithaca: New York State College of Human Ecology, 1980.

GEERKEN, MICHAEL, and GOVE, WALTER R. *At Home and at Work.* Beverly Hills: Sage Publications, 1983.

GEISEL, THEODOR SEUSS. *You're Only Old Once!* New York: Random House, 1986.

GIELE, JANET ZOLLINGER. "A Delicate Balance: The Family's Role in Care of the Handicapped." *Family Relations* 33 (January 1984): 85–94.

GILBERT, LUCIA A.; HOLAHAN, CAROLE KOVALIC; and MANNING, LINDA. "Coping with Conflict Between Professional and Maternal Roles." *Family Relations* 30 (July 1981): 419–426.

GIESEMAN, RAYMOND, and ROGERS, JOHN. "Consumer Expenditures: Results from the Diary and Interview Surveys." *Monthly Labor Review* 109 (June 1986): 14–18.

GLADOW, NANCY WELLS, and RAY, MARGARET P. "The Impact of Information Support Systems on the Well-Being of Low-Income Single Parents." *Family Relations* 35 (January 1986): 113–123.

GOLDBERG, WENDY A.; MICHAELS, GERALD Y.; and LAMB, MICHAEL E. "Husbands' and Wives' Adjustment to Pregnancy and First Parenthood." *Journal of Family Issues* 6 (December 1985): 483–503.

GOLDSCHMIDT-CLERMONT, LUISELLA. *Economic Evaluations of Unpaid Household Work: Africa, Asia, Latin America and Oceania.* Women, Work and Development, Series No. 14. Geneva: International Labour Organization, 1987.

GOODMAN, IRENE F. "Television's Role in Family Interaction." *Journal of Family Issues* 4 (June 1983): 405–424.

GOTSHALK, D. W. *Patterns of Good and Evil.* Urbana: University of Illinois Press, 1963.

GRANDORI, ANA. "A Prescriptive Contingency View of Organizational Decision Making." *Ad-*

ministrative Science Quarterly 29 (June 1984): 192–209.

GREENE, BOB. *Good Morning, Merry Sunshine.* New York: Atheneum, 1984.

GREIF, GEOFFREY L. "Children and Housework in the Single Father Family." *Family Relations* 34 (July 1985): 353–357.

———. *Single Fathers.* Lexington, Mass.: Lexington Books, 1985.

GRICAR, BARBARA GRAY, and BARATTA, ANTHONY J. "Bridging the Information Gap at Three Mile Island: Radiation Monitoring by Citizens." *Journal of Applied Behavioral Science* 19 (January 1983): 35–49.

GROSS, HARRIET ENGEL "Dual-Career Couples Who Live Apart: Two Types." *Journal of Marriage and the Family* 42 (August 1980): 567–576.

GROSS, IRMA H.; CRANDALL, ELIZABETH W.; and KNOLL, MARJORIE M. *Management for Modern Families.* New York: Appleton-Century-Crofts, 1973.

GUADAGNO, MARY ANN NOECKER. "Selected Factors Affecting Perceived Need for Life Insurance by Divorced Mothers." Ph.D. dissertation. Columbus: The Ohio State University, 1978.

GUBRUIM, JABER F. "Toward a Socio-Environmental Theory of Aging." *The Gerontologist* 12 (Autumn 1972, Part 1): 281–284.

HAAS, LINDA. "Role-Sharing Couples: A Study of Egalitarian Marriages." *Family Relations* 29 (July 1980): 289–296.

HAFSTROM, JEANNE L., and SCHRAM, VICKI R. "Chronic Illness in Couples: Selected Characteristics, Including Wife's Satisfaction with and perception of Marital Relationships." *Family Relations* 33 (January 1984): 195–203.

———. "Housework Time of Wives: Pressure, Facilitators, Constraints." *Home Economics Research Journal* 11 (March 1983): 245–256.

HAHN, GERALD J. "Evaluation of a Decision Based on Subjective Probability Estimates." *IEEE Transactions on Engineering Management* EM-18 (February 1971): 12–16.

HALL, A. D. and FAGEN, R. E. "Definition of Systems." *General Systems* 1 (1956): 18–28.

HALL, EDWARD T. *Beyond Culture.* Garden City, N.Y.: Anchor Books, 1977.

———. *The Hidden Dimension.* Garden City, N.Y.: Doubleday, 1966.

HANSON, SANDRA. "A Family Life-Cycle Approach to the Socio-economic Attainment of Working Women." *Journal of Marriage and the Family* 45 (May 1983): 323–338.

HANSON, SHIRLEY M. H. "Healthy Single Parent Families." *Family Relations* 35 (January 1986): 125–132.

HAPPEL, S. K.; HILL, J. K.; and LOW, S. A. "An Economic Analysis of the Timing of Childbirth." *Population Studies* 38 (July 1984): 299–311.

HARRIMAN, LYNDA COOPER. "Personal and Marital Changes Accompanying Parenthood." *Family Relations* 32 (July 1983): 387–394.

HARTMAN, ANN, and LAIRD, JOAN. *Family-Centered Social Work Practice.* New York: Free Press, 1983.

HAVELOCK, RONALD G. *Planning for Innovation.* Ann Arbor: The University of Michigan, Institute for Social Research, 1969.

HAYGHE, HOWARD. "Dual-Earner Families, Their Economic and Demographic Characteristics." In *Two Paychecks: Life in Dual Earner Families,* ed. by Joan Aldous. Beverly Hills: Sage Publications, 1982.

———. "Rise in Mothers' Labor Force Activity Includes Those with Infants." *Monthly Labor Review* 109 (February 1986): 43–45.

HECK, RAMONA K. Z. "A Preliminary Test of a Family Management Research Model." *Journal of Consumer Studies and Home Economics* 7 (June 1983): 117–135.

HEIDBREDER, ELIZABETH M. "Factors in Retirement Adjustment: White-Collar/Blue-Collar Experience." *Industrial Gerontology* 12–13 (Winter 1972): 69–79.

HELTSLEY, MARY E. "Coping—The Aged in Small Town, U.S.A." *Journal of Home Economics* 68 (September 1976): 46–50.

HENRETTA, JOHN C., and O'RAND, ANGELA M. "Joint Retirement in the Dual Worker Family." *Social Forces* 62 (December 1983): 504–520.

HILL, REUBEN. *Family Development in Three Generations.* Cambridge, Mass.: Schenkman, 1970.

———. "Life Cycle Stages for Types of Single Parent Families: Of Family Development Theory." *Family Relations* 35 (January 1986): 19–29.

HILL, WAYNE, and SCANZONI, JOHN. "An Approach for Assessing Marital Decision-Making Processes." *Journal of Marriage and the Family* 44 (November 1982): 927–941.

HIRA, TAHIRA K. "Socio-Economic Characteristics

of Families in Bankruptcy." *Canadian Home Economics Journal* 32 (Winter 1982): 26–31.

HOFSTEDE, GEERT. "The Poverty of Management Control Philosophy." *Academy of Management Review* 3 (July 1978): 450–461.

HOGARTH, ROBIN M., and MAKRIDAKIS, SPYROS. "Forecasting and Planning: An Evaluation." *Management Science* 27 (February 1981): 115–138.

HOLAHAN, CAROLE K. "The Relationship between Information Search in the Childbearing Decision and Life Satisfaction for Parents and Nonparents." *Family Relations* (October 1983): 527–535.

HOLDEN, CONSTANCE. "Counting the Homeless." *Science* 234 (October 17, 1986): 281–282.

HOLLAND, BARBARA. "The Day's Work." *Ms.* 6 (August 1977): 54–58, 79.

HOLYOAK, ARLENE, and MEINERS, JANE. "Time Allocation of the Handicapped and Their Spouses: Comparison with Families Including No Handicapped Members." In *The Balancing Act: Thinking Globally/Acting Locally,* Proceedings of a Workshop sponsored by the Family Economics/Home Management Section of the American Home Economics Association, ed. by Sharon Y. Nickols. Washington, D.C.: American Home Economics Association, 1985.

HOWELL, JOSEPH T. *Hard Living on Clay Street.* Garden City, N.Y.: Anchor Books, 1973.

HUBER, JOAN, and SPITZE, GLENNA. *Sex Stratification.* New York: Academic Press, 1983.

HUNTER, WOODROW W. "A Longitudinal Study of Preretirement Education." U.S. Department of Health, Education, and Welfare, Welfare Administration, Research Grants Branch Project #151. Ann Arbor: The University of Michigan, 1968.

HUTH, TOM. "$30,000 a Year 'Permits' Dissatisfaction." *The Washington Post,* May 13, 1973.

HYMAN, HERBERT H. *Of Time and Widowhood.* Durham, N.C.: Duke University Press, 1983.

IRESON, CAROL J. "Adolescent Pregnancy and Sex Roles." *Sex Roles* 11 (August 1984): 189–201.

JACKSON, MARY E., and TESSLER, RICHARD C. "Perceived Control over Life Events: Antecedents and Consequences in a Discharged Hospital Sample." *Social Science Research* 13 (September 1984): 287–301.

JACOBSON, D. S. "Stepfamilies: Myths and Realities." *Social Work* 24 (May 1979): 202–207.

JACOBSON, ROBERT L. "Most Students Are Satisfied with Their Education Survey Indicates, but Frustrations are Widespread." *The Chronicle of Higher Education* 31 (February 5, 1986): p. 1, 27–31.

JAFFE, A. J. "The Middle Years: Neither Too Young nor Too Old." *Industrial Gerontology,* Special Issue (September 1971): 1–90.

JOHNSON, FRANK A., and JOHNSON, COLLEEN L. "Role Strain in High-Commitment Career Women." *Journal of American Academy of Psychoanalysis* 4 (January 1976): 31.

JOHNSON, PHYLLIS J. "Divorced Mothers' Management of Responsibilities: Conflicts Between Employment and Child Care." *Journal of Family Issues* 4 (March 1983): 83–103.

———. "Non-Routine Management of Employment and Family Responsibilities by Divorced Mothers," Ph.D. dissertation. Columbus: The Ohio State University, 1978.

JOHNSON, PHYLLIS J., and FIREBAUGH, FRANCILLE M. "A Typology of Household Work Performance by Employment Demands." *Journal of Family Issues* 6 (March 1985): 83–106.

JUSTER, F. THOMAS; COURANT, PAUL N.; and DOW, GREG K. "A Conceptual Framework for the Analysis of Time Allocation Data." In *Time, Goods, and Well-Being,* ed. by F. T. Juster and F. P. Stafford. Ann Arbor: University of Michigan, Institute for Social Research, Survey Research Center, 1985.

KANDEL, DENISE B.; DAVIES, MARK; and RAVEIS, VICTORIA H. "The Stressfulness of Daily Social Roles for Women: Marital, Occupational and Household Roles." *Journal of Health and Social Behavior* 26 (March 1985): 64–78.

KANTOR, DAVID, and LEHR, WILLIAM. *Inside the Family.* San Francisco: Jossey-Bass, 1975.

KAPLAN, DEBORAH, and MEARIG, JUDITH S. "A Community Support System for a Family Coping with Chronic Illness." *Rehabilitation Literature* 38 (March 1977): 79–83.

KAST, FREMONT E., and ROSENZWEIG, JAMES E. *Contingency Views of Organization and Management.* Chicago: Science Research Associates, 1973.

———. "General Systems Theory: Applications for Organization and Management." *Academy of Management Journal* 15 (December 1972): 447–468.

KATAKIS, HARIS D. "The Systems Approach in the

Study of Family Interaction." *International Journal of Social Psychiatry* 22 (Summer 1976): 101–103.

KATZ, D., and KAHN, R. L. *The Social Psychology of Organizations*. New York: Wiley, 1966.

KEITH, PAT M. "A Comparison of the Resources of Parents and the Childless Men and Women in Very Old Age." *Family Relations* 32 (July 1983): 403–409.

KEITH, PAT M.; DOBSON, CYNTHIA D.; GOUDY, WILLIS J.; and POWERS, EDWARD A. "Older Men: Occupation, Employment Status, Household Involvement, and Well-Being." *Journal of Family Issues* 2 (September 1981): 336–349.

KELLY, ROBERT F., and VOYDANOFF, PATRICIA. "Work/Family Role Strain Among Employed Parents." *Family Relations* 34 (July 1985): 367–374.

KENT, MARILYN O. "Remarriage: A Family Systems Perspective." *Social Casework: The Journal of Contemporary Social Work* 61 (March 1980): 146–153.

KESHET, JAMIE KELEM. "From Separation to Stepfamily." *Journal of Family Issues* 1 (December 1980): 517–532.

KEY, ROSEMARY J. "Sequencing Techniques Used in Home Production Activities." M.S. thesis. Columbus: The Ohio State University, 1984.

KILPATRICK, ALLIE C. "Job Change in Dual-Career Families: Danger or Opportunity?" *Family Relations* 31 (July 1982): 363–368.

KINGSTON, PAUL WILLIAM, and NOCK, STEVEN L. "Consequences of the Family Work Day." *Journal of Marriage and the Family* 47 (August 1985): 619–629.

KNEELAND, DEBRA. "Meeting Across the Generations." *The Des Moines Register,* November 30, 1977.

KUHN, ALFRED, and BEAM, ROBERT D. *The Logic of Organization*. San Francisco: Jossey-Bass, 1982.

KYRK, HAZEL. *The Family in the American Economy*. Chicago: University of Chicago Press, 1953.

LA ROSSA, RALPH. *Conflict and Power in Marriage, Expecting the First Child*. Beverly Hills: Sage Publications, 1977.

LARSON, ERIK. "Working at Home: Is It Freedom or a Life of Flabby Loneliness?" *The Wall Street Journal,* February 13, 1985.

LARSON, JEFFRY H. "The Effect of Husband's Unemployment on Marital and Family Relations in Blue-Collar Families." *Family Relations* 33 (October 1984): 503–511.

LARSON, JOYCE M., and ACKERMAN, NORLEEN M. "Human Capital As Related to the Income of Households Recently Headed by Women: Descriptive Findings." In *The Balancing Act: Thinking Globally/Acting Locally,* Proceedings of a Workshop Sponsored by the Family Economics/Home Management Section of the American Home Economics Association, 1985.

LAWTON, M. POWELL. "The Elderly in Context." *Environment and Behavior* 17 (July 1985): 501–519.

LEAVY, RICHARD L., and HOUGH, OLGA B. "The Value and Cost of Children: Cross Generational and Sex Differences in Perceptions among Parents." *Home Economics Research Journal* 12 (September 1983): 57–62.

LEFCOURT, HERBERT M. "Belief in Personal Control: Research and Implications." *Journal of Individual Psychology* 22 (November 1966): 185–195.

LEWIS, JERRY M.; BEAVERS, W. ROBERT; GOSSETT, JOHN T.; and PHILLIPS, VIRGINIA AUSTIN. *No Single Thread*. New York: Brunner/Mazel, 1976.

"Life below the Poverty Line." *Newsweek* 99 (April 5, 1982): 20–23, 26, 28.

LINDER, STAFFAN BURENSTAM. *The Harried Leisure Class*. New York: Columbia University Press, 1970.

LITWAK, EUGENE. *Helping the Elderly*. New York: Guilford Press, 1985.

LONG, JUDY, and PORTER, KAREN L. "Multiple Roles of Midlife Women." In *Women in Midlife,* ed. by Grace K. Baruch and Jeanne Brooks-Gunn. New York: Plenum Press, 1984.

LOPATA, HELENA ZNANIECKA. "Widowhood: Social Norms and Social Integration." In *Family Factbook*. Chicago: Marquis Academic Media, 1978.

LOPATA, HELENA ZNANIECKA, and NORR, KATHLEEN FORDHAM. "Changing Commitments of American Women to Work and Family Roles." *Social Security Bulletin* 43 (June 1980): 3–14.

LOVINGOOD, REBECCA P., and MCCULLOUGH, JANE L. "Appliance Ownership and Household Work Time." *Home Economics Research Journal* 14 (March 1986): 326–335.

LUTZ, PATRICIA. "The Stepfamily: An Adolescent Perspective." *Family Relations* 32 (July 1983): 367–375.

LYNN, LAURENCE J., JR., and WORTHINGTON, MARK D. "Incremental Welfare Reform: A Strategy Whose Time Has Passed." *Public Policy* 25 (Winter 1977): 69–73.

MACIARIELLO, JOSEPH A. *Management Control: Systems*. Englewood Cliffs, N.J.: Prentice-Hall, 1984.

MAGEE, JOHN F. "Decision Trees for Decision Making." *Harvard Business Review* 42 (July–August 1964): 126–138.

MALHOTRA, NARESH K. "Information Load and Consumer Decision Making." *Journal of Consumer Research* 8 (March 1982): 419–430.

MALIK, R., and PROBST, G. "Evolutionary Management." *Cybernetics and Systems: An International Journal* 13 (1982): 153–174. Reprinted in *Self-Organization and Management of Social Systems,* ed. by H. Ulrich and G. J. B. Probst. Berlin: Springer-Verlag, 1984.

MALOCH, FRANCILLE, and WEAVER, C. R. "Orientation of Expenditures to Day of Pay." *Journal of Consumer Affairs* 5 (Summer 1971): 137–144.

MALSON, MICHELENE. "The Social Support System of Black Families." *Marriage and Family Review* 5 (Winter 1982): 37–57.

MANDELL, LEWIS. *Credit Card Use in the United States*. Ann Arbor: The University of Michigan, 1972.

MARET, ELIZABETH, and FINLAY, BARBARA. "The Distribution of Household Labor among Women in Dual-Earner Families." *Journal of Marriage and the Family* 46 (May 1984): 357–364.

MARKIDES, KYRIAKOS S, and MARTIN, HARRY W. *Older Mexican Americans*. Austin: The University of Texas, Center for Mexican American Studies, 1983.

MARKSON, ELIZABETH W.; LEVITZ, GARY S.; and GOGNALONS-CAILLARD, MARYVONNE. "The Elderly and the Community: Reidentifying Unmet Needs." *Journal of Gerontology* 28 (October 1973): 503–509.

MARSHALL, MARILYN. "The Gaither Quints: The Miracle of Multiple Births." *Ebony* 40 (December 1985): 31–40.

MCAULEY, WILLIAM J., and NUTTY, CHERI L. "Residential Preference and Moving Behavior: A Family Life-Cycle Analysis." *Journal of Marriage and the Family* 44 (May 1982): 301–309.

———. "Residential Satisfaction, Community Integration, and Risk Across the Family Life Cycle." *Journal of Marriage and the Family* 47 (February 1985): 125–130.

MCCARTHY, JAMES. "A Comparison of the Probability of the Dissolution of First and Second Marriages." *Demography* 15 (August 1978): 345–359.

MCCASKEY, MICHAEL B. "A Contingency Approach to Planning: Planning with Goals and Planning without Goals." *The Academy of Management Journal* 17 (June 1974): 281–291.

———. "Goals and Direction in Personal Planning." *The Academy of Management Review* 2 (July 1977): 454–462.

MCCONNEL, CHARLES E., and DELJAVAN, FIROOZ. "Consumption Patterns of the Retired Household." *Journal of Gerontology* 38 (July 1983): 480–490.

MCCROSKEY, JAMES C.; LARSON, CAROL E.; and KNAPP, MARK L. *An Introduction to Interpersonal Communication*. Englewood Cliffs, N.J.: Prentice-Hall, 1971.

MCHALE, SUSAN M., and HUSTON, TED L. "The Effect of the Transition to Parenthood on the Marriage Relationship." *Journal of Family Issues* 6 (December 1985): 409–433.

MCKENNA, JUDY, and NICKOLS, SHARON Y. "Planning a Retirement Security: A Study of Women in the Middle Years." Stillwater: Oklahoma State University, Family Study Center, [n.d.].

MCLANAHAN, SARA. "Family Structure and the Reproduction of Poverty." *American Journal of Sociology* 90 (January 1985): 873–901.

MCLAUGHLIN, STEVEN D. "Differential Patterns of Female Labor-Force Participation Surrounding the First Birth." *Journal of Marriage and the Family* 44 (May 1982): 407–420.

MESSINGER, LILIAN. *Remarriage: A Family Affair*. New York: Plenum Press, 1984.

MILLER, KIMBALL, and FIELD, CHARLES S. "Adolescent Pregnancy: A Combined Obstetric and Pediatric Management Approach." *Mayo Clinic Proceedings* 59 (May 1984): 311–317.

MIN, PYONG GAP. "An Exploratory Study of Kin Ties among Korean Immigrant Families in Atlanta." *Journal of Comparative Family Studies* 15 (Spring 1984): 59–75.

MODEL, SUZANNE. "Housework by Husbands: Determinants and Implications." *Journal of Family Issues* 2 (June 1981): 225–237.

MOLUMPHY, SUSAN D., and SPORAKOWSKI, MI-

CHAEL J. "The Family Stress of Hemodialysis." *Family Relations* 33 (January 1984): 33–39.

MONTGOMERY, JAMES E. "The Housing Patterns of Older Families." *The Family Coordinator* 21 (January 1972): 40–45.

MORGAN, LESLIE A. "Continuity and Change in the Labor Force Activity of Recently Widowed Women." *The Gerontologist* 24 (October 1984): 530–535.

MORRIS, EARL W., and WINTER, MARY. *Housing, Family and Society*. New York: Wiley, 1978.

MURPHY, MARTIN. "The Value of Nonmarket Household Production: Opportunity Cost Versus Market Cost Estimates." *The Review of Income and Wealth* 24 (March 1978): 243–255.

MUTRAN, ELIZABETH. "Intergenerational Family Support among Blacks and Whites: Response to Culture or to Socioeconomic Differences." *Journal of Gerontology* 40 (May 1985): 382–389.

MYERS-WALLS, JUDITH A. "Balancing Multiple Role Responsibilities During the Transition to Parenthood." *Family Relations* 33 (April 1984): 267–271.

NAISBITT, JOHN. *Megatrends*. New York: Warner Books, 1982.

NAMBOODIRI, N. KRISHNAN. "Sequential Fertility Decision Making and the Life Course." In *Determinants of Fertility in Developing Countries,* Vol. 2: *Fertility Regulation and Institutional Influences,* ed. by Rodolfo A. Bulatao and Ronald D. Lee. New York: Academic Press, 1983.

NELSON, LINDA. "Household Time: A Cross Cultural Example." In *Women and Household Labor,* ed. by Sarah Fenstermaker Berk. Beverly Hills: Sage Publications, 1980.

New York Times News Service. "Intellectual Sontag Comes to Grips with Cancer." *Ames Daily Tribune,* February 20, 1978.

NEWTON, JAN M. "Economic Rationality of the Poor." *Human Organization* 36 (Spring 1977): 52–55.

NICHOLS, MICHAEL P. *Turning Forty in the 80's*. New York: W. W. Norton, 1986.

NORD, WALTER R., and COSTIGAN, ROBERT. "Worker Adjustment to the Four-Day Week: A Longitudinal Study." *Journal of Applied Psychology* 58 (February 1973): 60–66.

NORRIS, RUBY TURNER. *The Theory of Consumer's Demand*. New Haven: Yale University Press, 1952.

NORTON, ARTHUR J., and GLICK, PAUL C. "One Parent Families: A Social and Economic Profile." *Family Relations* 35 (January 1986): 9–17.

NUSSBAUM, JOHN. "3 Orphans Win $1.3 Million in Fatal Chlorine Gas Leak," *The [Cleveland] Plain Dealer,* October 24, 1970, pp. 1A, 6A.

OAKLEY, ANN. *The Sociology of Housework*. New York: Pantheon, 1974.

O'BRYANT, SHIRLEY L. "Neighbors' Support of Older Widows Who Live Alone in Their Own Homes." *The Gerontologist* 25 (Spring 1985): 305–310.

O'DONNELL, LYDIA. "The Social Worlds of Parents." *Marriage and Family Review* 5 (Winter 1982): 9–36.

O'HARE, WILLIAM. "Keeping Track of the 'Truly Needy.' " *USA Today,* September 1984.

OLSON, DAVID H. and MCCUBBIN, HAMILTON I.; with BARNES, HOWARD L.; LARSEN, ANDREA S.; MUXEN, MARLA J.; and WILSON, MARC A. *Families: What Makes Them Work*. Beverly Hills: Sage Publications, 1983.

OLSON, GERALDINE I., and BEARD, DORIS M. "Assessing Managerial Behavior." In *The Balancing Act: Thinking Globally/Acting Locally,* Proceedings of a Workshop sponsored by the Family Economics/Home Management Section of the American Home Economics Association, ed. by Sharon Y. Nickols. Washington, D.C.: American Home Economics Association, 1985: 138–148.

OLSON, JOAN TOMS. "The Impact of Housework on Child Care in the Home." *Family Relations* 31 (January 1981): 75–81.

O'NEILL, NENA, and O'NEILL, GEORGE. *Shifting Gears*. New York: Avon Books, 1975.

O'RAND, ANGELA M., and HENRETTA, JOHN C. "Delayed Career Entry, Industrial Pension Structure, and Early Retirement in a Cohort of Unmarried Women," *American Sociological Review* 47 (June 1982): 365–373.

ORTHNER, DENNIS K., and PITTMAN, JOE F. "Family Contributions to Work Commitment." *Journal of Marriage and the Family* 48 (August 1986): 573–581.

OSMOND, MARIE WITHERS, and MARTIN, PATRICIA YANCEY. "A Contingency Model of Marital Organization in Low Income Families." *Journal of Marriage and the Family* 40 (May 1978): 315–329.

PALMER, JOHN L., and GOULD, STEPHANIE G. "The Economic Consequences of an Aging Society." *Daedalus* 115 (Winter 1986): 295–324.

PALOMA, M. M. "Role Conflict and the Married Professional Woman." In *Toward a Sociology for Women,* ed. by C. Safilios-Rothschild. Lexington, Mass.: Xerox College Publishing, 1972.

PAPERNOW, PATRICIA L. "The Stepfamily Cycle: An Experiential Model of Stepfamily Development." *Family Relations* 33 (July 1984): 355–363.

PARKER, MARIANNE, and FIREBAUGH, FRANCILLE M. "An Experience in Home Management." *Illinois Teacher* 15 (May–June 1972): 233–238.

PATTERSON, JOAN M. "Critical Factors Affecting Family Compliance with Home Treatment for Children with Cystic Fibrosis." *Family Relations* 34 (January 1985): 79–89.

PEACOCK, WINNIFRED E., and TALLEY, WILLIAM M. "Developing Leisure Competence: A Goal for Late Adulthood." *Educational Gerontology* 11 (Nos. 4–6, 1985): 261–276.

PEARCE, D., and MCADOO, H. "Women and Children Alone and in Poverty." Washington, D.C.: National Advisory Council on Economic Opportunity, 1981.

PERLMUTTER, JANE CLARKSON, and WAMPLER, KAREN SMITH. "Sex Role Orientation, Wife's Employment, and the Division of Household Labor." *Home Economics Research Journal* 13 (March 1985): 237–245.

PHILLIPS, GERALD M. "Consensus as Cultural Tradition: A Study of Agreements Between Marital Partners." In *Emergent Issues in Human Decision Making,* ed. by Gerald M. Phillips and Julia T. Woods. Carbondale: Southern Illinois University Press, 1984.

PISTRANG, NANCY. "Women's Work Involvement and Experience of New Motherhood." *Journal of Marriage and Family Living* 46 (May 1984): 433–447.

PLECK, JOSEPH H. "Husbands' and Wives' Family Work, Paid Work, and Adjustment." Working Paper 95. Wellesley, Mass.: Wellesley College, Center for Research on Women, 1982.

———. "The Work-Family Role System." *Social Problems* 24 (April 1977): 417–427.

———. *Working Wives/Working Husbands.* Beverly Hills: Sage Publications, 1985.

PLECK, JOSEPH H., and STAINES, GRAHAM L. "Work Schedules and Family Life in Two-Earner Couples." *Journal of Family Issues* 6 (March 1985): 61–82.

POORKAJ, HOUSHANG. "Social-Psychological Factors and 'Successful Aging.'" *Sociology and Social Research* 56 (April 1972): 289–300.

"Poverty Income Guidelines: Annual Revision." *Federal Register* 51 (February 11, 1986): 5105–5106.

PRATT, CLARA C.; SCHMALL, VICKI L.; WRIGHT, SCOTT; and CLELAND, MARILYN. "Burden and Coping Strategies of Caregivers to Alzheimer's Patients." *Family Relations* 34 (January 1985): 27–33.

PRESSER, HARRIET B. "Shift Work among American Women and Child Care." *Journal of Marriage and the Family* 48 (August 1986): 551–563.

RAINWATER, LEE. *Behind Ghetto Walls.* Chicago: Aldine, 1970.

RANK, MARK R. "Determinants of Conjugal Influences in Wives' Employment Decision Making." *Journal of Marriage and the Family* 44 (August 1982): 591–604.

RATHJE, WILLIAM L. "The Garbage Decade." *American Behavioral Scientist* 28 (September–October 1984): 9–29.

REGAN, MARY C., and ROLAND, HELEN E. "Rearranging Family and Career Priorities: Professional Women and Men of the Eighties." *Journal of Marriage and the Family* 47 (November 1985): 985–992.

REMPEL, JUDITH. "Childless Elderly: What Are They Missing?" *Journal of Marriage and the Family* 47 (May 1985): 343–359.

RETTIG, KATHRYN, and BUBOLZ, MARGARET M. "Interpersonal Resource Exchanges As Indicators of Quality of Marriage." *Journal of Marriage and the Family* 41 (August 1983): 497–509.

RETTIG, KATHRYN, and EVERETT, GLENDA. "Management, Crucial Subject Matter for the Home Economist in the '80's." *Canadian Home Economist Journal* 32 (Winter 1982): 17–20.

REXTROAT, CYNTHIA. "Women's Work Expectations and Labor-Market Experience in Early and Middle Family Life-Cycle Stages." *Journal of Marriage and the Family* 47 (February 1985): 131–142.

RICCI, ISOLINA. *Mom's House/Dad's House.* New York: Macmillan, 1980.

ROBINSON, JOHN P. "Housework Technology and Household Work." In *Women and Household Labor,* ed. by Sarah Fenstermaker Berk. Beverly Hills: Sage Publications, 1980.

ROSENFELD, RACHEL ANN. *Farm Women.* Chapel

Hill: The University of North Carolina Press, 1985.

ROSS, CATHERINE E., and MIROWSKY, JOHN. "The Social Construction of Reality in Marriage." *Sociological Perspectives* 27 (July 1984): 281–300.

ROSS, CATHERINE E.; MIROWSKY, JOHN; and HUBER, JOAN. "Dividing Work, Sharing Work, and In-Between: Marriage Patterns and Depression." *American Sociological Review* 48 (December 1983): 809–823.

ROSS, HEATHER L., and SAWHILL, ISABEL V. *Time of Transition*. Washington, D.C.: The Urban Institute, 1975.

ROWLAND, VIRGINIA T.; DODDEN, RICHARD A.; and NICKOLS, SHARON Y. "Perceived Adequacy of Resources: Development of a Scale." *Home Economics Research Journal* 14 (December 1985): 218–225.

RUFFIN, MARILYN DOSS. "Contribution of the Family to the Economic Support of the Elderly." *Family Economics Review* (October 1984): 1–11.

RUSHING, WILLIAM A. *Class Culture, and Alienation*. Lexington, Mass.: D. C. Heath, 1971.

RUSTAD, LYNNE C. "Family Adjustment to Chronic Illness and Disability in Mid-Life." In *Chronic Illness and Disability Through the Life Span,* ed. by Myron G. Eisenberg, LaFaye C. Sutkin, and Mary A. Jansen. New York: Springer Publishing, 1984.

SAFILIOS-ROTHSCHILD, CONSTANTINA. "Dual Linkages Between the Occupational and Family Systems: A Macrosociological Analysis." *Signs* 1 (Spring 1976): 51–60.

SANIK, MARGARET MIETUS, and MAULDIN, TERESA. "Single Versus Two Parent Families: A Comparison of Mother's Time." *Family Relations* 35 (January 1986): 53–56.

SANIK, MARGARET MIETUS, and STAFFORD, KATHRYN. "Boy/Girl Differences in Household Work." *Journal of Consumer Studies and Home Economics* 10 (September 1986): 209–219.

SARRI, ROSEMARY C. "Federal Policy Changes and the Feminization of Poverty." *Child Welfare* 64 (May–June 1985): 235–247.

SATHRE, FREDA S.; OLSON, RAY W.; and WHITNEY, CLARISSA I. *Let's Talk*. Glenview, Ill.: Scott, Foresman, 1973.

SATIR, VIRGINIA. *Peoplemaking*. Palo Alto: Science and Behavior Books, 1982.

SCHNITTGRUND, KAREN; DUNSING, MARILYN; and HAFSTROM, JEANNE. "Children and Money . . . Attitudes and Behavior of 52 Grandparent and Parent Families." *Illinois Research* 15 (Spring 1973): 12–13.

SCHOOLER, CARMI; MILLER, JOANNE; MILLER, KAREN A.; and RICHTAND, CAROL N. "Work for the Household: Its Nature and Consequences for Husbands and Wives." *American Journal of Sociology* 90 (July 1984): 97–124.

SCHULZ, JAMES H. *The Economics of Aging*. Belmont, Calif.: Wadsworth, 1976.

SCHULZ, JAMES H., and CARRIN, GUY. "The Role of Savings and Pension Systems in Maintaining Living Standards in Retirement." *Journal of Human Resources* 7 (Summer 1972): 343–365.

SCHWIEDER, ELMER, and SCHWIEDER, DOROTHY. *A Peculiar People: Iowa's Old Order Amish*. Ames: The Iowa State University Press, 1975.

SEBALD, HANS. "Adolescents' Shifting Orientation Toward Parents and Peers: A Curvilinear Trend over Recent Decades." *Journal of Marriage and the Family* 48 (February 1986): 5–13.

SEGALMAN, RALPH, and BASU, ASOKE. *Poverty in America*. Westport, Conn.: Greenwood Press, 1981.

SELIG, ANDREW L. "Crisis Theory and Family Growth." *The Family Coordinator* 25 (July 1976): 291–295.

SHAW, LOIS BANFILL. *Midlife Women at Work*. Lexington, Mass.: Lexington Books, 1986.

———. *Unplanned Careers: The Working Lives of Middle-Aged Women*. Lexington, Mass.: Lexington Books, 1983.

SHEEHY, GAIL. *Passages*. New York: Bantam Books, 1976.

SHEFFIELD, VIRGINIA K. A. "Managerial Standard Setting and Family Resource Distribution." M.S. thesis. Ames: Iowa State University, 1976.

SHIREMAN, JOAN F., and JOHNSON, PENNY R. "Single Persons As Adoptive Parents." *Social Service Review* 50 (March 1976): 103–116.

SIEBURG, EVELYN. *Family Communication, An Integrated Systems Approach*. New York: Gardner Press, 1985.

SIEGEL, JACOB S. "Demographic Aspects of Aging and the Older Population in the United States." U.S. Department of Commerce, Bureau of the Census, Special Studies Series P-23, No. 59. Washington, D.C.: U.S. Government Printing Office, 1982.

SIMON, HERBERT A. "Theories of Decision-Making in Economics and Behavioral Science." *The*

American Economic Review 49 (June 1959): 253–283.

SIMONS, RONALD L., and WEST, GALE E. "Life Changes, Coping Resources, and Health among the Elderly." *International Journal of Aging and Human Development* 20 (1984–1985): 173–189.

SLADE, MARGOT. "Working at Home: The Pitfalls." *The New York Times,* October 21, 1985.

SMITH, DRAKE S. "Wife Employment and Marital Adjustment: A Cumulation of Results." *Family Relations* 34 (October 1985): 483–490.

SMITH, HERBERT L., and CUTRIGHT, PHILLIPS. "Components of Change in the Number of Female Family Heads Age 15 to 44, an Update and Reanalysis: United States 1940–1983." *Social Science Research Journal* 14 (September 1985): 226–250.

SMITH, JEANNE WIELAGE, and BENINGER, ELIZABETH SMITH. "Women's Nonmarket Labor: Dissolution of Marriage and Opportunity Cost." *Journal of Family Issues* 3 (June 1982): 251–265.

SMITH, MARY M., and OLSON, PAMELA N. "Interfamily Transfers to Beginning and Elderly Families." *Home Economics Research Journal* 13 (December 1984): 184–191.

SMITH, SARAH JANE. "Personality Traits, Values, Expectations, and Managerial Behavior." M.S. thesis. University Park: The Pennsylvania State University, 1971.

SMITHERS, JANICE A. *Determined Survivors.* New Brunswick, N.J.: Rutgers University Press, 1985.

SMYER, MICHAEL A., and HOFLAND, BRIAN F. "Divorce and Family Support in Later Life." *Journal of Family Issues* 3 (March 1982): 61–77.

SOMMERS, PAUL, and MOOS, RUDOLF H. "The Weather and Human Behavior." In *The Human Context,* ed. by Rudolf H. Moos. New York: Wiley, 1976.

STACK, CAROL B. *All Our Kin Strategies for Survival in a Black Community.* New York: Harper and Row, 1974.

STAINES, GRAHAM L., and PLECK, JOSEPH H. "Work Schedule Flexibility and Family Life. *Journal of Occupational Behaviour* 4 (April 1986): 147–153.

STAMPFL, RONALD W. "Perceived Risk and Consumer Decision Making." *Journal of Consumer Studies and Home Economics* 2 (September 1978): 231–245.

STANLEY, SANDRA C.; HUNT, JANET G.; and HUNT, LARRY L. "The Relative Deprivation of Husbands in Dual-Earner Households." *Journal of Family Issues* 7 (March 1986): 3–20.

STEFFENSMEIER, RENEE HOFFMAN. "A Role Model of the Transition to Parenthood." *Journal of Marriage and the Family* 44 (May 1982): 319–334.

STEIDL, ROSE E. "Difficulty Factors in Homemaking Tasks: Implications for Environmental Design." *Human Factors* 14 (October 1972): 471–482.

STEIDL, ROSE E., and BRATTON, ESTHER CREW. *Work in the Home.* New York: Wiley, 1968.

STEIN, JESS, ed. *The Random House Dictionary of the English Language.* New York: Random House, 1967.

STEPHEN, BEVERLY. "Moment of Truth: Having a Second Child." *Working Woman* (April 1986): 131–133, 176.

STEPHENS, JOYCE. *Loners, Losers, and Lovers.* Seattle: University of Washington Press, 1976.

STEVENSON, JOANNE SABOL. *Issues and Crises During Middlescence.* New York: Appleton-Century-Crofts, 1977.

STOLLER, ELEANOR PALO. "Exchange Patterns in the Informal Support Networks of the Elderly: The Impact of Reciprocity on Morale." *Journal of Marriage and the Family* 47 (May 1985): 335–342.

STROBER, MYRA A., and WEINBERG, CHARLES B. "Strategies Used by Working and Nonworking Wives to Reduce Time Pressures." *Journal of Consumer Research* 6 (March 1980): 338–348.

TABOR, JOAN S., and BOWERS, JEAN S. "Factors Determining Credit Worthiness of Low Income Consumers." *Journal of Consumer Affairs* 11 (Winter 1977): 43–51.

TAEUBER, CYNTHIA M. "America in Transition: An Aging Society." U.S. Department of Commerce, Bureau of the Census, Special Studies Series P-23, No. 128. Washington, D.C.: U.S. Government Printing Office, 1982.

TAYLOR, ROBERT JOSEPH. "Receipt of Support from Family among Black Americans: Demographic and Familial Differences." *Journal of Marriage and the Family* 48 (February 1986): 67–77.

THOMAS, SANDRA; ALBRECHT, KAY; and WHITE, PRISCILLA. "Determinants of Marital Quality in Dual-Career Couples." *Family Relations* 33 (October 1984): 513–521.

THRALL, CHARLES ALEXANDER. "Household Technology and the Division of Labor in Families,"

Ph.D. dissertation. Cambridge: Harvard University, 1970.

THUROW, LESTER C. "The Optimum Lifetime Distribution of Consumption Expenditures." *The American Economic Review* 59 (June 1969): 324–330.

TITUS, SANDRA L. "Barriers to the Health Maintenance Organization for the Over 65's." *Social Science and Medicine* 16 (1982): 1767–1774.

TUBBS, STEWART L., and MOSS, SYLVIA. *Human Communication*. New York: Random House, 1983.

TURNER, RALPH H. *Family Interaction*. New York: Wiley, 1970.

TVERSKY, A., and KAHNEMAN, D. "Judgement Under Uncertainty: Heuristics and Biases." *Science* 185 (September 27, 1974): 1124–1131.

UNNI, V. K. "An Analysis of Entrepreneurial Planning." *Managerial Planning* 33 (July–August 1984): 51–54.

UPP, MELINDA. "Fast Facts and Figures About Social Security." *Social Security Bulletin* 49 (June 1986): 5–19.

VAN VELSOR, ELLEN, and O'RAND, ANGELA M. "Family Life Cycle, Work Career Patterns, and Women's Wages at Midlife." *Journal of Marriage and the Family* 46 (May 1984): 365–373.

VENTURA, JACQUELINE N., and BOSS, PAULINE G. "The Family Coping Inventory Applied to Parents with New Babies." *Journal of Marriage and the Family* 45 (November 1983): 867–875.

VISHER, EMILY B., and VISHER, JOHN S. *Stepfamilies: A Guide to Working with Stepparents and Stepchildren*. New York: Brunner/Mazel, 1979.

VOYDANOFF, PATRICIA, and KELLY, ROBERT F. "Determinants of Work-Related Family Problems among Employed Parents." *Journal of Marriage and the Family* 46 (November 1984): 881–892.

WAGNER, JANET, and HANNA, SHERMAN. "The Effectiveness of Family Life Cycle Variables in Consumer Expenditure Research." *Journal of Consumer Research* 10 (December 1983): 281–291.

WALKER, FLORENCE S., and PARKHURST, ANNE M. "Identification of Differences in Time Management." *Home Economics Research Journal* 11 (September 1982): 57–66.

WALKER, KATHRYN E., and WOODS, MARGARET E. *Time Use: A Measure of Household Production of Family Goods and Services*. Washington, D.C.: American Home Economics Association, 1976.

WALKER, ROSEMARY, and CUDE, BRENDA. "In-Store Shopping Strategies: Time and Money Costs in the Supermarket." *The Journal of Consumer Affairs* 117 (Winter 1983): 356–369.

WALLIS, CLAUDIA. "Children Having Children." *Time* 126 (December 9, 1985): 78–79.

WALSH, DORIS L. "Targeting Teens." *American Demographics* 7 (February 1985): 21–25, 41.

WARD, JOAN S., and KIRK, N. S. "The Relation Between Some Anthropometric Dimensions and Preferred Working Surface Heights in the Kitchen." *Ergonomics* 13 (November 1970): 783–797.

WARD, RUSSEL. "Informal Networks and Well-Being in Later Life: A Research Agenda." *The Gerontologist* 25 (February 1985): 55–61.

WEEKS, J. R., and CUELLAR, J. B. "The Role of Family Members in the Helping Networks of Older People." *The Gerontologist* 21 (June 1981): 388–394.

WEEKS, JOHN R. *Teenage Marriages*. Westport, Conn.: Greenwood Press, 1976.

WEINGARTEN, HELEN. "Remarriage and Well-Being: National Survey Evidence of Social and Psychological Effects." *Journal of Family Issues* 1 (December 1980): 533–559.

WEISS, ROBERT S. "The Impact of Marital Dissolution on Income and Consumption in Single-Parent Households." *Journal of Marriage and the Family* 46 (February 1984): 115–127.

WESTOFF, LESLIE ALDRIDGE. *The Second Time Around*. New York: Viking Press, 1977.

WINTER, MARY. "Management As a Mental Process: Implications for Theory and Research." Paper presented to North Central Regional Committee (NCR-116) on Family Resource Management, St. Louis, Missouri, 1986. (Home Economics Research Institute, Journal Paper No. 367, Iowa State University.)

WINTER, MARY, and BEUTLER, IVAN F. "Home Production As a Propinquous Activity." Paper presented to North Central Regional Committee (NCR-116) on Family Resource Management, Columbus, Ohio 1982.

WINTER, MARY, and MORRIS, EARL W. "Used Resources, Met Demands, and Satisfaction." Paper presented to North Central Regional Committee (NCR-116) on Family Resource Management, Columbus, Ohio, 1982.

WOLFGRAM, TAMMARA H. "Working at Home." *The Futurist* 18 (June 1984): 31–34.

"Women, Children, and Poverty in America." Working Paper. New York: Ford Foundation, 1985.

WOOD, VIVIAN, and ROBERTSON, JOHN F. "Friendship and Kinship Interaction: Differential Effect on the Morale of the Elderly." *Journal of Marriage and the Family* 40 (May 1978): 367–375.

ZICK, CATHLEEN D., and BRYANT, W. KEITH. "Alternative Strategies for Pricing Home Work Time." *Home Economics Research Journal* 12 (December 1983): 133–144.

ZUCKERMAN, BARRY S.; WALKER, DEBORAH K.; FRANK, DEBORAH A.; CHASE, CYNTHIA; and HAMBURG, BEATRIX. "Adolescent Pregnancy—Biobehavioral Determinants of Outcome." *The Journal of Pediatrics* 105 (December 1984): 857–863.

Cartoons

GUISEWITE, CATHY. *Cathy,* September 9, 1986. Reprinted courtesy Universal Press Syndicate.

JOHNSTON, LYNN. *For Better or Worse,* September 13, 1986. Reprinted courtesy Universal Press Syndicate.

KEANE, BIL. *The Family Circus,* January 22, 1974. Reprinted courtesy The Register and Tribune Syndicate.

No author. *Supermarkets and Men. The Futurist* 20 (March–April 1986).

TRUDEAU, G. B. *Doonesbury,* August 5, 1986. Reprinted courtesy Universal Press Syndicate.

Government documents

U.S. Department of Agriculture, Agricultural Research Service. "Cost of Food at Home Estimated for Food Plans at 4 Cost Levels, January 1986, U.S. Average." *Family Economics Review* (April 1986): 36.

———. Family Economics Research Group. "Updated Estimates of the Cost of Raising a Child." *Family Economics Review* (October 1987): 36–37.

U.S. Department of Commerce, Bureau of the Census, *Statistical Abstract of the U.S. for 1985,* 105th ed. Washington, D.C.: U.S. Government Printing Office, 1984.

———. *Statistical Abstract of the U.S. for 1986,* 106th ed. Washington, D.C.: U.S. Government Printing Office, 1985.

———. *Statistical Abstract of the U.S. for 1987,* 107th ed. Washington, D.C.: U.S. Government Printing Office, 1986.

———. Current Population Reports. "Household and Family Characteristics: March, 1983," Series P-20, No. 388, Washington, D.C.: U.S. Government Printing Office, 1984.

———. "Characteristics of Households and Persons Receiving Selected Noncash Benefits: 1984." Series P-23, No. 150. Washington, D.C., 1985.

———. "Demographic and Socio-economic Aspects of Aging in the United States. Series P-23, No. 138. Washington, D.C.: U.S. Government Printing Office, 1984.

———. "Earnings in 1981 of Married-Couple Families by Selected Characteristics of Husbands and Wives." Series P-23, No. 133. Washington, D.C.: U.S. Government Printing Office, 1984.

———. "Population Profile of the United States 1983/84." Series P-23, No. 145. Washington, D.C.: U.S. Government Printing Office, 1985.

———. "Money Income of Households, Families and Persons in the United States: 1983" Series P-60, No. 146. Washington, D.C.: U.S. Government Printing Office, 1985.

———. Money Income of Households, Families and Persons in the United States: 1984." Series P-60, No. 151. Washington, D.C.: U.S. Government Printing Office, 1986.

———. "Money Income and Poverty Status of Families and Persons in the United States, 1985." Series P-60, No. 154. Washington, D.C.: U.S. Government Printing Office, 1986.

U.S. Department of Commerce, Bureau of the Census, "Estimates of Poverty Income Including the Value of Noncash Benefits: 1985," Technical Paper 56. Washington, D.C.: U.S. Government Printing Office, 1986.

U.S. Department of Energy. *Annual Report to Congress.* Washington, D.C.: U.S. Department of Energy, 1985.

———. Energy Information Administration, National Energy Consumption Surveys. *Consump-*

tion and Expenditures, April 1982 through March 1983, Part 1, National Data. Washington, D.C.: U.S. Government Printing Office, 1984.

———. National Energy Information Center. *Energy Facts 1984*. Washington D.C.: U.S. Department of Energy, 1985.

U.S. Department of Health and Human Services, Public Health Service. "Current Estimates from National Health Interview Survey: United States, 1981." Series 10, No. 141. Washington, D.C.: U.S. Government Printing Office, 1982.

U.S. Department of Labor, Bureau of Labor Statistics. *CPI Detailed Reports*. Washington, D.C.: U.S. Government Printing Office, 1981.

———. "Three Budgets for a Retired Couple, Autumn 1981." *News,* USDL 82-266. Washington, D.C.: U.S. Department of Labor, 1982.

———. *CPI Detailed Reports*. Washington, D.C.: U.S. Government Printing Office, 1985.

———. "Consumer Expenditure Survey, Results from 1984." *News,* USDL 86-258. Washington, D.C.: U.S. Department of Labor, 1986.

Index